T0313400

# Cornish Wrecking, 1700–1860

## Reality and Popular Myth

Although the popular myth of Cornish wrecking is well-known within British culture, this book is the first comprehensive, systematic inquiry to separate out the layers of myth from the actual practices. Weaving in legal, social and cultural history, it traces the development of wreck law – the right to salvage goods washed on shore – and explores the responses of a coastal populace who found their customary practices increasingly outside the law, especially as local individual rights were being curtailed and the role of centralised authority asserted.

This groundbreaking study also considers the myths surrounding wrecking, showing how these developed over time, and how moral attitudes towards wrecking changed. Overall, the picture of evil wreckers deliberately luring ships onto the rocks is dispelled, to be replaced by a detailed picture of a coastal populace – poor and gentry alike – who were involved in a multi-faceted, sophisticated coastal practice and who had their own complex popular beliefs about the harvest and salvage of goods washing ashore from shipwreck.

CATHRYN J PEARCE holds a PhD in Maritime History from Greenwich Maritime Institute. A former associate professor of history with the University of Alaska Anchorage's Kenai Peninsula College, she is now with University Campus Suffolk where she continues to research on the relationship of coastal people with the sea.

# Cornish Wrecking, 1700–1860

## Reality and Popular Myth

Cathryn J. Pearce

THE BOYDELL PRESS

First published 2010
The Boydell Press, Woodbridge

ISBN 978 1 84383 555 4

The Boydell Press is an imprint of Boydell & Brewer Ltd
PO Box 9, Woodbridge, Suffolk IP12 3DF, UK
and of Boydell & Brewer Inc.
668 Mount Hope Ave, Rochester, NY 14604, USA
website: www.boydellandbrewer.com

A CIP catalogue record for this book is available
from the British Library

The publisher has no responsibility for the continued existence or accuracy
of URLs for external or third-party internet websites referred to in
this book, and does not guarantee that any content on such websites is,
or will remain, accurate or appropriate.

This publication is printed on acid-free paper

Printed in Great Britain by
CPI Antony Rowe Ltd, Chippenham Wiltshire

# Contents

# Figures, Maps and Tables

I dedicate this book to my family. It is especially dedicated to my father, Bert Pearce, my 'unassuming hero', without whom I never would have had the courage or the funds to begin this research so far away from Alaska. Sadly, he died suddenly just as I was beginning what had been a childhood dream, and I had to learn to carry on without his sage words and encouragement. He gave me his love of history, and supported me in my passion for maritime history even though he preferred lakes and streams to salt water. I miss him more than mere words can convey, but I know he is proud of me. Dad, here's the book that you wanted me to write. There will be more to follow, I promise.

# Preface and Acknowledgements

Wreckers. Cornish wreckers. It seems that the two terms have to go together; one cannot exist without the other. And yet, that really isn't true. There are Cornish people who are not wreckers, and wreckers who are not Cornish. Nevertheless, the popular notion of wrecking most surely connects the two. But who are they? Are they the despicable characters of popular belief, who lure ships ashore on the rocks using false lights? Or are they people altogether different who were somehow caught up with stories of evil-doing?

I first encountered stories of Cornish wreckers on my first trip to Cornwall. I had just finished two years of university and treated myself to a British holiday with a high school friend. Cornwall captured our imagination, with its fascinating geography and geology, its stone circles and Celtic crosses, and its relationship to the sea. We investigated every little tract we could find, hooked by the constant surprises. Like many visitors, we fell in love with the little seaside villages: Mousehole, Polperro, St Ives, Mullion Cove, and the Lizard. It was at the Lizard that I picked up a little booklet by John Vivian entitled *Tales of Cornish Wreckers*. I tucked it away in my growing collection of British history books, little realising that I would someday devote years of my life to the study of Cornish wreckers, and that questions arising from my reading of that modest collection of wrecking tales twenty years later would lead me to investigate this important aspect of Cornish and maritime history. This book is the result of that search, a journey which took me from my childhood home in Alaska, to my new student abode and maritime 'family' in Greenwich. From there I had many wonderful expeditions to Cornwall for my fieldwork. My research eventually led me to my husband and new home in England, and to this book. It is not an understatement to say that Cornish wrecking has changed my life immeasurably!

My involvement in this voyage has given me opportunities I could not have imagined, and I have met many people for whom I feel immense affection. Because of them, I have been able to 'sail in smooth waters'. To Joan Ryan, retired Humanities lecturer at the University of Greenwich, who was my sounding-board, and who helped me maintain my zeal through the years of research and writing. She has given so much of herself that she is a true friend in every meaning of the word. To her husband Mick Ryan, retired Professor of Penal Politics, also at Greenwich, with whom I enjoyed many long conversations about crime and wrecking. To Cori Convertito-Farrer, who listened patiently to effusive chatter about my research findings for entire train journeys between Greenwich and Kew. And to Professor Roger Knight, former Deputy-Director of the National Maritime Museum and now Professor of Naval History, Greenwich Maritime Institute (GMI), who introduced me to Capt. George Hogg and all those who were establishing the new National Maritime Museum Cornwall; and especially to Professor Sarah Palmer, Director of the GMI, whose continued enthusiasm and support meant more than I can ever say. She never wavered in her belief in me, for which I am eternally grateful. She is the best mentor I ever hoped to find. With much fondness to my friends and colleagues at GMI, especially Richard Bateman, Suzanne Bowles, Victoria Carolan, and Chris Ware, the 'usual suspects', your support was crucial to my success. Thanks for giving an Alaskan a sense of belonging when she moved so far from home.

To the wonderful and generous people who shared their research, ideas, and even their homes with me: Dr Helen Doe, University of Exeter, a fellow Cornish maritime historian; Michael Williams, Senior Lecturer in Law at the University of Wolverhampton, and his wife Julie; Capt. George Hogg and his wife Rosemary, who invited me down to Padstow and introduced me to the late Nick Darke, a nationally acclaimed playwright and self-avowed Cornish 'wrecker', and his wife Jane. And to Tony Pawlyn, the National Maritime Museum Cornwall, who graciously sent me the rough draft on his book on wrecking; Professor Glyndwr Williams, Queen Mary, University of London (Emeritus) for his encouragement and compliments; and all the participants at the International Commission of Maritime History seminars at King's College, University of London. Special thanks to Dr Alan Boraas, Professor of Anthropology at Kenai Peninsula College, University of Alaska Anchorage, who led me to think about the functions of myth. Our many conversations have been valuable to this study. Finally, I am much indebted to Dr David J. Starkey, University of Hull, who acted as my external examiner for my doctorate. His positive comments and support made this a better book. There are many more individuals not named who were also important to the success of this project.

No research project can be successful without the knowledge and support of the staff at the various archival repositories. Sincere appreciation goes to Alison Campbell and Ann Brown at the Cornwall Record Office; Angela Broom at the Courtney Library, Royal Institution of Cornwall; Liza Verity and Helen Pethers at the National Maritime Museum; and Kim Cooper, who even stayed late for me at the Cornish Studies Library, Redruth. And last, but not least, a very special thank you to my new husband, Robert Boyd, who worked hard on the illustrations and who put up with my nocturnal bursts of inspiration. Spouses of authors are truly unsung heroes. Special thanks are also due to Sarah Bryce, my copy-editor, for catching errors that were over-looked despite assiduous editing.

And finally, to add the bit that all authors need to do, any mistakes are purely my own, and there are still many questions to answer. Each topic could be a book of its own; limited space meant that I had to cut major amounts of material, to be used another day.

# Abbreviations

| | |
|---|---|
| AR | Arundell Papers, Cornwall Record Office |
| BL | British Library |
| BT | Board of Trade Records, The National Archives |
| CA | Croft Andrew Papers, Cornwall Record Office |
| CJ | *Journal of the House of Commons* |
| CRO | Cornwall Record Office |
| CUST | Records of the Boards of Customs, Outport Records, The National Archives |
| DJW | Journal of Christopher Wallis, Royal Institution of Cornwall |
| EN | Enys Papers, Cornwall Record Office |
| HB | Henderson Collection, Basset Papers, Royal Institution of Cornwall |
| HO | Home Office Papers, The National Archives |
| IOR | India Office Records, British Library |
| LG | London Guildhall Library |
| ML | Millaton Papers, Cornwall Record Office |
| MSA | Merchant Shipping Act of 1854 |
| MT | Ministry of Transport Records, The National Archives |
| P | Parish of Little Petherick Papers, Cornwall Record Office |
| PB | Prideaux-Brune Papers, Cornwall Record Office |
| PC | Privy Council Records, The National Archives |
| PP | Parliamentary Papers |
| QS | Quarter Sessions, Cornwall Record Office |
| RIC | Royal Institution of Cornwall |
| RO | R. Rogers & Sons, Solicitors Papers, Cornwall Record Office |
| RP | Rogers of Penrose Papers, Cornwall Record Office |
| SP | State Papers, The National Archives |
| T | H.M. Treasury Papers, The National Archives |
| TNA | The National Archives of the UK, Public Record Office |
| W | Willyams Papers, Cornwall Record Office |

# Introduction: A Reputation for Wrecking

'It is far harder to kill a phantom than a reality'
Virginia Woolf

In February 2002, BBC News issued headlines on its website: 'Timber galore for Cornish wreckers'. The Russian cargo ship *Kodima* foundered in heavy seas, spilling thousands of timber planks into the sea, which washed up on the beaches around Whitsand Bay. 'Scavengers have swarmed over a Cornwall beach to retrieve timber from a grounded cargo ship', the News announced, 'risking death in the waves. Tight laws control salvage, but the Cornish wreckers have a long heritage.' The articles go on to repeat oft-told tales of Cornish wreckers: the clergyman who asked his parishioners to wait for him to remove his robes, so 'we can all start fair', and the prayer repeatedly ascribed to the Cornish: 'Oh please Lord, let us pray for all on the sea; But if there's got to be wrecks, please send them to we.' The *Kodima* was the latest wreck to experience the activities of the wrecker, joining the 1997 wreck of the container ship CV *Cita*, which 'fill[ed] the sea with "gifts" for the islanders of Scilly'. In an interview cited by the article, Ed Prynn of St Merryn claimed: 'Everybody was down there with their diggers, right out in the surf. Nearly every house built after that had oak and teak beams. They won't stop us doing it – it's our culture. It's in our blood.'[1] And yet, in an additional article, the News cautioned: 'The coastguard is also warning people who are salvaging thousands of planks of pine wood washed up from the *Kodima* that the activity is illegal.'[2]

The wrecks of the *Kodima* and the *Cita* highlight an important truth. Even in the twenty-first century, crowds flock to the shoreline as soon as word is received that cargo is coming ashore. Some arrive on site simply to watch the proceedings, but others come in anticipation of 'free' goods. Likewise, the idea of 'finders keepers, losers weepers' seems to be inherent within our psyche. How often have we played the game, or have gone out beachcombing, hoping to find treasure that may have washed on the shore? We begin as children, searching for pretty shells, but even as adults we hope to find something

---

[1]   BBC News Online, 4 February 2002, news.bbc.co.uk/1/hi/uk/england/1801109.stm.
[2]   BBC News Online, 'Floods continue amid heavy rain', 4 February 2002, news.bbc.co.uk/1/hi/uk/1799659.stm.

of value or beauty, whether rocks, shells, or even floats from fishing nets or buoys, tags from crab pots or fenders lost from boats.

Shipwrecks such as the *Cita*, the *Kodima*, and even more recently the *Napoli* off the Devon coast (2007) and the timber cargoes which washed ashore from the *Ice Prince* in Sussex (2008) and the *Sinegorsk* in Kent (2009), show how much wrecking, or in modern parlance, 'scavenging', continues to be practised. Interestingly enough, however, media reports of the wrecks in Kent and Sussex describe the 'scavenging' activities of the local inhabitants, while the term 'wrecking' is reserved for the descriptions of the activity in Cornwall. The Cornish reputation for wrecking has been carried to us through media reports of shipwrecks, such as that of the *Kodima*, but also through television sit-coms such as BBC's *Doc Martin* and Dawn French's comedy *Wild West*. In literature, the vision of cruel wreckers was illustrated by the wicked Joss Merlin in Daphne du Maurier's *Jamaica Inn*, brought to the silver screen by Alfred Hitchcock in 1939, and then made for television in 1983. In opera, too, Ethel Smyth brought audiences her version of Cornish wreckers in 1909, and it is reprised every few years. The theme can also be found at Cornish tourist sites such as the multimedia show 'Return to the Last Labyrinth' at Land's End. This conception of the wrecker enjoys wide currency; its use in popular culture shows how pervasive it is within our national consciousness.[3]

Indeed, the BBC news stories of the *Kodima* highlighted several key themes of wrecking that continue to be emphasised in the media and litera-ture: 'salvaging' from the beach is still practised; people persist in believing it is their right to keep what they find; and the Government continues to issue warnings that 'wrecking' is illegal. In addition, the BBC's reports highlight some of the traditional tales associated with wrecking, including the wrecking prayers and the 'parson story'. Other tales that continue to be found within twenty-first-century popular narratives and tourist literature include the myth of Cornishmen who led donkeys or cows along the cliffs during dark and stormy nights with lanterns hanging around the animals' necks to deliberately lure ships to wreck on the hostile shore. Murder of the shipwreck victims and the plundering of corpses and cargoes complete the picture. No wonder the main question I'm asked, with much interest and glee, is 'Did they really do it?!', meaning, of course, did Cornish wreckers really lure ships ashore to their doom, and plunder the cargoes?

With these motifs so ingrained in British popular imagination, why has there not been more written on wrecking, particularly from an academic angle? Obviously wrecking is treated with sensationalistic enthusiasm in the ubiq-uitous shipwreck guides, but a serious, full-length account has been lacking. Why are there not more studies? The neglect of wrecking history involves

---

[3] See also Bella Bathurst, *The Wreckers: A Story of Killing Seas, False Lights and Plundered Ships* (London, 2005), chapters 4 and 7.

several fundamental issues. First, it is viewed as a 'popular' subject, which had been considered of antiquarian, romantic interest, rather than of scholarly merit. In this, the subject was viewed by academia with certain condescension, along with piracy, smuggling, highway robbery, and other tales of the romantic bent that were left to popular writers, written, as it has been so aptly put, 'from the ripping-good-yarns school of history'. It is only recently that these areas have begun to receive their proper due, as part of a greater movement towards an analysis of the social and cultural history of popular myths, beliefs and memory, brought on by society's interest since the mid-1960s in cultural themes.

Secondly, the topic of wrecking is a sensitive issue, in that the Cornish wrecker stereotype has created strong emotions in the Cornish, who have felt unfairly slandered by their being typecast as evildoers who would rather see a ship wrecked than sailing safely by their shores. They are still trying to come to terms with the label, a struggle that is at the root of their contradictory reactions. Do they celebrate or denigrate the practice of wrecking? What is the truth behind the stories? Were their ancestors truly evil, or were they simply opportunistic? It is an issue that needs to be taken seriously and requires fairness and objectivity.

Finally, wrecking history has been accused of being a less than 'substantial' subject because of a perceived dearth of primary sources.[4] However, this assessment is wrong. Although the subject might appear difficult to research, and although there is no direct evidence from the wreckers themselves, there are a multitude of excellent sources available. By assiduous investigation and 'beachcombing', we find that the historical record contains fragments of diverse materials that we can use to piece together wrecking history, including official government correspondence and records, Board of Trade wreck registers, legal cases involving right of wreck, personal correspondence, religious tracts, contemporary newspapers and literary sources. Little of this material had been used before this study, and hence many of the more popular works have relied on limited sources.

Nevertheless, the use of the extant sources in this study has not been without difficulty. Indeed, they often created downright frustration. Wrecker experiences at the hands of the law are difficult to determine: assize records are uncertain, not only because legal language can be obscure, but because the descriptions of the crimes prosecuted were imprecise. When labourer William Chapple of Madron was indicted for stealing 100 yards of canvas and ten yards of rope, were the goods taken from a warehouse or from a wrecked ship?[5] 'Trespass' can denote the theft of crops, yet it can also denote

---

4   Sara Wheeler, '"Whose Loot is it Anyway?" A review of Bella Bathurst's *The Wreckers*', *New York Times*, 17 July 2005.
5   QS/1/11/264–287, Bodmin, 10 July 1827.

wrecking. In addition, wrecking activity is often subsumed under the terms 'plunder', 'piracy', or simply 'theft'. 'Wrecking' is not a term used in prosecutions, although it is used in contemporary correspondence and media reports. Assize records are also very fragmentary, and little survives from the eighteenth-century petty sessions. Sources reporting shipwrecks are also fragmentary and lack essential detail. Journals, newspapers, and Lloyd's reports are relatively silent on the disposition of cargoes after shipwreck: the name of the ship, master, itinerary and types of cargo are often listed, but that is all. Likewise, news reports are not forthcoming, unless reporting on the rare moral panics against wrecking. Some sources offered enticing, teasing clues, only to end up a disappointment. Affidavits were collected by Penzance's Collector of Customs in 1776 regarding the plundering of Louis XVI's vessel *Marie Jeanne*, but unfortunately they were not copied into the letter-books, and have thus been lost.[6] Other missing records within collections foiled attempts to either corroborate cases or to add further detail. In spite of these difficulties, the many sources that are available are more than enough, with prudent use, to allow us to extend our understanding beyond the accepted stereotype of the Cornish wrecker, and to see the reality of wrecking in the coastal communities of Cornwall and beyond.

### Myths of Wrecking: Conceptual Clarifications

The Cornish today, in speaking of their connection with their wrecker past, may argue that the harvesting of wrecks is 'in their blood', as did those present at the wreck of the *Kodima*. Yet, the heritage which they claim does not include all of the same activities that were performed in the past, at least not unequivocally. Indeed, there is much confusion over what 'wrecking' and 'wreckers' really are. Is wrecking the deliberate wrecking of a ship for its cargo? Is it benign beachcombing? Are wreckers evil characters bent on destruction, murder, and theft? Or are they harmless 'harvesters' and beachcombers, as the Cornish assert?

In 1867, Admiral W.H. Smyth published his *The Sailor's Word-book: an Alphabetical Digest of Nautical Terms*. He opined that 'wrecker' was 'a name which includes both meritorious salvors of ships in distress, and the felonious brutes who merely hasten to wrecks for plunder'.[7] Interestingly enough, he does not include the one image most often brought up: that of the mythic wrecker using false lights.[8] However, the *Oxford English Dictionary* fills this

---

[6]   CUST 68/42. Penzance Board to Collector, 23 July 1776; 28 September 1776; 19 October 1776.
[7]   W.H. Smyth, *The Sailor's Word Book, an Alphabetical Digest of Nautical Terms* (London, 1867).
[8]   See film versions of Daphne du Maurier's *Jamaica Inn*, and the 'Return to the Last Laby-

void by including the practice of false lights in its definition, treating it not as a mythic image, but as an actual practice.[9]

Thus, the terms 'wrecker' and 'wrecking' denote different activities and nuances of behaviour, differences that are not always apparent in discussions of the practice. Accordingly, to clarify its conceptual framework for this book, 'wrecking' incorporates both the mythic – the image of men deliberately luring ships ashore by using false lights – and the reality. The actual activities can be divided into three categories (see Figure 1), all of which are distinct from the practice of legal salvage.[10] The first category comprises the attack and plunder of a vessel, which includes a form of deliberate wrecking – the cutting of a ship's cables – but it also includes the opportunistic assault on a vessel and her cargo once she lay aground. The second category consists of the taking or 'harvesting' of wrecked goods.[11] This activity can be further subdivided into the actions of either the immediate taking of wrecked goods at the time of the wreck, or the taking of wrecked goods after they had been turned over to the authorities for salvage. Finally, the third category comprises the harvesting of goods that had been washed ashore after the shipwreck event, or that had come ashore in the absence of a clear shipwreck, which was the most widespread form of wrecking.

These generally opportunistic activities can be difficult to separate for analysis; they often occurred simultaneously. Moreover, contemporary informants were not necessarily concerned to distinguish between these forms of wrecking practices. For example, the term 'plunder', with its negative cultural connotation, often conflated relatively benign beach harvest with the aggressive attack of shipwrecks. To aid clarity of exposition and prevent confusion, this book therefore uses as far as possible the following terminology: 'mythic wrecker' to refer to the invented persona; 'plunderers' for those who attacked a vessel and its cargo; and 'harvesters' for those who collected goods provided by the sea as a result of wreck. The term 'salvors' refers to those involved in salvage activities.

The concept of 'myth', too, needs to be discussed, as its use can be contentious. 'Myth' is neither being used in its simpler, more popular understanding

---

rinth' exhibit at Land's End. Both show examples of the wrecker with the lantern.

9    OED online, accessed 6 June 2002.

10    The act of legal salvage requires that the salvor be a volunteer who assists in the saving of a vessel or its cargo from immediate danger. By law, they are entitled to a salvage payment up to the value of the property that is saved. See Geoffrey Brice, *Maritime Law of Salvage*, 3rd edition (London, 1999), Section 1–01. The boundaries between legal and illegal salvage were, however, sometimes blurred. See Chapter 4.

11    The term 'harvest' has been adapted from a description of wrecking by Rev. Robert Hawker in his *Footsteps of Former Men in Far Cornwall* (London, 1903), whereby he describes wreckers as 'those daring gleaners of the harvest of the sea' (129), to allow for the differences between the violent attack of a ship and the picking up of wrecked goods from the beach as it washes ashore.

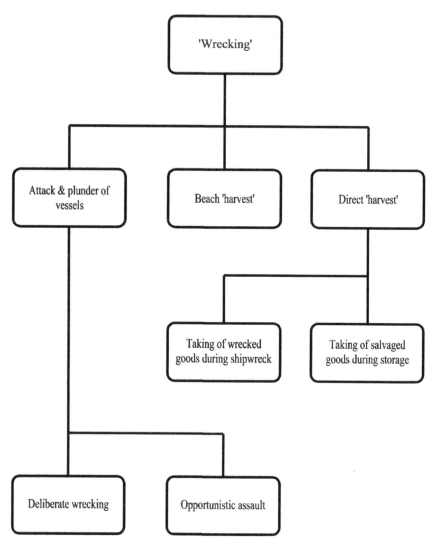

Figure 1. Wrecking Activities

to signify something that is untrue, nor in its folkloric definition of sacred origin narratives.[12] Instead, this book uses the meaning defined by Peter Burke, who emphasises the 'richer, more positive sense of a story with a symbolic meaning, involving characters who are larger than life, whether they are heroes or villains'.[13] The wrecker myths discussed in this book originate with actual cases and beliefs that have a taken on a mythic status, in that they are used by popular society to symbolically convey messages of cultural significance. It is not the purpose of this study, however, to focus on those wrecker myths that are part of the corpus of folkloric narratives, such as the false lights stories. Rather, they will be the subject of another book.

This book has two overarching, intertwined objectives: to establish the historical reality of wrecking and to achieve an understanding of the myth itself as an historical phenomenon. It covers the period from 1700 to 1860, as this era saw the height of documented wrecking activity, the passage of the majority of shipwreck legislation, and the solidification of wrecking as myth. It examines the most widely held beliefs about wrecking that pervade British culture and that are included in popular sources and traditional tales. It then analyses those beliefs in light of the historical evidence. In doing this, it illuminates the multifaceted aspects of the wrecking practices and their place within popular culture that heretofore have been hidden. Consequently, it also investigates the interplay between the social groups who were involved, and we can see that rather than having a precise understanding of the differences between salvage practices and wrecking, these groups often operated in the shadowy world between legality and illegality. This highlights larger questions of the position of the law in popular society and of increasing State control over shipwrecked goods, a control underscored by taxation concerns. Thus this study also focuses on the greater questions of the struggle and mediation between the ruling elite and the 'country people' of Cornwall, and the centrifugal forces of national power and control – a mediation that took place not only on the economic front, but socially, culturally, and nationally.[14]

This book takes as its central focus the practice of wrecking in the Penwith peninsula of western Cornwall, an area that includes Penzance. The Penzance district Customs records are the most complete, and incorporate the area of Mount's Bay and Land's End, a region of major wrecking activity, thus

---

[12]   See William G. Doty, *Mythography: The Study of Myths and Rituals* (Tuscaloosa, Alabama, 2000) and Bob Trubshaw, *Explore Mythology* (Loughborough, 2003).

[13]   Peter Burke, *Varieties of Cultural History* (Cambridge, 1997), 51. See also Roland Barthes, *Mythologies*, trans. Annette Lavers (London, 1972) for a further discussion of myths, and their meaning and function.

[14]   The Isles of Scilly are also included within this study, albeit peripherally, as are other areas of Cornwall outside of the Penwith Peninsula. They are not politically part of the county, but they are a part of the Duchy of Cornwall, and during the eighteenth century the Custom's outport of Penzance had nominal jurisdiction over Scillonian Customs' revenue.

making it an ideal case study, although material from other districts is incorporated when needed. Wreckers in other Cornish districts, such as that of the far northeast corner near Morwenstow, Parson Hawker's territory, may have had slightly different experiences as they did not have the same level of law enforcement and Customs activity as did Mount's Bay and Land's End, but the documentary record is not as complete. Nevertheless, the study of Mount's Bay offers a comparative framework for areas both inside and outside of Cornwall, for wrecking was practised along the entire British coastline. Indeed, anti-wrecking legislation was enacted in reaction to activity occurring in other areas of the British Isles. Thus we can draw general conclusions about wrecking nationally, as well as situating the practice more firmly within the history of crime.

This study, in its focus on wrecking as a maritime activity, is philosophically at home within maritime history, an overarching field which is 'concerned with the interrelationship of people, things, and events on land and sea ... man's relationship with the sea in all its facets, with all its connections'.[15] It takes advantage of what has been described as postmodernism's 'rich residue [left] on the shore, encouraging historical beach-combing'.[16] This has allowed for a more sophisticated study of wrecking than has heretofore been attempted. Descriptive language has been analysed to interpret elite perspectives of wreckers and wrecking, and a related intellectual development, the 'cultural turn', has been beneficial for illuminating the perceptions of the ruling elite, which in turn not only influenced their policy-making, but was central in the solidification of the wrecking myth into popular consciousness. The tools of the cultural turn have been useful in highlighting the modes of communication used in reporting wrecking, the representation of wreckers given in national media, and 'the interaction between structures of meaning – narratives, discourses – and the ways in which individuals and groups use them and thus express themselves'.[17] These concepts are particularly beneficial when examining the shifting meanings of criminality and the relationships between the various levels of society that were involved in wrecking or in the attempted subjugation of wrecking. Another important concept gleaned from 'beach-combing' is that 'cultural products and practices are performative as well as reflective', meaning that they do not just reflect social experience', but they 'also

[15] Sarah Palmer, 'Seeing the Sea: The Maritime Dimension in History', *Inaugural Lecture Series*, University of Greenwich, 11 May 2000, 9. See also Frank Broeze, ed., *Maritime History at the Crossroads: A Critical Review of Recent Historiography*, Research in Maritime History 9 (St John's Newfoundland, 1995), xvix.

[16] Felipe Fernández-Arnesto, 'Epilogue: What is History Now?', in David Cannadine, ed. *What is History Now?* (London, 2002), 149.

[17] Miri Rubin, 'What is Cultural History Now?', in David Cannadine, ed. *What is History Now?*, 81.

construct it,[18] a process which we will see clearly illustrated in this enquiry. Thus the merging of methodologies and approaches allows us to have a more nuanced understanding of the complexities of wrecking.

### Developing the Stereotype: Representations of Wrecking in Literature

Exactly when the Cornish stereotype of the wrecker made its appearance within popular consciousness is difficult to determine. We do know that by the mid-eighteenth century it was firmly entrenched, and was being reacted to. Writers who commented on wrecking are of two camps: adherents and sceptics. Conflating the differing forms of wrecking, the adherents claim that deliberate wrecking was actually practised in the past, and that there is truth in the stereotype. Sceptics of deliberate wrecking claim it is a myth developed out of the Victorian's penchant for dark Gothic fiction, a genre in which wreckers fit so well.[19] However, its genesis goes back much further. It can be traced through the more general popular accounts of Cornish history and shipwrecks written after the first in-depth study of the county, Richard Carew's *The Survey of Cornwall* (1602). Although Carew's book does not remark on wrecking, other than to state that the finders of wrecks 'by the common custom alloweth a moiety for his labour',[20] the wrecker stereotype is found in subsequent narratives. The first history to express negative comment on wrecking may have been one of the earliest sources to have invented or cemented the Cornish, or in this case Scillonian, reputation. In 1724, Daniel Defoe anonymously published his best-selling *Tour through the Whole Island of Great Britain*, in which he described Scillonian wreckers as 'fierce and ravenous people … they are so greedy, and eager for the prey'.[21] With the popularity of Defoe's writing, the imagery of 'fierce and ravenous people' was situated in the popular mind, and set the debate into the twenty-first century. Subsequent Cornish and Scillonian histories all responded to the existence of the 'Reputation', beginning with Robert Heath's *The Isles of Scilly* in 1750.

---

[18] Sarah Maza, 'Stories in History: Cultural Narratives in Recent Works in European History', *The American Historical Review*, 101, no. 5 (December 1996), 1495.

[19] See Peter Pern, ed., *Cornish Notes and Queries: Reprinted from the* Cornish Telegraph (London, 1906), 292–297; *Mariner's Mirror*, 70 (1984), 44, 388.

[20] Richard Carew of Antony, *The Survey of Cornwall*, ed. F.E. Halliday (originally published London,1602: London, 1953, 1969), 104.

[21] Daniel Defoe, *A Tour through the Whole Island of Great Britain*, intro. G.D.H. Cole and D.C. Browning (originally published London, 1724; London 1962, 1974), 243. There were probably earlier descriptions of the Cornish and Scillonian reputation, but thus far they have not been located. Literary critics accept that Defoe did not visit the Isles of Scilly, thus he could not have witnessed this activity (vii–xvi). However, Defoe must have been aware of the reputation in order to draw upon it, although most likely he embellished it to emphasise their foreignness, to the detriment of the Scillonians.

Heath's tone is unmistakable, claiming that Defoe 'had made so free with the Characters of these People, and Islands that he never saw, nor could possibly be informed of, in so unfaithful a Manner, except by the Dictates of his own Imagination....'[22] Heath's call for defence of the Scillonians was literally adopted in the writings of Rev. John Troutbeck in 1796, which use Heath's exact wording. In 1822, Rev. George Woodley, on the other hand, explicitly denies that the Scillonians were involved in any wrecking, preferring to claim that they were only involved with legal salvage.[23] As with the Isles of Scilly, many nineteenth-century Cornish local histories were written and published by clergy as part of the antiquarian movement. These histories also reacted to the 'Reputation', casting a moralistic, censuring tone upon the practice. The works include Rev. Richard Polwhele, *A History of Cornwall* (1803–08) and Rev. John Whitaker, who, in his *The Ancient Cathedral of Cornwall Historically Surveyed* (1804), took the opportunity to censure the locals of Breage for the practice he called 'so hostile to every principle of Christianity',[24] the taking of wrecked goods from the shore. Fortescue Hitchins and Samuel Drew's *A History of Cornwall* (1824) emphasised that the Cornish were no longer inhuman wreckers who wished to see victims perish; instead they had been 'broken from fierce barbarians into men'.[25] In 1852, Rev. H.J. Whitfield utilised the deliberate wrecking myth as factual evidence to proclaim the defeat of Catholicism (represented by the drowned followers of St Warna, the Scillonian patron saint of shipwrecks and wrecking) by triumphant Protestantism.[26] Rev. Coulthard of Cury and Gunwalloe followed suit in 1912 when he used wrecking as an example to illustrate the violence of the past, but 'when we contrast it with the present it fills the mind with hopefulness, and reveals the vast latent possibilities in human nature for improvement and progress.'[27] Thus these works stressed not only cultural evolution, but religious evolution,

---

[22] Robert Heath, *The Isles of Scilly: the First Book on the Isles of Scilly* (originally published London, 1750; reprinted Newcastle-upon-Tyne, 1967), 53–54.

[23] Rev. John Troutbeck, *A Survey of the Ancient and Present State of the Scilly Islands, &c.* (Sherborne, 1796), 157; Rev. George Woodley, *A View of the Present State of the Scilly Islands: Exhibiting their Vast Importance to the British Empire* ... (London, Truro, 1822), 164. William Borlase's *Observations on the Ancient and Present State of the Islands of Scilly, and their Importance to the Trade of the Great Britain* ... (Oxford, 1756), does not mention wrecking at all.

[24] Rev. Richard Polwhele, *The History of Cornwall, 1760–1838.* Reprint of 1802–1808 and 1816 edition, Vol. III, Book 2 (Dorking, 1978), 49; Rev. John Whitaker, *The Ancient Cathedrals of Cornwall Historically Surveyed*, Vol. I (London, 1804), 338.

[25] Fortescue Hitchins and Samuel Drew, *The History of Cornwall: From the Earliest Records and Traditions to the Present Time* (Helston, 1824), ii. Fortescue Hitchins began the work, but died before it could be completed. Then, in the meantime, the printer, William Penaluna had the papers which were utilised for Penaluna's own *The Circle, or Historical Survey of Sixty Parishes and Towns in Cornwall* (Helston, 1819). Penaluna then asked Samuel Drew to complete Hitchins original work, which was accordingly done.

[26] Rev. H.J. Whitfield, *Scilly and its Legends* (originally published Penzance, 1852; facsimile reprint: Felinfach, 1992), 178–183.

[27] Rev. H.R. Coulthard, *The Story of an Ancient Parish: Breage with Germoe, with Some Account*

in which the barbarities of the past are used as points of reference to emphasise the progress, humanitarianism, and enlightened religion of the Victorian
age. They also subsequently were used to cement the Cornish 'Reputation'
and stereotype.

Contemporary writings are thus useful in tracing perception, and in tracing
the development of the stereotype of the wrecker and his place within popular
myth. Indeed, it is very difficult to separate out fact from fiction in these
histories, as many of these accounts were written in an era when objective
history had not yet been born, when myths and legends were taken as fact and
were more important as morality tales and as works of literature. As a case in
point, the most damning element in the wrecker myth, the use of false lights,
enters the factual realm in the mid-nineteenth century with Cyrus Redding's
historical narrative *An Illustrated Itinerary of the County of Cornwall* (1842).
Redding prefaces his account with the validity principle, that 'it is true, we
were told, and have no reason to doubt the correctness of our information.'[28]
By 1892, national histories written in the Whig tradition, such as that by
William E.H. Lecky, could state authoritatively that the crime 'strikingly
indicative of the imperfect civilisation of the country, was the plunder of
shipwrecked sailors, who were often lured by false signals upon the rocks.'[29]
The charge even appears in an otherwise well-researched modern article on
wreck law.[30] Hence it took little for a mythic story to enter wrecking history
as fact, although this does not preclude a folkloric genesis for the initial false
lights motif.

Two folklorist-clergy writers whose works have also muddied the waters
between the fact and fiction of wrecking, and who are thus major players in
the development of the 'Reputation', are Robert Hawker, vicar of Morwenstow, and Sabine Baring-Gould, rector of Lew Trenchard in Devon. Both
wrote histories, collected folklore, and employed it within their fiction. Baring-
Gould borrowed much from Hawker, particularly the stories of the smuggler-
wrecker 'Cruel' Coppinger, whom Baring-Gould fictionalised in his *In the
Roar of the Sea* (1892). He also wrote a biography of Hawker, which created
much uproar and which was eventually exposed as fictional.[31] In his treat-

---

of its Armigers, Worthies, and Unworthies, Smugglers and Wreckers, its Traditions and Superstitions (Camborne, 1913), 81.
[28] Cyrus Redding, *An Illustrated Itinerary of the County of Cornwall* (London, 1842), 189; see
also Alfonse Esquiros, *Cornwall and its Coasts* (London, 1865), 177–178; Rev. Alfred Hayman
Cummings, *The Churches and Antiquities of Cury and Gunwalloe in the Lizard District, including
Local Traditions* (Truro, London, 1875); Coulthard, *The Story of an Ancient Parish*, 81.
[29] William E.H. Lecky, *A History of England in the Eighteenth Century*, Vol. II (London, 1892),
113.
[30] Frederick C. Hamil, 'Wreck of the Sea in Medieval England', in A.E.R. Boak, ed., *University
of Michigan Historical Essays* (Ann Arbor, 1937), 18–19.
[31] Rev. Sabine Baring-Gould, *The Vicar of Morwenstow: Being the Life of Robert Stephen Hawker,
M.A.* (London, 1899). It was denounced in a series of newspaper articles. See BL Add.37825,

ment of wrecking, Hawker alludes to the practice of deliberate wrecking in his *Footprints of Former Men in Far Cornwall* (1870), but most of his wrecker stories are fairly innocuous, unless he is censuring those whom he felt were remiss in performing their duties of lifesaving. However, as Hawker's son-in-law Charles Byles notes, Hawker had the 'mystifying habit of concealing his identity by vague allusions to "ancient writers" who never existed', thus it is unclear what wrecker allusions are folklore, and what is invention.[32] Like Hawker, Baring-Gould showed his belief in the myth of deliberate wrecking even in his supposedly non-fictional works, such as *The Book of Cornwall* (1899).[33]

Besides Hawker and Baring-Gould, there are two important Cornish folkloric works that record local wrecking stories, and which are crucial to the continuation of the popular myth. They were collected as part of a greater folklore movement in the nineteenth century, when folklorists thought it imperative to salvage stories before they disappeared. They mourned the demise of a past that was losing ground to industrialisation, a process very evident within Cornwall. Thus Robert Hunt produced *Popular Romances of the West of England* (1865) and William Bottrell wrote the three-volume series *Traditions and Hearthside Stories of West Cornwall* (1873), though only Bottrell's second volume contains wrecking stories. Even though Hunt's collection was published before Bottrell's, the primary story, 'Pirate Wrecker and the Death Ship', was collected by Bottrell and shared with Hunt.[34] Unfortunately, it is difficult to determine how much the stories were influenced by earlier fictional works, including the work of Hawker. The stories, however, contain pervasive folkloric beliefs, such as that of false lights and the sightings of a phantom ship, symbols portending death.[35] These collections are an invaluable source for studying popular culture, and for illuminating beliefs

---

Philip Hedgeland papers: 'Some remarks upon two recent memoirs of R. S. Hawker, Late Vicar of Morwenstowe'. See also Piers Brendon, *Hawker of Morwenstow: Portrait of a Victorian Eccentric* (London, 1975, 2002).

[32] Rev. Robert S. Hawker, *Cornish Ballads and Other Poems*. Ed. with an intro. by C.E. Byles (London, 1904), 15, x. Original manuscript, BL Add.37825, Philip Hedgeland papers: 'Some remarks upon two recent memoirs of R. S. Hawker, Late Vicar of Morwenstowe'. For a discussion of Hawker's role in developing the literary representation of wrecking, see Simon Trezise, *The West Country as a Literary Invention: Putting Fiction in its Place* (Exeter, 2000), 51–52.

[33] Rev. Sabine Baring-Gould, *The Book of West Cornwall* (London, 1899; Reprinted 1981), 266.

[34] Robert Hunt, *Popular Romances of the West of England; or the Drolls, Traditions, and Superstitions of Old Cornwall* (London, 1865), 137–140; William Bottrell, *Traditions and Hearthside Stories of West Cornwall*, vol. II (Penzance, 1873), 247–249.

[35] Hunt, Bottrell, and Baring-Gould relate many different stories of false lights, lanterns, and phantom ships which were interpreted as harbingers of death. Cathryn Pearce, 'Lured by False Lights: Cornish Wrecking and Victorian Myth', paper read at the 5th International Congress of Maritime History, University of Greenwich, 23–27 June 2008. See also Hunt, *Popular Romances*, 135–36, 144–146; Bottrell, *Traditions and Hearthside Stories*, 141, 145; Baring-Gould, *The Book of West Cornwall*, 266.

regarding shipwrecks and wrecking, although for reasons already indicated they must be used with caution.

One of the most important non-fictional works that has added to the mythology of wrecking is Michael Oppenheim's chapter in the *Victoria County History of Cornwall* (1906).[36] Unfortunately, the scholarship within this chapter is seriously flawed. Although he employed important primary sources such as State, Chancery, and Admiralty papers, for wrecking he relied on partially fictionalised works, such as William J. Hardy's *Lighthouses: Their History and Romance*.[37] This failure led, for example, to the transmogrification of an innocent case of the misfortune of shipwreck in 1681 on St Agnes, Isles of Scilly, into a 'factual' depiction of deliberate wrecking by the lighthouse keeper.[38] Oppenheim's chapter is, in turn, the source for many of Cornwall's well-known historians who have described wrecking in their works, such as Charles Henderson and A.K. Hamilton Jenkin.

Most Cornish histories use Henderson, an Oxford-trained Cornish historian specialising in medieval history. Before he died at the age of 33, he published several articles on Cornish wrecking which are at their strongest for the medieval period.[39] Unfortunately, he did not employ documents on wrecking for the later periods, but rather relied on the work of Oppenheim. Likewise, Hamilton Jenkin, the author of such well-known books as *The Cornish Seafarer: The Smuggling, Wrecking & Fishing Life of Cornwall* (1932), *Cornwall and its People* (1945), and *News from Cornwall* (1946), used both Oppenheim and Henderson, as did John Rowe in his unparalleled study on Cornwall in the Industrial Revolution.[40] The use of these texts continues in popular studies of shipwrecks and wrecking in Cornwall. However, it is necessary to emphasise their reflexivity. Stories of wreckers related by Cornish informants can easily be traced directly back to these sources. Thus, as with newspapers, they have had a major role in myth-making, and the 'ability to alter the pattern of history'.[41]

---

36  Michael Oppenheim, 'Maritime History', in *Victoria County History of Cornwall*, Vol. I (London, 1906), 475–511.

37  William J. Hardy, *Lighthouses: Their History and Romance* (London, 1895).

38  Cathryn Pearce, '"Neglectful or Worse': A Lurid Tale of a Lighthouse Keeper and Wrecking in the Isles of Scilly', *Troze: The Online Journal of the National Maritime Museum Cornwall*, 1, no. 1 (September 2008).

39  Sir Arthur Quiller-Couch in Charles Henderson, *Essays in Cornish History*, ed. by A.L. Rowse and M.I. Henderson (Oxford, 1935. Reprinted Truro, 1963), Foreword, n.p. Henderson's most quoted article on wrecking is 'Cornish Wrecks and Wreckers: Plundered Ships and Sailors', *The Western Morning News and Mercury*, Monday 21 January 1929.

40  John Rowe, *Cornwall in the Age of the Industrial Revolution* (Liverpool, 1953). Fortunately Rowe also utilised other primary sources in his account, and so escaped some of the serious errors of the other works.

41  Owen Davies, 'Newspapers and Popular Belief in Witchcraft and Magic in the Modern Period', *Journal of British Studies*, 37 (April 1998), 149.

Not all recent works have contributed to the making of the popular myth, although they are inextricably tied to the 'Reputation'. In reacting disapprovingly to the adherents of the 'Reputation', apologists such as Alfonse Esquiros, in his *Cornwall and its Coasts* (1865), Jonathan Couch, in *The History of Polperro* (1871), and C.F.C. Clifton, in *Bude Haven* (1902), addressed the conflation of the myths of deliberate wrecking with other aspects of the wrecker stereotype, and defended the Cornish by emphasising their role in lifesaving and the humane treatment of shipwreck victims. Couch and Clifton also railed against what they felt was a slanderous reputation created by fiction writers, a charge that would be brought up in several debates regarding the truth or falsity of the Cornish use of false lights that would rage in the pages of the *Cornish Telegraph* and the *Mariner's Mirror* in the twentieth century.[42] There is no doubt that the wrecker theme was popular among Victorian writers. Indeed, James Cobb's Methodist novel *The Watchers on the Longships* (1876), which has as its central character a deliberate wrecker and which was located amongst the Cornish mining communities, was reprinted at least 35 times.

Wrecking as a cultural construct has thus been given meaning according to the era and cultural milieu in which it has been used. Most of the earlier views of the wrecker are firmly situated in Victorian morality tracts, to illustrate moral depravity in the face of religious evolution, or, within literature, as a symbol of marginality, to show the 'march of progress' with the arrival of civilising influences.[43] Additionally, the stories have also been used as entertainment, whether as backdrops for boy's adventure novels, gothic romances, or theatre and opera. Wrecking has also been the subject in the long-running debate on the truth or falsity of the myths, rather than the focus of an attempt to understand it as an activity of the coastal populace. Indeed, both wrecking as a practice and wrecking as a narrative have been taken out of their contemporary context by popular writers, transmogrified and sensationalised, to create the popular view of wreckers that has become common currency.[44]

Few recent works have attempted to treat wrecking in a more sophisticated, systematic manner, with three notable exceptions. Based on the theoretical framework established by E.P. Thompson and the Warwick school, John Rule

---

[42] Esquiros, *Cornwall and its Coasts*, 177–178; Jonathan Couch, *The History of Polperro: a Fishing Town on the South-Coast of Cornwall* (first published 1871; Newcastle-upon-Tyne, 1965), 44; C.F.C. Clifton, *Bude Haven: Bencoolen to Capricorno: A Record of Wrecks at Bude, 1862 to 1900* (Manchester, 1902), 13, 52. For the false lights debate, see Pern, *Cornish Notes*, 292–297; and *Mariner's Mirror*, 70 (1984), 44, 388.

[43] Helen Hughes, "'A Silent, Desolate Country': Images of Cornwall in Daphne du Maurier's *Jamaica Inn*', in Ella Westland, ed., *Cornwall: The Cultural Construction of Place* (Penzance, 1997), 68–75.

[44] See Cathryn Pearce, review of Bella Bathurst's *The Wreckers*, in *International Journal of Maritime History*, 17, no. 2 (December 2005), 411–412.

presented his seminal chapter on wrecking in *Albion's Fatal Tree* (1975).[45] It is the most frequently cited source on wrecking in eighteenth-century crime studies.[46] He argues that wrecking fits within a recurring theme of the social history of the late eighteenth to early nineteenth centuries: that of popular custom versus legal prohibition. It takes its place alongside the activities of smuggling, poaching, and food riots. Rule subsequently refined his views on wrecking to include it within his discussion of social crime in the rural south, a concept that he defines as a 'criminal action which is legitimised by popular opinion'.[47] However, he did not return to the subject to give it an in-depth inquiry. Thus this study responds to and refines the model of wrecking developed by Rule, particularly that of the 'social crime' thesis. It is not, however, intended to be one more study of protest crime. Rather it is an analysis of an important coastal activity whose serious study is a long overdue.

On a slightly different tack, Philip Payton identified wrecking as a constituent element of Cornish ethnic identity. He argues that wrecking formed a 'nice paradox juxtaposing the supposed savagery of remote West Barbary with the modernity of global maritime communication ... it was played out in a contest between wreckers and government officials, the former insistent upon the exercise of ancient privileges and the latter equally insistent upon the rule of the law'.[48] In other words, wrecking was just one example of the particularism and individuality of the Cornish. Payton also recognises the value of John Vivian's little booklet *Tales of Cornish Wreckers*, which highlights the conflict between the locals and government. Indeed, Vivian's work in bringing together wrecking stories for the tourist market has resulted in a very useful source, although his thesis highlighting the conflict between the Government and the Cornish is hidden among the tales.[49]

Wrecking as a topic, therefore, has been used in the literature in a variety of ways, whether to point out the depravity of the wreckers and so to sustain the wrecking myth or to defend the Cornish by pointing out that wrecking was on the wane, as a result of moral enlightenment. Wrecking has also been treated with a more sophisticated approach, in discussions of social crime, or

---

[45] 'Wrecking and Coastal Plunder', in Douglas Hay, Peter Linebaugh, et al., *Albion's Fatal Tree: Crime and Society in Eighteenth-Century England* (London, 1975, 1988), 167–188. Only in France has the topic been given full-length scholarly treatment. See Alain Cabantous, *Les côtes barbares: Pilleurs d'épaves et sociétés littorales en France, 1680–1830* (Fayard, 1993).

[46] Clive Emsley, *Crime and Society in England, 1750–1900* (London, 1996), 3–4; J.A. Sharpe, *Crime in Early Modern England, 1550–1750* (London, 1984, 1992), 12–13; and Peter King, *Crime, Justice and Discretion in England 1740–1820* (Oxford, 2003), 6.

[47] John G. Rule, 'Social Crime in the Rural South in the Eighteenth and Early Nineteenth Centuries', *Southern History*, 1 (1979), 138–139; John G. Rule and Roger Wells, *Crime, Protest and Popular Politics in Southern England, 1740–1850* (London, 1997), 153–168.

[48] Philip Payton, *Cornwall: A History* (Fowey, 2004), 172. See also John Vivian, *Tales of Cornish Wreckers* (Truro, 1969).

[49] Vivian, *Tales of Cornish Wreckers*.

as an example of Cornish particularism. However, it has not, except for Rule's work, been studied as an important subject in its own right, nor has there been any attempt to establish an accurate portrayal of wrecking in relation to the reflective and performative properties of the myth. This book provides that much needed corrective.

The structure of the book is as follows: Chapter 1 gives context to wrecking by investigating Cornish geography and the general historical background of the county, thus showing the importance of the maritime realm. Chapter 2 focuses on the development of wreck law and the rights of wreck in the medieval and early modern period, since these were the foundation for legal concepts arising in the eighteenth and nineteenth centuries. Chapter 3 analyses the legal reaction to wrecking in the eighteenth and nineteenth centuries, and traces the development of wreck legislation. This includes the elite attempt to clarify definitions of wrecking offences and a consideration of the shifting sense of the criminality of wrecking. Chapter 4 examines the 'country people' of Cornwall and assesses their custom of wrecking. It considers the identity of those involved and their motives; the economic significance of wrecking; and the social crime debate. Chapter 5 appraises the concept of popular morality, and evaluates not only the levels of violence, but the evidence and mechanisms for wrecker restraint. Chapter 6 investigates the criminality of wrecking, by analysing prosecutions and convictions for various wrecking offences. It also traces the effect of developing forms of law enforcement and the wreckers' mediation with authority. Chapter 7 furthers the investigation of the communal practice of wrecking, by examining the role and responsibility of the lords of the manors and their relationship to not only the 'country people', but to each other, as also to the Government. Chapter 8 traces the effects on local wreck rights of the growth of central government bureaucracy, especially that of HM Customs and the Board of Trade. Chapter 9 focuses on the use of language and sensationalism by the press and clergy, which solidi-fied the wrecker stereotype and resulted in the survival of the popular myth.

# Cornwall and the Sea

THE dictionary definition of wrecking does little to illustrate the gruel-ling labour and danger involved; neither does it truly portray the condi-tions. Wrecking, salvaging and lifesaving – concomitant activities – were particularly dangerous when they took place at the height of a gale, often in the hours of morning before dawn. Curtains of wind and rain lashed at the wreckers, obstructing vision and making footholds on the cliff face perilous. Cold and wet hands grasped at the rocks for balance as they tried to reach for the slippery hands of survivors or for the bodies of those who died or for the cargo as it slammed ashore. Hearing, too, was impaired by the howl of the gale and the cacophony of sounds coming from the sea; indeed, the wind drowned out the calls of survivors and of fellow wreckers. Backs ached with the strain of hauling bodies and cargo ashore; hogsheads full of wine or brandy (456 pounds in weight) or tobacco (almost 1000 pounds) were water-logged, making them even heavier. Backs were further compromised by the exertion it took to haul the goods from the heavy and dangerous surf, and up steep and craggy cliffs out of the reach of the sea. Some wreckers, salvors and lifesavers were not so lucky, and were swept off the cliffs, dragged under by the violence of the sea, to be pounded against the rocks along with the shattered and broken remains of the ship.

Such scenes played out every winter along Cornwall's coast, although most often wrecking and salving were much less labour-intensive, occurring well after the ship was wrecked, as the cargo and remains of the vessel washed ashore over miles of coastline. In that case, it was only a matter of walking along the shore, picking up items deposited on the beach by the gale or a high tide. Likewise, goods lost from smuggling ventures would also wash ashore, to be collected by those fortunate enough to be first on the scene. These authentic wrecking scenes belie the more popular, but inaccurate, image of deliberate wrecking; they also belie what has become a more prominent, land-based view of Cornish history.

In 1930 Sir Arthur Quiller-Couch emphasised the remoteness of Corn-wall; its almost island status, its foreign ways, and the slow development of its road system. He gave a view of the almost total isolation of the Cornish, citing Wilkie Collins's visit in 1851, when the Cornish looked on in suspicion

Map 1. Cornwall and the Isles of Scilly

at the stranger in their midst.[1] This representation conformed to his perceived vision of his native Cornwall, and accentuated his attempts at promoting Cornish particularism – the uniqueness of Cornwall and its Celtic culture. It is within this vision of uniqueness and isolation that the activity of wrecking is placed by popular culture. However, this representation is centred on a land-based view, and fails to take into account Cornwall's thriving maritime-based economy in the eighteenth and nineteenth centuries, and the influence of the sea on Cornwall's identity. The sea is a resource, whether as a seaway for trade, a fishing ground, or provider of wrecks; the Cornish took advantage of all those resources. As one historian put it, 'England possessed the fortune to sit athwart one of the busiest trade routes in the world.'[2] And sitting centrally along those trade routes was Cornwall. Thus, the foundation of Cornwall's reputation for wrecking lay in its location and its relationship with the sea.

## Geography

Visitors to Cornwall discover that the sea figures prominently; it is never far from sight. Indeed, the county is surrounded by the sea on three sides: by the English Channel, the Celtic Sea, leading to the Bristol Channel, and the Atlantic Ocean. Its fourth side is bounded by the River Tamar, which effec-tively cuts it off from Devon. With the smaller Penwith Peninsula attached to

[1]   William Harding Thompson, *Cornwall: A Survey of its Coast, Moors, and Valleys, with Suggestions for the Preservation of Amenities.* Preface by Sir Arthur Quiller-Couch (London, 1930), n.p.
[2]   Richard Price, *British Society, 1680–1880: Dynamism, Containment, Change* (Cambridge, 1999), 57.

its westernmost reaches, Cornwall extends 80 miles from east to west; it is 40 miles from north to south at its widest along the Devon border. Significantly, no part of the county is over 18 miles from the sea. Isolating it from the more populous, central parts of England, Cornwall's physical features also give it a sense of remoteness. Granite makes up the majority of the land mass, making for a rough, almost desolate terrain. The interior is dominated by a rocky spine consisting of granite moors, the most famous being Bodmin Moor. The Penwith Peninsula, too, has high moorland and granite outcroppings at its centre; its hard-rock cliffs are carved by the sea's uncontrollable power.

This relative isolation also preserved other elements: the Neolithic stone circles, quoits, and monoliths, left by a mysterious, unknowable ancient population, mistakenly presumed by some early antiquarians to be the work of giants or Druids;[3] the stone remnants of Iron Age villages on the moors; and the stone Celtic crosses by the roadside, evidence of early Celtic missionaries from Ireland and Wales who left their names on landmarks and villages. This isolation is also credited with maintaining Cornwall's distinctive, widely dispersed settlement patterns. Rather than clustering in small nucleated villages as was common in parts of England, many Cornish lived in isolated homesteads near the fields they tilled. The result is Cornwall's characteristic maze of tiny lanes 'narrow, deep-set, and twisting, that take little or no account of what happens in the next parish, but pursue their sequestered way independently'.[4] These lanes not only linked the homesteads; they also connected the surrounding countryside to the few market towns such as Penzance and St Ives, and to the shoreline.[5] The Cornish continued to live in these small villages despite Cornwall's population growth through the nineteenth century. Indeed, the parish of Gwennap, one of the richest of the mining districts, located in the western half of Cornwall, had a population of 10,465 in 1851. But it did not have a single settlement larger than a village, and this was not unusual.[6]

Visitors to Cornwall are also struck by the topography and weather, especially if they happen to enter the county in autumn or winter. Celia Fiennes, visiting in 1698, picturesquely described most of the towns she visited, remarking that they lie 'down in a bottom, pretty steep ascent ... that you would be afraid of tumbling with nose and head foremost'. The treach-

---

3   See William Borlase, *Observations on the Antiquities of Cornwall* (1756) and *Antiquities, Historical and Monumental, of the County of Cornwall* (1769).
4   W.G.V. Balchin, *Cornwall: An Illustrated Essay on the History of the Landscape* (London, 1954), 112.
5   The most important markets in the eighteenth and nineteenth century included Truro, Bodmin, Launceston, Stratton, Lostwithiel, St Ives, Mousehole, Penzance, Fowey, Helston, and Marazion.
6   John G. Rule 'The Labouring Miner in Cornwall c. 1740–1870: a study in social history' (unpublished Ph.D. thesis, University of Warwick, 1971), 194.

erous ascent into the towns was usually coupled with pelting wind and rain. Indeed, because of Cornwall's location, almost every season witnesses gales: 'they fall upon the land in all their violence and frequently occasion considerable mischief', Fiennes explained.[7] As Victorian writers Fortescue Hitchins and Samuel Drew stressed, 'nearly three-fourths of the year the wind blows from some of the intermediate points between north-west and south-east; and those winds which issue from the south-west, not only bring rain, but also violent gales, from which mariners too frequently suffer.'[8]

## The Dangers of Shipwreck

With the prevailing weather patterns and Cornwall's location jutting out into the sea, shipwreck along its coasts was inevitable. The numbers of wrecks are almost impossible to estimate, although several scholars have attempted to do so by establishing shipwreck databases, drawing their data from such diverse sources as *Lloyd's List*, newspapers, logs, journals, correspondence, and archaeological remains. Case studies of Dutch and English East India Company shipping losses show that between 3 and 5 per cent of shipping was lost every year from the late seventeenth to early nineteenth century. *Lloyd's List* reported over a thousand wrecks or losses in the short period from 1770 to 1775.[9] These figures are for overall wrecks and losses. Important for this study, however, are the shipwrecks along the British coastline. Over a quarter of a million ships may have been lost along the British coast since records began.[10] In 1810, W.H. Mallison, arguing for a society to aid shipwrecked seamen, suggested that over 3000 to 4000 lives were lost annually on the British coast, an appalling number.[11] Although popular belief holds that Cornwall has more shipwrecks than any other coastal county, this is not the case. The east coast of England experienced a greater number of shipwrecks than did the more notorious Cornwall. This is accounted for by the sheer amount of traffic between the Baltic and England, as well as the coasting coal trade. On the south coast, Kent heads the list with the most shipwrecks overall, especially when the infamous Goodwin Sands are taken into account.

---

[7]   Celia Fiennes, *The Journeys of Celia Fiennes*, ed. Christopher Morris (London, 1947), 265.
[8]   Fortescue Hitchins and Samuel Drew. *The History of Cornwall: From the Earliest Records and Traditions, to the Present Time*. Vol. I (Helston, 1824), 557.
[9]   Peter Earle, *Sailors: English Merchant Seamen, 1650–1775* (London, 1998), 110.
[10]  Richard Larn, *Cornish Shipwrecks: The Isles of Scilly*, Vol. 3 (Newton Abbott, 1971), 210. The results of Larn's research can be found at www.shipwrecksuk.com, although his earlier work was published by Lloyd's Register as *Shipwreck Index of the British Isles*, 5 Volumes (1995–98).
[11]  W.H. Mallison. *Plan of an Institution for Rendering Assistance to Shipwrecked Mariners, Preserving their Lives, and the Property of Merchants, When Wreck Occurs* (London, 1810), 29.

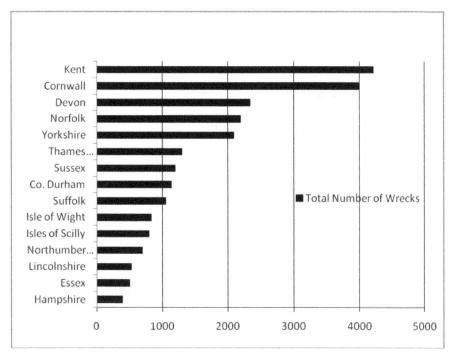

Figure 2. Total Number of Shipwrecks, by County. Source: compiled from Richard Larn and Bridget Larn, *Shipwreck Index of the British Isles*, 5 vols. (London, 1995–98).[a]

[a] These figures must be used with some caution, as the index for Cornwall and the Isles of Scilly may be more complete than figures for the rest of England. Larn utilised more diverse sources for Cornwall such as the *Lloyd's Register*, *Lloyd's List*, newspapers, and archival collections, while his figures for the rest of England are drawn primarily from *Lloyd's List*. However, the large numbers shown for the east coast, despite fewer sources searched, indicate that the margin may be even wider.

While popular writers have asserted that a small number of shipwrecks may have been caused by deliberate wrecking, by luring ships ashore with false lights, there is no evidence to substantiate this claim.[12] Indeed, evidence of deliberate wrecking is limited to a few cases of insurance fraud and the occasional cutting of ships' cables. Rather, the 'usual reasons' for shipwreck, as identified by the Parliamentary Select Committee on Shipwreck (1836), included concerns that the select committee hoped to alleviate, among them the defective construction of ships; inadequate equipment; poor repair;

[12] See, for instance Bella Bathurst, *The Wreckers: A Story of Killing Seas, False Lights and Plundered Ships* (London, 2005), xvii.

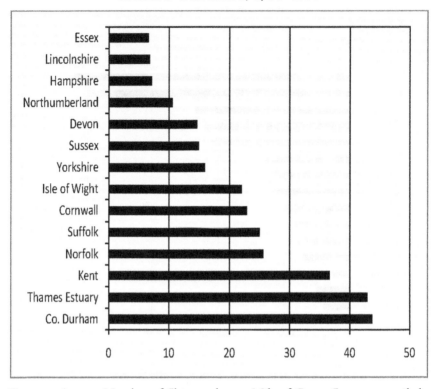

Figure 3. Average Number of Shipwrecks per Mile of Coast. Source: compiled from Larn, *Shipwreck Index of the British Isles*, 5 vols.

improper or excessive loading of cargo; inappropriate ships for the cargoes being carried; incompetent masters and officers, including problems with drunkenness and lack of navigational knowledge; poor marine insurance; the lack of harbours of refuge to lay-to during bad weather; and poor charts which either misplaced navigational hazards, or omitted them altogether.[13]

Although Cornwall has a hazardous coast, neither the Select Committee of 1836, nor the Select Committee of 1842 considered the county's location in causing shipwrecks, other than to listen to testimony as to the lack of harbours of refuge and proper lighting on the north Cornish coast.[14] Indeed, most of its attention was on the east coast of England, an area that saw the worst of the shipwreck statistics, and which was important for the coastal coal trade. Despite this, none could deny that the Cornish coast was dangerous, having its share of shipwrecks. Land's End, especially, was dangerous to navi-

[13]  PP, *Report from the Select Committee Appointed to Inquire into the Causes of Shipwrecks: with the Minutes of Evidence, Appendix and Index*, 15 August 1836, v.
[14]  PP, *First Report from the Select Committee on Shipwrecks; Together with Minutes of Evidence, Appendix and Index*, 10 August 1843.

gation. Hitchins and Drew aptly described the conditions 'to which sailors are too frequently exposed' along Land's End in the nineteenth century: 'Between the projecting promontories, the bays in some places are very deep: and in stormy weather, when ships get within the headlands, it is with the utmost difficulty that they can escape being driven on the rocks.' They continue:

> Another inconvenience arises from the particular form which the land assumes, and from the rapidity of the tides near the Land's End. Presenting rather a point, than a bold and extended shore to vessels coming from the Atlantic, it is not always that mariners can know with certainty which channel they have entered, until they find themselves unexpectedly thrown upon a leeward shore ...[15]

If ships were blown to the north of Land's End, from the Celtic Sea towards the Bristol Channel, they found a north coast bereft of safe harbours, except for the Hayle estuary, St Ives, and Padstow, the few important ports. (See Map 2.) Indeed, throughout the nineteenth century, the situation on the north coast was cause for an extensive debate on the future locations of lighthouses and harbours of refuge. In 1829, the Padstow Harbour Association for the Prevention of Shipwrecks issued a report recounting the conditions:

> The character of the shore from the Land's End to Hartland Point, a distance of twenty-four leagues, is marked by a continuation of rocky inaccessible cliffs, broken at intervals by sandy beaches of equal fatality; and a ground sea is incessantly thrown in from the Atlantic Ocean, at times augmented to a powerful degree by the north-westerly gales so prevalent in the winter season. The whole of this part of Cornwall is therefore naturally dreaded by navigators, and proves fatal to those, who, either from ignorance of their situation, or a fear of the difficulties of access, do not avail themselves of the security fully presented to them by the only harbour on the coast; but vainly endeavouring to beat off, and losing ground on every tack, they are inevitably wrecked either to the eastward or westward of the port, and generally with the loss of all lives on board ...[16]

Sabine Baring-Gould, with his characteristic Victorian romanticism, described the north coast: it is emphatically "'the cruel sea," fierce, insatiate, hungering for human lives and stately vessels, that it may cast them up mumbled and mangled after having robbed them of life and treasure.'[17]

A ship blown towards the south coast, and into the English Channel, met with a very different coastline. The south Cornish coast has a gentler topography, including more wooded valleys, with many small fingers of the Channel reaching inland to create natural harbours. (See Map 3). The ports

---

[15]  Hitchins and Drew, *History of Cornwall*, Vol. I, 541.
[16]  PB/6/234, Report of the Proceedings of Padstow Harbour Association for the Prevention of Shipwrecks, 1829.
[17]  Sabine Baring-Gould, *The Vicar of Morwenstow: Being the Life of Robert Stephen Hawker, M.A.* (London: 1899), 33.

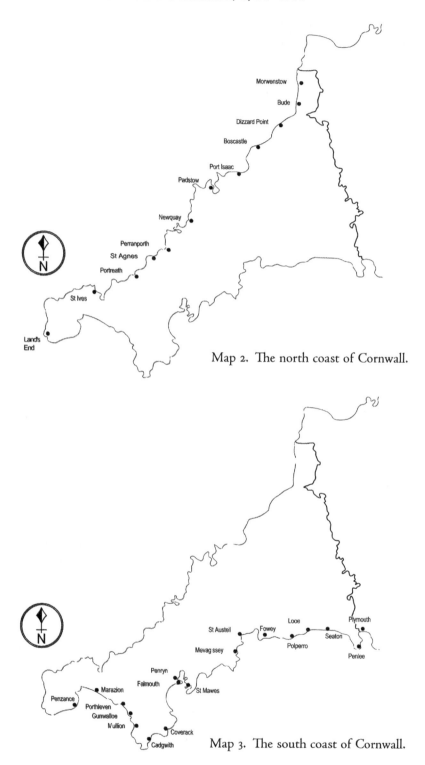

Map 2. The north coast of Cornwall.

Map 3. The south coast of Cornwall.

of Mount's Bay, Falmouth, Looe, Polperro, and Fowey were frequently used as safe harbours during gales. However, the south coast, too, had its dangers. The Lizard, the furthest most southern point in Great Britain, which juts out into the English Channel, was a particularly perilous stretch. Again, Hitchins and Drew vividly describe the terrors of the Lizard:

> Through the fury of the winds and seas, and the awful darkness with which the tempests of Cornwall are often accompanied, ships are frequently driven on shore, particularly foreigners, and beaten to pieces at the base of the projecting point. When these melancholy catastrophes happen at night, the howling of the storm, and the roaring of the waves, prevent the cries of the perishing seamen from being heard, while the darkness that reigns conceals the mournful scene from every eye. The disaster is only known in the morning by the fragments of the wreck, which are seen beating against the rocks, and the mangled bodies of the seamen that are distinguished among the crags, or seen occasionally lifted up by the surges of the boiling deep ...[18]

With such a dangerous coast, Cornwall and the Isles of Scilly were some of the first areas to see the establishment of regular lighthouses, beginning with the Lizard Lighthouse in 1619. The Killigrew family built the original structure with permission from the Corporation of Trinity House.[19] St Agnes Light in the Isles of Scilly followed in 1680, the first built by Trinity House proper. These lighthouses were followed by the Eddystone Light (1698), built by Henry Winstanley, and Longships off Land's End, built almost one hundred years later by Lt Henry Smith with Trinity House approval. By the end of the eighteenth century, these four lighthouses were the only aids to navigation operating on the entire Cornish coast, and were considered by many to be insufficient. 'Primitive' coal fires still lit the Lizard and St Agnes until the end of the eighteenth century, which had several disadvantages. They not only reflected less light, but the lighthouses lacked unique signals, so they could not be distinguished from each other until oil lamps and revolving reflectors were fitted in 1790 and 1811 respectively.[20] Indeed, Cornwall only became properly lighted at the end of the nineteenth century.

Shipwreck was thus a major reality both for mariners and for the Cornish people. However, we need to realise that certain locations within Cornwall experienced more shipwrecks than others, just as there were certain districts which gave more opportunity for the harvest of wrecked goods. Based on figures given in the Larn's *Shipwreck Index* , the areas experiencing the most shipwrecks in the period from 1700 to 1865 include: on the south coast,

[18]  Hitchins and Drew, *History of Cornwall*, Vol. II, 382.
[19]  For a complete discussion concerning the debate surrounding the establishment of the Lizard Lighthouse, see Howard Fox, 'The Lizard Lighthouse', *Journal of the Royal Institution of Cornwall*, 6, pt 14 (1879), 319–336. The lighthouse was rebuilt on two promontories in 1751.
[20]  Cyril Noall, *Cornish Lights and Ship-Wrecks, including the Isles of Scilly* (Truro, 1968), 11, 16.

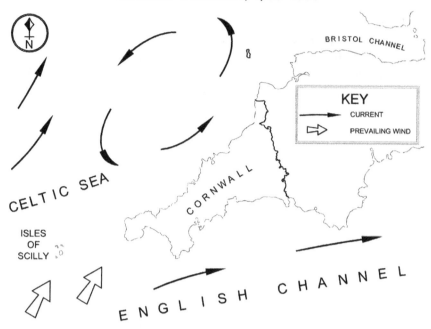

Map 4. Prevailing Winds and Currents of the Cornish Coast.

Mount's Bay (243), Land's End (236), Falmouth (121), and the Lizard (91); and on the north coast, St Ives (153), Newquay (67), Padstow (196), and Bude Haven (74) were the most dangerous. Many of these wrecks occurred at harbour mouths, especially of those ships which encountered difficulty at sea and attempted to limp into the nearest safe haven. Additionally, the locations where wrecked materials and victims washed ashore were dependent on the winds, currents, and tides. (See Map 4). This record of shipwrecks, and the county's resultant wrecking activity, has added additional fuel to the argument for Cornish particularism. It solidifies an image of remoteness and barbarity, both of the people and of the topography.

## Cornwall's Maritime Trade

Despite Cornwall's distinctive features and apparent isolation, this is not a comprehensive picture by any means. Rather, Cornwall's history contains a paradox. While it had an economy and society that was isolated from the rest of the country before the mid-nineteenth century, it was involved in the international market-place, and was thus open to external influences. Cornwall, like the rest of the coastal British Isles, had developed a thriving international maritime trade which was active until the end of the nineteenth century, a trade which brought a variety of goods to, and – in the case of shipwreck –

onto its shores.[21] Thus wrecking was just one of many activities that made up Cornwall's maritime dimension, but it was an activity that was implicitly connected with maritime trade.

Cornwall's overall economy during the medieval period relied on the sea, whether for trade, food, smuggling, piracy, or wrecking.[22] Its ports had welcomed and feared the arrival of strangers for centuries, even back into the midst of the ancient world, when local folklore claims that Phoenicians called to trade for Cornish tin.[23] Indeed, Cornwall's trading ties with Brittany, Wales, and Ireland, as well as Iberia and the Mediterranean, were part of a much older tradition going back thousands of years – perhaps initially stronger than that resulting from their land-based relationship with the rest of England.[24] Such trade increased exponentially with the Industrial Revolution of the eighteenth century, which came early to Cornwall because of its mining industry.[25] Falmouth, Looe, and other smaller Cornish ports were major participants in the southern European trades, clearing 149 ships to Spain and Portugal between 1715 and 1717, out of a total of 513 ships that set sail from England, the majority of the others departing from larger ports such as London, Exeter, Bristol, Liverpool, and Plymouth. In the same years, the Cornish ports sent 47 vessels to Genoa, Leghorn, Marseilles, and Venice in the Mediterranean out of a total of 177 English ships involved in the trade.[26]

Cornwall's major exports came mainly from its mining and fishing industries, produced by those who made up its wrecking population. In particular, tin, gold, copper, slate, and china clay were either loaded onto foreign ships, or carried by the Cornish themselves in Cornish ships to either foreign or domestic ports. Roman records from the first century BC indicate that the tin trade had long been in existence, and it became of increasing significance to Rome itself.[27] By the medieval period, tin exports had increased substantially, as had the number of mines, where tin-streaming was being replaced by underground mining. The production of tin continued to increase, even through the upheavals of such political events as the Hundred Years' War,

---

[21] For an excellent discussion of Cornwall and the Southwest's falling position in the British maritime economy, see David J. Starkey, 'Growth and Transition in Britain's Maritime Economy, 1870–1914: The Case of South-West England', in David J. Starkey and Alan G. Jamieson, eds., *Exploiting the Sea: Aspects of Britain's Maritime Economy since 1870* (Exeter, 1998), 7–36.

[22] John Hatcher, *Rural Economy and Society in the Duchy of Cornwall, 1300–1500* (Cambridge, 1970), 32.

[23] Malcolm Todd credits Tudor antiquary John Twyne with the Phoenician trade thesis, who 'thus started a hare whose elusive shade is still hunted on the wilder shores of archaeological romance'. *The South West to AD 1000* (London and New York, 1987), 13.

[24] Barry Cunliffe, *Facing the Ocean: The Atlantic and its Peoples, 8000BC–AD 1500* (Oxford, 2001), especially Chapter 1; Balchin, *Cornwall*, 25.

[25] John Rowe, *Cornwall in the Age of the Industrial Revolution* (Liverpool, 1953), Chapter 1.

[26] Ralph Davis, *The Rise of the English Shipping Industry in the 17th and 18th Centuries* (London, 1962, 1972), 243, 256.

[27] Todd, *The South West*, 188; Philip Payton, *Cornwall: A History* (Fowey, 2004), 47, 52.

the Anglo-Spanish War, and the English Civil Wars. By the end of the seventeenth century mining was the single most important industry, overtaking other Cornish economic activities such as agriculture and fishing.[28] Significant factors in the success of the Cornish tin industry were its near monopoly, and its importance in the manufacture of pewter.[29] Indeed, mining in some areas of Cornwall was the dominant economy, amassing most of the available labour and capital.[30] By the late eighteenth century, the East India Company had become a major purchaser of Cornish tin.[31] Thus the Cornish 'tinner' became emblematic of Cornwall's labour force as well as a key figure of the wrecking myth.

Beginning in the seventeenth century, advances in technology allowed copper to be mined at deeper levels, and thus by the early nineteenth century it overtook tin as Cornwall's primary mineral export.[32] Production did not slow down until the mid-nineteenth century, when discoveries overseas forced the price of copper down, resulting in the mass emigration of the Cornish miners, termed 'Cousin Jacks', to the newly discovered seams.[33] Also, by the eighteenth century the discovery of china clay in Cornwall and the increasing demand for luxury goods such as Wedgwood pottery fuelled the mining and export of the commodity, leading to the establishment of new ports such as Charlestown and to the extension of others, such as Porthleven. In the nineteenth century, the export of minerals was joined by the export of mining equipment, such as the Cornish beam engine and pumping engine, produced in several of Cornwall's foundries.

Cornwall's agricultural produce, too, was exported by sea, beginning in the mid-seventeenth century, although never in large quantities. Most agriculture was for subsistence, although excess crops were exported after the Civil Wars to foreign markets such as France and Spain, and to domestic markets such as Plymouth, Exeter, Bristol, and London. Although minerals were Cornwall's most visible export during the eighteenth and nineteenth centuries, and mining directly employed one-third of the working population, with others working in support and ancillary services, arable agriculture continued to be the major employer of labour.[34] Thus farmers made up

---

[28] Payton, *Cornwall*, 84, 132.

[29] Rowe, *Cornwall in the Age of the Industrial Revolution*, 14–15; Payton, *Cornwall*, 153.

[30] James Whetter, *Cornwall in the 17th Century: An Economic History of Kernow* (Padstow, 1974, 2002), 172.

[31] Rowe, *Cornwall in the Age of the Industrial Revolution*, 177; Payton, *Cornwall*, 185; D. Bradford Barton, *A History of Tin Mining and Smelting in Cornwall* (Truro, 1965; repub. Exeter, 1989), 17.

[32] Payton, *Cornwall*, 155.

[33] See Arthur C. Todd, *The Cornish Miner in America* (originally published Truro, 1967; reprinted: Spokane, Washington, 1995).

[34] Edwin Jaggard, *Cornwall Politics in the Age of Reform, 1790–1885* (London, 1999), 10, 11. According to the occupational census of 1851, in the county as a whole there were 85,509

a majority of Cornwall's population. Corn, wheat and barley predominated, with some oat crops grown inland. With the increasing Cornish population, however, demand began to outstrip supply, which lessened the amount of crops available for export. Indeed, Cornwall's total population leapt during this period, from 140,000 people in 1750, to 192,000 in 1800, and up to 342,000 by 1841, creating a greater demand for locally grown produce.[35] The majority of the population increase was in the mining districts, particularly Illogan, Gwennap, Camborne, Breage, Kenwyn, and Kea.[36] Shortages from a series of harvest failures led to food riots by hungry miners, most notably in 1789, 1793, 1795–96, 1801–03, 1812, 1831, and 1847. The miners insisted that the grain first be sold at a reasonable price locally, and only then should any excess be exported for additional profit.[37] These same harvest failures can be linked to upsurges in wrecking activity.

Besides mining and agriculture, fishing was one of the most important economic activities in the period, and it made up a significant sector of Cornwall's international exports.[38] Important centres included Fowey, Polperro, Mevagissey, Mousehole, and Newlyn on the south coast, and St Ives, Newquay, Port Isaac, and Padstow on the north coast, although almost all areas of the coast had a fishery, if only for subsistence. Fishing communities involved in the export trade required large quantities of salt, which constituted a major import item. During the seventeenth century, the pilchard catch grew to become the dominant fishery, as the pilchard shoals increasingly concentrated along the Cornish coast, and ports such as Mevagissey and St Ives profited.[39] The harvest of mackerel, herring, rays, conger, and hake was also important, and made up a large portion of the exports for Brittany, Spain, and other Mediterranean countries.[40]

men over the age of twenty; only 24 per cent, or 20,483, were considered miners. Rule, 'The Labouring Miner', 14.

[35] Norman J.C. Pounds, 'The Population of Cornwall Before the First Census', in E. Minchinton, ed., *Population and Marketing*, Exeter Papers in Economic History 11 (Exeter, 1976).

[36] Jaggard, *Cornwall Politics*, 12.

[37] CUST 68/16 Penzance Collector to Board, 22 March 1794; Jaggard, *Cornwall Politics*, 13; John Rule, 'Some Social Aspects of the Cornish Industrial Revolution', *Exeter Papers in Economic History*, 2 (1970), 71–106. This action has been labelled by E.P. Thompson as an example of 'moral economy of the crowd'. See. E.P. Thompson, 'The Moral Economy of the Crowd', in *Customs in Common: Studies in Traditional Popular Culture* (New York, 1993), 185–258.

[38] Rowe, *Cornwall in the Age of the Industrial Revolution*, 263.

[39] For a discussion of Cornish shipping carrying pilchard harvests to the Mediterranean, see David H. Kennett, 'The *Magic*: A West Country Schooner in the Mediterranean, 1833–9', in Stephen Fisher, ed., *West Country Maritime and Social History: Some Essays* (Exeter, 1980), 101–126. The *Magic* had four voyages carrying pilchards between St Ives and Venice (107, 119). See also Rowe, *Cornwall in the Age of the Industrial Revolution*, 263–265

[40] Payton, *Cornwall*, 152.

The pilchard industry was considered so important, and often very uncertain, that from the end of the seventeenth century to the beginning of the nineteenth century, the Government gave a bounty on fish exported to foreign markets, particularly to the Mediterranean. Writing in 1824, Hitchins and Drew argued that the bounty was necessary to keep the industry alive; they also pointed out the ways in which fishing was tied to other important elements in the Cornish economy. Fishing supported boat-builders, rope-makers, coopers, and net weavers; and masons, carpenters, and smiths who built the fish cellars. Farmers used fish offal and salt in agriculture, while the fisheries 'form an excellent nursery for seamen; which is another valuable consideration for England, whose prosperity depends upon its naval power, and the extension of its commerce'. Hitchins and Drew emphasised the place of the fisheries within the Cornish maritime environment:

> Connecting together the multitudes who are actually employed in taking fish, the sailors who bring salt to the ports, those who carry the annual produce to the Mediterranean markets, and the collateral branches of trade which associate with each department, we behold many thousands of seamen, who are prepared for an emergency that may demand their aid.[41]

The fishermen, however, were not involved simply in the fishery. Many were also involved in an activity often associated in the literature with wrecking – smuggling. There seems little doubt that smuggling in Cornwall, as elsewhere, was rife in the eighteenth century, with its defeat being the primary occupation of the Customs.[42] In the mid-eighteenth century the small fishing village of Polperro, for instance, was an infamous centre of smuggling. It was the home of Zephaniah Job, one of the most skilled smuggler-businessmen, who kept detailed books of his transactions. Prussia Cove, too, was made famous by the exploits of Captain Harry Carter, who wrote up his autobiography.[43] Smuggling was a well organised, complex business venture integrating nearly all levels of society, which included far-reaching distribution networks, was financed through the use of extensive credit, and had large shipbuilding operations. However, smuggling in south-east England was much more complex and far-ranging than in Cornwall, whose markets were mainly local.[44] The fishermen-smugglers of Cornwall tended not to be prosecuted, being either

[41] Hitchins and Drew, *History of Cornwall*, 551.

[42] Edward Carson, *The Ancient and Rightful Customs: A History of the English Customs Service* (London, 1972), 48.

[43] Most of Job's records were burnt after his death, but a few survived and are lodged in the Royal Institute of Cornwall, Courtney Library. See also Jeremy Rowett Johns, *The Smugglers' Banker: The Story of Zephaniah Job of Polperro* (Polperro, 1997); Captain Harry Carter, *The Autobiography of a Cornish Smuggler (Captain Harry Carter of Prussia Cove), 1749–1809* (London, 1900).

[44] Paul Muskett, 'English Smuggling in the Eighteenth Century' (unpublished Ph.D. thesis, Open University UK, 1996); See also Cal Winslow, 'Sussex Smugglers', in Douglas Hay, Peter

too poor or unable to pay fines, or being too old to be impressed into the Navy upon conviction.[45] Smuggling also shares a recurring theme with wrecking: 'the defence of [what was seen as] a legitimate form of livelihood against the increasing intrusion of governmental control and direction.'[46]

Wrecking and smuggling were not Cornwall's only maritime ventures considered illegal by central government. Ports such as Fowey developed a reputation not only for the ability of its seamen, but for piracy as well. Fowey ships engaged in an undeclared war with the Cinque Ports during the reign of Edward II (1307–27), when they attacked Rye and Winchelsea. During the Wars of the Roses, they were known to attack English shipping, and shipping of other countries, such as the Normans and Bretons of France, and the Spanish.[47] Fowey ships were also involved in piracy while ostensibly carrying pilgrims to Spain in the fifteenth century, taking advantage of opportunity.[48] Cornish piracy continued during the unrest preceding the Tudor regime and during the undeclared war against Spain in the sixteenth century; piracy converted to privateering after war was declared. Certainly, Cornwall produced several famous West Country sea-dogs, notably Sir Richard Grenville of the *Revenge*. The tradition of piracy and privateering persisted into the eighteenth century, when Cornish and other West Country ports became the centre of privateering activity against France in the Channel between 1777 and 1783 and during the Anglo-Dutch War of 1780–83.[49] Indeed, during the Anglo-Dutch War, letters of marque were issued to thirty British vessels from Falmouth, fifteen from Penzance, eleven from St Ives, and a smaller number from Fowey, Gweek, Looe, Padstow, Penryn, St Austell, and Truro.[50]

Cornwall's maritime activities ranged beyond the export sector – and wrecking, piracy and privateering – to include a small shipbuilding industry. According to the 1805 Parliamentary survey on shipwrights, Cornwall had thirty-four shipyards employing an average of ten men per yard. The largest shipyards in Falmouth were supported through the building and repair of the Post Office packets.[51] Smuggling gave impetus to the shipbuilding industry

Linebaugh et. al., *Albion's Fatal Tree: Crime and Society in Eighteenth-Century England* (London, 1975), 119–166.

[45] Tony Pawlyn, 'Fishermen Smugglers', paper read at the First Cornish Maritime History Conference, National Maritime Museum Cornwall, 25 September 2004.

[46] Payton, *Cornwall*, 173.

[47] Payton, *Cornwall*, 90.

[48] Francis Davey, 'Cornish Medieval Piracy', paper read at the First Cornish Maritime History Conference, National Maritime Museum Cornwall, 25 September 2004.

[49] David J. Starkey, *British Privateering Enterprise in the Eighteenth Century* (Exeter, 1990), 204, 38.

[50] David J. Starkey, 'British Privateering against the Dutch in the American Revolutionary War, 1780–1783', in Stephen Fisher, ed., *Studies in British Privateering, Trading Enterprise and Seamen's Welfare, 1775–1900* (Exeter, 1987), Table 2, 12.

[51] Helen Doe, 'Small Shipbuilding Businesses during the Napoleonic Wars: James Dunn of Mevagissey, 1799 to 1816' (unpublished M.A. dissertation, University of Exeter, 2003), 15.

in Mevagissey at the turn of the eighteenth century; its shipyards built 39 per cent of the Cornish-built ships in 1805, most of them smuggling cutters, although ironically, they also built revenue cutters. Padstow, Falmouth, Polperro, and Fowey also had active shipyards. Cornish shipbuilders turned out many other types of vessels, ranging from small fishing smacks to larger ocean-going trading vessels. Cornish-built and Cornish-registered shipping was involved in such wide-ranging commercial activities as the fruit trade from the Azores and West Indies; the dried cod trade from Newfoundland; and the hide trade from Brazil. The goods were carried to major English ports such as Liverpool, London, and Bristol.[52]

It is difficult to calculate the total amount of Cornish shipowning by port during this period, but some figures are instructive. Fowey, one of the most studied ports, offered a significant shipbuilding business that allowed for local investment. Ownership in local vessels was based on the normal 64th shareholding system, and most of the shares in the vessels were local. Because Fowey had a smaller amount of local capital for investing in shipping compared to the larger ports such as London and Liverpool, ships needed more shareholders. Between 1841 and 1880, there were 319 vessels registered locally, and a potential of 20,416 shares. As well, women investors in Fowey were important for shipping: they held over 2,505 shares, 12 per cent of the total. These figures are enlightening in that they show that women were supporting not just their family members, but the entire community whose livelihoods depended on the locally owned ships.[53] Table 1 below gives a comparison of Fowey's shipping with that of ports outside Cornwall:

Table 1. Ships Registered as of 31st December 1850

| Port | No of Vessels | Total Tonnage | Av Ship Size in tons |
|------|---------------|---------------|----------------------|
| Exeter | 182 | 18358 | 101 |
| Fowey | 137 | 10724 | 78 |
| King's Lynn | 180 | 19763 | 110 |
| Whitby | 399 | 63028 | 158 |
| Whitehaven | 220 | 35129 | 160 |

Special thanks to Helen Doe for sharing her data with me.

[52] Helen Doe, 'Cornish Ships and Shipbuilding in the Nineteenth Century', paper read at the First Cornish Maritime History Conference, National Maritime Museum Cornwall, 25 September 2004. Doe utilised the Cornwall Ship Database, developed by George Hogg, which is held at the National Maritime Museum Cornwall. The database contained 2620 entries of Cornish ships as of September 2004.
[53] Helen Doe, 'Waiting for Her Ship to Come In? The Female Investor in Nineteenth Century Sailing Vessels', *Economic History Review*, 63, No. 1 (Feb. 2010).

In 1850, Cornish-registered shipping only equalled 2 per cent of the total for England and Wales. (See Table 2). However, the figures are also useful in comparing registry across the major Cornish ports: the south coast ports account for over 48 per cent of registries, while the north coast has approximately 40 per cent. Fowey and St Ives, both large Cornish shipbuilding areas, account for the largest number of local shipowners.

Table 2. Cornish Registry by Port, 1850

| Port | Shipping Registered ['000 net tons] | | % of Cornish Total |
|---|---|---|---|
| Scilly | 6.8 | | 12 |
| *South Coast* | | | |
| Penzance | 9.2 | | 16.3 |
| Falmouth | 7.3 | | 12.9 |
| Fowey | 10.7 | | 19.0 |
| *South Coast Total* | | 27.2 | 48.2 |
| *North Coast* | | | |
| Padstow | 8.2 | | 14.6 |
| Hayle | – | | – |
| St Ives | 10.2 | | 18.0 |
| Truro | 3.9 | | 7.0 |
| *North Coast Total* | | 22.3 | 39.6 |
| Cornwall Total | | 56.3 | |
| England and Wales Total | | 2,721.3 | |
| Cornwall % of Total Shipping | | | 2.0 |

Tables adapted from David J. Starkey, 'Growth and Transition in Britain's Maritime Economy, 1870–1914: The Case of South-West England', in David J. Starkey and Alan G. Jamison, eds. *Exploiting the Sea: Aspects of Britain's Maritime Economy since 1870* (Exeter, 1998), 16–17.

In comparison with other English ports, those of Cornwall and the South-west did not have as large a trade. The largest Cornish ports of Falmouth and Penzance were relatively small when compared with those elsewhere in Britain, even within the Southwest region, where Bristol and Plymouth dominate.[54] (See Table 3 below). However, the location of the Cornish ports on the major trade routes of both the English and Bristol Channels was more

---

[54] See Starkey, 'Growth and Transition'; Gordon Jackson, 'Seatrade', in John Langton and R.J. Morris, eds., *Atlas of Industrializing Britain, 1780–1914* (London, 1986), 94–105; Gordon Jackson, 'Ports 1700–1840', in Peter Clark, ed., *The Cambridge Urban History of Britain*, Vol. II: *1540–1840* (Cambridge, 2000), 705–731; Sarah Palmer, 'Ports 1840–1950', in M.J. Daunton, ed., *The Cambridge Urban History of Britain*, Vol. III: *1840–1950* (London, 2000), 133–150; Jacob M. Price, 'Competition between Ports in British Long Distance Trade, c. 1660–1800', *Puertos y Sistemas Portuarios (Siglos XVI–XX): A Clas del Coloquio Internacional* El Sistema Portuario Español, Madrid, 19–21 October 1995, 19–36.

important than their existence as trading ports in their own right. Indeed, their trading activities were essential regionally, and local shipping had its share of shipwrecks.

Of particular significance on the south coast were Penzance and Falmouth; both were centres of Customs districts, and thus centres of law enforcement to combat wrecking. In 1814, the Customs collector described Penzance as an 'extensive Port' ranging from Cape Cornwall to the Lizard, which is 'the first Port at the entrance of the British Channel (attached to the main Land), by which means it is much resorted to by Vessels bound to different Ports of the United Kingdom and other Ports which put in, under distress Circumstances …'.[55]

Indeed, the range of Penzance's own trade by 1820 was impressive:

> the business carried on at the Port, which consists of the following Trades, namely, – importations of Timber &c from Norway – D° from British Colonies & Plantations in America, – Hemp, Iron, Tallow &c from Russia, – Salt from France for the use of the Fisheries, – Fruit & o$^r$ Produce from the Islands of Guernsey & Jersey – Provisions & o$^r$ produce from Ireland. – Exportations of Pilchards, to the Mediterranean, – Tin to Russia and Turkey, – Oil & Dregs of Oil, to Ireland; together with the Coasting Trade Inwards and Outwards, Viz$^t$ Coals, Culm, Slate & Stone, & O$^r$ Merchandize.[56]

Falmouth became the major port in Cornwall after recognition of its strategic importance and deep harbour led to its establishment as a Post Office packet base in 1689, a position it held until 1850. The Royal Navy and merchant vessels used the port extensively throughout the eighteenth and nineteenth centuries as a rendezvous point: 'the masters and supercargoes of both outward and homeward bound ships resort hither, to receive final instructions from their owners, by which they ascertain the state of British and foreign markets, and to regulate their future proceedings accordingly'.[57] This gave rise to the saying: 'Falmouth for orders'. The Packet Service was established to transport mail overseas to Spain and the Mediterranean when the French wars closed overland routes. By the 1760s it expanded with the establishment of North American ports and it later extended its services to include South America, Madeira, and the western Mediterranean. At the height of the Napoleonic Wars, the Packet Service operated over forty ships which sailed from Falmouth on mail runs.[58]

The Packet Service was clearly of major economic importance to Falmouth. The ships, rather than being government-owned and operated, were contracted

---

55  CUST 68/21, Penzance Collector to Board, 20 April 1814.
56  CUST 68/26, Penzance Collector to Board, 17 July 1820.
57  Hitchins and Drew, *History of Cornwall*, Vol. II, 262.
58  J.C.A. Whetter, 'The Rise of the Port of Falmouth, 1600–1800', in Stephen Fisher, ed., *Ports and Shipping in the South-west* (Exeter, 1971), 20–22.

from local shipowners and businessmen, thus bringing in opportunities for
the shipyards and local investment.[59] The Packets were also heavily involved
in trade. Defoe, describing Falmouth while on his *Tour through the Whole
Island of Great Britain* in the 1720s, claimed that 'there is a new commerce
between Portugal and this town, carried on to a very great value'.[60] Goods
such as textiles, spirits, tobacco, sugar, fruit, silk, and lace were imported into
Falmouth, boosting the economy. The Packet Service was so important to
Falmouth and Great Britain that it stimulated the improvement of overland
transport routes to provide faster links to London.[61] The service not only
performed the transport of mail; its vessels were also involved in privateering
and action with the enemy during the French wars.[62]

Described by Hitchins and Drew as having more trade activity than any
other port in the county, Falmouth also had a special trade privilege; it was the
exclusive tobacco and wine port in Cornwall and Devon. As well, Falmouth's
foreign trade during this period was similar to that of Penzance, landing
goods from North America, Spain, Portugal, Holland, Russia, France, and
the Baltic, the Mediterranean, South America, Ireland, and other domestic
ports.[63] Falmouth's exports included pilchards, tin, and corn. Indeed, it was
the prime exporter of pilchards, shipping out over half of the average total of
30,000 hogsheads per year between 1747 and 1756.[64]

The ports of the north coast were not as large as were Penzance and
Falmouth from the eighteenth century onwards, although they saw a fair
amount of trade past their shores heading in from the Atlantic into the
Bristol Channel. St Ives, Hayle, and Padstow were the most important ports,
with St Ives and Padstow being the centre of Customs districts for the north
coast. These ports were also major harbours of refuge for shipping caught
on the lee shore as they were heading up channel. Indeed, Richard Carew
said of St Ives in the sixteenth century: 'the town and port of St Ives are
both of mean plight, yet with their best means, and often to good and necessary purpose, succouring distressed shipping'.[65] St Ives' trade began to increase

[59] Whetter, 'Falmouth', 21. Some of the packets were owned in whole or in part by their
commanders. Tony Pawlyn, *The Falmouth Packets, 1689–1851* (Truro, 2003), 31.
[60] Quoted in Whetter, 'Falmouth', 21 from Daniel Defoe, *A Tour through the Whole Island of
Great Britain* (originally published 1724, London, 1948), 238.
[61] Whetter, 'Falmouth', 23. A turnpike road was constructed in 1754 from Falmouth to Truro
and then on to Grampound. It was eventually extended from Truro to Launceston to create
the present A30. Whetter also says that the first horse-drawn coaches were used in Falmouth
in 1770, and eventually, by 1788, mail and passenger coaches were running between London and
Falmouth (23).
[62] Payton, *Cornwall*, 163; Pawlyn, *Falmouth Packets*.
[63] Hitchins and Drew, *History of Cornwall*, Vol. II, 262.
[64] Whetter, 'Falmouth', 24. Unfortunately, most of Falmouth's port books are no longer extant,
so the volume of trade for the eighteenth century is unknown except for this brief period. Most
of the tin and corn was carried to domestic markets.
[65] Richard Carew, quoted in Hitchins and Drew, *History of Cornwall*, Vol. II, 343.

after the construction of its pier in 1770, whereby it exported pilchards and copper ore. Its imports consisted of timber, iron, salt, and Welsh coal, mainly to support the industries of its hinterland. Likewise, Padstow saw a heavy export of copper, tin, and pilchards, while importing salt, timber, and coal. Hayle, also one of the north coast's larger ports, was primarily involved with the export of minerals.[66]

Table 3. Cornish Coastal Trade by Port, 1850

| Port | Shipping Registered ['ooo net tons] | | % of Cornish Total |
|---|---|---|---|
| Scilly | 12.2 | | 1.17 |
| *South Coast* | | | |
| Penzance | 212.7 | | 29.6 |
| Falmouth | 103.5 | | 14.4 |
| Fowey | 141.3 | | 19.9 |
| *South Coast Total* | | 457.5 | 63.9 |
| *North Coast* | | | |
| Padstow | 67.2 | | 9.3 |
| Hayle | 61.0 | | 8.5 |
| St Ives | – | | – |
| Truro | 119.7 | | 16.7 |
| *North Coast Total* | | 247.9 | 34.5 |
| Cornwall Total | 56.3 | | |
| Devon Total | 108.9 | | |
| England and Wales Total | 2,721.3 | | |
| Southwest % of Total Shipping | | | 6.1 |

Tables adapted from David J. Starkey, 'Growth and Transition in Britain's Maritime Economy, 1870–1914: The Case of South-West England', in David J. Starkey and Alan G. Jamison, eds. *Exploiting the Sea: Aspects of Britain's Maritime Economy since 1870* (Exeter, 1998), 16–17.

Although always volatile depending on the whims of markets and policies, Cornwall's mineral and maritime trade economy received severe blows in the mid-nineteenth century which affected the living conditions of those involved, and hence had an impact on wrecking activity. The Cornish industrial economy ultimately failed in the nineteenth century as a result of an inability to diversify and its overspecialisation in mining and its ancillary businesses. The pilchard industry collapsed because of over-fishing, and because the shoals no longer migrated in the same numbers along the Cornish coast.[67]

[66] For an overview of Cornwall's main ports, see Cyril Noall, *The Story of Cornwall's Ports and Harbours* (Truro, 1970).
[67] Alan Southward, Gerald Boalch and Linda Maddock, eds, 'Climatic Change and the Herring and Pilchard Fisheries of Devon and Cornwall', in David J. Starkey, ed., *Devon's Coastline and Coastal Waters: Aspects of Man's Relationship with the Sea* (Exeter: University of Exeter Press, 1988).

Agricultural depression also periodically hit the population, culminating with the 'Hungry Forties' potato blight. As well, the expansion of Cornish international maritime trade came to a standstill, ironically because of the county's location. Despite sitting 'athwart one of the busiest trade routes in the world', Cornwall lacked the large centres of population that were needed for markets, and it lacked the centres of industry and capital that allowed Bristol, Liverpool, and the ports of the east coast to gain prominence. Indeed, by the mid-nineteenth century, much of Cornwall's industry and its investors had shifted to larger ports out of Cornwall, particularly those involved with shipbuilding and fishing.[68] The Packet Service, too, was lost by Falmouth in 1850, primarily because Falmouth lacked a modern dock and was considered too far away from the industrial centres of London, the Midlands, and the north.[69]

These factors affected the Cornish economy so much that it was plunged into a prolonged economic depression. Thus, beginning in the 1830s, one of Cornwall's heaviest exports was its own people. The mining region of Breage and Germoe lost 27 per cent of its population between 1841 and 1851.[70] Some Cornish ports profited from the 'emigration trade'; Padstow acted as a primary port of embarkation for Quebec between 1829 and 1857, and the emigrant vessels returned laden with Canadian timber.[71] While emigration took some pressure off the land, the cycles of depression still persisted, therefore poverty continued as a causative factor in wrecking, which it had been throughout the period studied. As well, returning timber ships were particularly unseaworthy in the mid-nineteenth century, and thus cargoes of wrecked timber were found washed up on the shores of Cornwall.[72]

## Cornwall and British Trade Policy

Cornwall's extensive maritime trade did not only derive from the local economy. Cornwall profited from the State's interest in promoting commerce and raising revenue. The aim of British commercial imperialism to exploit its geographical location and its empire, to become the 'warehouse of the world', led to a system of re-export that brought tremendous quantities of goods into English ports.[73] The policy of the State to divert trade through British ports was crucial to the development of the Atlantic economy. Re-export accounted

---

[68] Whetter, 'Falmouth', 25; Starkey, 'Growth and Transition', 20, 29–31.
[69] James Whetter, *The History of Falmouth* (Redruth, 1981), 54.
[70] Denys Bradford Barton, *Essays in Cornish Mining History* (Truro, 1968), 69.
[71] Payton, *Cornwall*, 233.
[72] For a discussion of the problems of timber carriers, see PP, *Report from the Select Committee on Shipwrecks of Timber Ships; with Minutes of Evidence, 1839*, vol. xvii. See also CRO W/43 Willyams Papers, 1826.
[73] Price, *British Society*, 57.

for 60 per cent of British trade by the 1770s, and 'by this means England created for herself a great confluence of commodities out of flows in both directions, which otherwise need not have touched her shores at all'.[74] Indeed, the sheer amount of trade in consumer products was a defining factor in the power of the British Empire during this period.[75] This is especially evident in the history of shipwreck. Many of the wrecks along the Cornish coast consisted of shipping carrying cargoes not destined for British markets, yet when they fell afoul of the Cornish coast, and were required to enter ports for repairs or were unfortunate enough to be wrecked and salvaged, the remnants and goods were taxed and sold according to British law.

The role of collecting duties fell to HM Customs Service. Although the Customs Service had existed since the beginning of the English state, it gained increasing powers when the permanent administration was established in 1671, and when it was consolidated in 1715. Indeed, the growth of Customs was part of the increasing centralisation and bureaucratisation that was occurring in England.[76] The Customs Service was mainly responsible for collecting duties, enforcing quarantine laws, and applying the Navigation Laws and Ship's Registry. However, the detection and defeat of smuggling was 'the "raison d'être" of a large part of the Service'.[77] Customs officers also had duty as Receivers of Wreck, which entailed salvaging shipwrecked property. Thus they become major players in the story of wrecking.

Smuggling, as well as the Customs' interest in shipwrecked goods, arose through the increasing taxation on imported commodities. Taxes were seen by the Government as necessary for two purposes: to protect locally made goods and to collect funds to finance the wars against France. From 1688, the importation of French goods such as brandy, silk, and lace was prohibited, and heavy duties were placed on tea and tobacco. Thus smuggling, which had hitherto been focused on wool, came to centre on what were considered French luxury goods, along with tea and tobacco.[78] Duties were also placed on the importation of food stuffs, raw materials, and manufactured goods. By 1704–05, the overall rate of duties had climbed by 15 per cent, and by 1760, over 800 different Customs Acts defining duties had been passed. Commodities which had the highest duties included luxury goods such as tea, which was taxed at between 65 per cent and to 119 per cent, and tobacco, which was

[74] Dwyryd W. Jones, *War and Economy in the Age of William III and Marlborough* (Oxford, 1988), 49.

[75] Maxine Berg, *Luxury and Pleasure in Eighteenth-Century Britain* (Oxford, 2005), 8.

[76] See William J. Ashworth, *Customs and Excise: Trade, Production, and Consumption in England 1640–1845* (Oxford, 2003) and John Brewer, *The Sinews of Power: War, Money and the English State, 1688–1783* (Cambridge, Massachusetts, 1990).

[77] Carson, *Ancient and Rightful Customs*, 12.

[78] Ashworth, *Customs and Excise*, 40.

taxed in 1794 at five times its value.[79] The determination of duties was not only of major significance for fiscal revenue, but it was also allied to the Navigation Acts. Higher duties were placed on goods carried in foreign vessels. As a consequence of protectionism, goods such as timber from North America and sugar from the West Indies were given colonial preference, and thus had lower duties. Goods imported into Britain via foreign vessels had higher customs duties.[80] The North American timber trade, for instance, was given preferential treatment after the end of the Napoleonic Wars. The wars had shown that the Baltic timber trade was too vulnerable to enemy action and blockades, and so preference was given to North American timber. Thus, in 1811 the first duties on Baltic timber were enforced, while colonial timber was imported duty-free.[81] This change of policy would have an effect on wrecking and salvage practices.

Between the late seventeenth century and the mid-Victorian period, the long list of dutiable goods grew exponentially, including, besides the high value consumer goods already mentioned, more mundane articles such as glass, soap, timber, playing cards, dice, and medicines.[82] Indeed, by the 1840s, there were over 700 dutiable items. By 1860, despite trade liberalisation, over 400 items continued to be subject to Customs duties. This number was finally decreased to 48 at the end of that year after the signing of Cobden's free-trade treaty with France, which limited duties to goods such as flour, wine, and brandy, and manufactured sugar and tobacco.[83]

An awareness of the role of Customs and their responsibility to collect duties is critical for understanding the Government's reaction to the phenomenon of wrecking. For wrecking, the claiming of shipwrecked goods by local inhabitants, had two different consequences: one fiscal and one cultural. Wrecking denied the Government income from Customs duties, income which, along with excise taxes, supported the State.[84] Customs only had authority to stop the plunder of dutiable goods. But equally, wrecking gave the populace the opportunity to obtain what were defined as luxury goods by the Government. These goods, such as sugar, wine, and tobacco, had high duties placed upon them, not only because they were an 'income elastic demand' whereby consumption, and therefore profits, would increase when the economy pros-

---

79 Brewer, *Sinews of Power*, 211, 21; Elizabeth Evelynola Hoon, *The Organization of the English Customs System, 1696–1786* (originally published 1938, Newton Abbot, 1968), 36.
80 Sarah Palmer, *Politics, Shipping and the Repeal of the Navigation Laws* (Manchester, 1990), 40–42; Hoon, *English Customs*, 32.
81 Palmer, *Navigation Laws*, 57–58. The duties on Baltic timber were reduced in 1821 and a low duty was placed on colonial timber, but there continued to be a difference of 45s per load (58).
82 Ashworth, *Customs and Excise*, 40; Lucy Brown, *The Board of Trade and the Free Trade Movement, 1830–1842* (Oxford, 1958).
83 Price, *British Society*, 91.
84 Brewer, *Sinews of Power*, 95–101.

pered, but also because the high duties, and therefore higher prices, would confine their consumption to the elites.[85] Wrecking made these goods available to the poor. Indeed, there existed between the Customs officers and the populace an awareness of shifting power, centred around the contest for control over of those luxury goods – cultural capital – which came through wrecking. This is evident in the fact that Customs would rather destroy goods that were seen as being too damaged to be 'worth the duty', rather than let them be claimed by the common people.[86] Yet for the coastal populace of Cornwall, reliant on the precarious harvests of mining, fishing, and agriculture, the sea offered in wrecks the opportunity for unexpected bounty. Each group of participants had their own idea of what constituted their interests and rights, and to some extent they shifted their claims to accommodate each other. Thus wrecking is a story of interrelationships, of symbolic – and real – violence; of claims to cultural – and real – capital; of the shifting definitions of wrecking and its consequent perception of criminality, all being enacted within the context of Cornwall's extensive maritime dimension.

---

[85] M.J. Daunton, *Progress and Poverty: An Economic and Social History of Britain, 1700–1850* (Oxford, 1995), 523; Maxine Berg and Elizabeth Eger, eds., 'The Rise and Fall of the Luxury Debates', in *Luxury in the Eighteenth Century: Debates, Desires and Delectable Goods* (Basingstoke, 2003), 8.
[86] CUST 68/139, Penzance Collector to Board, 6 June 1795.

2

# 'Dead Wrecks'
# and the Foundation of Wreck Law

*where a man, a Dog or a Cat escape quick out of a Ship, that*
*such Ship nor Barge, nor any Thing within them, shall be adjudged*
*wreck*

Statute of Westminster (1275)

T
HE news reports from the wreck of the *Kodima* in 2002 show us that even in the twenty-first century, people still believe in the precept of 'finders keepers' when it comes to items found on the beach. Indeed, this is one of the core tenets of wrecking – people believe they have the right to goods that have washed ashore – that it was a 'custom' practised 'from time immemorial'. In the mid-nineteenth century, David Williams, the Coastguard's Inspecting Commander at Padstow, testified during the Select Committee on Shipwrecks that the 'country people' called shipwrecked goods a 'godsend'. He defended them emphatically: 'they were not thieves'; they would only take objects that had been thrown upon the shore. His opinion was echoed by John Bulley, commanding officer on the Isle of Wight, who reported that the wreckers told him that: '"We considered it a right when those things come on shore to take home what we can get." He added: 'They do not call it stealing.'[1] What is so remarkable is that this belief has persisted into the twenty-first century in the face of almost a thousand years of legislation to the contrary. This is not all. Existing side-by-side with the belief in 'godsend' or 'providence' is another belief, more rooted in law – that of the claim to 'dead wrecks', meaning wrecks in which there were no survivors.[2] The claim to 'dead wrecks' became the root of one of the persistent myths of Cornish wrecking: that wreckers would murder any survivors to ensure those claims.

How could the popular conviction be maintained, if, as it has been argued, the belief 'in the legitimacy of appropriating wreck goods has no basis in fact',

---

[1]  PP, *First Report from the Select Committee on Shipwrecks; Together with Minutes of Evidence, Appendix and Index* (1843), vol. ix, 302, 310.
[2]  See CUST 68/6, 16 January 1768 and CUST 68/12, 20 May 1782.

that 'the legal position was clear'?[3] To make matters even more complex and contradictory, as late as the nineteenth century common people also recognised their manorial lords' rights to claim wreck according to feudal law. Thus popular belief shows shifting perceptions of wreck rights; those perceptions were multiple and simultaneous and were not always in accordance with the law. And yet, beliefs also reflected accommodation to some facets of the law. The origin of this difference in perceptions lay in the medieval and early modern periods, when the foundation of the dominant elite's legal definition of 'wreck' and the legal claim to wrecked goods were established. Indeed, these important principles, and the popular beliefs connected to them, influenced the rights of wreck in eighteenth and nineteenth centuries.

### *Wreccum maris*: The Rights to 'Wreck of the Sea' in Common Law

Who legally owns the wrecked goods that wash ashore? Is it the finder? The owner of the ship or cargo? The survivors? The owner of the land where it is found? Or is it the monarch? Rather than being clear-cut, the legal position of *wreccum maris*, or 'wreck of the sea,' was ill-defined for centuries; it went through several incarnations before being solidified. By the end of the seventeenth century, the groundwork had been laid to establish the dispensation of shipwrecked goods by recognising proprietary rights, meaning the original owner's rights to the goods, as well as what is called the 'right of wreck' or the 'liberty' of wreck. Thus rather than identifying wreck as anything that washed ashore, the legal definition took a step further to define wreck according to possession. Accordingly, to describe the process in a simplified manner, goods washing ashore were to be collected and handed over to either the lord of the manor where they washed up, or given to another local official, such as the coroner. They were to be held for a requisite 'year and a day', to await claiming by the rightful owners. If the goods were claimed, then the owners were required to pay the finders a salvage reward. Salvage rewards were the only dispensation given to the finders – usually the 'country people'. Their rights to the goods were not considered despite their popular belief. Rather, if the goods were not claimed, then those goods were legally deemed 'wreck', to be awarded to either the lord of the manor, or to the Crown, depending on who had the 'rights of wreck'. Goods claimed by their proprietary owners were not legally labelled 'wreck'. (See Figure 4 below.) This is an important distinction, as usage of the term is dependent upon its context, whether it applies to shipwrecked goods generically, or whether it is used in its more specific legal sense.

---

3    John Rule, 'Wrecking and Coastal Plunder', in Douglas Hay, Peter Linebaugh, et. al, *Albion's Fatal Tree: Crime and Society in Eighteenth-Century England* (London, 1975), 177.

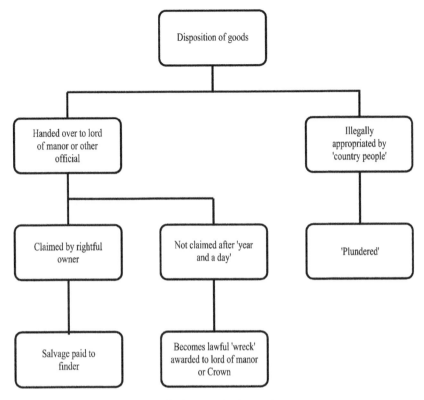

Figure 4. Legal Disposition of Shipwrecked Goods.

During the medieval era, feudal claims to 'wreck of the sea' were affirmed, even before the legal concept of 'wreck' was defined. In the thirteenth century, the renowned jurist Henry de Bracton, who wrote the first treatise on English common law, maintained that wreck was originally subject to 'natural law', in other words, wreck belonged to the finder. However, by the time of his writing, all *wreccum maris* was the property of the Crown, 'by virtue of the prerogative', to be granted by the monarch as a privilege to a chosen few.[4] The country people's claims to wreck, however, most likely originated before regnant control was gained, and were more in line with 'natural law'. Even so, their claims signify their lack of adherence to, or even knowledge of, the royal prerogative.

The transition from natural law to royal prerogative occurred before the reign of Edward the Confessor, when Saxon kings sought to gain control and unify England. The king claimed as his prerogative not only *wreccum maris* – goods which have washed ashore – but also flotsam, jetsam, lagan, derelict,

---

[4] Henry de Bracton, quoted in Sir William Holdsworth, *A History of English Law*, Vol II (London, 1938), 273; Vol. VII, 495.

and 'royal fish', especially whales. Flotsam were goods found floating on the sea, deriving from a ship that has sunk; jetsam, that which might have been cast out of a ship to lighten her when in danger; lagan, goods that have been cast out of a ship but which have been tied to a buoy or cork so they could be found again and recovered; and derelict applied to vessels that have been abandoned.[5] The right to wreck in the early medieval era also occasionally included the right to claim survivors, who were either enslaved or held for ransom. This was experienced by Wilfred, Bishop of York and his followers, who survived a shipwreck on the Sussex coast in AD 666, only to be attacked by locals intent on taking them for slaves. They succeeded in escaping. Less lucky, Harold Godwinson was taken prisoner by Count Guy of Normandy as 'spoil of the sea', until he fell into the hands of Duke William of Normandy.[6] Enslavement was a real danger to the shipwrecked in other areas of the world through to the nineteenth century, particularly off the Barbary Coast of Africa.

Numerous records illustrate the king's granting of wreck rights, or 'liberties', to church officials, powerful magnates or lords of the manor, and even ports, as part of their manorial rights. Many of the early grants were specifically given to ecclesiastical benefices: Canute gave the right of 'port, ferry, and wreck' to Christchurch Canterbury in 1023. [7] Ramsey Abbey was granted wreck by Edward the Confessor, though a court case from 1129 regarded the privilege as dating from Canute.[8] Likewise, William the Conqueror verified the wreck rights granted to the abbot of Abbotsbury by Edward.[9] The Cinque Ports, originally established by the king in 1155, were given royal rights, including their own courts, the right to appropriate lost property or cattle, and the right to seize all wreck, flotsam, jetsam, and lagan, in return for ships and defence.[10]

5   James C. Hannen and W. Tarn Pritchard, *Pritchard's Digest of Admiralty and Maritime Law*, 3rd edition, Vol. II (London, 1887), 2317; William Palmer, *The Law of Wreck, Considered with a View to its Amendment* (London, 1843), 3; Michael Williams, 'A Legal History of Shipwreck in England', unpublished manuscript. *Annuaire de Droit Maritime et Océanique* (Tomexu, 1997), 71–92. Special thanks to Mr Williams for supplying this article. The above categories were legally codified in Sir Henry Constable's case (1601).
6   Frederick C. Hamil, 'Wreck of the Sea in Medieval England', in A.E.R. Boak, ed., *University of Michigan Historical Essays* (Ann Arbor, 1937), 12.
7   Rose Melikan, 'Shippers, Salvors, and Sovereigns: Competing Interests in the Medieval Law of Shipwreck', *Journal of Legal History*, 11, no. 2 (September 1990), 172; Hamil, 'Wreck of the Sea', 3. A good article outlining the role of the Church in controlling wrecking and saving ships from wreck is R.F. Wright, 'The High Seas and the Church in the Middle Ages, Part II', *Mariner's Mirror*, 53, no. 1 (February 1967), 115–135. However, Wright fails to take into account the Church's participation in wrecking and the struggle for wreck rights.
8   Melikan, 'Shippers, Salvors', 172; Case 256, Ramsey *Cart.* c. 1116–29 Sept 1129, in R.C. van Caenegem, ed., *English Lawsuits from William I to Stephen (Nos. 1–345)* (London, 1990), 220–221; and R.C. van Caenegem, ed., *Royal Writs in England from the Conquest to Glanvill: Studies in the Early History of the Common Law* (London, 1959), 482.
9   van Caenegem, *Royal Writs in England from the Conquest to Glanvill*, 482.
10   Holdsworth, *A History of English Law*, Vol. I, 559; R.G. Marsden, ed., *Select Pleas in the Court of Admiralty (AD 1547–1602)* Vol. II (London, 1897), xxii–xxiii, xxxix.

Many other seaports also enjoyed similar rights as evidenced by Yarmouth, Dunwich, and Southwold.

By the end of the reign of Henry II in 1135, the Crown had granted away most of its right to wreck along the entire English coast in return for support or favours. Moreover, feudal lords who had not been explicitly granted the liberty of wreck by the monarch had taken the rights by utilising the legal principle of 'prescription', claiming they had practised the right to wreck from 'time immemorial', a concept that will be discussed later in this chapter. But what exactly was involved with the claiming of wreck rights?

### 'Dead Wrecks' and the Development of Statutory Wreck Law

During the medieval era, the monarchs and law courts began to refine what was involved with the legal taking of 'wreck'. At issue were several key questions that were fraught with conflict. What legally constitutes 'wreck'? How is legal ownership of the wrecked goods determined? And which law courts had jurisdiction over wreck cases? The expansion of wreck law resulted in what is undeniably one of the most important legal developments from this period, that entitlement to wrecked goods belongs to the original – the proprietary – owner, a right that was not initially recognised. Until the law's solidification in 1771, however, proprietary owners were not legally guaranteed they would gain claim to their lost goods.

The most quoted definition of wreck rights comes from Edward I's Statute of Westminster (1275), where it is stated that 'where a man, a Dog or a Cat escape quick out of a Ship, that such Ship nor Barge, nor any Thing within them, shall be adjudged wreck'.[11] In other words, if there were any survivors, shipwrecked goods could not be claimed as 'wreck'. The ship or cargo was defined as wreck, eligible to be claimed by those holding wreck rights, *only* when there were no survivors – in other words, a 'dead wreck'. Thus, the popular belief that the country people had claim to 'dead wrecks' had its genesis in the legal definition of 'wreck'.

The Statute of Westminster is one of the most frequently repeated pieces of legislation in the literature on wreck, as if it were the earliest pronouncement of wreck law in England, but it is not. Rather, wreck law went through substantial changes before being codified by statute and before guaranteeing proprietary rights. 'From antiquity', a clerk for King Stephen wrote, 'it had been held as law along the sea-coast that in the case of shipwreck, if the survivors have not repaired her within a fixed period of time, the ship and whatever may have been landed falls without challenge under the lordship of

---

[11]  3 Edw. I c. 4 in *The Statutes at Large*, 24 vols, Vol. 1, ed. D. Pickering (Cambridge, 1762), 79.

that land as "wreck".[12] Therefore, time – limited to three days – and not the existence of survivors, defined 'wreck' according to custom.[13] Henry I (r. 1100–35) took exception to that archaic rule and brought the focus onto survivors by stipulating if anyone survived shipwreck, then that individual would have the right to the wrecked goods.[14] This decree laid the groundwork for all future legislation, shifting emphasis from the rights of the lords to the rights of survivors and proprietary owners of the ship and cargoes.

Henry II (r. 1154–89) has the reputation for being the father of English common law, but he may have modelled many of his policies on the work of his grandfather, Henry I.[15] Certainly this may be the case for wreck law, since Henry I's decree is the first extant definition of wreck in England. Henry II, following Henry I, issued a charter in 1174 that shows the beginnings of the familiar language of the Statute of Westminster, emphasising that if anyone escaped alive from a ship, then the ship could not be claimed as wreck. However, Henry II's charter added a time limit: if the goods were not claimed by the survivors within three months, then the goods could be constituted as wreck and granted to those who had wreck rights.[16] Richard I (r. 1189–99) further refined the definition of wreck by allowing survivors to keep their property, and emphasised that if the property's owners did not survive, it should be given to the owner's heir or heirs.[17]

By 1236, during the reign of Henry III (r. 1216–72), the main body of what would be Edward I's Statute of Westminster had taken shape. Henry's charter called for the 'abolition of bad customs' and prescribed that 'if ever a ship be in peril within the King's dominions whether on the sea-coast of England, or of Poitou, or of the isle of Oléron, or of Gascony', and if anyone survived, then 'all the goods and chattels in the said ship shall remain and belong to their former owners, and shall not be lost to them as wreck'. It also introduced the now familiar 'animal clause', which further stipulated that if there were no survivors, 'but an animal escape alive or be found living in the ship' then

> the goods and chattels found in the ship shall be delivered to by the King's bailiffs, or by the bailiffs of those upon whose land the ship was in peril, to four good men to be kept by them for three months, so that, if the owners come within that term and claim the said goods and prove that they are theirs, the said goods should be restored to them; but in default of such claim the goods

[12] Suit 303, van Caenegem, *English Lawsuits*, 255–256.
[13] Hamil, 'Wreck of the Sea', 13.
[14] Suit 303, van Caenegem, *English Lawsuits*, 255.
[15] Stephanie L. Mooers, 'A Reevaluation of Royal Justice under Henry I of England', *American Historical Review*, 93, no. 2 (April 1988), 341.
[16] Sir William Blackstone, *Commentaries on the Laws of England*, Vol. 1, 9th edition, ed. R. Burn (London, 1783), 291–293; Rule, 'Wrecking and Coastal Plunder', 177–178. Unfortunately Rule misread Blackstone and confused the legislation, claiming for Henry II's charter some of the provisions of the Statute of Westminster.
[17] Melikan, 'Shippers, Salvors', 173.

shall be the King's as wreck, or shall go to the person possessing the liberty of wreck.[18]

Thus, Edward carried through to his statute the important point identified by Henry I, Henry II, and Henry III by defining what was *not* a wreck: the presence of survivors, even if those survivors were not human. The only substantial difference between the acts is the time allotted for the owners to claim their property. Henry III gave them three months, while Edward I lengthened the time to 'a year and a day', which was more in keeping with the maritime law of other countries.

Of course, at the heart of the legislation was the issue of who held the rights to wreck, but increasingly the original owners of the property were recognised as having proprietary claim. The presence of live animals, emphasised by Henry III and carried forward by the Statute of Westminster, indicates this. Lord Hale, a premier chief justice of the King's Bench in the seventeenth century, argued that this precept was significant because otherwise it was 'lex odiosa' – an abhorrent law – if it were 'to add affliction to the afflicted',[19] which would occur if the owners were denied their shipwrecked property. Lord Coke, also from the seventeenth century, construed that the statute was 'only declaratory of common law; and the case of a man, a dog, or a cat escaping were only put for example of circumstances by which the property might be identified'.[20] By 1777, the eminent jurist Lord Mansfield agreed that the clause was only evidentiary, and that the survival of animals did not exclude proprietary claims from being established in other ways.[21]

Despite the argument that the surviving animal clause was only meant to be evidentiary, some writers have asserted that it had a more gruesome use; it gave incentive for wreckers to kill animals, and surviving victims, as they were escaping to assure a 'dead wreck'.[22] A story is told that after the wreck of a ship in the Isles of Scilly in the mid-nineteenth century, two salvors threw the surviving dog off the wreck to ensure their claim.[23] William Palmer, a barrister of the Inner Temple in 1843, suggested that this clause might have 'encouraged the atrocious cruelty of obstructing the escape of shipwrecked persons', and

---

[18] 20 Henry III, m. 4, 25 May 1236, in *Calendar of Charter Rolls*, Vol. I: *Henry III AD 1226–1257* (London, 1903), 219–220.
[19] Quoted in Palmer, *Law of Wreck*, 10; see the transcript of the case in Stuart A. Moore, *A History of the Foreshore*, 3rd edition (London, 1888).
[20] Quoted in Palmer, *Law of Wreck*, 14.
[21] Michael Williams, 'Manorial Rights of Wreck', unpublished paper read at the Nautical Archaeology Society, University of Plymouth, March 1995.
[22] Charles Henderson, 'Cornish Wrecks and Wreckers: Plundered Ships and Sailors,' *The Western Morning News and Mercury*, 21 January 1929; *Essays in Cornish History*. ed. A.L. Rowse and M.I. Henderson. Foreword by Sir Arthur Quiller-Couch (Oxford, 1935. reprinted Truro, 1963), 172; F.E. Halliday, *A History of Cornwall* (London, 1959), 261.
[23] John Fowles, *Shipwreck: Photography by the Gibsons of Scilly* (London, 1974), 2.

that it might even be the foundation of the 'barbarous superstition', used by Sir Walter Scott in *The Pirate*, 'that a man saved from drowning would do his preserver some capital injury'.[24] These stories are, however, unverified and may say more about reflexive myth-making rather than be evidence of actual incidences originating with a misinterpretation of the law.

But what if no living thing escaped? Proprietary rights of the legal owners were often ignored anyway; the advent of a 'dead wreck' gave further inducement to the owners of wreck rights to invoke the statute to lay their claim. This is one of the major differences between wreck law on the Continent and in England: feudal interests were dominant in England, while commercial interests had more control on the Continent, at least during the medieval period.[25] This is not to say that owners had no recourse. Cargoes were sometimes returned through intervention of the monarch. In particular, both Henry III and Edward II were known to have ordered the return of goods.[26] By the sixteenth and seventeenth centuries, however, the law gradually began to observe the rights of previous owners, even if they had yet to have legal recognition. Finally, in 1771 a decision by Lord Mansfield and the King's Bench in Hamilton *v.* Davis gave proprietary rights to the owner, even if nothing escaped alive, provided that the identity of the owner or his successors and his title to recovered goods could be established. Thus it was only in the late eighteenth century that we get a nullification of the 'dead wreck' claim. Initially, however, if there were no survivors, wreck was allocated to the owner of the wreck rights.

After the Statute of Westminster, if 'a man, a Dog or a Cat escape quick out of a Ship', and the goods were not classified as 'wreck', then the owner had 'a year and a day' to identify and claim the cargo. Until formal ownership of the goods was established within the set time, wreck law set out clear instructions as to what was to become of the cargo. Beginning with Henry II's charter, unclaimed goods should be placed in the care of 'four good men' by the king's bailiffs, or by the bailiffs of the manorial lord, to be held for three months; if the goods were not claimed, then possession would revert to the owner of wreck rights. Under Edward I's Statute of Westminster, the sheriff, coroner, or king's bailiff was given responsibility over the goods which were to be kept 'on view'. The following year, in 1276, Edward I issued his *De Officio Coronatoris*, 'Of what things a Coroner shall inquire'. Specifically, the coroner

[24] Palmer, *Law of Wreck*, 14. The same superstition is recorded by Rev. Robert Hawker of Morwenstow, who claimed his parishioner, Peter Barrow, told him the couplet 'Save a stranger from the sea; And he'll turn your enemy.' *Footprints of Former Men in Far Cornwall* (London, 1870), 189. It is possible that this superstition came from Scott, whom Hawker read prodigiously.

[25] Melikan, 'Shippers, Salvors', 163.

[26] Hamil, 'Wreck of the Sea', 17.

was given the responsibility to gather a jury to evaluate the value of the wreck for salvage purposes.[27] The coroners would legally hold this duty until the Coroner's Act of 1887. In practise, however, the technicalities of the law were often not followed. Rather, control was left in the hands of the lord of the manor upon whose lands the shipwrecked goods were found, and it was up to them to hold the goods until they were claimed by the proprietary owners.[28]

Another significant act that upheld the claim of proprietary owners, yet also recognised a claim by the finders, came in 1353 in the reign of Edward III.[29] The act reiterated that shipwrecked goods which were not legally defined as wreck should be restored to their proprietary owners, but it also required that a reward, or salvage, be given to the finders. Indeed, the act even gave salvors the right to place a lien on the goods saved if any disagreement erupted between the parties. Disputes were to be decided by a jury if the case came under common law, or by the Court of Admiralty in the case of shipwreck at sea.[30] Thus, for the first time, salvors' rights were included in law. Although the amount of salvage was not specified, salvors customarily received a moiety, meaning half the goods or half their value.[31] It is unclear how the moiety originally came to be established, but it is certain that the subordinate classes through to the nineteenth century took care to protect their salvage rights, even to the point of dividing the goods before turning them over to the proper authorities. As well, entitlement to salvage became an important point of contention for the country people, which will be discussed in Chapter 4.

Although it is difficult to determine all of the influences that caused the shift from feudal to commercial rights in regard to wreck, it is clear that there was some influence from other maritime law codes, in particular from the Rolls of Oléron. Legal historians have emphasised the importance of the Rolls, but there are many debates surrounding it, including its provenance, when it came in use in England, how much it was used, over what distance it was practised, and how much it influenced modern English common law and admiralty law. Sir Travers Twiss, in his introduction to the *Black Book of the Admiralty* in 1873,[32] argues that the Rolls probably came into England from

---

[27]  4 Edw. I st. 2, in *The Statutes at Large*, Vol 1, 114.
[28]  Coroners did not assume responsibility over wreck until at least the English Civil War, and even then their function was mainly to investigate deaths. See Jeremy Gibson and Colin Rogers, *Coroners' Records in England and Wales*, 3rd edition (Bury, Lancashire, 2009), 5. There is also some debate as to whether this statute is 'genuine', and even if it is, legal historians claim that it was 'merely directory', as no further statutes mention it. Sir George Hill, *Treasure Trove in Law and Practice: From the Earliest Time to the Present Day* (Oxford, 1936), 197–198.
[29]  27 Edw. III c. 1, in *The Statutes at Large*, Vol 2, 87.
[30]  Palmer, *Law of Wreck*, 23.
[31]  Marsden, ed., *Select Pleas in the Court of Admiralty*, Vol. II, xxi, no. 7 and xxxv; Palmer, *Law of Wreck*, 23; Williams, 'A Legal History of Shipwreck in England', 3.
[32]  Sir Travers Twiss, ed. *The Black Book of the Admiralty*, Vol II (London, 1873), xliv–lvi.

the duchy of the Aquitaine sometime during the reign of Richard I in the twelfth century, and thus may have begun influencing maritime courts sometime thereafter.[33] Whenever they were adopted, by the end of the medieval period they had become accepted as common maritime law in every country that bordered the Atlantic Ocean or North Sea. The newly instituted Admiralty Court in England used them from the mid-fourteenth century to deal with cases arising on the sea. A key characteristic of the Rolls is the emphasis they placed on the rights of merchants and cargo owners over the rights of the holders of *wreccum maris*. Unclear, however, are the provenance and date of Law Codes 26 and 27, clauses which are concerned with wreck. Neither one was included within the original English manuscripts, though they appear later in the fourteenth century. These codes are very similar to Henry III's act of 1236. Printed in English in 1536 by Thomas Petyt, Code 26 states that if

> the mayster and the maryners or one of them escapeth and is saved, or the marchauntes or a marchaunte, the lorde of the place ought not to hinder the saving of the fragments and the marchaundise of the said shyp by those who shall have escaped, and by those to whom the vessell or the marchaundise belong.

Code 27 asserts

> that if the mayster, maryners, and marchaunts dye, theyr goods are cast on the coast, or remayne in the sea, without any pursuyte on the parte of those to whom they belong, for they know nothynge; in such a case the whiche is very piteouse, the lord ought to set persons to save the said goodes, and those goodes the lord ought to guard and place safely, and afterwards he ought to make known to the relations of the dead drowned the misfortune, and paye the said salvors after the labour and paid that they shall have taken, not at his own expense, but at the expense of the thynges saved, and the residue the which remayneth the said lorde ought to guard, or have guarded entirely till a yere, unless those to whom the said goods belong come sooner. And the ende of a yeare passed or more, yf it pleaseth the said lorde to wayte, he ought to sell publicly, and to the highest offrer, the said thynges, and from the money received he ought to have prayer made to God for the dead ...[34]

As can be seen, the Rolls of Oléron allow the owner to claim shipwrecked goods even when there were no survivors, as well as allocating for salvage. Unfortunately, the lineage of the laws, and their influences, are almost impossible to follow because of the lack of extant sources.

---

[33] For an additional discussion of the Rolls of Oléron, see Timothy Runyan, 'The Rolls of Oléron and the Admiralty Court in Fourteenth Century England', *American Journal of Legal History*, 19 (1975), 95–111; Paul Studer, *Oak Book of Southampton*, 2 vols. (Southampton, 1910–11), 54–103; Louis F. Middlebrook, 'The Laws of Oléron', *Marine Historical Association*, 1, no. 10 (22 April 1935), 171–183.

[34] Twiss, *The Black Book of the Admiralty*, Vol. II, 463.

## Disputes over *Wreccum maris*

Despite the existence of statute and common law that defines wreck and right of wreck, ultimately, at a grassroots level the issue was not nearly so straightforward, and people were not willing to give up their 'natural rights' of wreck, nor were they willing to allow neighbouring lords, or even the Crown, to appropriate wrecked goods. Medieval legal records are rife with contested cases – between Crown and the Church, between Crown and lords of the manor, between neighbouring lords, between cargo owners and lords, and even between lords and the common people.[35]

Each change in legislation did not go unchallenged. Indeed, the Abbot of Battle argued that Henry I's decree, guaranteeing the rights of the survivors, was nullified upon Henry's death. The Archbishop of Canterbury filed a lawsuit against the abbot in an attempt to uphold the decree. At the centre of the dispute was a wrecking incident that occurred in 1139, during the reign of Stephen (1135–54). A ship from Romney found itself in peril and wrecked upon the shore of Dengemarsh, an area claimed by Battle Abbey; the crew escaped, but the ship and cargo did not. According to the abbot, the wreck was the property of Battle Abbey, and so it was taken by force. As the abbot pronounced, 'while King Henry could at will change the ancient rights of the country for his own time, that fact should not establish anything for posterity except with the common consent of the barons of the realm', a clear challenge to royal authority. The abbot offered to give up his claim of immediate wreck if the other barons agreed to do the same on their own lands, and thus support Henry I's decree. No one was willing to give up their rights, and Stephen clearly did not have their backing to enforce the decree. The abbot left him with this threat, indicating the power of the barons' feelings over their right of wreck: 'Not for long may you wear the crown of England, O king, so please it God, if you destroy even such a small liberty given our church by King William and respected by your other predecessors.'[36]

One of the most far-reaching legal disputes over wreck, however, occurred when Edward I attempted to secure the rights of *wreccum maris* that his antecedents had granted away, the results of which had significant consequences for wreck law in the eighteenth and nineteenth centuries. Beginning in 1274, Edward sent justices around England to make inquiries and to institute *quo warranto* proceedings, intended to challenge manorial wreck rights by investigating by what authority lords claimed the 'liberty', or privilege. In this investigation into wreck rights, however, even those lords who could not produce

---

[35] Melikan, 'Shippers, Salvors', 172.
[36] Suit 303, van Caenegem, *English Lawsuits*, 119; H.W.C. Davis, 'The Chronicle of Battle Abbey', *English Historical Review*, 29 (July 1914), 434.

their charters claimed they had practised *wreccum maris* from 'time immemorial'. Edward maintained that those rights were only to be practised by
special royal warrant; in reality, however, he could do nothing. There were too
many feudal lords who claimed the liberty. In one important case, Edward
summoned the Abbot of Tavistock to court and asked by what right he was
claiming wreck on the Isles of Scilly. The abbot answered that he 'and all his
Predecessors had enjoyed them without Interruption for Time immemorial;
and therefore desires that his Right may be tried by a Jury'. It was, and the jury
found that 'said Abbat, and all his Predecessors, had enjoyed all the Wreck
that happened in all the aforesaid Islands for Time immemorial: except *Gold*,
*Whale*, *Scarlet Cloth*, and *Fir*, or *Masts*, which were always reserved to the
King in the respective Grants of those Islands',[37] thus thwarting Edward's
challenge. With so many claims against him, Edward was forced to concede,
and in 1290 he issued his far-reaching compromise: he would recognise the
lord's 'prescriptive' rights to wreck if they had been practised for one hundred
years, that is, from 1189. The decree read that:

> All those which claim to have quiet possession of any franchise before the time
> of King Richard, without interruption, and can show the same by a lawful
> inquest, shall well enjoy their possession; and in case that such possession be
> demanded for cause reasonable, our lord the king shall confirm it by title.[38]

Thus this compromise resulted in a clear legal designation for the phrase 'from
time immemorial', and it also defined the key legal doctrine of prescriptive
rights. The doctrine of prescription was fundamental in all of the important
legal battles involving the rights to wreck for the lords of the manor, the Duchy
and the Crown in the eighteenth and nineteenth centuries, as we will see.

The feudal lords had forced Edward I into a compromise about their right
of wreck, but another pivotal battle brewed. In whose jurisdiction would
wreck cases and claims be tried, the courts of common law or the Admiralty
Court? This dispute would also have far-reaching consequences. Edward III
created the Admiralty Court to adjudicate cases that arose on the high seas.
By definition, these cases occurred outside of English counties, and hence
beyond the jurisdiction of common law courts, which were required to call
local county juries. The Lord High Admiral was the major office-holder in the
Admiralty, chosen by the king from the feudal nobility. As the office took on
greater legal administration, the office of vice-admiral was formed to handle
legal affairs. During the wars in France, Edward extended the Admiralty to
include an admiral of the north and an admiral of the west. Initially given

---

[37]  Assize Roll, taken before John de Berewick and other Justices at the Court of Launceston at
Michaelmas Term, *Anno* 30 Edw. I, quoted in Robert Heath, *The Isles of Scilly: The First Book
on the Isles of Scilly* (originally published London, 1750, reprinted Newcastle-upon-Tyne, 1967),
65.
[38]  Hamil, 'Wreck of the Sea', 6.

a wage, the admirals were also awarded a share in wreck and prize rights.[39] In consequence, they received what was termed 'droits of Admiralty' – claim to any shipwrecked goods that would normally be received by the monarch. The Admiralty Court soon began to challenge the common law courts over jurisdiction, especially in cases arising from disputes over the foreshore, which included disagreement over the actual body of law the courts would follow. The Admiralty Court took as its corpus maritime law as practised by other maritime nations, including the Laws of Rhodes and Oléron, the Hanseatic League ordinances, and the Consolato del Mare. The common law courts based their decisions on English precedent and statute. Technically, the Admiralty Court dealt with cases concerning piracy, smuggling, shipwrecks, and anything concerning the waterways as well as the sea.[40]

By the reign of Richard II, even the monarch noticed that the powers of the Admiralty Court were growing too fast. Richard sought to curb them beginning in 1383, when he turned his attention to the actions of the Admiral of the West, who was interfering with the havener in Cornwall. This conflict is easy to understand – haveners were officials employed by either the Earl of Cornwall, or the monarch in the absence of an earl, to oversee the maritime affairs of the Duchy, including wrecks. The havener 'was bound to take and answer for the same, and all former haveners used so to do, the admirals or any others not being used to meddle therein as the king is particularly informed'.[41] The request was not enough, and Richard followed with statutes that were passed in 1389 and 1391 to limit the powers of the Admiralty. 13 Richard II, Statute I, c. 5 stated that the admirals were not to 'meddle from henceforth of anything done within the realm but only of a thing done upon the sea'. Two years later, upon request from the Commons, Richard ordained an additional statute:

> That of all manner of contracts, pleas, and quarrels, and all other things rising within the bodies of the counties, as well by land as by water, and also of wreck of the sea, the admiral's court shall have no manner of cognizance, power nor jurisdiction ... [but they] shall be tried, determined, discussed, and remedied by the laws of the land, and not before nor by the admiral, nor his lieutenant in any wise.[42]

Nonetheless, even statutes did not curb the Admiralty. Frustrated, Henry IV passed an additional statute in 1400 imposing a penalty on those who attempted to use the Admiralty court in lieu of the common law courts;

---

[39] Runyan, 'The Rolls of Oléron', 96–104; Marsden, *Select Pleas in the Court of Admiralty*, Vol. II, xxxix–xli; Williams, 'A Legal History of Shipwreck in England', 4–5.

[40] Runyan, 'The Rolls of Oléron', 109.

[41] Quoted in Hamil, 'Wreck of the Sea', 22.

[42] 15 Rich. II c. 3, quoted in Hamil, 'Wreck of the Sea', 23. A more in-depth discussion of this conflict is found in Hannen and Pritchard, *Digest of Admiralty and Maritime Law*, xiv–xvii.

there were petitions to the parliaments of 1402 and 1410 to enforce these laws, but to no avail. The king relented in 1426 when the Duke of Bedford was appointed Admiral, but even then, he was not to have judicial powers over wreck of the sea. Henry emphasised that wreck cases were to be heard by common law.[43] Despite this royal counteraction, by the sixteenth century the Admiralty Court commonly heard and investigated most wreck cases.

An example of the conflict between the courts occurred in 1535 in the reign of Henry VIII when Thomas Sleighter was arrested for receiving goods pillaged from the cargo of a wrecked ship on the Essex coast. Anthony Hussey charged him with stealing over 550 pounds of wax and four staves worth £16 6s 8d. Sleighter was condemned to pay the value of the goods, as well as the legal costs of his co-plaintiffs.[44] This complaint was heard in the Admiralty Court, but Sleighter sued for cognisance of the common law court. The writ of supersedeas, issued in the name of Henry VIII, condemned the Admiralty Court for hearing the case, citing the statute of Richard II. Even though the royal writ 'command[ed]' that they 'stay further proceedings' and that the statute should be 'inviolably observed', the Admiralty Court passed sentence on Sleighter anyway and delivered its verdict with the fine.[45] In this case, the Admiralty Court was successful in claiming jurisdiction in a wreck case, despite royal condemnation.

In the seventeenth century, the common law courts reacted and grew increasingly assertive in their bid to curb the power of the High Court of Admiralty. According to *Sir H. Constable's Case*, heard in 1601, the Admiralty Court was limited to hearing cases only arising on the high seas: "The Admiralty has no jurisdiction over wreck of the sea, for that must be cast on the land before it becomes wreck'.[46] The Admiralty was left, instead, with authority to try salvage cases. At the end of the seventeenth century, even the Admiralty Court admitted that it had gone beyond its jurisdiction in wreck cases, thus leaving wreck in the control of the common law courts.[47] This, by definition, also left criminal cases arising from the plunder of wrecks to the common law courts. Eventually, through case law, the common law courts determined that 'wreck' cast upon the land came under the cognisance of the common law courts, while other shipwrecked goods, not *legally* defined as 'wreck', but meaning flotsam, jetsam, lagan, and derelict, came under the jurisdiction of the Admiralty, and could be claimed as droits of Admiralty.[48]

---

43  Hamil, 'Wreck of the Sea', 23.

44  R.G. Marsden, ed. *Select Pleas in the Court of Admiralty*, Vol. I: *The Court of Admiralty of the West (AD 1390–1404) and the High Court of Admiralty (AD 1527–1545)* (London, 1897), 186.

45  Marsden, *Select Pleas in the Court of Admiralty*, Vol. I, 185.

46  Hannen and Pritchard, *Digest of Admiralty and Maritime Law*, 2319.

47  Marsden, *Select Pleas in the Court of Admiralty*, Vol. I, 186.

48  Palmer, *Law of Wreck*, 2–3; Hannen and Pritchard, *Digest of Admiralty and Maritime Law*,

This was to have important consequences for court cases in the eighteenth and nineteenth centuries.

Despite the establishment of wreck law and the resolution of legal jurisdiction for wreck law cases, the law continued to be disregarded by all levels of society, which demonstrates a lack of authority on the part of the Crown. Indeed, there is evidence that the survivor clause of the Statute of Westminster was not adhered to, and quite possibly many people were not even aware of its existence. Indeed, even the 'year and a day' clause was not followed; ships and goods that were not legally defined as 'wreck' were seized by the holders of *wreccum maris*, including royal officials, sheriffs, lords of the manor, and ecclesiastical officials. Numerous cases occur in the *Calendar of Patent Rolls* where royal writs were required to force the return of goods to their proprietary owners.[49] Sometimes, however, royal writs were not needed. In 1219, a shipwreck off Bridlington Bay, Yorkshire yielded one survivor. The sheriff ordered that all the goods taken from the wreck be restored. The survivor was lucky. William Martyn had the opposite experience. In 1298 Martyn lost one of his vessels near Sandwich after a voyage to Flanders, losing expensive armour as well as other goods. He claimed the cargo was plundered, and he sought recourse in the courts, asking that his property be returned. He was to be disappointed as no action was taken.[50] In 1302, Thomas de la Hyde, the Duke of Cornwall's steward, and William de Talcarn, the havener, along with thirty other men, were charged with illegally carrying away goods from the wreck of a Spanish ship. They were found guilty of obstructing the owner from claiming his ship and cargo.[51]

Even ships and property belonging to reigning monarchs were appropriated as wreck despite the presence of survivors. In January 1525, the *St Anthony*, carrying the king of Portugal's bullion, plate, and silver, wrecked in a storm off Gunwalloe, on the south coast of Cornwall. Forty-five men survived and made it onto the beach, where they commenced with salvage duty. Helping them for two days after the wreck were 'the country folk'. Francis Person, the Portuguese factor, reported that three local magistrates, William Godolphin of Godolphin, Thomas Seynt Aubyne (St Aubyn) and John Mylaton (Millaton), captain of St Michael's Mount, arrived and attacked them, carrying off over £10,000 in goods. The factor appealed to the king of England's Court of Star Chamber, and provided a list of the stolen goods which indicated the sheer wealth of the wreck: copper, silver bullion, silver vessels, a chest of ready money; precious stones, pearls, chains; rich clothes of Arras; Holland cloth and linen; satin,

---

2316–2319. See the court cases *The King v. Two Casks of Tallow* (1837) and *The King v. Forty-nine Casks of Brandy* (1836).
[49] Hamil, 'Wreck of the Sea', 18.
[50] Richard Larn, *Shipwrecks of Great Britain and Ireland* (Newton Abbot, 1981), 20.
[51] *Calendar of Patent Rolls*, 1307–13, in Maryanne Kowaleski, ed., *The Havener's Accounts of the Earldom and Duchy of Cornwall, 1287–1356*, Vol. 44 (Exeter, 2001), 25.

velvet, and silk; musical instruments; the king of Portugal's personal armour; and guns of brass and iron. The defence put forth by the Cornish magistrates illustrates defamation of the reputation of the 'country people', a stratagem of symbolic violence that will appear again in this book. The magistrates denied they had been involved in attacking the vessel, instead claiming that the officer in charge of the cargo, Diego de Alvero, had feared that the cargo would be plundered by the 'country people' and had thus called for the assistance of the magistrates. They said that Alvero then implored them to purchase some of the goods so the shipwrecked sailors could procure supplies. Godolphin and Millaton declared they only bought £20 worth of goods, and that they had been involved with salvage, and so claimed salvage payments.[52]

The above case shows that the reputation of the 'country people' for 'plunder' and fear of their actions were familiar enough to the magistrates that they could use it to cover their guilt, even if the country people were innocent in the plunder of the St Anthony. Indeed, extant records of litigation from the medieval era are rife with cases of 'wrecking by plunder' by common people, tracing back as far as the thirteenth century. In 1201, Sigur of Liskeard, in Cornwall, charged Amand, a clerk, and Amand's son Eustace with robbery. He claimed that 'in the king's peace and in robbery they took his chattels from his ship which was in peril, namely wine and corn and salt and other chattels'. The jurors were asked if they suspected the accused were robbers – they did not. Amand and Eustace were acquitted, 'because Sigur is dead and no one sues against them'.[53] One wonders what would have been the verdict if Sigur had not died before the case was tried. For the most part, however, those guilty of plundering vessels without having the rights to *wreccum maris* were not identified in the records, despite the copious cases enumerated in the Patent and Close Rolls,[54] an indication of the number of conflicts over popular belief in the right of wreck. It is unclear, however, as to what 'plunder' really meant, as the entries are too brief.

The king, as well as merchants, and the holders of the liberty of wreck all had trouble with country people who believed they had customary rights over the shipwrecked goods that they found. In Kent in 1395, a serjeant-at-arms claimed that he had attempted to investigate a wreck, but he could not deal with the local inhabitants, that 'neither ship, gear, nor goods came to his hand, neither did he for his life dare to arrest aught of them, except some jardels

---

[52] Henderson, *Essays in Cornish History*, 173–175; Henderson, 'Cornish Wrecks and Wreckers', A.K. Hamilton Jenkin, *Cornwall and Its People* (Newton Abbot, 1970), 46–47. See also John Chynoweth, 'The Wreck of the *St Anthony*', *Journal of the Royal Institution of Cornwall*, new series, 5 (1968), 385–406.

[53] Doris Mary Stenton, ed., *Pleas Before the King or His Justices 1198–1202* Vol. II: *Rolls or Fragments of Rolls from the Years 1198, 1201, and 1202* (London, 1952), 80.

[54] Hamil, 'Wreck of the Sea', 19.

of wool and some cloths.'[55] There were also cases involving outright murder, although there is no evidence that the murders were motivated by the survivor clause from the Statute of Westminster to ensure a 'dead wreck'. The *Calendar of Patent Rolls* records that in 1286 a ship wrecked at Dengemarsh. The plunderers killed a merchant on board, Vincente E. Stefne, and then escaped with the cargo.[56] A similar incident occurred off the coast of Suffolk when a ship belonging to Newcastle and Berwick merchants wrecked in 1353. The plunderers claimed that they killed the crew because they thought they were enemy Scots.[57] Sometimes it was not clear exactly what happened, and an area's reputation might colour the report. In 1283, a Shoreham ship wrecked in St Ives Bay, Cornwall. The survivors tried to make it to shore, but their boat was swamped and all were drowned. However, 'Later it was said some of the men came ashore alive but were slain by the people of the country.'[58]

The law, as it has been outlined, differentiated between those who had rights to wreck, and those who did not. Much of the court activity regarding wreck, and subsequent punishment, involved those who were 'disenfranchised': the common people. Commoners who came upon wreck were expected to bring it to their local lords or to the local sheriff. If they did so, they could expect their moiety of the goods as salvage. If they failed to do so, and if they hid the goods, then they could expect penalties. According to the Statute of Westminster, people who were in illegal possession of wrecked property could be punished with imprisonment and a fine, although it appears that fines were more common. In the case of Leiston Abbey, in Suffolk, amercements – fines – placed on individuals caught taking wreck, were actually more profitable for the abbot than was the taking of wreck itself.[59] This is also true of Duchy lands in Cornwall. Havener's accounts contain detailed lists of those fined, along with the amounts the people were expected to pay. In the early fourteenth century, fines brought in annually up to four times the value of the sale of wrecked goods. Fines ranged from two shillings to four shillings and up, the exact amount probably based on the value of the goods taken.[60] Between 1301 and 1306, the annual average for wreck was 36.8 pence; fines for pillagers amounted to 146.1 pence and profits from salvage amounted to 18.3 pence, making wreck fines 30 per cent of the Duchy maritime revenues. Some years

---

55  Quoted in Hamil, 'Wreck of the Sea', 19.
56  *Calendar of Patent Rolls, 1281–1292*, 256, cited in Hamil, 'Wreck of the Sea', 18; Larn, *Shipwrecks of Great Britain*, 19.
57  *Calendar of Patent Rolls, 1350–1354*, 389–390, 453–454, 458–459, in Hamil, 'Wreck of the Sea', 19.
58  James Whetter, *Cornwall in the 13th Century: A Study in Social and Economic History* (Gorran, Cornwall, 1998), 94.
59  Bertram Schofield, 'Wreck Rolls of Leiston Abbey', in *Studies Presented to Sir Hilary Jenkinson*, ed. J. Davies Conway (Oxford, 1957), 369.
60  Kowaleski, *Havener's Accounts*, 25.

no wrecks were recorded, and thus no fines. The reasons for the differences are twofold. As the Duchy survey of 1337 stated, 'Regarding the annual value of wreck of the sea, nothing can be estimated because the profit arising from it falls fortuitously by chance, sometimes more, sometimes less …'. In addition, when the office of havener was given to non-Cornish individuals, who in turn farmed out their duties, profits for wreck, especially by fine, fell drastically.[61]

Paying fines for appropriating wrecked property could be difficult for poorer people to manage, but worse penalties could be instituted. Ecclesiastical and maritime law, as opposed to the common law under which wreck law was eventually subsumed, had much harsher penalties than mere fining. The ecclesiastical councils of Nantes (1127) and the Lateran (1179) both prescribed excommunication. The Rolls of Oléron took this a step further:

> And he who … shall take any of the goodes of the said poor persons shipwrecked, lost and ruined against theyr desire and wyll, he is excommunicated by the church, and ought to be punysshed as a thief, yf he make not restitution briefly; and there is neither custome nor statute whatever that can protect them against incurring the said penalty.

If the miscreants used violence, the penalty was much harsher:

> Likewise, yf a shyp is lost in stryking against any coast, and chaunceth that the crew imagine to escape and save themselves and come to the bank halfdrowned, thinking that some one wyll ayde them, but it chaunceth that sometyme in many places there are inhuman felons, more cruel than dogs or wolves enraged, the whiche murder and slaye the poor sufferers, to obtain theyr money, or clothes or other goodes; such manner of people the lorde of the place ought to seize and inflict on them justice and punishment, both as regards their persons, and their goodes, and they ought to be cast into the sea and plunged in it, until they are half dead, and then they ought to be dragged out, and stoned, and massacred as would be done to a dog or a wolfe. This is the judgement.[62]

It is not known if this penalty was actually carried out. By the eighteenth century, however, as we will see, the penalty under English common law for wrecking by plunder changed from fines based on the value of the wrecked goods to the penalty of death, though, fortunately for those convicted, not in the manner prescribed by the Rolls of Oléron.

Thus, it was in the medieval and early modern eras that the rights to *wreccum maris* were established and developed. The granting of those rights to the dominant elites – to both lords of the manor and ecclesiastical officials – laid the foundation for the legal framework that would be drawn upon during wreck disputes of the eighteenth and nineteenth centuries. Important

---

[61] Kowaleski, *Havener's Accounts*, figured from Table 1, Annual Revenues and Expenses in the Havener's Accounts, 66–67, 23.
[62] Twiss, *The Black Book of the Admiralty*, Vol. II, 463, 465.

concepts in wreck law, too, were instituted, with the development of the legal definition of 'wreck' (and 'prescription'), its consequent codification with the inclusion of a salvage clause, and the settlement of wreck jurisdiction within the courts of common law. However, the legal status was not as clear as has been argued, especially in the minds of the disenfranchised commoners. Although they had no legal claim, in practise they continued to appropriate 'the gifts of the sea' from 'time immemorial', most likely with little interference, and were thus able to hold on to their belief that the wreck washing ashore was 'providence', a gift from God. In addition, they also embraced some facets of the law, and developed their own popular beliefs, such as their rights to 'dead wrecks', although there is no evidence that this clause instigated indiscriminate murder of shipwreck victims. Indeed, the law does not necessarily influence a person's behaviour, nor can it be used to demonstrate the actual practices of the time. Rather as a prescriptive form of evidence it shows how the dominant elite *wanted* wreck law to be observed, but as the wealth of cases shows, this rarely happened. It would be left for the legislators of the eighteenth and nineteenth centuries to solidify wreck law and to attempt to bring about legislation to combat what they described as 'so barbarous a Practice', the appropriating of wrecked goods and materials by the subordinate classes.

# 3

# Wrecking and Criminality

*to prevent the cargo from becoming prey to the populace*

O n Tuesday, 14 December 1708, several men representing the East India
Company left its sumptuous headquarters on Leadenhall Street in the
City of London. Making their way through traffic, pedestrians, and filth
laying in the gutters of the narrow, grimy streets, they headed to the House
of Commons, then situated in a modest two-storey, turreted ex-chapel, part of
the old Palace of Westminster. Upon arriving, they placed before the members
copies of three letters sent post-haste from Cornwall, delivered to Secretary
Thomas Woolley as he had been working late on Saturday night. The letters
described a 'melancholly Account' then occurring: the East India Company's
ship *Albemarle* had run aground during a storm the previous Tuesday night
on her return from the East Indies. She was breaking to pieces near Polperro,
on the south coast of Cornwall. She and her consort, the *Rochester*, were, as
Woolley described them, rich ships. She carried within her hold indigo, coffee,
pepper, and bale goods, including silk and calico. Joseph Bullock, one of the
supercargoes, had written in panic that 'the Savage Inhabitants are ready to
plunder what they have gott & cutt their throats too.'[1]

Woolley inaccurately concluded that after the ship went aground, she was
attacked 'by the people of the Country getting on board and plundering what
they could and then cutting her Cables for that some of the Country people
were overheard on the road threatening they would do so if she was not
ashore by the time they got thither'.[2] This was just speculation, but it shows
the extent of the fear the East India Company had regarding the dire situation of the wrecked vessel. Indeed, the ship had already parted her anchors by
the force of the wind and had been driven onto the rocks; she did not need

---

[1]  India Office Records [IOR] E/1/198 Letter Books Misc, Woolley to Addis, 14 December
1708, 74–75; James Derriman, 'The Wreck of the *Albemarle*', *Journal of the Royal Institution of
Cornwall*, new series II, I, pt 2 (1992), 129.
[2]  IOR E/1/198 Letter Books Misc. Woolley to Capt Staines of the *Rochester*, 25 December
1708, 97; Derriman, 'The Wreck of the *Albemarle*', 130.

further assistance to become a total wreck.[3] Despite the dispatch of soldiers to protect the wreck, the 'country' did, however, abscond with the silk and other bale goods that had washed ashore. Coffee, too, was harvested from the beach, and sold in Polperro at 12 pence a pound.[4]

After the letters were delivered to the Commons, a bill entitled 'to prevent the Embezzlement of Goods and Merchandizes cast away upon, or near, the Coast of Great Britain' – or, as worded by Woolley, 'to prevent such Rapine & violence for some time to come'[5] – was ordered to be prepared. The drafting committee was impressive. It consisted of Sir Gilbert Heathcote, Director of the new East India Company, who had risen from the ranks to become a major financier of the Bank of England; William Lowndes, the redoubtable Secretary of the Treasury; Francis Scobell, MP for St Germans in Cornwall, a member of the Middle Temple; and Hugh Boscawen, the influential Cornish MP from the borough of Tregony, who was the nephew of Lord Godolphin, the Lord Treasurer.[6] Boscawen, at the time of the bill's introduction, was also the Warden of the Stannaries and High Steward of the Duchy of Cornwall, thus he had an interest in the events occurring in Polperro. After four months, the bill was finally introduced on 9 April 1709 by the counsel for the East India Company, John Hungerford. Despite this initial interest, however, and the influence of the men involved, the bill was dropped. Unfortunately, it is no longer extant, so the measures introduced against wrecking are unknown, but they could not have been important to the Commons overall. Rather, most of House's focus lay in passing legislation to supply the continuing European wars, and in political in-fighting, which culminated in the downfall of the Whig ministry in 1710. The emergency had passed. Nothing was done about wrecking issues for another six years.[7]

Although the plunder of shipwrecks was legally a felony, merchants and traders were unhappy with the state of the law and sought stronger measures. Thus this bill was one of eight initiated in House of Commons in the eighteenth century, with another seventeen bills introduced in the nineteenth century that included wrecking clauses. (See Appendix 1) As the legislation multiplied, important distinctions in wrecking offences were itemised. An analysis of these changes shows that attitudes towards wrecking were

3   IOR E/1/198 Letter Books Misc. 'Letter to All High Constables, Pettie Constables Head-boroughs and all other officers', n.d. [25 December 1708], 98.

4   IOR E/1/198 Letter Books Misc. Woolley to Wright, Addis, Beawes, Bullock and Bisse, 16 December 1708, 85–86.

5   IOR E/1/198 Letter Books Misc. Woolley to Addis, 14 December 1708, 74–75; Derriman, 'The Wreck of the *Albemarle*', 133.

6   *CJ*, Vol. XVI, 14 December 1708, 47; Derriman, 'Wreck of the *Albermarle*', 132–133; *Oxford Dictionary of National Biography Online*, accessed 10 February 2009.

7   *CJ*, Vol. XVI, 20 December 1708, 51; 9 April 1709, 195; 14 April 1709, 201. It was rare for bills to be printed before 1714, thus most of them have not survived.

not constant. Rather, wrecking, like other crimes, can be defined as 'social constructions changing over time and between societies, social groups, and individuals'.[8] Indeed, the legal transformation of wrecking emphasised the protean concerns of the merchants and legislators, illuminating their role not only in the criminalisation of wrecking but in the constantly shifting levels of punishment the crime incurred. Their view of wrecking, of course, never embraced the precept of 'finders keepers'; that idea would remain intact within the populace. Rather, their actions in creating anti-wrecking legislation gave birth to an alternative modern myth, that all wrecking activity was a hanging offence.

## 12 Anne st. 2 c. 18 (1714)

At the beginning of the eighteenth century, the basic tenets of wreck law remained unchanged from the early modern period. What had changed were the ways special interest groups were able to lobby Parliament, a transformation that occurred after 1688. A now annual standing parliament held longer sessions, and extended levels of legislative activity.[9] Thus merchant interests became increasingly visible, assisted by the expanding number of merchants and financiers who took the most active roles within parliament.[10]

In early 1714, merchants petitioned the Commons for another wrecking bill. The preamble states that in returning from dangerous voyages, trading vessels 'have unfortunately near home run on shore, or been stranded on the coasts thereof; and that such ships have been barbarously plundered by her Majesty's Subjects, and their cargoes embezzilled'.[11] But rather than accentuating the financial losses of the shipping interests, the preamble underscored the 'great loss of her Majesty's revenue', an ample reminder that most general parliamentary acts had the monetary interest of the kingdom at their heart.[12] The preamble also alleges that others besides the East India Company wanted to stop wrecking activity, for 'great complaints have been made by several merchants, as well as her Majesty's subjects as foreigners, trading to and from this Kingdom'. As bills were normally introduced by MPs whose constituencies brought the petitions, the merchants of Liverpool may have been behind the bill. William Clayton, a prominent Liverpool merchant, was not only on

---

[8]  Peter King, *Crime, Justice, and Discretion in England, 1740–1820* (Oxford, 2000), 6.

[9]  John Brewer, *The Sinews of Power: War, Money and the English State, 1688–1783* (Cambridge, Massachusetts, 1990), 231.

[10]  Peter Jupp, *The Governing of Britain, 1688–1848: The Executive, Parliament and the People* (London, 2006), 61.

[11]  Preamble 12 Anne st. 2, c. 18 (1713), *The Statutes at Large*, 24 vols. Vol. 13, ed. D. Pickering (Cambridge, 1762), 121.

[12]  Brewer, *Sinews of Power*, 246.

the drafting committee, but he presented the bill to the Commons and the Lords for approval.

The 1714 bill was more successful than that of 1708; it passed into law as 12 Anne st. 2 c. 18, confirming the Statute of Westminster's definition of wreck, as well as confirming 4 Edw. I st. 2, which outlined the role of juries in determining salvage. However, in other ways, 12 Anne was groundbreaking. It specified important distinctions in wrecking offences and itemised the penalties for each.

Table 4. Wrecking Offences – 12 Anne, st. 2, c. 18 (1714)

| Offence | Penalty |
| --- | --- |
| Entering a distressed ship without permission | Double satisfaction or House of Correction-12 months |
| Obstructing the saving of a ship or goods | Double satisfaction or House of Correction-12 months |
| Defacing the marks on goods | Double satisfaction or House of Correction-12 months |
| Carrying off goods without permission | Forfeit triple the value |
| Deliberate Wrecking – making holes in ship | Felony without Benefit of Clergy Death |
| Deliberate Wrecking – stealing the pump of the ship, etc. | Felony without Benefit of Clergy Death |

This statute sought to legislate against anyone who forced themselves on board to plunder the ship or to claim salvage rights. It also granted officials the legal authority to forcefully resist anyone who attempted to board with those intentions. 'Double satisfaction' – fines – were assessed to discourage criminal activities and to convince perpetrators to relinquish the goods. Most people could not afford to pay the fines; the threat of the house of correction was expected to be deterrent enough.[13] If anyone was involved in deliberate wrecking, by staving holes in the side of the ship, or by stealing the means of pumping out the ship as she was taking on water, they could receive the penalty of 'felony without benefit of clergy'. In other words, for the first time in statute law, the penalty of death was given for deliberate wrecking.

The escalation of penalties is unsurprising given the fact that during Anne's reign, Parliament passed numerous statutes that showed similar language. The new wrecking legislation was enacted at a time when the climate of opinion was turning towards criminal reform. Reformers who influenced the legislation sought to improve the nation's morality; they were disturbed by what they perceived as an important failing of the legal system – a lack of 'systems of

[13] J.M. Beattie, *Crime and the Courts in England, 1660–1800* (Oxford, 1986), 457.

punishment that would discourage crime and prevent the hordes of immoral and debauched individuals ... from going on to even worse offences'.[14] Indeed, this particular statute highlights the characteristic reaction of merchants and legislators to wrecking events; they hastily created laws designed to meet the threat, or perceived threat, to shipping. 12 Anne shows all of the characteristics of an 'emergency' act; it was to be in effect for a limited time – three years – and it contained the typical 'minute details' codifying specific activities to be criminalised. It is unclear what the precipitating factors were behind the bill's introduction, unfortunately, for the shipwreck records for the first quarter of the eighteenth century are very sketchy. However, since the act gained passage at the instigation of the Liverpool merchants, and was pushed through by their representative, there may have been a wrecking incident on the Wirral peninsula. Located on the seaway into Liverpool, it was an area notorious for shipwrecks, and consequently, for wreckers.

As was the case for many emergency acts whose continuance was believed by Parliament to be a necessity to ensure the 'bulwarks of public order',[15] 12 Anne was made perpetual in 1718 by the passage of 4 Geo. I c. 12. The statute specifically stressed that it be read in 'all parish churches and chapels on the coast' on the Sundays before Michaelmas, Christmas, Lady Day, and Midsummer Day, to educate and warn those who were involved with wrecking.[16] However, as David Macpherson remarked in his *Annals of Commerce* in 1805 regarding 12 Anne, 'we are truely sorry to remark, that notwithstanding this good law, there have been frequently barbarous infractions of it, more especially on the farther south-western shores of England, which seem to want a stronger enforcement'.[17] He could also have added that the clergy did not follow through in educating the populace, as Rev. Eden admitted in 1840. Eden had been unaware of the clause that required the reading of the act until he was informed by a Customs officer after the wreck of a ship on the Essex coast.[18] These instances show that despite passage of the statute, it is questionable how much the 'country people' knew about the law or whether it made any inroads into their belief system.

Although 12 Anne detailed the wrecking offences and applied more stringent punishment, the merchants and traders of the City of London did not believe the statute had gone far enough. Together with 'other Merchants and

---

[14] Beattie, *Crime and the Courts*, 496.
[15] See Leon Radzinowicz, *A History of English Criminal Law and its Administration from 1750*. 4 vols. Vol I: *The Movement for Reform* (London, 1948), 17–18, for a discussion of emergency acts.
[16] 4 Geo. I c. 12
[17] David Macpherson, *Annals of Commerce: Manufactures, Fisheries and Navigation, with Brief Notes*. 4 vols (London, 1805), Vol. III, 39–40.
[18] Rev. Robert Eden, *An Address [on Ephes.iv.28] to Depredators and Wreckers on the Sea Coast* (London, 1840), 15.

Traders of Great Britain', which suggests they were involved in a widespread petitioning campaign, they presented their grievances to the Commons in March 1735/36. They protested about the 'barbarous Custom of plundering of ships wrecked or driven on the Shore … and treating the Mariners in a most cruel Manner, if they offer the Least Resistance'. The petitioners also resorted to comparisons with other countries to goad Parliament into action: 'in other Nations, effectual Provision is made for preventing such Attempts, by appointing officers to take care of Ships wrecked, and to render just accounts to the Proprietors of their Goods saved'. Hence, one of their key grievances was the absence of authority during the shipwreck event, which they argued increased the depredations. Further, although the petitioners recognised that Britain had laws that classified wrecking as a felony, they argued that it was impractical to convict offenders because of defects in the laws. They did not, however, reveal what those defects were. The petition gained enough parliamentary attention that a drafting committee was appointed, with City of London Alderman Micajah Perry, a third-generation tobacco merchant with considerable ties to the Atlantic world, as the principle.[19] Assisting him was Sir John Barnard, also a prominent merchant in the City who had extended his business into marine insurance.[20] All of the merchants who served in the House were called forward to serve on the committee after the bill's second reading. [21]

Notwithstanding this initial activity the bill never moved forward and was dropped. Unfortunately, the 1735/36 bill is no longer extant, and it is unknown what provisions the committee suggested. However, the following year the Commons again took up the issue of wrecking. Although the *Commons Journal* makes no mention of petitioners, it is probable that the substance of the bill from the previous year was brought back, especially since it was presented by the same MP, Alderman Perry. This second bill, as well, never made it into law. It made it to its engrossed form, and was approved by the Commons, but it never returned from the Lords.[22]

Despite its failure to pass, an analysis of the 1737 bill makes clear the interests of the merchants and the MPs involved, and what they perceived were the major wrecking crimes. Like 12 Anne, the bill shows evidence that it was formed as a reaction to a wrecking event. It shows comprehensive detail, cataloguing new wrecking crimes and intensifying the severity of the penalties.

[19] Peter Linebaugh, *The London Hanged: Crime and Civil Society in the Eighteenth Century* (Cambridge, 1992), 155–156.
[20] *Oxford Dictionary of National Biography Online*, accessed 29 March 2009.
[21] The bill is entitled 'To render the Laws, now in being, more effectual for the saving and recovering Ships and Goods wrecked, or driven on Shore, by distress of weather or otherwise'. CJ, Vol. XXII (1732–37), 2 March 1735/6, 603–604.
[22] The bill is entitled 'for the better preserving of all such Ships, and Goods thereof, which shall happen to be stranded upon the Coasts'. CJ, Vol. XXII (1732–37), 805, 858, 863, 879, 883.

Table 5. Wrecking Offences – 1737 Wreck Bill

| Offence | Penalty |
| --- | --- |
| Embezzling goods | £20 fine and treble the value of goods |
| Robbery of victim/if offender not caught within one year | inhabitants of the hundred shall make full satisfaction, not exceeding £100 |
| Murder of victim/if offender not caught | inhabitants of the hundred to pay £100 and one moiety for His Majesty and one moiety for person who sues |
| Wounding or stripping live victims or dead bodies | Felony: Transportation |
| Entering a distressed ship without permission | £20 fine or gaol-12 months |
| Obstructing the saving of ship and goods | £20 fine or gaol-12 months |
| Defacing ownership marks on goods | £20 fine or gaol-12 months |
| Entering a distressed ship with weapons and beating a superior officer or anyone preserving the ship | Felony: Transportation |
| Deliberate Wrecking – cutting or destroying the ship or any part of the tackle, furniture, goods or cargo | Felony: Transportation |
| Stealing salvaged goods | Felony: Transportation |

The committee also responded to the key complaint voiced in the merchants' petition, namely the lack of authority. At the time, the only person authorised to issue search warrants valid between counties was the Lord Chief Justice. Application also had to be made by the owners of the shipwrecked cargo to the High Court of Admiralty for a commission of enquiry to search for stolen goods. All these procedures took time and decreased the likelihood that the shipwrecked goods would be recovered. Thus the local magistrates were to be given the power to search for stolen goods, and to arrest and prosecute offenders.

The 1737 bill contained several controversial issues that may have led to its defeat. Of especial contention was the question of culpability. Should the hundred or parish pay indemnities to shipwreck victims if the offenders were not caught? Additionally, a curious aspect of this bill was that in spite of the immense amount of legislation applying capital punishment for crimes involving property, this bill actually *downgraded* the penalty for deliberate wrecking from death to transportation. With no known convictions under 12 Anne, it is difficult to ascertain why the decision was made. However, it could be that transportation provided the courts with an alternative to capital punishment, and thus 'made the discretionary application of increasing capital statutes tolerable'.[23] Unfortunately for those involved with wrecking, when the merchants and Parliament took up the issue again, they were not in as generous a mood.

## 26 Geo. II c. 19 (1753)

The passage of 26 Geo. II c. 19 signified a change in attitude towards wrecking from earlier attempts at legislation. It brought wreck law more in line with other offences that had been legislated during this period when it imposed the death penalty for theft from a wreck. Between 1722 and 1731, thirty-one statutes prescribing capital punishment had been passed, including the infamous 'Black Act' against deer poaching, which was so loosely defined it could be used against any perceived crimes against property.[24] Indeed, 26 Geo., like many acts, was supplementary; it built on previous legislation that had defined wreck crimes so narrowly that additional statutes had to be passed to include other possible forms of the crime. Legislators also reassigned defined crimes as felonies, with the attendant death penalty, in an attempt to fight crime through deterrence and punishment.

Scholarly opinion has it that the passage of 26 Geo. II as a capital statute was not necessarily a 'matter of conscious public policy'. Instead, it has been argued that this statute, like others approved in the same period, incurred little debate, that 'most of the changes were related to specific, limited property interests ... [o]ften they were the personal interest of a few members, and the Lords and Commons enacted them for the mere asking'. Thus the prevailing view of the wreck law is that it is one of many statutes passed in order 'to make *every* kind of theft, malicious damage or rebellion an act punishable by death'.[25] This argument is, however, misleading. Although 26 Geo. II was enacted 'for the asking', in this case at the request of the merchants, traders and insurers of the City of London, the bill *did* incur discussion before it was approved.

The merchants claimed that they had too much profit-loss from wrecking activities; they believed that the existing laws 'were too gentle'. Arguing that the act of 12 Anne 'has, by Experience, been found not to answer the salu-

---

[23] Beattie, *Crime and the Courts*, 519.
[24] Ian Gilmour, *Riot, Risings and Revolution: Governance and Violence in Eighteenth-Century England* (Pimlico, 1992), 7; E.P. Thompson, *Whigs and Hunters: The Origin of the Black Act* (London, 1975, 1990), 21–24.
[25] Douglas Hay, 'Property, Authority and the Criminal Law', in Douglas Hay, Peter Linebaugh, et.al., *Albion's Fatal Tree: Crime and Society in Eighteenth-Century England* (London, 1975, 1988), 20–21; Radzinowicz, *A History of English Criminal Law*, Vol. I, 35.

tary Ends thereby proposed', they wished for 'a more effectual Remedy'.[26] The prologue indicates that their previous points were still of utmost concern:

> whereas, notwithstanding the good and salutary Laws now in being against the plundering and destroying Vessels in Distress, and against taking away shipwrecked, lost, or stranded Goods, many wicked Enormities have been committed, to the Disgrace of the Nation, and to the grievous Damage of Merchants and Mariners of our own and other Countries …

Thus, the bill sought to allay some of these concerns. Magistrates were to be given the powers of search and seizure outlined in the failed 1737 bill. To combat the charge that the laws were 'too gentle', the following wrecking crimes were either added or had their penalties redefined:

Table 6. Wrecking Offences—26 George II, c. 19 (1753)

| Offence | Penalty |
| --- | --- |
| Plundering, stealing, taking away any goods belonging to a wrecked ship | Felony without Benefit of Clergy Death |
| Beating or wounding with intent to kill or destroy survivors | Felony without Benefit of Clergy Death |
| Obstructing the escape of survivors | Felony without Benefit of Clergy Death |
| Deliberate Wrecking: Putting out false lights | Felony without Benefit of Clergy Death |
| Stealing of goods of small value without violence | Petty larceny |

We can see, however, that the reluctance of MPs to assign capital punishment for *all* of the enumerated wrecking offences is substantiated by an important clause added by special rider before the bill was passed: if the goods were considered of small value, and were stolen 'without Cruelty or Violence', as in the case of harvesting, then the offender would be persecuted for petty larceny.[27] Thus, the death penalty was *not* invoked for all forms of wrecking, as has been alleged in much wrecking discourse.[28] Rather, legisla-

---

[26] The bill is entitled 'to enforce the Laws against Persons, who shall Steal or Detain Shipwrecked Goods; and for the Relief of Persons suffering losses thereby'. *CJ*, Vol. XXVI (1750–54), 589.

[27] 26 Geo II c. 19, section 2. The line 'and no barbarity is used in taking them' is quoted in T. Williams, *Everyman His Own Lawyer*, 2nd edition (London, 1818), 523; John Rule, 'Wrecking and Coastal Plunder', in Hay, Peter Linebaugh, et. al., *Albion's Fatal Tree*, 168. See *CJ*, Vol. XXVI (1750–54), 532, 541, 589, 596, 615, 625, 670, 709, 733, 774, 816, 818, 821 and *Journal of the House of Lords*, Vol. XXVIII (1753–56), 125.

[28] Even Hay alludes to the overarching penalty of death for all forms of wrecking in 'Property, Authority and the Criminal Law', 20, although Rule in the same volume mentions the differing sentences, 'Wrecking and Coastal Plunder', 168.

tors invoked capital punishment only for those crimes involving violence or the threat of violence.

The 1753 wrecking statute also included an important clause that was far-reaching. Indeed, this clause has had an impact on wrecking myth as profound as the Statute of Westminster with its 'dead wreck' clause, for here we find enshrined in law for the first time the foremost wrecking myth: the use of false lights to deliberately cause shipwreck. Thus 'any Person or Persons [who] shall put out any false Light or Lights, with Intention to bring any ship or Vessel into Danger' shall suffer death. Why was this particular offence singled out at this time?

Popular writers have argued that the clause is confirmation that the practice existed. After all, 'when was a law ever passed against a nonexistent crime'?[29] Yet, the manner in which it was passed as a last-minute add-on is telling. Someone determined that a clause regarding false lights needed to be appended to the bill; it was not in the original. It is impossible to know whether or not the members *believed* that the crime actually existed. Because offences were defined very specifically, the clause may have been included to safeguard against its possibility, especially since shipwrecks had occurred from the accidental placement of lights.[30] Indeed, the one 'specific recorded case' of the use of false lights cited as occurring in Wales in 1774 is inaccurate; it had been falsified by overzealous newspaper reporters.[31] There are no cases indicating that this crime had actually occurred. Indeed, although several statutes had been passed for lighthouses that mention false lights, none of the clauses dealt with the possibility of using such lights for deliberate wrecking.[32] Thus, the presence of the clause cannot be used as verification that the crime existed; it lacks the authority that investigators have wished to ascribe it. It is perhaps more revealing, however, that in none of the literature or debate on wreck law throughout the eighteenth and nineteenth centuries is the issue of deliberate wrecking by using false lights mentioned. Instead, the concerns dealt almost completely with opportunistic wrecking.

Although the momentum for the wrecking legislation came from the London merchants, there was Cornish interest in the bill, linking local

---

[29] Jeremy Seal, *Treachery at Sharpnose Point: Unraveling the Mystery of the* Caledonia's *Final Voyage* (New York, 2001), 197; Bella Bathurst, *The Wreckers: A Story of Killing Seas, False Lights and Plundered Ships* (London, 2005), 10–11.

[30] See CUST 68/28, 5 January 1821. The inclusion of the clause may also be from one reported instance that is no longer extant. Clive Emsley, *Crime and Society in England, 1750–1900* (London, 1996), 251.

[31] Rule, 'Wrecking and Coastal Plunder', 180; Geoffrey Place, 'Wreckers: The Fate of the *Charming Jenny*', *Mariner's Mirror*, 76, no. 2 (1990), 167–168.

[32] 8 Eliz. c. 13; 26 Geo. III c. 101; 28 Geo. III c. 25. As well, no one was ever convicted under the wrecking clause. Special thanks to Michael Williams, Senior Lecturer in Law, University of Wolverhampton, for conducting a search of prosecutions under statutory law.

interests with national concern.[33] George Borlase, steward for Lt General Richard Onslow's Cornish manors, corresponded with his employer about the upcoming bill while the debate occurred in the Commons.[34] Borlase offered his support, but then complained that he felt the bill was 'very defective'. His recommendations, he believed, would make a more 'effectual remedy against the practice of wrecking'. He stressed that he had been a frequent witness of wrecking events, which would 'shock humanity'; the punishments considered by the bill would not stop the wreckers. He identified them as the local tinners: 'as soon as they observe a Ship on the coast they first arm themselves w$^{th}$ sharp axes and hatchetts and leave their tyn works to follow those ships'. He added emphatically, 'Sometimes the ship is not wrack'd but w$^r$ this or not the mines suffer greatly.'[35]

It is here that Borlase's self-interest becomes explicit. Not only was he a shareholder in the local tin mines, but he was also attempting to seize wreck rights for Onslow's manor of Lanisley, near Penzance, which were legally held by the Arundells, an important gentry family in the area. Hence he had many reasons to be concerned with the outcome of the legislation.[36] Borlase recommended that the bill contain a clause that would nip 'this infamous practice in its very budd' by 'laying the loss of all wages due and some further penalty on every labouring tynner who sh$^d$ leave his Tynwork in order to go to wreck would contribute to keep them home and break the neck of it'. He also maintained that 'no person sh$^d$ be allow'd to attend a wreck arm'd with axes or the like unless lawfully required … for … [t]hey'll cut a large trading vessell to pieces in one tide and cut down everybody that offers to oppose them. Therefore there sh$^d$ be some provision against this.'[37]

Borlase's suggestion to extract wages was, of course, too narrowly defined and only fitted the Cornish situation. It is difficult to see how this could be covered in the wreck bill, or even if it should. As far as his second suggestion, however, future bills would include provisions against the gathering of crowds at wrecks, but for this particular statute, Borlase's counsel went unheeded. Indeed, in spite of the passing of the more stringent act and the application of the death penalty for violent wrecking, Borlase continued to disapprove. Seven years later, he complained to Onslow about its lack of efficacy:

---

[33] Although Cornwall returned forty-four MPs to Parliament before the Reform Act of 1832, they rarely argued for Cornish interests. See Philip Payton, *Cornwall: A History* (Fowey, 2004), 210–211.

[34] Onslow was MP for Guildford in Surrey. He was also the brother of the current Speaker of the House, Sir Arthur Onslow.

[35] Borlase to Onslow, 1 February 1753; 5 March 1753, in Thomas Cornish, ed., 'The Lanisley Letters: to Lt. General Onslow from George Borlase, his Agent at Penzance, 1750–53', *Journal of the Royal Institution of Cornwall*, 6, pt 22 (1880), 374, 377.

[36] This conflict will be covered in Chapter 7.

[37] Borlase to Onslow, 15 March 1753, in Cornish, 'Lanisley Letters', 379.

'notwithstanding the late act there is as much occasion for soldiers here as ev$^r$. last Wednesday night a Dutchman was stranded near Helstone every man saved and the ship whole, burthen 250 tons, laden with claret in 24 hours the Tinners cleared all'.[38]

The existence of later bills show that the merchants continued to pursue further actions to combat wrecking, especially since there was little evidence to show that the preceding legislation had any effect on wrecking activity. Thus legislators returned to the issue of local culpability. On 17 March 1775, Edmund Burke presented a bill to the Commons for his Bristol merchant constituents. Drawing on similar statutes that had been passed, Burke argued that the hundred was more capable of controlling wrecking within its borders, much more so than it could control other more 'minor' offences, such as the killing and maiming of cattle, cutting trees, or the destroying of hedges and gates, which under existing law already held the hundred liable. He was thus seeking to place wrecking on the same footing. Additionally, Burke's bill sought to issue rewards of £40 to those who were involved in the capture and conviction of offenders: if they were killed while pursuing offenders, then the reward would be paid to their executors. Burke and his committee also introduced a new clause: the making of a felony, to be punishable by transportation, for the taking of buoys, a 'wicked Practice [which] hath prevailed'.[39]

No action was taken on the bill in 1775, but Burke presented it again in April 1776 with few changes. He introduced petitions from his Bristol constituents, the Master, Wardens and Commonality of the Society of Merchant Venturers of Bristol, and the Merchants and Insurers of Bristol, who claimed that they had incurred large monetary losses because the laws had not been effective. The Merchant Venturers of Bristol, an organisation that continues to wield much political clout even in the twenty-first century, opined that wrecking offences were not included within the same class of law as other 'malicious Attacks upon Property', and that it was not 'as in other Cases, the Interest of those whose local Situation enables them best to prevent, or prosecute and punish such offences'. The Merchants and Insurers of Bristol suggested, in particular, that rewards be offered to those 'who by their local situation, are best able to render Assistance, that then such would warmly exert themselves as well as preserve the lives of our brave Seamen'.[40]

---

[38] Borlase to Onslow, 21 February, 1760, in Cornish, 'Lanisley Letters', 379.

[39] A Bill [with the Amendments] for the preventing the inhuman Practice of Plundering Ships that are Shipwrecked on the Coast of Great Britain; and for the further Relief of Ships in Distress on the said Coasts, in Sheila Lambert, ed., *House of Commons Sessional Papers of the Eighteenth Century*, Vol. 27, George III Bills, 1774–75 and 1775–76 (Delaware, 1975), 107–109.

[40] It is unclear whether the bill was first introduced in response to the lobbying effort, or whether the lobbying effort occurred in support of the bill. *CJ*, Vol. XXXV (1774–76), 705, 725, 738.

There was also a petition in opposition. Indeed, this is the only wreck bill where the wording of the petitions is extant, giving us an indication as to the major issues under debate. On 30 April 1776, the 'Justices of the Peace, Gentlemen, Clergy, Land-Owners, and Land-holders, of the several Hundreds or Commotts of *Kidwely, Carnawllan,* and *Derlis,* all situate on the Sea Coast of the County of *Caermarthen*', stated their concerns about the bill. They claimed that the existing laws were sufficient; the only remedy needed was the legal appointment of persons who could give immediate notice to the local magistrates of the impending shipwreck so that 'the Mischiefs of Plundering might be prevented, and the necessary relief afforded, under the Power of the Act passed in the 26th of his late Majesty....' They argued that preventive means would be more effective than either penalising the hundreds or disciplining the wreckers. They were particularly concerned that the hundreds would be penalised 'although every possible Effort of the Magistracy has been exerted to prevent it'; thus they requested that the bill not be passed.[41]

The debate within the Commons is enlightening; it shows their concerns with national reputation, culpability of the hundreds, and the importance of trade, despite the backdrop of the War of American Independence. The deliberations were held over two days. Burke opened up the proceedings by arguing that there was 'scarcely a winter passing but our public prints contained accounts which were a disgrace to any civilized country' and that commercial countries such as Great Britain, 'which prided itself so much on national honour, should take care to do every thing possible in its power to discourage such outrageous proceedings'. Although the gentlemen agreed with his concerns, most felt that the hundreds should not be penalised for wrecking activity; it would cause 'much suffering among the innocents', and 'a few of the most profligate persons in a hundred were to profit by public rapine and plunder, and all the reputable industrious inhabitants, persons who abhorred the act as much as those really plundered, were to be made responsible for the loss'.[42]

The ruling elite recognised that not all country people consented to wrecking, and that local attitudes towards it were much more multifaceted than has been argued.[43] The opinions also indicate that not all MPs were members of a 'ruthless Hanoverian ruling class acting in its own interests against [those] who were resisting that class's assault on customary rights'.[44] Others, however, felt that the hundreds should be liable. Lord Mulgrave,

---

[41]  CJ, Vol. XXXV (1774–76), 738.

[42]  'Debate on Mr. Burke's Bill to prevent the Plundering of Shipwrecks', 27 March, 30 April 1776 in *Cobbett's Parliamentary History (1774–76)*, Vol. XVIII, 1298–1302.

[43]  See Rule, 'Wrecking and Coastal Plunder', 167–188; John G. Rule, 'Social Crime in the Rural South in the Eighteenth and Early Nineteenth Centuries', *Southern History*, 1 (1979), 135–153. The concept of wrecking as a social crime will be further discussed in Chapter 4.

[44]  Emsley, *Crime and Society*, 19, footnote 33, in discussion of E.P. Thompson's *Whigs and*

a member of the Admiralty Board and its primary representative in the Commons, was, in particular, adamant that he would be for any bill that would prevent 'such scandalous practice'. He argued that the 'vice' had become so 'flagrant', and that 'the only way to curb it is by punishments properly suited to the nature of the offence', thus

> every man who lived in the hundred where a ship was wrecked if the loss was made good by the hundred, would find an interest in protecting the wreck; for by doing so he would protect his own property; that this was the very reason why the hundred was compelled to make good robberies committed on the highway, in order to make them more ready to assist in apprehending the offenders; or more active in discovering them.

James Adair had a more eloquent way of putting it: that 'pecuniary temptations should be resisted by pecuniary punishments'.

Several gentlemen suggested that the bill was not needed; the responsibility for preventing wrecking already belonged to the forces of local control, to the magistrates and 'gentlemen of the neighbourhood'. Philip Rashleigh, the Cornish member from Fowey, claimed that 'such melancholy accidents, he was sorry to say, too frequently happened; yet he could affirm that the plundering of ships was generally prevented by the assiduity and exertions of the neighbouring gentlemen'. Likewise, Sir George Yonge, also from a maritime county, argued that 'the execution of the present laws depended on the magistrates; wherever any injury therefore was sustained, it was owing to their neglect'. Thus he could not support Burke's bill. He felt that passing new laws without ensuring their 'punctual execution, was doing nothing'. It is evident that most of the MPs present were reluctant to force penalties on the hundreds, despite their concern over the effect wrecking had on Great Britain's reputation. Burke recognised that his bill was lost. In his closing argument, he opined on the state of British law:

> that gentlemen affected great caution in the present case, though it was well known we had laws enacted on the most trivial occasions. We had some against pulling a stake out of a hedge; others against touching paling; others, still more extraordinary, against disturbing a thorn. All those, according to the language of this day, were, it seems, of more consequence in the estimation of some gentlemen, than the destroying, pillaging, or purloining the cargo of a vessel worth thousands of pounds.

Burke's closing remarks were harsh. Members were not necessarily against the condemning of wrecking as such; they were against culpability being laid at the door of the hundreds. Thus, the bill failed with a vote of 55 to 43.[45]

---

Hunters. See also Brewer, *Sinews of Power*, xix–xxi for a discussion of the attempts of proponents of limited government to curtail the growth of bureaucracy.

[45] 'Debate on Mr. Burke's Bill', *Cobbett's Parliamentary History*, 1302; CJ, Vol. XXXV (1774–76), 749.

The Burke wreck bill was controversial, time-consuming, and costly for the lobbyists. The petitions showed the existence interregional lobbying, having almost identical wording.[46] Indeed, while the debate was in progress, the petition of the 'Merchants, Traders, and principal Inhabitants of the Town and County of Poole' was presented to the House, with the exact same wording as the petition from the City of Bristol.[47] Despite the intensive debates and lobbying, however, the issue of local culpability was still too contentious, especially in coastal regions such as Carmarthen and Cornwall. Richard Gully, sheriff of Cornwall, wrote to the mayor of Fowey that he had heard of the bill at a public meeting in Bodmin. He warned that the bill 'would be most partial and oppressive to Maritime Counties and to the County of Cornwall in particular' and they feared 'a similar attempt'. The mayor of Fowey was asked to consult with his MP 'to oppose such an unjust Attempt', but also to assure him that the county of Cornwall was interested in cooperating with other parts of the country, as long as the laws were based on 'equal and just principles'.[48]

### Nineteenth-century Wreck Law

The problem of wrecking was not brought up in the Commons again until the beginning of the nineteenth century, despite an attempt by local Cornish magistrate John Knill to introduce a plan against wrecking in 1792 that made it only as far as the Home Office.[49] Legislation passed in the years between 1776 and 1817 was concerned more with fraud by merchants, accused of wrecking their ships for insurance claims, or with issues of jurisdiction between common law courts and the Admiralty in issues of salvage.[50] Little of this involved the plundering of wrecked vessels. In 1817, Whig MP Lord Brougham resurrected the old debate when he requested to bring in a bill revisiting the culpability of the hundreds, but this attempt, like the others, failed.[51] Unfortunately there is little extant from this bill, other than its announcement in *The Times*.

The following year, John Hearle Tremayne, a Cornish MP, made another attempt to reform the wreck statutes by bringing forth a modification of Knill's wreck bill from 1792.[52] This bill had a different genesis; it was not a product of merchant-lobbyists. Rather it developed out of the concerns of

---

46  Brewer, *Sinews of Power*, 233.
47  *CJ*, Vol. XXXV (1774–76), 749.
48  CA/B/42/26. Richard Gully, Sheriff of Cornwall, to the Mayor of Fowey, 5 March 1777.
49  J.J. Rogers, *John Knill, 1733–1811* (Helston, 1871), 20.
50  43 Geo. III c. 113 (1803); 48 Geo. III c. 130 (1808); 49 Geo. III c. 122 (1809).
51  *The Times*, 27 June 1817.
52  CA/B/46/49. Knill's Wreck Bill, 1792; CA/B42/66, Scheme for Preventing Plundering at Wrecks, 15 November 1792.

local magistrates, who wanted stronger authority and better organisation to prevent plundering during the shipwreck event. They suggested that a 'wreck police' be appointed by the magistrates, made up of a port agent, assistant agent, official salvors and a local lawyer who could act as a solicitor and notary. Placed into the hands of Lord Sidmouth, the Home Secretary, by Sir William Lemon and Tremayne in January 1818, it was passed on to Lord Liverpool. Sidmouth expressed reservations about the proposals, that they 'are very crude, & evidently inadmissible' but he admitted that 'the Subject is an important one'.[53]

Reworked, the bill reached the Commons on 5 June and was presented by Davies Gilbert, MP for Bodmin. Specifically, the bill sought to repeal the acts of 12 Anne, 26 Geo. II and 48 Geo. III, which dealt with preventing fraud by merchants and shipowners. To combat plundering, the bill highlighted the proposal put forth by Knill, and also suggested by the merchants of Carmarthen in 1776, whereby a permanent salvage and lifesaving corps would be made up of special constables from the parishes, controlled by the justices and local churchwardens. The bill gave additional powers to the local justices, to allow them to appoint agents and subagents to perform salvage duties. In addition, for the first time, the bill included a special oath to be given to the agents and special constables that they will 'faithfully and honestly ... execute the duties imposed ... for the more effectual preservation of Property in Cases of Wreck'.[54]

The 1818 bill also sought to regulate for the first time the behaviour of those who attended but did not participate in the shipwreck event, harkening back to a suggestion made by Borlase in 1753 and refined by Knill in 1792. The agents were to be given authority to disperse crowds; if the crowds did not leave the scene, they could be charged with misdemeanour. Offenders could be brought before any local JP, committed to gaol, and if convicted, could be sentenced to 'hard labour on the river *Thames* or other navigable river in *Great Britain*' or committed to the local gaol to serve a sentence of hard labour. For those found guilty of deliberate wrecking, including the use of false lights, the capital punishment clause was carried over from 26 Geo. II. However, the bill sought to downgrade the punishment for those found guilty of violent assault and plunder by removing capital punishment and replacing it with transportation. Hence this new bill reflected the changes in attitudes toward penal law. Nonetheless, the bill never had a chance to be read a second time. It was introduced on 5 June 1818 and the Prince Regent dissolved Parliament on the 10th, calling for new elections. Accordingly, the bill was defeated by postponement, and was never resurrected.[55]

---

53   BL, Liverpool Papers Add.38270, Sidmouth to Liverpool, 23 January 1818.
54   The bill is entitled 'for the more effectual Preservation of Property, in cases of Wreck....'
55   *CJ*, Vol. XXXVIII, 5 June 1818, 423.

The 1818 bill stood at a crossroads in the criminalisation of wrecking. It emphasised prevention rather than deterrence and punishment, although those aspects were still present. After that year, wreck legislation, as well as other constructs of criminal and penal law, took on a different form that reflected changes in the attitude of the ruling elite. Henceforward, the Commons were concerned with reform and consolidation. By the nineteenth century parliaments began to view criminal law from a national perspective, rather than from a reactive local perspective as they had in the eighteenth century.[56] Thus, the presence of the merchant was much less visible; that of the legislator more so. The influence of such reformers as Sir Robert Peel and Lord John Russell was seen first-hand. In 1826, Peel, who led the way towards consolidating criminal law, was behind the passing of 7 & 8 Geo. IV c. 30, which combined and amended the laws 'relative to malicious Injuries to Property'. While ostensibly dealing with various forms of criminal activity such as setting fire to churches, destroying silk and cotton goods and machinery, the statute also singled out the crimes of 'setting fire to or destroying a ship'; 'damaging a ship, otherwise than by Fire'; and 'Exhibiting false signals to a ship &c, destroying a shipwrecked Vessel or Cargo, &c'. The two former sections were concerned with the destruction of ships for insurance fraud; only the latter section dealt with wrecking offences by consolidating the laws against deliberate wrecking and plunder. However, despite parliamentary movement towards abolishing capital punishment, which had already been enacted on crimes such as shoplifting, theft, and the sending of threatening letters, wrecking and plunder continued on the books as capital felonies. They would have to await the administration of Lord John Russell before any modification towards lessening penalties would be forthcoming.

In 1837, Russell, then Home Secretary, pushed for more radical, far-reaching reforms in criminal and penal law – in particular the lessening of the number of capital offences on the books. Although not all capital offences were abolished, as was argued for by a strong abolitionist cause,[57] plundering of ships did receive parliamentary attention. Indeed, by the passage of 7 Will. & 1 Vic. c. 86, the statute to 'amend the Laws relating to Burning or Destroying Buildings and Ships', the death penalty for the plundering of vessels was finally repealed, twenty-nine years after it was originally suggested in the failed 1818 bill.[58] The crime, though still considered a felony, would thenceforward be punishable with transportation 'beyond the seas, for any term not exceeding *fifteen years*, nor less than *five years*'. If the court decided against transportation, the act allowed the offender to be imprisoned up to five years. Interest-

---

[56] Emsley, *Crime and Society*, 13.
[57] V.A.C. Gatrell, *The Hanging Tree: Execution and the English People, 1770–1868* (Oxford, 1994), 23.
[58] CJ, Vol. XCII (January–July 1837), 218, 245, 420, 514, 523, 549, 660, 663, 670.

ingly enough, despite the lack of evidence for the use of false lights, the revised statute continued and confirmed the offence as a capital felony.[59]

Although recognising the need to reform the punishment for wrecking offences, in 1843 William Palmer, barrister of the Inner Temple, took umbrage at the almost total mitigation of the penal law in his treatise on wreck law:

> For, whatever the disposition may be felt to spare the life of an offender who aims only at property without striking at life, many will question the propriety of making the *forcibly, unlawfully and maliciously impeding any person endeavouring to save his life from a vessel in distress or wrecked* only punishable with transportation or imprisonment. This seems carrying to an extreme limit the disputed rule that attempts to murder should not be punishable by death … For to wilfully omit to render every practicable assistance to the ship-wrecked is inhuman barbarity; to maliciously contribute to their destruction bears the stamp of the most atrocious murder …[60]

Palmer argued that if any person 'wilfully and maliciously' obstructed anyone who was attempting to save life from shipwreck, then the offender should be subject to nothing less than transportation or imprisonment for life. He was also a proponent of making the hundreds liable for any plunder and used as an example the attack and plunder of the *Jessie Logan* at Boscastle that year. He claimed that 'the law of France, making the *communes* responsible for the plunder of wrecks if effected by force or a mob, seems in this respect worthy of our imitation.'[61]

Palmer's suggestions were realised in 1846 when the first major bill for the consolidation of the laws of wreck and salvage was passed.[62] It was part of an effort in the mid-nineteenth century to overhaul and consolidate the legal code, especially that which concerned merchant shipping. Specifically, it offered another attempt to repeal the acts of 12 Anne and 26 Geo. II, in addition to other acts dealing with salvage. For the first time the position of Receiver-General of Droits of Admiralty was given jurisdiction to oversee the provisions of the act, underscoring the increasing bureaucratisation and governmental control involved with wreck law. From thenceforward, anyone finding wreck, including lords of the manor who held rights to wreck, were required to report their finds and deliver any wreck, or goods found flotsam, jetsam, lagan, or derelict, to the Receiver upon penalty of £100 and loss of claim to any salvage. As well, the Receiver was required to report to the lord of the manor any wreck found on the lord's lands. The Receiver and

---

[59] See Emsley, *Crime and Society*, 251.
[60] William Palmer, *The Law of Wreck, Considered with a View to its Amendment* (London, 1843), 48.
[61] Palmer, *Law of Wreck*, 53.
[62] 9 & 10 Vic. c. 99. CJ, Vol. CI (1846), 814, 858, 1069, 1090, 1124, 1200, 1202, 1261, 1276, 1303; See also John Jagoe, *The Wreck and Salvage Act, 9 & 10 Vict, c.99, with a Copious Analysis, Notes, Proceedings and Forms …* (London, 1846).

Customs officers could seize any goods that were not reported and delivered. The Receiver was also given the ultimate authority to give orders during the shipwreck event, and ultimate control over custody of wrecked goods.

Another area gaining the attention of the legislators in their attempt to combat wrecking was the control of marine stores. The penalties for neglecting the regulation were fines of £20 for the first offence, and £50 for each subsequent offence. The act also consolidated wrecking penalties, and maintained the punishment of transportation if the convicted cut away or defaced buoys. However, if the offender was convicted of stealing goods or ships' tackle, attacking or impeding persons attempting to save the ship, then the penalty was a fine of £50. If a justice were to 'proceed summarily with the case without any information to convict', however, and if the penalty was not paid, then the offender could be given a gaol sentence of less than six months. Hence, by the mid-nineteenth century, there was a continuing lessening of the penalties. For wreck plundering 'by riotous and tumultuous assemblage', the long move towards finding the hundreds liable was finally realised. Thenceforward, the hundred would have to pay full compensation to the owners of the ship and cargo. Plunderers apprehended would be convicted under 7 & 8 Geo. IV c. 31 – 'An Act for consolidating and amending the laws in England relative to remedies against the Hundred'. As well, noticeably absent in the new statute was the false light clause. It finally disappeared from the enumeration of wrecking offences.

The 1846 Wreck and Salvage Act formed the lead-up to the more powerful Merchant Shipping Act of 1854. As Inner Temple barrister George Morley Dowdeswell stated, 'we cannot but regard the Merchant Shipping Act with favour, as the most valuable attempt to arrange, condense, simplify, and amend the old enactments'. He further pointed out that 'if defects be found, which are in truth inevitable, great forbearance and indulgence should be extended to them, and we should receive this measure in a grateful spirit, remembering the chaos from which it has redeemed us'.[63] Probably the most important aspect of this act was the solidification of government regulation and control within the shipping sector.[64] Of particular note was the extension of the duties and overall importance of the Board of Trade, initially given by the Mercantile Marine Act of 1850.[65] Shipping regulations, including wreck law, had been

---

[63] George Morley Dowdeswell, *Merchant Shipping Acts, 1854 & 1855, with a Readable Abridgement of the Former Act, and an Explanation of the Law Relating to It* (London, 1856), 2.

[64] See Roger Prouty, *The Transformation of the Board of Trade, 1830–1855: A Study in Administrative Organization in the Heyday of Laissez-Faire* (London, 1957), 34; and David M. Williams, 'James Silk Buckingham: Sailor, Explorer and Maritime Reformer', in Stephen Fisher, ed., *Studies in British Privateering, Trading Enterprise and Seamen's Welfare, 1775–1900* (Exeter, 1987), 99–119.

[65] 13 & 14 Vic. c. 93.

spread out over nine departments prior to consolidation.[66] To create more efficiency, the Marine Department, within the Board of Trade, was given authority over areas as diverse as the examination of officers, shipping classification, and the institution of courts of inquiry regarding shipwrecks.

The Merchant Shipping Act also consolidated and amended the legal code with regard to wrecking. By repealing the act of 1846 that gave authority to the Receiver-General of the Droits of Admiralty, the new code handed that authority to the office of the Receiver of Wreck, appointed by the Board of Trade from HM Customs, the Coastguard, or Inland Revenue. Thus all matters with regard to wreck were ostensibly taken from the Admiralty and placed within the Board of Trade. The Receiver was given the same duties originally assigned to the Receiver-General; all wreck washed ashore was to be delivered to the Receiver, and if any of it was stolen, hidden away, or refused to be delivered, then the offender could be charged a penalty of £100 or less. The Receiver was also given authority to take any suspected wreck by force, if necessary, and also to use force to quell any plundering activity, 'with power to command all Her Majesty's subjects to assist him; and if any person is killed or hurt in resisting the receiver or any person thus acting under his orders, the receiver or such other person is indemnified.'[67] This section closed a crucial loophole in the legal code, whereby the authorities, in particular Customs officers, had been stifled in their attempts to stop plundering activity because of concerns over authority and fears of litigation if any wreckers were injured.[68] As far as wrecking offences, the Merchant Shipping Act confirmed previously enacted penalties; in this, there was no change. Those guilty of plundering wrecks, stealing any part of the ship or cargo, or interfering with lifesaving were subject to a penalty of not less than £50, along with 'any other Penalty or Punishment he may be subject to under this or any other Act or Law.'[69]

At first blush, it would appear that there was much anxiety about wrecking, especially when placed in the context of the eighteenth-century fears of riot and concern about property. Twenty-five pieces of legislation involving wreck were introduced to the House of Commons between 1708 and 1854, and nineteen of the bills became law. However, rather than indicating a generalised concern on the part of the dominant classes, most of the eighteenth-century legislation involved the special interests of merchant groups and their lobbyists. Indeed, as it has been argued, 'the most active proponents of government intervention became the powerful traders rather than the officials

---

[66] Prouty, *Transformation of the Board of Trade*, 5.
[67] Dowdeswell, *Merchant Shipping Acts*, 5; MSA, s. 444.
[68] See PP, *First Report from the Select Committee on Shipwrecks* (1843), testimony of Captain Samuel Sparshott, 10 August 1843, 219.
[69] MSA, s. 478.

themselves'.[70] Even so, they had difficulty in getting either new or reforming wreck legislation through the House of Commons, and overall, the merchants' attempts at legislation were lukewarm at best. Despite the costs involved in lobbying and presenting bills to Parliament, the small number of attempts pales to insignificance compared to the campaigns of other special interest groups who were concerned about the effect of government policy on their trades.[71]

The presentation of only eight bills in the eighteenth century, during an era that saw up to 200 bills passing in a parliamentary session that were for the most part local and specific, indicates that wrecking was not of major parliamentary importance. Rather governmental apprehension over smuggling was more intense because of its obvious drain on revenue.[72] Indeed, only four bills regarding wrecking were passed; only two included important changes in wreck law. It is likely that most of the bills were presented in consequence of a reaction to a perceived 'emergency'. As Sir Robert Peel observed in 1826 regarding eighteenth-century criminal law: 'If an offence were committed in some corner of the land, a law sprang up to prevent the repetition, not of the species of crime to which it belonged, but of the single and specific act of which there had been reason to complain.'[73]

The nineteenth-century legislative involvement, however, indicated differing priorities on the part of government. Of the seventeen bills introduced, only two could be considered directly concerned with wrecking; six contained clauses regarding the fraudulent burning of ships; three were Customs Acts; five were involved with consolidation; and one verified Admiralty jurisdiction. Indeed, eleven of the bills were heard in the last 33 of the 150 years under study, from 1821 to 1854, and are directly attributed to the reform and consolidation movements of Peel and Russell. Thus, legislators in the nineteenth century were more concerned with reforming criminal law, strengthening the grip of the government over Customs duties, and gaining control over shipping, and hence profits; wrecking clauses were embedded within other legislation.

Through the legislation passed at the beginning of the eighteenth century and extending through the mid-nineteenth century, the penalties for wrecking came full circle: from fines to capital punishment to transportation and back to fines. The dominant classes, in this case the merchants, attempted to control rights to shipwrecked goods, and prescribed punishment for any perceived deviance, which was not necessarily accepted by the country people. Wrecking

---

[70] Brewer, *Sinews of Power*, 248.

[71] Brewer, *Sinews of Power*, 233, 236–237. The most active campaign was that of the leather trades between 1697 to 1699, whereby over 150 petitions were launched from over 100 locations to force the repeal of leather duties (233).

[72] Edward Carson, *The Ancient and Rightful Customs: A History of the English Customs Service* (London, 1972), 12.

[73] Quoted in Emsley, *Crime and Society*, 251.

in itself was considered theft, of that there was no debate among the elite, but the definitions of criminality and punishment shifted. They determined which behaviours constituted criminality, behaviours for the most part which were violent, although the legislation and consolidation attempts show that they were not satisfied and the laws were never truly clarified. However, rather than simply being an instrument of class power, as has been asserted in much criminal law discourse,[74] the law continued to recognise rights of the finders through the principle of salvage. Hence, 'criminal law may more fruitfully be described as a multi-use right within which the various groups in eighteenth-century society conflicted with, cooperated with and gained concessions from each other'.[75]

The definitions of wrecking crimes were not only contested by the country people, but they were also sources of confusion to the local authorities who attempted to put them into action, notably Customs officials and magistrates.[76] As George Dowdeswell remarked,

> upon turning to the volumes of statutes during the late reigns ... a feeling of astonishment will be excited, that such a subject [merchant shipping legislation, and by association wreck law], should have been dealt with piecemeal by the vast number of Acts ... exhibiting no system, general principle, or harmony, and frequently confused, obscure, and inconsistent ... To the experienced lawyer ... no easy task ... but for the student, and more especially to the mercantile man ... the attainment of even a moderate knowledge was attended with such difficulty as to deter many from its pursuit.[77]

If for the 'mercantile man' simple understanding was almost impossible, little chance was left for country folk to comprehend or follow those same laws even if they wished to. Thus the country people made attempts to interpret and justify their own actions through reference to the law, just as they had during the medieval and early modern periods. Nevertheless, it is with this growth in legislation and the increasing governmental bureaucracy, along with the development of regulatory controls regarding salvage, that wrecking became transformed.

---

[74] See Hay, 'Property, Authority and the Criminal Law'. This issue has been at the centre of debates within crime history, centring on the topic of the 'Bloody Codes'. See also Thompson, *Whigs and Hunters*; John Langbein, 'Albion's Fatal Flaws', *Past and Present*, 98 (1983), 96–120; and King, *Crime, Justice and Discretion*.
[75] Peter King, 'Decision Makers and Decision-Making in the English Criminal Law, 1750–1800', *Historical Journal*, 27 (1984), 53.
[76] CUST 68/6, 27 April 1768.
[77] Dowdeswell, *Merchant Shipping Acts*, 1. See also Peter King, *Crime and the Law in England 1750–1840: Remaking Justice from the Margins* (Cambridge 2006), 16, 24–25.

# 4

# *The Cornish Wrecker*

*let's all start fair!*

IN 1907, Henry Shore, a retired Royal Navy commander who had served in Fowey with the Coastguard, published a collection of stories after he had interviewed the locals about smuggling. In Shore's fictional 'society', created, he said, to protect their identity, the men huddled together over their pints to reminisce about smuggling in the 'old days'. Wherever there are tales of smuggling, there are tales of wrecking, and thus the story is told:

> I mind when I was a bit of a nipper, mother used to teach us hymns of a Sunday afternoon. But the one I remember best was one old dad taught us, as we sat on his knee, 'Twas about a passon up Padstow way, time wrecking was allowed back-along. Well, one Sunday morning – leastaways that's what old dad used to say, a ship got on to the Gull Rock while the folk was at church, and old Ephraim Blowey – that was the sexton, having been bred to the sea, always kept his weather eye liftin' seawards, and twigged it in a moment, and shouts, 'Wreck!' and the congregation was on their feet in a jiffy. But the passon, being a conscientious man and werry [sic] strict about doing things right and proper, was all for fairplay –
>
> > Stop! Stop! cried he, at least one prayer,
> > Let me get down, and all start fair.
>
> I did hear that was one of Wesley's favourites.[1]

The 'parson story' has to be one of the most common tales found in the anthology of wrecking outside of the false-light narratives; it is ubiquitous in popular histories of Cornish shipwrecks. The earliest version thus far discovered is in James Silk Buckingham's autobiography, published in 1855, where he was told the story during a visit to St Mary's, Isles of Scilly. He was informed it was true, 'occurring less than fifty years ago'.[2] It is almost certain that the

---

[1]   Commander Henry N. Shore, RN, *Old Foye Days: An Authentic Account of the Exploits of the Smugglers in and Around the Port of Fowey* (London, 1907), 65.
[2]   James Silk Buckingham, *Autobiography of James Silk Buckingham*, Vol. I (London, 1855), 176. A similar account is told as far afield as Pembrokeshire. Dilys Gater, *Historic Shipwrecks*

genesis of the tale is of an earlier provenance, but it is unknown where it may have originated. It is narrated, like many tales, as a true story, unique to the location of the teller. However, it is in fact a migratory tale. Versions are found from Padstow and Germoe in Cornwall to the Isles of Scilly to Pembroke-shire in Wales, and undoubtedly in many other places besides.

The message contained within the parson stories, underscored by the humorous ways in which they are told, is that the religious and moral leaders acknowledged and took part in wrecking; it was an accepted communal pursuit. Likewise, John Rule, in his seminal articles on wrecking, argued that it was a 'social crime' – criminal activity communally accepted despite its illegality. His was the first academic study of the practice, and as such has been the sole source for wrecking discussion in other histories of crime. Therefore, his labelling of wrecking as a 'social crime' has been widely accepted and used as an illustration of communal solidarity in protecting perceived customary rights. But rather than analysing wrecking activity by recognising its differing forms, he opts to consolidate the practices, and defines wrecking simply as 'the illegal appropriation of cargo and materials of shipwrecked vessels'.[3] He admits that he did not distinguish between violent and non-violent practices.[4] However, the categorisation of such wrecking behaviours into their dominant forms is necessary to distinguish the levels of violence, to assess motivations, and to break down the stereotype of the wrecker. Indeed, as pointed out in Chapter 3, statutory wreck law of the eighteenth and nineteenth century recognised these distinctions.

The concept of wrecking as a 'social crime' can be used, albeit with caution. The definition of wrecking communities, and the subsequent view of the communal acceptance of wrecking, is oversimplified to fit within the social crime debate that occurred in the late 1970s and 1980s. Although the model acknowledges social class differentiation within rural society as including the 'better off', those populations are assigned to the margins, with the focus firmly on the poorer class.[5] The effect is to create a narrower, more mono-lithic society that not only condoned, but also openly supported wrecking, and which was motivated by poverty. Indeed, the definition of 'community' is limited only to those who *actively* engaged in wrecking, but does not include

*of Wales* (Llanrwst, Gwynedd, 1992), 14. An enquiry was sent into *Notes and Queries* in 1857 asking for further information; unfortunately no one responded (second series, 3, no. 74, 30 May 1857), 439.

3   John G. Rule, 'Wrecking and Coastal Plunder', in Douglas Hay, Peter Linebaugh, et. al., *Albion's Fatal Tree: Crime and Society in Eighteenth-Century England* (London, 1975), 169.

4   John G. Rule, 'Social Crime in the Rural South in the Eighteenth and Early Nineteenth Centuries', *Southern History*, 1 (1979), 138–139, 146. Reprinted in John Rule and Roger Wells, *Crime, Protest and Popular Politics in Southern England, 1740–1850* (London, 1997), 153–168 and discussed in John Rule, *Cornish Cases: Essays in Eighteenth and Nineteenth Century Social History* (Southampton, 2006).

5   Rule, 'Social Crime', 139.

any other members of the village or parish, nor those who were involved in wrecking on some occasions and in legitimate salvage activities on others.[6] It is only through this constraint that wrecking's inclusion as a social crime is sustainable, which brings into question the degree of communal acceptance, and the degree to which wrecking is a 'social crime'. Through this model, then, the stereotype of the communally accepted wrecker, who stands defiant against the dominating upper classes by defending his customary right, has been created and utilised within crime histories.[7] But by focusing on the 'lower orders' of the community, the interplay and involvement of the multiple layers of society is masked.

## Wrecker Identity

Who were the wreckers? Rather than consisting of only the 'lower orders', wreckers came from all levels of society, from the gentry to the 'middling sorts' to the lowest labourer; they were men, women, and children; and they were involved in differing forms of wrecking. Within Cornwall, the reputation for wrecking rests most squarely on the miners, or 'tinners' in the colloquial, who were described on numerous occasions as being especially involved in the attack and plunder of ships. Indeed, their involvement is undisputed.[8] The mining region of Breage and Germoe on Mount's Bay in particular had a ruthless reputation for wrecking, as evidenced by the couplet: 'God keep us from rocks and shelving sands; And save us from Breage and Germoe men's hands!'[9]

Because of contemporary emphasis on tinners, speculation has arisen that they were the main, and perhaps only, participants in wrecking. Even Rule contemplates whether the attitude of miners would differ from that of seamen toward shipwrecked sailors.[10] Certainly Commodore Walker would have agreed with this assessment in 1745, for he found that the inhabitants of the fishing village of St Ives were very accommodating when his ship *Boscawen* was wrecked:

> The people of the seacoast of Cornwall have for some years undergone the censure of being savage devourers of all wrecks, that strike against their coasts.

---

[6]  Rule, 'Social Crime', 141.

[7]  See John Briggs, Christopher Harrison, et. al., *Crime and Punishment in England: An Introductory History* (London, 1996, 1998), 91; Frank McLynn, *Crime and Punishment in Eighteenth-Century England* (London, 1989), 200.

[8]  See George Borlase to Lt Gen. Onslow, 5 March 1753, in Thomas Cornish, ed., 'The Lanisley Letters: to Lt. General Onslow from George Borlase, his agent at Penzance, 1750–53', *Journal of the Royal Institution of Cornwall*, 6, pt 22 (1880), 374; CUST 68/16, 22 November 1795.

[9]  The earliest use found is that in Arthur P. Salmon, *The Cornwall Coast* (London, 1910), 151.

[10]  Rule, 'Wrecking and Coastal Plunder', 183–184.

How weak a creature is general belief, the dupe of idle fame! Humanity never exercised its virtues more conspicuously than in this instance, in the inhabitants and people of St. Ives. They flocked down in numbers to our assistance, and at the risk of many of their own lives, saved ours.[11]

Although Walker was grateful to the St Ives inhabitants, he still feared that his ship would be plundered, 'and accordingly it happened, for in the night the miners came down, and were setting about sharing the wreck amongst them'. The miners, he wrote, 'are a people the civil power are scarcely answerable for, at least for their good manners, as they live almost out of the districts of human society'.[12] The people of the village of Gwithian, too, won accolades from the local press in 1817. They saved victims from the wreck of the brig *Mary* only to have their hard work laundering the wrecked seamen's clothes come to naught when neighbouring miners from Camborne entered town and stole the clothes while they were hanging out to dry.[13] Emphasis on the tinners' involvement came, however, not necessarily because of their famed sense of independence and propensity for collective action,[14] but rather from the sheer numbers of mines and miners that were located close to prime wreck areas such as Mount's Bay and the Penwith Peninsula.

Examples such as these lend countenance to the popular belief – sometimes stated as fact – that only miners, and not fishermen, were involved in wrecking.[15] Indeed, a lesson plan on wrecks and wreckers stated: 'It has been said that fishermen would rarely, if ever, take part in wrecking. Why do you think this was so?'[16] But placing tinners and fishermen into such binary oppositions is a false construct. Reality was much more fluid. Tinners were often part-time fishermen, as well as part-time farmers.[17] Fishermen, too, were involved in differing seasonal subsistence activities – and they were involved

---

[11] Commodore George Walker, *The Voyages and Cruises of Commodore Walker* (London, 1760, 1928), 90–91.

[12] Walker, *Voyages and Cruises*, 91.

[13] *West Briton*, 28 March 1817, cited in R.M. Barton, ed. *Life in Cornwall in the Early Nineteenth Century, Being Extracts from the West Briton Newspaper in the Quarter Century from 1810 to 1835* (Truro, 1970), 75.

[14] Philip Payton, *Cornwall: A History* (Fowey, 2004), 170; Rule, 'Wrecking and Coastal Plunder', 181.

[15] Cyrus Redding, *An Illustrated Itinerary of the County of Cornwall* (London, 1842), 186; Jonathan Couch, *The History of Polperro, a Fishing Town on the South-Coast of Cornwall* (first published 1871; Newcastle-upon-Tyne, 1965), 44.

[16] Lesson plan 'Treasure Island – Related Topics: Wrecks and Wreckers', www.stockportmbc. gov.uk/treasure_island/wrecks.htm repeated many of the unverified wrecker stories. Accessed 6 December 2001.

[17] In 1778, for instance, W. Pryce wrote of the miners that, 'Our county being altogether maritime, and the miners being situated in the most narrow of it ... many of our adroit tinners are equally conversant with naval and subterranean affairs. So true is this, that in St. Ives and Levant during the fishing season, they are wholly employed upon the water, to the great hindrance of the adjacent mines; and when the fishing craft is laid up against the next season, the fishermen again become tinners.' W. Pryce, in *Mineralogia Cornubiensis* (1778), 97, quoted

in wrecking. Evidence points to fishermen's complicity in both legal and illegal salvaging and in harvest activities. Fishermen often had the advantage of being first on the scene of a wreck by virtue of the availability of their boats. Most coastal wrecks occurred slightly offshore, and although fishermen often answered the call for lifesaving, many were known to 'help themselves' with goods from the ship.[18] Shipwrecked goods were also frequently found floating, and even entangled in nets. Although the goods were technically the property of either the owner of the ship and cargo, the insurance company, or if unclaimed, the Admiralty, fishermen kept them for their own use – a form of wrecking. Fishermen were also prime participants in smuggling, and occasionally their smuggling activities encompassed wrecking. There are cases in which Customs officers had difficulty determining under which crime to charge offenders. They preferred to take possession of goods under the charge of smuggling, simply because they would be given a reward more lucrative than if the goods were wreck, which would then be subject to salvage charges.[19]

Other populations involved in wrecking included the clergy, giving some credence to the parson stories. Clergy involved in wrecking included Rev. James Cumming of Lansallos in 1708 and Rev. Thomas Whitford of Cury in 1739.[20] Richard Polwhele, vicar of Newlyn and St Anthony, remarked in 1826 that when he arrived at the vicarage for the first time he discovered large amounts of wrecked wine in the cellar. In 1846, the *Royal Cornwall Gazette* alluded to the participation of clergy when it reported on the wreck of the *Samaritan* that 'it was lamentable that there should be found amongst these miserable wretches men who stand up in the pulpit and preach the word of God'.[21] Finally, Rev. Troutbeck of Scilly is credited, though it is not verified, with the prayer: 'We pray Thee, O Lord, not that wrecks should happen, but that if any wrecks should happen, Thou wilt guide them into the Scilly Isles for the benefit of the poor inhabitants.'[22] Like the parson story, the prayer has been identified with many Cornish districts. Thus, the participation of some clergy is well substantiated, although others stood aloof and attempted to preach to their parishioners on the evilness of wrecking in all its forms, such

in John G. Rule, 'The Labouring Miner in Cornwall, c. 1740–1870: A Study in Social History', (unpublished Ph.D. thesis, University of Warwick, 1971), 76.

[18] For example, CUST 68/15, May 1791; CUST 68/24, 10 April 1818.

[19] CUST 68/24. Customs Officers to Collector, 10 April 1818.

[20] East India Company [IOR] E/1/199, 100–101, Woolley to Bullock, 9 June 1711; James Derriman, 'The Wreck of the *Albemarle*', *Journal of the Royal Institution of Cornwall*, new series II, I, pt 2 (1992), 142; CUST 68/1. Penzance Collector to Board, 2 February 1739/40. Unless otherwise stated, all references to CUST 68 are Penzance Collector to Board.

[21] Richard Polwhele, *Traditions and Recollections: Domestic, Clerical and Literary*, Vol. II (London, 1826), 377.

[22] Cited in E.L. Bowley, *The Fortunate Isles: The Story of the Isles of Scilly* (St Mary's, 1945), 144.

as Rev. G.C. Smith of Penzance and Rev. Richard Lyne of Little Petherick.[23] Some were even involved in a more active role, such as Rev. John Trefusis, who, with the help of other local magistrates and their assistants, was able to save the cargo of the *Fanny* near Padstow in 1809.[24]

Analysis of other sources highlights additional populations who were involved in wrecking. John Bray, a former salvage agent, shipowner, and constable of Bude, identified individuals and occupations in his account of shipwrecks on the north coast. Spanning from 1759 to 1830, and describing some thirty-six shipwrecks, Bray's work named farmers, labourers, shoemakers, blacksmiths, smugglers, coopers, even an excise-man, as known wreckers. He also mentioned 'country people' in general, including 'scores of men, women and children' who surged down to the beach to harvest wrecked goods such as bell-metal, beeswax, and morocco leather, along with food stores.[25] Carpenters, butchers, and yeoman were described as carrying away goods from the wreck of the *Two Friends* in Whitsand Bay in 1749, and the *Gentleman's Magazine* reported that townsfolk who had been appointed as guards plundered a London brig near Looe.[26] From Bray's account, from accounts of the press, and descriptions from the clergy, we can see that women and children were involved as well as men. The *General Evening Post* of London reported in January 1751 that at a wreck of a brigantine near Looe, 'Even the children were proud to stagger under the Burden of a painted board.'[27] Rev. G.C. Smith described the people of Predannack, near Mullion, an area 'sadly infested with wreckers'. He was particularly concerned about the women and children who were seen working to break up vessels: 'the hardships they endure (especially the women) in winter to save all they can, are almost incredible.'[28]

Finally, the remaining population implicated in wrecking are the gentry and local lords of the manor. Although not included in the social crime model, the involvement of this population was central to many wrecking activities, as will be discussed in further chapters. Some commentators actually cast

[23] Most notable are the sermons published by Rev. G.C. Smith entitled *The Wreckers; Or, a Tour of Benevolence from St. Michael's Mount to the Lizard Point* (London, 1818), extracts of which were published in *The Times*, 22 September 1818, and Richard Lyne of Little Petherick's 'Exhortation against wrecking after the sermon in Little Petherick Church', P 185/2/3, 1 March 1818. Also published in Cornwall was a moral commentary written by Rev. James Walker, *A Dialogue between the Captain of a Merchant Ship and a Farmer Concerning the Pernicious Practice of Wrecking* ... (London, 1768).
[24] Richard Larn and Bridget Larn, *Shipwreck Index of the British Isles*, Vol. 1 (London, 1995), n.p.
[25] John Bray, *An Account of Wrecks, 1759–1830 – On the North Coast of Cornwall*. Edited and transcribed by A.K. Hamilton Jenkin (Cornwall, 1975). Original mss, British Library, Add.37826.
[26] CRO RS/1/1068; *Gentleman's Magazine*, 17 January 1751 (Vol. 31), 41.
[27] *General Evening Post*, January 1751, cited in John Vivian, *Tales of Cornish Wreckers* (Truro, 1969), 9.
[28] Smith, *The Wreckers*, 8–9.

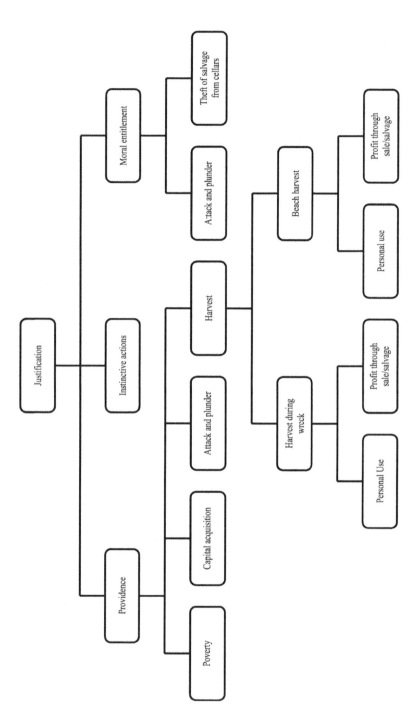

Figure 5. Focal Points of Justification and Resulting Actions.

blame on the gentry, accusing them of being unrepentant examples to their tenants and 'country folk'.[29] The Arundells, Bassets, and St Aubyns, together with a few other lesser gentry, all practised some forms of wrecking, as they controlled wreck rights along large portions of the Cornish coast.[30] Although their right of wreck was legal, the ways in which it was practised often were not. Rather lords of the manor frequently claimed goods for their own use, without either reporting the finding of the goods to Customs, or without waiting the requisite year and a day for the potential owner to claim them.[31] Just as in the case of the clergy, however, wrecking was practised by some lords of the manor and not by others. Some, indeed, were insistent on holding to the letter of the law.[32]

The evidence that wrecking was performed by all social classes, male and female, adult and child, could be taken as verification of communal solidarity, and used to support the 'social crime' thesis. However, this does not necessarily indicate that wrecking was performed by cultural and communal consensus. None of the populations discussed wholly approved of wrecking. The coastal population had differing views and degrees of acceptance on the forms of wrecking involved.

### Focal Points of Wrecker Justification

Justification and motivation for various wrecking practices are more multifarious than has been argued. They can be centred on three major focal points: that of 'providence', 'moral entitlement' and 'instinctive actions'. (Figure 5 sets out the key relationships in diagrammatic form.) Of course, not all wrecking was justifiable. Some activities included deviant behaviour brought on by alcohol and mindless rioting and looting. There were also those who practised petty theft; shipwrecks gave them additional opportunities.[33]

### Providence

Most wrecking discourse includes some discussion of the customary belief in 'providence', in that God 'constantly intervened in human affairs'. This provi-

---

[29] See Redding, *An Illustrated Itinerary*, 187–188.
[30] The Duchy of Cornwall ostensibly controlled most of the Cornish coast, but their involvement in protecting wreck rights was negligible from the medieval period until the mid-nineteenth century. See Chapter 7 for further discussion of the role of the lords of the manor.
[31] See CUST 68/5, 29 October 1763.
[32] See W/43, Willyams to Bowles, 23 November 1826; Bowles to Willyams, 12 December 1826; Willyams to T.R. Avery, 6 December 1826.
[33] Peter King, *Crime and Law in England 1750–1840: Remaking Justice from the Margins* (Cambridge, 2006), esp. Chapter 8.

dential system of thought was deeply embedded within the cultural and religious psyche of the nation; it was 'an ingrained parochial response to chaos
and crisis, a practical source of consolation in a hazardous and inhospitable
environment, and an idea which exercised practical, emotional, and imagi-
native influence'.[34] Thus it was behind the well-documented popular belief
that whatever washes ashore belongs to the finder as a divine gift.[35] Indeed,
the argument that wrecking was a social crime is based upon the communal
acceptance of this principle.[36] Deliberate wrecking by cutting a ship's cables
was justified perhaps by a more perverse sense of providence, however, than
was normally suggested by custom.[37] Allied with providence was the motive
of poverty, used mainly to justify harvest activities, although it was occasionally applied to behaviour that was more violent.

It is difficult to correlate wrecking events with general economic down-
turns and the increase of poverty, but a few patterns are evident. The most
active periods for reported plundering cases were the late 1740s, the 1790s,
and the 1840s. In 1748, the *Jonge Alcida* was plundered near Porthleven; in
1749, the *Squirrel* was attacked and burnt in Mount's Bay, and the cargo of
the *Rose in June* was destroyed 'by the Mobb, who came in such Numb' twas
impossible to resist'. In 1749, *Two Friends* was demolished at Whitsand Bay
near Plymouth, and the *Endeavour* was barely saved by the militia at the same
location in 1750.[38] During those two years, harvests failed both at sea and on
land. Grain prices were high, and the prices of copper and tin fell, so much
so that tin could hardly be sold.[39] Thus it was a particularly difficult time for
those on the margins.

The 1790s, as well, appear to have seen an upsurge in wrecking, or at least
in reported attempts of wrecking. Three months before the infamous Corn
Riots in 1794, the *Fly* was plundered at Mount's Bay.[40] The following year, the
Customs collector reported that the brig *John* was plundered at Poljew Cove
and the militia killed two of the wreckers.[41] The tinners were the most vocal
part of the population during this period, and have achieved much notoriety
for their activities in pursuing what E.P. Thompson describes as the 'moral

[34] Alexandra Walsham, *Providence in Early Modern England* (Oxford, 1999, 2003), 2–3.
[35] For example: PP, *First Report from the Select Committee on Shipwrecks*, 10 August 1843, Testimony of Capt. Samuel Sparshott, RN, 225, Testimony of Capt. David Peat, RN, 249.
[36] Rule, 'Wrecking and Coastal Plunder', 174, 182.
[37] There are only four recorded cases in Cornwall where ships' cables were cut.
[38] CUST 68/2, 2 February 1749; CUST 68/2, 20 December 1749; CUST 68/2, 20 September
1749; CRO RS/1/1068, 1069. Account of loss of *Two Friends* at Whitsand Bay, 1749; *Western
Flying Post*, 19 March 1750.
[39] John Rowe, *Cornwall in the Age of the Industrial Revolution* (Liverpool, 1953), 43.
[40] CUST 68/16, 9 February 1794.
[41] CUST 68/16, 14 December 1795.

economy of the crowd'.[42] Their situation was fairly grim in the 1790s; it was exacerbated by grain prices and the falling price of tin. Thus, by November 1795, Christopher Wallis, a Helston solicitor, wrote that 'the mines in general are very poor', and that 'the necessities of life' are 'such an enormous price'.[43] So when a rich prize washed upon their shores, it was no wonder that the miners felt compelled to act. The *John* was laden with a valuable cargo of linen and woollen drapery, a large quantity of cutlery, silver and plated ware, iron in bars, port, and puncheons of rum, ham, and cheese.[44] For people who were suffering from poverty, this indeed, could be seen as 'providence'.

The plunder of the wrecks of the *Jessie Logan* in 1843 off Boscastle, and in 1846 of the *Eliza* near Bude and the *Samaritan* near Bedruthan Steps came at a particularly difficult time economically for Cornwall. It was the height of the 'Hungry Forties', and Cornwall, like Ireland, suffered through the failure of the potato crop, especially during 1845–47.[45] Two famous forms of a rhyme indicate the conditions:

> The *Eliza* of Liverpool came on shore,
> To feed the hungry and clothe the poor.[46]

> The *Good Samaritan* came ashore,
> To feed the hungry and clothe the poor.
> With barrels of beef and bales of linen,
> No poor soul shall want for a shilling.[47]

Poor economic conditions were clearly a factor in the sporadic outbreaks of plundering, although all wrecking activity cannot be attributed to poverty.

## Wrecking and Cultural Capital

Shipwreck was also seen as 'providence' not only for bringing goods to those in need, but for bringing goods which were too costly or considered too culturally valuable for the country people to acquire. The eighteenth century was a period when social status was conveyed by conspicuous consumption, allied to the widespread trade in luxury items that came at a time when the elite were adopting the ideals of civility.[48] Beginning in the late sixteenth century, sumptuary legislation was introduced to limit to the elites the availability of

---

42 E.P. Thompson, Chapter 4: 'The Moral Economy of the English Crowd in the Eighteenth Century', and Chapter 5: 'The Moral Economy Reviewed', in *Customs in Common: Studies in Traditional Popular Culture* (New York, 1993), 184–258, 259–351.
43 DJW/1/3. Christopher Wallis Journal, 7 November 1795.
44 CUST 68/16, 5 December 1795.
45 Payton, *Cornwall*, 214.
46 Vivian, *Tales of Cornish Wreckers*, 3.
47 A.K. Hamilton Jenkin, *Cornwall and its People* (Truro, 1932; reprinted Newton Abbot, 1970), 66.
48 Maxine Berg and Elizabeth Eger, 'The Rise and Fall of the Luxury Debates', in *Luxury in the Eighteenth Century: Debates, Desires and Delectable Goods* (Basingstoke, 2003), 7. Luxury,

commodities that were deemed luxuries. In turn, the legislation as practised 'became centred on protectionist regulation, import and export regulations and quality controls'.[49] The commodities included colonial-produced items such as sugar, tea, and tobacco. As well, as part of the protectionist policy any goods arriving in foreign ships had higher duties placed on them, and thus were even more expensive.[50] The cost of goods could be prohibitive, especially with the increasing customs and excise duties. Labouring-class budgets often had little leeway for any expenditure beyond rent and food; when common people did attempt to consume luxuries purchased legally, such as tea and sugar, it easily could put them in debt.[51] This was the case, for example, for an Oxfordshire labourer whose yearly budget exceeded his income by £5; tea and sugar accounted for £2 10s, only one pound less than his house rent for the year.[52] Thus these goods were not only considered economic capital, but they were cultural capital as well.[53] Wrecking, along with smuggling, therefore, was a means not only of acquiring economic and cultural capital, but also of avoiding the heavy direct and indirect taxation. Elizabeth Bonham, in her collection of Cornish tales, described several wrecks that washed ashore during the Napoleonic Wars: 'the "tea wreck"', she claims, 'was a wonderful piece of good fortune', for 'very few of them ever indulg[ed] in that expensive beverage'. Likewise, the 'coffee wreck', afforded the inhabitants a taste of 'the delicious stimulant for the first time'.[54]

By the mid to late eighteenth century, these luxury items had become increasingly available to the middling and lower classes, despite much contemporary debate as to their moral and economic effects, and this lessened their value as cultural capital.[55] It is debated how much the poor were able to partake in the greater market, especially in Cornwall, but tea and coffee in particular became everyday commodities. Additionally, growth in consum-

---

however, as Berg and Eger point out, is a concept full of debated meanings and values that held the attention of eighteenth-century writers.

49   Alan Hunt, *Governance of the Consuming Passions: A History of Sumptuary Law* (New York, 1996), 371; M.J. Daunton, *Progress and Poverty: An Economic and Social History of Britain, 1700–1850* (Oxford, 1995), 523.

50   Sarah Palmer, *Politics, Shipping and the Repeal of the Navigation Acts* (Manchester, 1990), 43.

51   Richard Price, *British Society, 1680–1880: Dynamism, Containment and Change* (Cambridge, 1999), 34.

52   Roy Porter, *English Society in the Eighteenth Century* (London, 1982, 1990), 92.

53   Cultural capital is a concept coined by Pierre Bourdieu to express a non-economic meaning 'to all the goods, material and symbolic, without distinction, that present themselves as *rare* and worthy of being sought after in a particular social formation.' *Outline of a Theory of Practice* (Cambridge, 1977), 178.

54   Mrs Elizabeth Bonham, *A Corner of Old Cornwall*, introduced by E.J. Oldmeadow (London, 1896), 170.

55   Maxine Berg, *Luxury and Pleasure in Eighteenth-Century Britain* (Oxford, 2005), 32. See also Neil McKendrick, John Brewer and J.H. Plumb, *The Birth of Consumer Society: The Commercialization of Eighteenth-Century England* (London, 1982).

erism meant an unprecedented increase in manufacturing and shipping to international markets, shipping which sometimes ran afoul of the dangerous coastline and fell into the hands of wreckers.

## Wrecking and Economic Capital

Wrecking certainly brought consumable goods to the coastal populace, but it also occasionally afforded an additional means to make a small profit. Cornwall did not have as organised a system for the sale of smuggled and wrecked goods as did Sussex, Kent, and Cheshire, simply because Cornwall was too far away from the major population centres.[56] However, there is evidence that shipwrecked goods entered the economy, although how their sale affected the economy cannot be discerned. Frank McLynn states in his study of eighteenth-century crime that 'It is no exaggeration to say that the entire economy was fuelled by wrecking', but there is no evidence for this assertion.[57] It can be argued, however, that *shipwrecks* were important to the economy if taken as a whole, to include salvage, repair, and the sale of shipwrecked goods through auction.

Unfortunately, there is not enough extant evidence describing the illegitimate sale of wrecked goods or their markets to reconstruct the complex networking which must have underpinned wrecking. Only small clues are available. The *Sherborne Mercury* reported in 1758 that a quantity of silk and cochineal from the wreck of the *Gracia Divina* in the Scillies was offered for sale in Penzance.[58] Helston solicitor Christopher Wallis wrote in his diary in 1796 that 'the staves from the Hercules, Cap[n] Wood, wrecked at Gunwalloe were this day sold by people calling themselves salvors at Helston for about ~£8pm, they were sold in great quantities and delivered openly in the street at Helston'.[59] Likewise, in 1819, also at Helston, John Burnell, the supervisor of Excise, reported that he had been '[i]nformed, very Credibly, that large Quantities [of nuts from the *Montreal Packet*] were carried through Helston in open Day & quite exposed nearly all Day on the 19th [December] without any Notice being taken thereof by any of the Officers'.[60] The nuts were most likely offered for sale.

---

[56] See the case of the wreck of the *North* on the Goodwin Sands, and the extent of disbursement of her cargo in 'Wrecking at Deal', *The Times*, 19, 20, 22, 23, 25, 29, 31 October, 6 November 1866; Association for the Protection of Commercial Interests as respects Wrecked and Damaged Property, *Report on the Subject of Wreck and Salvage on the Coast of Kent* (London, 1867); and PP, *First Report of the Constabulary Force Commissioners* (1839), vol. XIX, which describes extensive wreck distribution between Cheshire and Liverpool (56).

[57] McLynn, *Crime and Punishment*, 200.

[58] *Sherborne Mercury*, 11 December 1758, cited in Larn and Larn, *Shipwreck Index*, Vol. 1, n.p.

[59] DJW/1/4, Christopher Wallis Journal, 2 January 1796; Rule, 'Wrecking and Coastal Plunder', 173.

[60] CUST 68/26, John Burnell, Supervisor of Excise, Penzance, to Lords of the Treasury, 27 December 1819.

Likewise, clothing, such as that stolen by the tinners from the wrecked seamen of the *Mary* in 1817, may have entered a second-hand clothes market.[61] Clothing was one of the most commonly stolen items in eighteenth-century England, in both urban and rural locations.[62] It was not uncommon for individuals to be stripped and robbed, or for laundry to be pilfered, especially as it was hanging out to dry.[63] The theft of clothes from shipwrecks and shipwreck victims can be seen as part of a more widespread criminal activity, based not only on poverty and the lack of cheap new garments, but on a desire for more luxurious fashion. Indeed, 'second-hand clothing, legally or illegally acquired, was assured of sale and had a guaranteed value'.[64]

Marine store dealers profited through the sale of wrecked goods. In 1848, Michael M'Allister and Michael Flagherty, marine dealers from St Just, were indicted for stealing copper sheathing, yellow metal, bolts and stores from the wreck of the *L'Adele* at Land's End.[65] Although this is the only evidence found from within Cornwall, it is assuredly not the only time that wrecked goods came into the hands of marine dealers. Indeed, two years previously, the act of 9 & 10 Vic. c. 99 had been passed, with clauses regulating the sale of marine stores in an effort to combat wrecking. As well, the 1867 wreck of the *North* at the Goodwin Sands showed the extent of activity of dealers in Kent.[66]

Evidence for the sale of goods also comes from the experiences of purchasers who had their merchandise apprehended by Customs, not seized as *wrecked* goods, but seized as potentially smuggled contraband. Such was the experience of Jane Hewitt of Penzance in 1807 when she purchased a small amount of sugar at Scilly that had been given to some islanders as salvage payment in kind.[67] Likewise, in 1812, Scillonians salvaged a cargo of tallow, were paid in kind, but had their tallow seized by Customs as being smuggled when they attempted to trade it for bread.[68] Goods were also sold to itinerant traders, as evidenced by a seizure of oranges and a cart made by Customs officers in 1824. Thomas Palmer, who was 'a Stranger in the Neighbourhood', claimed that he had sold out of cheese, and took the opportunity to buy oranges 'in small quantities from Individuals' who had picked them up from an unidenti-

---

[61] *West Briton*, 27 March 1817.
[62] J.M. Beattie, *Crime and the Courts in England, 1660–1800* (Oxford, 1986), 187.
[63] Beverly Lemire, 'The Theft of Clothes and Popular Consumerism in Early Modern England', *Journal of Social History*, 24, no. 2 (1990), 260, n. 47, 274.
[64] Lemire, 'The Theft of Clothes', 265.
[65] *West Briton*, 30 June 1848. Cited in Larn and Larn, *Shipwreck Index*, Vol. 1, n.p.
[66] 'Wrecking at Kent', in *The Times: Report on the Subject of Wreck and Salvage*.
[67] CUST 68/39, Petition of Jane Hewitt to Commissioners of Customs, 19 September 1807; Penzance Collector to Board, 19 September 1807.
[68] CUST 68/51, Charles B. Selby, Minister of St Agnes and St Martin's, to Commissioners of Customs, London, 18 November 1812; John Julyan, Land-waiter, Penzance, to Board, 27 November 1812; Charles B. Selby to Penzance Collector, 12 January 1813; Penzance Board to Collector, 15 April 1813.

fied wreck. They were seized as contraband.[69] It is likely that some wreckers also found customers for excess spirits in the same market as for smuggling items,[70] but wrecked goods were not nearly so available to sell since they were acquired opportunistically.

## Harvest

Although much wrecking activity undeniably occurred at times of dearth, and wrecked goods offered people a reprieve from hunger and want, whole ship-wrecks were rare, and wrecks containing valuable items, such as those carried by East India vessels, were rarer still. Rather, most wrecking activity involved simple beach harvest. Descriptions of wreckers as harvesters occur frequently within the local histories written by clergymen, which give some indication as to the activity's communal acceptance. Rev. Robert Hawker, the famous vicar of Morwenstow on the north Cornish coast, described the wreckers of his parish as 'a watcher of the sea and rocks for flotsam and jetsam, and other unconsidered trifles which the waves might turn up to reward the zeal and vigilance of a patient man', those 'daring gleaners of the harvest of the sea'.[71] Rev. Harvey of Mullion apologised for his flock of wreckers by admitting that 'while the dwellers of our coasts would not scruple to appropriate portions of wrecked timber and the like, no kind of dishonesty is felt or intended'.[72]

That harvesting was accepted, or at least occasionally overlooked, is also substantiated through Customs records. Indeed, it is through the activity of harvest that a shifting power dynamic is found, whereby accommodation of Customs to the coastal populace is most evident. Although Customs were continually apprehensive about possible plunder and violence, they were more concerned about smuggling and their own salvage operations; relatively benign harvest activities were disregarded. Indeed, wrecking-as-harvest was a form of 'tolerated illegality', which became 'so deeply rooted and so necessary to the life of each social stratum, that it had in a sense its own coherence and economy'.[73] Thus, although the country people had no legal rights over wrecked goods, 'they benefited, within the margins of what was imposed on them by law and custom, from a space of tolerance, gained by force or obstinacy'.[74] As the Penzance collector explained to the Customs board in 1817, salving the

---

[69] CUST 68/29, 26 November 1824.
[70] The major market for smuggled spirits in Cornwall was with the mining population. See Mary Waugh, *Smuggling in Devon and Cornwall, 1700–1850* (Newbury, Berkshire, 1991, 2003), 8, 13.
[71] Rev. Robert S. Hawker, *Footprints of Former Men in Far Cornwall* (London, 1903), 186, 129. See also descriptions by Rev. E.G. Harvey, *Mullyon: Its History, Scenery and Antiquities* (Truro, 1875), 51; Rev. John Shearme, *Lively Recollections* (London, 1917), 7.
[72] Harvey, *Mullyon*, 52.
[73] Michel Foucault, *Discipline and Punish: The Birth of the Prison* (London, 1977), 82–83.
[74] Foucault, *Discipline and Punish*, 82.

cargo of the *Resolution* was 'a Measure, in our judgment, more beneficial to the Revenue & the Parties interested than the pursuit & attempt to apprehend the petty Depredators....'.[75] Likewise, Customs were not concerned about the harvest that occurred after the wreck of the *Montreal Packet* in 1820, when the cargo of nuts was spewed over miles of beach. The riding officer from Breage admitted that 'it is natural to suppose that small quantities must be taken away by the Country People, which could not possibly be prevented'.[76] Indeed, in the cases reported within Customs correspondence, wreckers were not even apprehended.[77] Likewise, Elizabeth Bonham explained that 'the custom-house officers and the preventive men arrived on the scene in due course, but as a rule they were not overstrict, and very often the pilfering went on almost under their noses'.[78]

Another aspect of harvest activity that shows its communal acceptance is found through popular wrecking conventions. Although most evidence has been lost, some references deserve attention. Wreckers often made sure that they divided their proceeds amongst themselves. Thus in 1812, Samuel Gilbert helped himself to eight barrels of butter that washed ashore on the manor of Lanherne. Although he 'appropriated a part of it for his own use', he 'distributed the other to the People who assisted him in taking it up'.[79] When four Sithney fishermen and a labourer came across a box which washed on the beach at Loe Bar in March 1817, they swore in an affidavit that they had divided the contents into shares. The labourer William Williams received 'seven silver coins or dollars, one double Louis, a coat, a great coat, a black silk waistcoat, a pair of pantaloons, a pair of mixed silk stockings, and a belt or girdle'. Unfortunately, the affidavit does not list the other shares.[80]

One other known convention, still practised in the twenty-first century, is that of laying claim to wrecked goods by moving them above the waterline, a custom Cornish playwright Nick Darke described in his 'wrecking' activities, especially when he collected wood from the shore. He stated that other local inhabitants immediately recognised his claim, and left it alone until he could collect it.[81] In the eighteenth and nineteenth centuries, this practice was

---

[75] CUST 68/23, 20 May 1817.
[76] CUST 68/26, Stephen Bate, riding officer, Breage, and John Bennet, riding officer, Mullion, to Penzance Collector and Comptroller, n.d. January 1820.
[77] William Davey, the only wrecker to be arrested for plundering the *Resolution*, was released for lack of evidence. See CUST 68/23, 20 May 1817. Thomas Hitchen was prosecuted by Customs for the plunder of the *Marie Jean* and attack on a Customs Officer in 1776, although the results of his trial are no longer extant. See CUST 68/48.
[78] Bonham, *A Corner of Old Cornwall*, 169. This assessment is also supported by the lack of harvest reports in the Customs records. See Figure 6 in the next chapter.
[79] CUST 69/1, Agnes Wright, Lanherne, to John Buller, Custom House London, n.d. February 1813.
[80] RP/244, Case Papers: taking of items washed up on Loe Bar from Wrecked Vessel, 1817.
[81] Nick Darke, in *The Wrecking Season*, filmed and produced by Nick Darke, 2005.

more complex because of procedures involved with legitimate salvage operations, including the auctioning of goods to raise funds to pay salvage and duty. Nevertheless, Sabine Baring-Gould, in his *Book of Cornwall*, describes the process:

> The usual course at present is for those who are early on the beach, and have not time to secure – or fear the risk of securing – something they covet, to heave the article up the cliff and lodge these where not easily accessible. If it be observed – when the auction takes place – it is knocked down for a trifle, and the man who put it where it is discerned obtains it by lawful claim. If it be not observed, then he fetches it at his convenience.[82]

The evidence supporting the justification of providence and poverty is thus well substantiated, and indicates a certain level of acceptance of harvesting and hence supports its categorisation as a social crime. Indeed, even an analysis of the terms used to describe the activity supports the assertion. Those who recognised the legitimacy of harvest utilised the verb to 'appropriate', while those who denied its legality – the ruling elite and the press – used the verb to 'plunder'.

## Moral Entitlement

The second major focal point of wrecker justification is 'moral entitlement', a concept that has hitherto been overlooked.[83] Moral entitlement takes customary wrecking to an additional level, by incorporating the defence of customary salvage practices, which is dismissed in the social crime model because salvage is not an illegal activity. However, wreckers felt motivated to rectify perceived wrongs occurring after salvage operations, and thus enacted a form of social protest by undertaking wrecking activity. Although Rule admits that 'customary notions about entitlement to salvage sometimes blur the edges of definition of wrecking', he argues that 'the basic distinction between salvors and wreckers is, however, a clear-cut one'. The division is based on what are deemed different motivations: 'salvors rescued wrecked or stranded property in order to receive a share from the legitimate owners or insurers: wreckers appropriated property for their own use'. His argument is furthered by suggesting that salvors, when they became involved in clashes with the law, were claiming, not their customary 'right of wreck, but right of salvage'.[84]

Although motives may have occasionally been distinct on the part of salvors, outcomes were not nearly so straightforward, and analysing the activities separately ensures a false dichotomy. Salvors and wreckers were not neces-

---

[82]  Sabine Baring-Gould, *A Book of Cornwall* (London, 1899, 1981), 267.
[83]  'Moral entitlement' is closely allied to E.P. Thompson's 'moral economy', but 'entitlement' is more descriptive for this particular belief.
[84]  Rule, 'Wrecking and Coastal Plunder', 172–173.

sarily even separate individuals, as witnessed by several men who had salved brandy near St Michael's Mount in 1756. They handed over 'a peice of fforeign Brandy Brackish [sic]' for salvage, and they received 7 guineas payment, a substantial amount. But what they failed to inform the bailiff was that they had found two other 'peices' of brandy, which were not brackish, and carried them to the pier on the Mount, where they secreted them away for their own use.[85]

Of use in understanding the concept of moral entitlement is Antonio Gramsci's notion of 'popular morality', which is 'understood as a certain whole (in space and time) of maxims of practical conduct and customs … There exist imperatives which are much stronger, more tenacious and more effectual than those of official morality.'[86] The concept of salvage fits within this model of popular morality, and it may have originated with the 'concept of reward for due labour [which] lay at the heart of much folk activity', a notion which has at its source traditional society's 'emphasis on reciprocal dues and responsibilities.'[87]

The justification of moral entitlement thus developed when the custom of reciprocity broke down, when customary salvage practices were threatened by increasing governmental control in the late eighteenth and early nineteenth centuries. Traditionally, local magistrates and lords of the manor, who paid salvors either half the goods or half the value of the goods, controlled salvage activities; payment was often immediate.[88] Indeed, salvors often took it upon themselves to divide their finds on the spot between themselves and the lords of the manor, such as with mahogany from the wreck of the *William and Ann* in 1743.[89] Wrecking and salvage had a close relationship, and cannot be disassociated from each other. Salvors argued that their customs were legitimate, but owners of cargoes and the authorities often perceived their actions as illegal wrecking.

Analysis of salvage reports filed by Customs shows the numbers of those who were considered legitimate salvors. The salvage charges for the French brig *Le Harmeçon* in 1817 listed 153 individuals, all of whom were involved in salvaging the vessel for three days and two nights.[90] 124 people were involved

[85] AR/15/68, Connerton: Copies of Court Presentments, mostly concerning wrecks in Penwith, 1695–1759.

[86] Quoted from Alastair Davidson, *Antonio Gramsci: the Man, his Ideas* (Australia, 1968), 86, in Bob Bushaway, *By Rite: Custom, Ceremony and Community in England, 1700–1880* (London, 1982), 12.

[87] Robert W. Bushaway, 'Ceremony, Custom and Ritual: Some Observations on Social Conflict in the Rural Community, 1750–1850', in Walter Minchinton, ed., *Reactions to Social and Economic Change, 1750–1939* (Exeter, 1979), 26, 22.

[88] On the Isles of Scilly, the moiety was customarily divided into thirds: one-third for the salvors, one-third for the Duchy of Cornwall, and one-third for the leasor of the Islands.

[89] AR/15/96, Legal Opinion by John Belfield concerning wreck found, c. 1743.

[90] CUST 68/23, 24 February 1817.

in salving nuts from the *Montreal Packet* in 1820, and 60 persons were involved in salving the *Neptunus* in 1833, labouring under 'almost perpendicular' cliffs and risky conditions, only to find that the crew were all drowned, and the cargo of salt was barely worth preserving.[91] Although salvage payments were dependent upon goods salvaged, quality, quantity, and the value assessment of either Customs, the owners of the goods or, if contested, the local magistrates, some figures are suggestive. In 1780, 30 shillings were paid for the salvage of each hogshead of wine from the Dutch ship *Lands Welvaaren*, while in 1782, £3 8s were paid out per pipe of wine salvaged from the *Tortington*, and in 1817, 153 individuals were paid a total of £683 14s 3d for three days and two nights of salvage work on the wreck of *L'Harmeçon*.[92] Thus salvaging, whether by the customary half the value or half the goods in kind, or by legally figured rates, was lucrative. A common day labourer at the port of Penzance in 1813 in the middle of the period, for instance, could only expect to earn 2s 6d per day.[93]

That salvors were concerned to protect their customary rights and to demand immediate payment is well established, and many cases of conflict between Customs and the local populace have been played out. In 1740, salvors from the Scillies refused to hand over what they perceived were their moiety of wrecked goods to Customs, and thus led the revenue cutter on a merry chase through the islands.[94] There are many instances that show the failure of the Government to pay salvage, or where salvage payments were deferred for a long time, thus denying the salvors their due. In 1763, salvage charges were finally submitted to the Commissioners of Customs for the salvage of an Algerian xebec wrecked off the Lizard two years previously.[95] An even longer delay was experienced by fishermen from the Isles of Scilly in 1793; they were still waiting for payment three years later.[96] Actions such as these would hardly be incentive for people to salvage goods, and indeed show why salvors transgressed the law to protect their interests. As Thomas Davies, a Customs officer from Porthleven, complained when he attempted to seize wrecked brandy in 1768:

> myself & the other Officers under my Direction attempted to have it put into a Warehouse, & the King's Lock put thereon, but the people that have saved it w[d] not submit to it insisting y[t] we as Officers of the Revenue had nothing to do with Goods under the above Circumstances, & w[d] not permit us to lock it

---

[91] CUST 68/26, Tobias Roberts, Salvage Account of *Montreal Packet*, 1 January 1820; CUST 68/32, Richard Pearce, Salvage Account of sloop *Neptunus*, 11 December 1833.

[92] CUST 68/11; 68/12.

[93] CUST 68/21, 5 March 1813.

[94] CUST 68/1, Copy of an affidavit for the King's Bench, sworn at St Mary's, 24 April 1740.

[95] CUST 68/5, 17 January 1763. Likewise, the owners of the cargo were also anxious to see satisfaction. TNA T 1/426/19–93: Secretary of State's Office, 3 December 1763.

[96] CUST 68/16, Petition of William Hickens of Scilly to the Custom's Commissioners, 27 May 1793. This particular delay was caused by a disagreement between Customs and Excise.

up but drew it off in to small Casks & carried it off by force. I attempted to take one of the small Casks, when one Edw^d Pascoe lifted up a large Stick in order to strike me, & declared I should have nothing to do with the Brandy, in Consequence of which I was obliged to desist ...[97]

Customs records also show that some officials, whether they were ship's agents appointed to oversee salvage operations or ship's officers, accepted that mediation over salvage could restrain plundering activity, and thus indicated their recognition of the code of moral entitlement. When the *Triton* wrecked in Mount's Bay in 1774, the country people, 'who were assembled in an amazing Number', entered into an agreement with the shipping agent to assist in salvage for the payment of half of the cargo. When the Customs collector arrived, he was informed of the agreement and asked to concur; he refused because of the duties that were owed. However, he was also told that if he did not agree, 'there would be none of the Cargo saved for the Proprietors, that the Country would carry it all off'.[98] The Commissioners of Customs reluctantly admitted that the agreement was legitimate, and that the salvors could be paid in kind, although they did not wish to set an official precedent.

The relationship between moral entitlement and wrecking was thus well understood by shipping agents. They were concerned that salvage payments were fair and paid in a timely manner; otherwise they realised that people would take what they considered to be their fair share. Indeed, Richard Pearce is credited with reducing the plundering of wrecks in Mount's Bay in the early nineteenth century.[99] Pearce remarked in 1820 that he had paid salvage immediately, 'in the firm expectation that prompt payment would operate in a very great degree to prevent Plunder at Wrecks in future', and by 1833 he claimed that his 'personal exertions having in most cases put a stop to the disgraceful system of Plunder at Wrecks'.[100] Richard Oxnam, too, was credited with working with the country people over salvage payments 'in order to prevent plunder' after the wreck of the *Neptune* in 1782.[101] Even the outright plundering of a vessel was seen by some authorities as a reaction to the Government's failure to pay salvage on earlier shipwrecks, and hence played out the motive of seeking restitution for the violation of moral entitlement. William Kent, an agent for the wrecked galliot *Good Hope*, wrote in to the Commissioners of Customs, stating that he believed the plunder of the *Resolution* in 1817 could be directly attributed to the non-payment of salvage fees from

97   CUST 68/6, 27 April 1768.
98   CUST 68/8, 21 February 1774.
99   Vivian, *Tales of Cornish Wreckers*, 37.
100  CUST 68/27, Richard Pearce to Commissioners of Customs; CUST 68/32, Richard Pearce, Penzance, to Commissioners of Customs regarding salvage of the Swedish sloop *Neptunus*, 11 December 1833.
101  CUST 68/12, Penzance Collector to Board, 7 September 1782.

the *Good Hope*, which had wrecked the year previously.[102] The relationship between wrecking and salvage was so close that local magistrates and MPs, in seeking legislation to combat wrecking on a national level, proposed improvements in salvage law and called for more timely salvage payments.[103] The Government's transgression of 'moral entitlement' to salvage appears to have been one of the more important points of justification for wrecking activity on the part of those who wished to be legitimate salvors.

## Wrecking and Plunder Activity

The justification of providence and issues of poverty do not explain why, on occasion, entire ships or their cargoes were plundered and deliberately destroyed. Customs reported in 1749 that the snow *Squirrel* of North Yarmouth ran aground in Mount's Bay, 'when the Country immediately boarded her striped the M$^r$ of everything valuable then carryed off what Brandy they could and in the hurry Satt fire to the rest of the Cargoe so that the whole ship is now in flames'.[104] John Vivian also relates that a writer to the *General Evening Post* complained in 1754 that '[t]he unheard-of manner of proceeding of these barbarians is not only plundering, but setting on fire and destroying what they could not carry off of the valuable cargo of the *Bordeaux Trader* as well as burning the ship'.[105] Likewise, the plundering and burning of the *Concord* of Calais, which ran aground in the Bristol Channel in January 1769, reached the notice of Lord Weymouth and the Lords of the Treasury.[106]

Clearly, these activities indicate additional motives that can only be surmised, including that of simple deviant behaviour and thievery. However, it is possible that the wreckers sought to keep the goods out of the hands of Customs, just as Customs destroyed goods that 'were not worth the duty' to keep them out of the hands of the country people. In 1741, for example, Customs destroyed a whole cargo of tobacco, both by burning large amounts and by taking the rest out to sea and flinging it overboard.[107] Customs also attempted to destroy the salved remains of the *Le Landais* in 1837 when the agent abandoned them as 'not worth the duty'. As the Customs Collector

[102]  CUST 68/23, William Kent to S.R. Lushington, HM Treasury, n.d. 1817; See also CUST 68/16, Penzance Collector to Board, 7 June 1793, whereby salvors on Scilly were refused salvage payments because of conflicts between Customs and Excise over salvage revenue. Customs was even petitioned by William Hickens asking that the salvors get paid: 'the poor Fishermen the salvers at present in the greatest distress from the very great failure of the present Mackral Fishery ...'.
[103]  CA/B/46/99, Essay Against Wrecking; TNA HO 44/33, J.H. Rees, Magistrate at Llanelly, to Rt Hon. Lord John Russell, re: 'Inefficient State of the Law rel. to Saving Wrecks on the Coast', 29 July 1839.
[104]  CUST 68/2, 20 December 1749.
[105]  *General Evening Post*, February 1754, cited in Vivian, *Tales of Cornish Wreckers*, 10.
[106]  T1/469/106–109, Lord Weymouth to Lords of the Treasury, 31 October 1769.
[107]  CUST 68/1, 3 December 1741.

reported: 'any attempt on our part to destroy them, even if practicable, would be the signal for a general attack on the Officers from thousands of half-civi- lized Miners assembled'. The coastguard officers destroyed the salved goods anyway, by overturning vessels in which alcohol had been collected, staving in casks and shooting their firearms into the air.[108] These are not exceptional examples. The Customs House Letter books are full of requests by out-ports such as Penzance, Falmouth, and Padstow to destroy goods that had not been claimed. Tobacco, alcohol, and other stores were all eventually destroyed, since duty had not been paid.[109] This activity could hardly have garnered the support of the country people, who believed they had a right to the goods in the first place, especially to 'dead wrecks'.[110] Likewise, Customs were not seen by the country people as having authority over wrecks. As Officer Thomas Davies from Porthleven complained, 'Gentlemen as well as the common people give out that the Officers of the Customs have nothing to do with Goods that are thrown in before the Sea.'[111] Their opinion could have some merit, as legally Customs only had jurisdiction over dutiable goods.

Of course, not all behaviour occurring at shipwreck events was premedi- tated, and thus cannot be considered communally sanctioned. E.P. Thompson has argued that crowds often maintained control of their behaviour, and thus he sees rioting as a form of political voice.[112] However, in the case of wrecks, because crowds were not necessarily led by 'ring leaders', nor did many people have clear objectives other than to harvest goods, order could, and did, break down, especially with the presence of alcohol. Additionally, some actions were instinctive and involuntary; not all human behaviour is controlled by conscious decisions. Indeed, behaviours which 'are often described as meaningless or irrational, i.e. at variance with prevailing values and modes of conduct', can be explained by the concept of *Eigensinn*, or 'wilfulness', whereby individuals caught up in wrecking activities may have behaved in ways that they did not intend.[113]

---

[108] CUST 68/33, Penzance Collector to Board, 3 October 1837; HO 73/3, Alexander Shairp to Comptroller General, Coast Guard, Penzance, 4 October 1838.

[109] See CUST 68, Penzance; CUST 67, Falmouth; and CUST 69, Padstow.

[110] See CUST 69/7, J.D. Bryant, Receiver of Droits, Padstow, to Receiver General of Droits of Admiralty, 29 December 1852, regarding the extraordinary lengths Customs took to keep wrecked tobacco out of the hands of the common people. He estimated that if it had been carried off 'it would have displaced so much Duty paid Tobacco', thus he argued that he had saved '£2000 & upwards of Revenue', yet the actual cost of salvage and destruction of the goods left him with a deficit.

[111] CUST 68/6, 27 April 1768.

[112] Thompson, *Customs in Common*, 71.

[113] Sigurdur Glylfi Magnusson, 'Social History-Cultural History-Alltagsgeschichte-Microhis- tory: In-Between Methodologies and Conceptual Frameworks', *Journal of Microhistory* (2006), accessed at www.microhistory.org, 2 January 2009. See also Alf Lüdtke, *The History of Everyday Life: Reconstructing Historical Experiences and Ways of Life*, trans. William Templer (Princeton, 1995), 16.

Thus wrecking justification and motivation came from differing directions, and some activities were more accepted than others. For the most part, common people rather than being 'lawless' had their own understanding of the law, which informed their behaviour and acceptance of wrecking. Indeed, Bray's shipwreck account is useful in showing the nuances of communal acceptance and the shades of popular morality. Although Bray was a salvage agent, charged with protecting cargoes, and consequently was in direct competition for salvage awards for everything he 'put in the sillar', he still tended to show compassion towards the country people, especially if the excise men were involved. Only in cases where violence occurs, or where wreckers stormed the cellars where the shipwrecked goods were held, does Bray show any enmity. When it comes to the 'country people' harvesting goods from the beach, he is less judgmental.[114]

The custom of wrecking was clearly important, and the coastal populace of Cornwall, whether they were gentry or labourers, resisted the encroachment of Government control on what they perceived as their customary rights, whether those rights were for wreck or salvage. In this they could be said to accept, and even promote, varying forms of wrecking. Clearly, beach harvest was the most widely accepted and justified 'social crime', but other forms of wrecking, particularly the violent attack and plundering of vessels, are not so easily subsumed within that paradigm. Furthermore, many inhabitants were involved with legitimate salving and lifesaving, and as such were in conflict with those who only had wrecking in mind.[115] Wreckers were neither a monolithic population practising a socially accepted crime nor were they involved in wrecking simply as a way to assuage their poverty. Rather they were a diverse population whose justifications and motivations for wrecking activity illustrate a more complex popular morality than has heretofore been recognised – a popular morality that also informed their behaviour during wrecking events.

114 Bray, *An Account of Wrecks, 1759–1830*, 8.
115 See CUST 68/16, 9 February 1794.

# 5

# *Wrecking and Popular Morality*

*the grim hell-hounds prowling round the shore*

WHILE serving as second mate aboard the *Britannia*, William Falconer was shipwrecked off Cape Colona in the Levant. He returned home to write and publish his most famous poem, *The Shipwreck*, in 1762. While ostensibly reflecting his experiences, he used his pen in his third version to castigate and shame those who populated England's shore. Northumbria, he opined was:

> Where the grim hell-hounds, prowling round the shore,
> With foul intent the stranded bark explore:
> Deaf to the voice of woe, her decks they board,
> While tardy justice slumbers o'er her sword.[1]

Although Falconer singled out Northumbria, and other writers have targeted regions such as the Dorset coast,[2] the reputation of the 'grim hell-hounds' rests most squarely on Cornwall and the Isles of Scilly.[3] Indeed, Falconer is preceded in using such rhetoric by Daniel Defoe, who described the Scillonians in 1724 as

> a fierce and ravenous people … they are so greedy, and eager for the prey, that they are charged with strange, bloody, and cruel dealings, even sometimes with one another, but especially with the poor distress'd seamen when they come ashore by the force of a tempest, and seek help for their lives, and where they

---

[1]  Canto ii, 282–285, 3rd version (1769) in William Falconer, *A Critical Edition of the Poetical Works of William Falconer*, ed. William R. Jones (Lewiston, Queenstown, Lampeter, 2003), 72, 121.

[2]  See Thomas Francklyn, Rector of Langton-Herring and Vicar of Fleet, Dorset. *Serious Advice and Fair Warning to All that Live Upon the Sea-Coast* (London, 1761); and Anon, *The Wreckers, or a View of What Sometimes Passes on our Sea Coast: Written by a Clergyman of the Church of England, etc.* (London, c.1820).

[3]  John G. Rule, 'Wrecking and Coastal Plunder', in Douglas Hay, Peter Linebaugh, et. al., *Albion's Fatal Tree: Crime and Society in Eighteenth-Century England* (London, 1975), 169. See also William Hardy, *Lighthouses: Their History and Romance* (London, 1895). Hardy discusses wrecking, but *only* in relation to Cornwall.

find the rocks themselves not more merciless than the people who range about them for their prey.[4]

Although many fictional wrecking narratives utilise the motif of the deliberate wrecker preying on shipping by using false lights, the work of Falconer and Defoe represents what has become an associated literary motif: that of crowds of wreckers swarming upon shipwrecks and their victims. Between the existence of literary narratives and the use of similar hyperbole and motifs by the press, an entrenched cultural construct of the wrecker has been developed whereby the wrecker is portrayed as immoral and the epitome of evil.[5] It is this stereotype which has grabbed the public imagination, and thus is more widespread than the archetype of the wrecker protecting his customary rights. This malevolent figure is not romanticised like that of the smuggler or the highwayman; rather he must always be overcome.[6] But to what extent is Falconer's vision of 'a bloodhound train, by rapine's lust impell'd' an accurate depiction? [7]

The foundation of this stereotype rests on beliefs of the ruling elite and moral observers that the country people – the 'lower orders' – were 'lawless'. Commentators such as Rev. H.R. Coulthard of the parish of Breage claimed that miners thought themselves above the law because they came under the jurisdiction of the Duchy of Cornwall's Stannary Courts. The Stannary Courts, held in the mining districts, supposedly protected miners from prosecution by common law, allowing them instead to be tried by a jury of other miners. But at the same time, the miners were denied the legal protection of the common law courts.[8] Coulthard argues that this situation was the reason for 'the oppression and consequent debasement of the Miners', which created a sense of lawlessness that contributed to their wrecking proclivities. Thus, he contends that 'it may well have been said of the Miners of Cornwall, as far as wrecking was concerned, "wheresoever the carcase is, there will the vultures be gathered together"'.[9] This assessment indicates that

4   Daniel Defoe, A Tour through the Whole Island of Great Britain, intro. G.D.H. Cole and D.C. Browning (London, 1724, 1974), 243.
5   The role of the press in creating moral panics and solidifying the reputation of the wrecker will be covered in Chapter 9.
6   See Gillian Spraggs, Outlaws & Highwaymen: The Cult of the Robber in England from the Middle Ages to the Nineteenth Century (London, 2001); David Brandon, Stand and Deliver! A History of Highway Robbery (London, 2001).
7   Falconer, 'The Shipwreck', canto ii, 843.
8   Graham Haslam, 'Evolution', in Crispin Gill, ed., The Duchy of Cornwall (Newton Abbot, 1987), 27–28. The last Stannary Court case, held according to Stannary Law, was heard in 1896.
9   H.R. Coulthard, The Story of an Ancient Parish: Breage with Germoe, With Some Account of its Armigers, Worthies and Unworthies, Smugglers and Wreckers, its Traditions and Superstitions (Camborne, 1913), 39, 79. The relationship of the Stannary Courts and wrecking needs to be examined.

miners had few constraints to their violent plundering behaviour, but how far is this appraisal distorted?

The eighteenth and early nineteenth centuries were well known for outbreaks of popular violence. Indeed, in 1769, Benjamin Franklin recorded that:

> I have seen within a year riots in the country about corn; riots about elections; riots about workhouses; riots of colliers; riots of weavers; riots of coalheavers; riots of sawyers; riots of Wilkesites; riots of government chairmen; riots of smugglers, in which Custom-house officers and excisemen have been murdered, the King's armed Vessels and troops fired at.[10]

Franklin's observations may have been exaggerated, but he lived at a time when there was a popular morality 'that legitimised direct physical confrontation as a means of maintaining personal authority and of solving personal and public wrongs'.[11] Wrecking needs to be seen within this cultural context of violence.

Although there are many forms of violence – from personal violence to symbolic violence – most scholarly focus has been on the study of collective violence, defined as 'social interaction involving threatened or real physical damage to persons or property, carried out by a group of individuals whose efforts are coordinated, either by improvising on the spot, or through prior planning'.[12] Social historians have probed behind the attitudes and explanations of the elite, who labelled the crowd, or 'mob', as an amorphous, faceless 'barbaric' entity that threatened the public order, to understand the mob's social make-up, motives and the function of riots and protests. In these studies 'from the bottom up', scholars have discovered that at the root of many protests was a reaction to protect collective rights and customs against elite and government encroachment, by invoking their rights as 'free-born Englishmen'. Rather than being unrestrained, however, protests involved constraints that limited the level of violence, particularly in social protests such as food riots and for grievances as wages, enclosures, and impressment. Violence, if it erupted, was typically limited to the destruction of set targets, such as property, rather than the destruction of lives.[13] Thus, those involved in protest carried with them a

---

[10] A.H. Smyth, ed., *The Writings of Benjamin Franklin* (New York, 1907), x, 239, quoted in Ian Gilmour. *Riot, Risings and Revolution: Governance and Violence in Eighteenth-Century England* (London, 1992), 15.

[11] Clive Emsley, *Hard Men: The English and Violence since 1750* (London, 2005), 12; Peter King, *Crime and the Law in England, 1750–1784: Remaking Justice from the Margins* (Cambridge, 2006), 227.

[12] William Beik, 'The Violence of the French Crowd from Charivari to Revolution', *Past and Present*, 197 (November 2007), 78.

[13] George Rudé, *The Crowd in History: A Study in Popular Disturbances in France and England, 1730–1848* (London, 1964, 1981); John Brewer and John Styles, *An Ungovernable People? The*

popular ethic that informed their behaviour.[14] They had grievances for which they sought restitution, often against people whom they knew, and they saw themselves as righteous in their actions, with 'pride of legitimacy', all which acted to 'prevent theft or wanton brutality during a riot'. Indeed, the primary social constraint may have been what has been termed their 'intimate social relations', in that 'rioters, magistrates, and victims acted in a milieu of face-to-face familiarity'.[15]

Like other participants of collective violence, wreckers justified their actions by invoking custom, and viewed encroachment by officials such as Customs officers as threatening their traditional rights. Wreckers instituted their moral entitlement to salvage, too, which was clearly a form of social protest against government control, as was discussed in the previous chapter. Wrecking populations were also involved in collective protest; Cornish tinners had a strong record of food protests, for instance, and were a key population for E.P. Thompson's model of the 'moral economy of the crowd'.[16]

Overall, however, violent wrecking differed from that of other customary riot behaviour and thus the explanatory models have crucial differences.[17] Foremost, wrecking events were rarely protest movements as such. Rather, wrecking was primarily a form of economic pursuit, based on opportunism. Neither were wrecking activities in response to market-driven forces as was the case with food rioting, although both were influenced by poverty. Nor were wreckers involved in close social and intimate relationships with the 'victims', as were the perpetrators of other forms of collective violence that had clear objectives. Wrecking also had no clear political agenda, other than the few protests which erupted over late or missing salvage payments and a generalised challenge to authority. But was the level of wrecking violence as limited by social constraints as other forms of rioting? And if so, what other internal constraints may have been involved?

If we are to believe popular culture about wreckers, violence was endemic; there was no popular morality to limit the level of violent behaviour. One of the most enduring myths involves the murder of shipwreck victims, not only to ensure 'dead wrecks', but as part of the violent proclivity and avarice of the wrecker. One of the most vivid literary images we have was written by

*English and their Law in the Seventeenth and Eighteenth Centuries* (London, 1980); Adrian Randall, *Riotous Assemblies: Popular Protest in Hanoverian England* (Oxford, 2006).

[14] E.P. Thompson, 'The Moral Economy of the Crowd', in *Customs in Common: Studies in Traditional Popular Culture* (New York, 1993), 212.

[15] John Bohstedt, *Riots and Community Politics in England and Wales, 1790–1810* (Cambridge, Massachusetts, 1983), 41.

[16] Thompson, 'Moral Economy of the Crowd'; Barry Reay, ed., *Popular Cultures in England, 1550–1750* (London, 1998), Chapter 6 'Riots and the Law'; John G. Rule, *The Labouring Classes in Early Industrial England, 1750–1850* (London, 1986), Chapter 14, 'The Protesting Crowd: Riots and Disturbances'.

[17] Bohstedt, *Riots and Community Politics*, 35, 37, 41, 198–201.

Daphne du Maurier, where her villain, Joss Merlyn, drunkenly admits to his niece Mary Yellan that

> 'I've killed men with my own hands, trampled them underwater, beaten them with rocks and stones ... There was a woman once, Mary; she was clinging to a raft, and she had a child in her arms; her hair was streaming down her back. The ship was close in on the rocks, you see, and the sea was as flat as your hand; they were all coming in a live, the whole bunch of 'em ... She cried out to me to help her, Mary, and I smashed her face in with a stone ... I watched them drown in four feet of water ...'

He added chillingly, 'Did you ever hear of wreckers before?'[18]

The sinister wrecking scenes of the novel were made even more pervasive by the filmic images brought forth by the 'Master of Suspense', Alfred Hitchcock, when *Jamaica Inn* was released worldwide in 1939. Popular culture, too, incorporates the belief that if wreckers did not kill their victims outright, they at least ignored their fate and let the sea take its sacrifices. Although these views are common tropes within literature, they have become part of British popular culture and are promoted as fact.

The actual occurrence of violent attacks on shipwrecks and shipwreck victims is almost impossible to determine because of the sketchiness of the qualitative sources; not all attacks had witnesses who recorded the activities. As well, the frequency was dependent on the location of the wreck coming ashore; most wrecks occurred slightly offshore, and were difficult to access. Nonetheless, a few statistics are useful. As Figure 6 shows, in Mount's Bay, near Breage and Germoe, there were only eleven cases of outright attack reported by Customs out of 155 wrecks from the period 1738–1860: eighteen shipwrecks were described as protected, and 119 were reported as having some salvage activity. Thus, only 7 per cent could be considered as having come under violent attack. For the majority of wrecks, no details were given.

More frequently, the accounts record only pieces of wrecked timber or barrels of goods that had washed ashore, thus there were few opportunities for large numbers of wreckers to gain full access to vessels wrecked offshore. It is also telling that there are few contemporary descriptions of the plunder and attack of vessels as opposed to the regular reporting of other forms of popular violence and protest, such as food riots, even though these actions involved the same populations. It is clear that a popular morality was involved, even on the part of the so-called 'ungovernable' miner, and was a key social constraint. Indeed, the same popular ethic that justified wrecking contained restrictions governing against levels of violence. The belief in moral entitlement contained within it an ethic of fairness and reciprocity which erupted into violence only in response to official aggression or broken agreements to

---

[18] Daphne du Maurier, *Jamaica Inn* (London, 1936, 1976), 116–117.

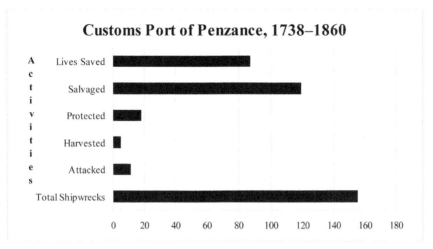

Figure 6. Shipwreck Activities, Mounts Bay (Customs Port of Penzance), 1738–1860.

Source: CUST 68, Penzance Collector to Board. The figures are necessarily rough as shipwreck activity was underreported. Missing years include 1743–47, and there are limited entries from 1845–60.

salvage.[19] Even so, it was a limited form of violence, and nothing like the images touted in modern popular culture. Thus, there is little hard evidence to prove the charge of murder, although robbery of shipwreck victims sometimes occurred.[20] Certainly the attempted robbery of two victims from the wreck of the East India Company ship *President* in Mount's Bay in 1683 was well disseminated, and would have added to Cornwall's growing reputation.[21] However, the more violent behaviour and mistreatment of shipwreck victims 'may have been exceptional', as '[t]here are few recorded cases of such direct inhumanity'.[22]

### Lifesaving

By looking at the data from the Penzance Customs district additional conclusions can be drawn about the behaviour and mentality of the coastal populace.

---

[19]  Robert Shoemaker, *The London Mob: Violence and Disorder in Eighteenth-Century England* (London, 2004, 2007), Chapter 6.
[20]  CUST 68/2, 20 December 1749; *Calendar of Home Office Papers*, No. 1460, 24 September 1764, 447–448; T1/450–31, H.S. Conway to the Lord's Commissioners of the Treasury, 15 January 1766; Richard Larn and Bridget Larn, *Shipwreck Index of the British Isles*, Vol. 1 (London, 1995), n.p., wreck of the *Jane*, 13 December 1827.
[21]  See William Smith, *A full account of the late ship-wreck of the ship called the* President, *which was cast away in Mountz-bay in Cornwal on the 4th of February last, as it was deliver'd to his Majesty (both in writing and discourse) by William Smith and John Harshfield …* (London, 1684).
[22]  Rule, 'Wrecking and Coastal Plunder', 176.

It is evident that in 77 per cent of the reported shipwreck cases lifesaving activity occurred, which meant that members of the coastal populace put themselves at personal risk. These figures belie the serious charge that the Cornish wreckers were guilty of murdering shipwreck victims, or at least of ignoring their fate and leaving them to die.[23] It is this charge that Rev. Hawker of Morwenstow bemoaned in his poetry, such as the 'Croon of Hennacliff'. Written after the wreck of the *Bencoolen* in 1862, it falsely accused the Bude lifeboatmen of neglect of duty:

> Cawk! Cawk! then said the Raven
> I am fourscore Years and Ten:
> Yet never, in Bude Haven,
> Did I croak for rescued Men!
> They'll save the Captain's Girdle
> And Shirt, if Shirt there be,
> But leave their Blood to curdle,
> For my Old Dame and Me![24]

Concurrent with wrecking, lifesaving was obviously already present as part of popular morality, and had been from time immemorial, the two activities not being mutually exclusive. As well, although most of the men concerned with lifesaving were pilots and fishermen, whole communities were drawn in once the wreck and the victims came ashore. Indeed, town and parish accounts record funds released to shipwreck survivors. Such figures show that the saving of lives from shipwreck was costly. Survivors had to be given clothing and provisions, and were frequently afforded transportation to their homes or home ports, expenses that were not reimbursed through salvage payments.[25] Penryn's town account book for 1652–1795 shows 'several payments of 6d to poore men having lost their shippe', including seven Englishmen, who were also given a pass from the mayor of Penzance 'to travell to Great Yarmouth', and on 29 March 1653/54, thirteen Englishmen were paid 6s 5d after being shipwrecked on the Lizard.[26] The corporation of Looe, likewise, paid out one shilling in 1669–70 to '3 poore men yt lost their ship in Mount's Bay', and one shilling to three men who were shipwrecked off Land's End. Looe also paid relief the same year to three men who lost their ship on the Goodwin Sands in Kent. The following year, the East Looe mayor gave four shillings to eight

---

[23] See Thurstan C. Peter, *A Compendium of the History and Geography of Cornwall, by the Reverend J.J. Daniell*, 4th edition by Thurstan C. Peter (Truro, London, 1906), 465; Richard Larn, *Cornish Shipwrecks: The Isles of Scilly* (Newton Abbot, 1971), 21; John Fowles, *Shipwreck: Photography by the Gibsons of Scilly* (London, 1974), 2.

[24] BL Add.37825, Handwritten copy of the 'Croon of Hennacliff' by Rev. Robert Hawker.

[25] See CUST 68/45, Board to Penzance Collector, 26 June 1790; CUST 68/48, 1 October 1799; CUST 68/55, 13 January 1820.

[26] Roland J. Roddis, *Penryn: The History of an Ancient Cornish Borough* (Truro, 1964), 79.

shipwrecked Dutchmen.[27] St Ives, too, gave money in 1698 to two Irishmen shipwrecked off Zennor, and to an unfortunate ship's captain who had lost all his worldly possessions during a wreck.[28] William Penaluna emphasised the effort of the inhabitants of Falmouth to assist the victims of the wreck of the *Queen* transport in 1814, when

> some proceeded to the fatal spot to aid the half naked fugitives, others made preparations at home for their reception. Even the poorest inhabitants took the blankets from their beds ... All seemed to vie with one another in acts of humanity, according to their respective abilities, and their general conduct deserves the warmest testimonies of approbation.[29]

The ability of the coastal populace to combine wrecking and lifesaving practices is also evidenced in a letter Joseph Banfield wrote to John Knill in 1792, describing the 'plundering' of the Dutch frigate *Brielle* near Coverack. The men from Coverack brought the Dutch crew on shore 'with great alacrity and activity tho there was a great sea & they ran some risk of the boats and their lives very humanely brought all the ships company together with the Soldiers safe to land excepting only some few who were unfortunately drowned'. Banfield wanted to highlight that 'the first part of this business did the Coverack men great credit, as to the accounts given in the papers of their plundering the people of their cloaths as they came on shore I believe is totally destitute of the truth'. The 'plundering' occurred the following day after the pieces of wreck had washed onshore and only then did the local people gain Banfield's censure. He remonstrated that "'tis true they have humanity enough to save men's lives at the hazard of their own: when that is done, they look upon all the rest as their own property'.[30] Banfield's account underscores the argument that the concept of providence was not exclusive of more humanitarian endeavour, and further indicates the existence of a popular morality that included lifesaving and charity to the shipwrecked. The populace's actions in plundering were a form of reciprocity, where payment in kind was extracted for their assistance, especially considering that salvage was not paid for lifesaving; it was paid out only for the salving of goods. Banfield's description additionally shows another important issue that clouds attempts to assess

---

[27] Mayor's Account, 1669–70 in Austin L. Browne, *Corporation Chronicles: Being Some Account of the Ancient Corporations of East Looe and of West Looe in the County of Cornwall* (Plymouth, 1904), 71; CRO X/155/371, Mayor's Account, Borough of East Looe, 1700–01.

[28] St Ives Borough Accounts, 1693–98, in Arthur P. Salmon, *The Cornwall Coast* (London, 1910), 241.

[29] William Penaluna, *The Circle, or Historical Survey of Sixty Parishes and Towns in Cornwall* (Helston, 1819), 155.

[30] HO 43/4, from Joseph Banfield to Mr Knill, 28 February 1792, Falmouth. Extract of letter, Rule 'Wrecking and Coastal Plunder', appendix, 187.

wrecking activity: the use of pejorative terminology, or 'symbolic violence', by the press when dealing with the country people.[31]

Some of the most riveting descriptions of the lifesaving endeavours of the Cornish are included in John Bray's manuscript, in which he enumerated shipwrecks off Bude from 1759 to 1830.[32] His account is a balance of wrecking and lifesaving, and, as editor A.K. Hamilton Jenkin acknowledges, many lives were lost in the attempt to save victims as the lifeboat was still unknown in Bude even in 1840. Thus, many of those who wrecked – harvested – were involved with saving the lives of the shipwreck victims first, putting their own lives in danger before collecting their due. And for those who could not reach the victims, real anguish was felt. Bray describes a ship from Drogheda, in Ireland, which ran aground near Bude with a cargo of butter. Unfortunately, the seas were so high that none could approach her: 'The poor souls was making a dismal noise stritching out for help, and we could not give them the least assistance. When one part of the ship would part,' Bray wrote, 'the poor men would get on it, then would a sea wash them off.' He continues:

> At last the mast fell and it was soon over, all the poor men drownded. The parts of the ship, the butter and peeces of the mast all coming on shore, it was a danger to take hold of anything in the sea for everything was drove (in) so violent that unless great ceair (care) our legs might been broke. One of the unfortunate men lash't himself to the mast and the rope cut him into two parts, the poor man's heart and liver and hand was sceen lying on the rocks at Marclake, a very wisht sight God knows.[33]

Bray tried to save what he could, bringing the body of the supercargo ashore, which was soon joined by three more bodies. The ship's agent, Edward Fox, ordered him to arrange for their burial at Poughill, using ten of the thirteen gold guineas found in the supercargo's pocket to pay internment costs. Bray thought nothing of it to keep the supercargo's silver watch; and Fox gave Bray the remaining three guineas and the supercargo's gold ring for his troubles.[34]

Bray also matter-of-factly describes the near loss of his own life in a life-saving incident, one which he had seen foretold in a dream that came twice in one night. Bray informed his companion that he could not sleep anymore, and 'if he would not go, I should'. About 4 a.m., the two men rode to Wide-mouth Bay, and at their first view of the bay, discovered a scene similar to

---

[31] The use of symbolic violence by the press will be discussed in Chapter 9.

[32] John Bray, *An Account of Wrecks, 1759–1830 – On the North Coast of Cornwall*, edited and transcribed by A.K. Hamilton Jenkin (Cornwall, 1975), 12.

[33] Bray, *An Account of Wrecks*, 12. This might have been the wreck of the *Ability* in December 1824. The *Royal Cornwall Gazette* reported that hundreds of people watched helplessly from the cliffs as the vessel and crew were lost, a disaster that could have been avoided if they had been able to send a line out to the ship. Larn and Larn, *Shipwreck Index*, Vol. 1, n.p.

[34] Bray did not keep the silver watch, however. He 'gave the watch to old Mr. Bryant to send it to Stratton to have it cleaned – and never sceen it afterwards', *An Account of Wrecks*, 13.

that of Bray's dream. A brig was heading toward them, its 'sails all to shatters'. They plunged their horses over the sand dunes to the beach, arriving just as the ship struck:

> I saw the poor sailors lashing a yard along-side the ship, broadside against the seas. In a small time, I saw the sailors get on the yard and then they jumped off into the sea … I rode out and got them as they swimmed, my horse swimming too. Sometimes the sea would break all over us. I ordered the men to hold fast all together, so they did, and by the help of God I brought seven of them safe to land.

One of the victims informed Bray that one of the crew was still left, and thus Bray headed his horse back into the surf, and into the undertow:

> At last I saw a very great sea coming. I stopped my breath, stooped down my head to sea and it broke very high over me. However I soon saw the poor man on his back at the bottom, lifting up both his hands. I sprung off my horse and seized the man by his jacket collar. He at that moment seized my great coat sleeve and held so fast as if he was sensible. I was under water at the time, but I held my breath and at the same time he held fast by the near stirrup. The moment I came above water, a very great roule of sea knocked my horse with all four legs up, and I and the poor sailor under the horse. However, by the providence of God, my horse was soon on his belly and turned all about towards shore and swimmed with the poor sailor and I to land.

Bray succeeded in saving most of the crew, and the next morning, when he rode out to see the sailors 'they was all very much recovered, and if I could have swalloed gould (*swallowed gold*) I might have had it. They gave me as many limmons and oranges as I could bring home.'[35] As Simon Trezise aptly comments, 'This description is just as exciting as Du Maurier's fiction. … If Bray's account was as well known as *Jamaica Inn*, the modern Cornish could use it to help re-write their history and re-adjust the stereotyping of the wrecker.'[36]

Bray's account is not the only evidence showing the coexistence of wrecking and lifesaving. Defending the Bude lifeboatmen in response to Rev. Hawker's charge of dereliction of duty after the wreck of the *Bencoolen*, C.F.C. Clifton describes the distress felt by the villagers after onshore winds and rough seas prevented the lifeboats from launching: 'the village is thrown into mourning, as if the lost men had been friends rather than strangers'. But then he adds: 'Frequently, however, a wreck is regarded as a rather pleasant and exciting incident in a long dull winter. *But that is only when it is attended with no loss of life* [emphasis his]. I question whether there is any other place along the

35 Bray, *An Account of Wrecks*, 15–16.
36 Simon Trezise, 'The Sea-Dog, the Smuggler and the Wrecker: Literary Representations of Maritime Life in the West Country' (unpublished conference paper, University of Exeter, 20 October 2001), 31.

coast where shipwrecked sailors are more tenderly cared for than at Bude'.[37] Although Clifton's staunch advocacy of Bude is obviously biased, Bray's account, written in a much more honest tone, corroborates Bude's humanitarian impulses.[38]

The wreck of the H.M.S. *Anson* in 1807 on Loe Bar, Porthleven, gives another example of the lifesaving propensities of a population accused of barbarous wrecking. Thomas Tegg, the leading publisher of shipwreck narratives in the nineteenth century, took the opportunity to praise the humanity of the local Cornish inhabitants:

> We are happy to hear that the inhabitants of Helston, and its neighbourhood, have, in this instance, as well as the late one of a transport, which was also wrecked, rescued the character from those odious epithets of savage and barbarian, which have heretofore been thrown upon them, for by their unexampled and hazardous activity, all the crew that remained on board, and escaped a watery grave by not being precipitate getting on shore, were landed by eleven o'clock.[39]

Cyrus Redding, a Cornish journalist and founder of the *West Briton* newspaper, also used the *Anson's* experience to argue against Cornwall's reputation for brutality:

> Nothing can be more untrue than the charge of Cornish barbarity, since in no part of England shipwrecked persons meet with greater kindness ... On the wreck of the *Anson* frigate, thirty years ago, not only were the survivors kindly treated, but the efforts made to assist in the escape of the crew were all which were possible in such a dreadful scene.

Redding goes on to relate the story of an act of bravery by an unidentified man, whom he believed was a 'methodist teacher, a humble man', who was swept out to sea with his horse while attempting to rescue a third person. The man 'found in this way the proudest death and interment that is destined for humanity, – losing his life in the act of trying to save a fellow-creature from destruction, and having the bosom of the ocean for his sepulchre'. Therefore, Redding tersely argues, 'the charge of want of hospitality or kindness in the Cornish to shipwrecked persons, then, is not true'.[40] Likewise, the much-decorated Henry Cuttance of Gunwalloe is singled out by Rev. Cummings as

---

[37] C.F.C. Clifton, *Bude Haven: Bencoolen to Capricorno: A Record of Wrecks at Bude, 1862 to 1900* (Manchester, 1902), 19.

[38] Bray, *An Account of Wrecks*.

[39] EN/P/462, *The Loss of His Majesty's Frigate Anson, which was Wrecked Within Three Miles of Helston, December 28, 1807, and About Fifty Persons Lost ...* (Thomas Tegg, n.d.), 8–9. Tegg was the leading publisher of shipwreck narratives, which were increasingly popular in the nineteenth century. Keith Huntress, *Narratives of Shipwrecks and Disasters, 1586–1860* (Ames, Iowa, 1974), xiii–xviii.

[40] Cyrus Redding, *An Illustrated Itinerary of the County of Cornwall* (London, 1842), 187.

one of the most active in saving lives on the south coast, having attended not only the wreck of the *Anson* and the transport *Susan and Rebecca* in the same year, but nearly all the wrecks from that period until at least 1870.[41] These cases of lifesaving are emphasised in reaction to the Cornish reputation for violent wrecking, a charge that the apologists believe is unfair. Their defence is supported by the historical record. Thus, there is little evidence for the truth of the couplet related to Rev. Hawker justifying the murder of shipwreck victims: 'Save a stranger from the sea/ And he'll turn your enemy.'[42]

The wreck of the *Anson* also initiated two other achievements of Cornish humanity. The tragedy affected two witnesses who sought to improve the conditions of shipwreck in their own way. First, Thomas Grylls of Helston drew up an act that would allow parish officers to bury shipwreck victims in consecrated ground. The 'Burial of Drowned Persons Act' was introduced to Parliament by Cornish MP John Hearle Tremayne, and it was passed in June 1808.[43] Previous to the legislation, shipwreck victims were buried on the shore near where they were discovered. If the bodies landed on manors with the right of wreck, the lord of the manor would pay men for the labour of burial. The presence of so many who had lost their lives in dire circumstances and who lacked a Christian burial must have been the foundation of many a ghost story. But with the passage of the act, burials came under the purview of the local vicar. Indeed, Rev. Hawker wrote extensively of his experiences burying shipwreck victims, and the memorials which he erected in the churchyard at Morwenstow stand to this day.[44]

Second, Henry Trengrouse of Helston was badly distressed by the large loss of life from the *Anson* tragedy, especially by the victims' failed attempts to swim ashore. He described the Loe Bar sands that would not allow the victims to get to their feet before they were washed back out to sea by the 'out-haul'. He also recollected the loss of a Danish brig in Porthleven Bay in which 'the people on the shore, by hallooing and waving their hats, directed her to an eligible spot' where they were able to save the crew. But, he opined, 'notwithstanding vessels come in so close before taking to the ground, – yet

[41] Rev. Alfred Hayman Cummings, *The Churches and Antiquities of Cury and Gunwalloe in the Lizard District, including Local Traditions* (Truro and London, 1875), 142–146. Cummings claims that Cuttance was the first Englishman to be decorated for bravery by foreign royalty, having been awarded a silver cup by the king of Norway in 1846.

[42] Rev. Robert S. Hawker, *Footprints of Former Men in Far* Cornwall (London, 1870, 1903), 190. There certainly could be reasoning behind the couplet, especially since shipwreck victims could bring disease, especially plague. The couplet has been popularised with frequent citation of Hawker's work, beginning with Rev. Sabine Baring-Gould's *The Vicar of Morwenstow: Being the Life of Robert Stephen Hawker, M.A.* (London, 1899), 106. See also J. Saxby Wryde, *British Lighthouses: Their History and Romance* (London, 1913), 280.

[43] 48 Geo. III c. 75; Penaluna, *The Circle*, 231.

[44] See Robert S. Hawker and C.E. Byles, *The Life and Letters of R.S. Hawker (Sometime Vicar of Morwenstow) by his Son-in-Law C.E. Byles* (London, 1906).

without the assistance of a rope, destruction is almost inevitable, for the afore-said reasons, – the power of the breakers – and the looseness of the sand'. Trengrouse determined that getting a rope to the victims was critical, as they would be too overcome with terror to think clearly. Thus he began to work on his rocket apparatus, designed to shoot ropes onto the endangered ship so that a cradle could be used to carry the victims to shore.[45] Trengrouse's 'Traveller' began showing up in salvage accounts in 1821, when it was used successfully to save life from the *Peggy*, driven on shore near Porthleven. He was awarded £5 5s salvage 'for the saving the lives and property being ship-wrecked, and without the Assistance of which it would not have been possible to receive from the Vessel on the high Clift any of the Peggy's Cargo'.[46]

Therefore, a form of humanitarianism, allowing for the coexistence of life-saving and wrecking, was present within Cornish coastal society and acted as a constraint to limit the level of violence towards shipwreck victims. Local inhabitants believed in their duty to save lives, and developed customs by which they performed many acts of bravery. As a form of popular morality, it is likely that it had its foundations within the popular religion that was practised by the Cornish, a religion that had at its roots a conservative form of Anglicanism emphasising the notion of providence. Although many Cornish had limited access to formal religious instruction because they lived in isolated villages without incumbent clergy, and outside of the influence of clergy found in the larger villages,[47] they had nonetheless developed a popular morality that contradicts the argument that they were 'barbaric', 'Godless', and preyed on shipwrecks with alacrity.

### Methodism and Evangelicalism

A second social constraint on wrecking activities, which intersects with tradi-tional popular morality, was that of Methodism and evangelicalism. Indeed, Methodism is often credited with the defeat of wrecking, and hence is argued by many to be the key social constraint. In 1913, Saxby Wryde wrote with hyperbolic force that 'truly there was needed the strong arm of a religious body to subdue and govern a population that for centuries had yielded itself to the influence of wrecking and smuggling', as if the population were entirely

---

[45] CRO X/498/58, Henry Trengrouse Papers: *Shipwreck Investigated, for the Cause of the Great Loss of Lives with which it is Frequently Attended; and a Remedy Provided in a Portable, Practi-cable Life Preserving Apparatus; Which is Calculated For, and Is Necessary to Become, a Part of Every Ships Equipment* (Falmouth, 1817), 21.
[46] CUST 68/27, Tobias Roberts, Salvage Charges for *Peggy*, to Commissioners of Customs, 3 March 1821.
[47] Philip Payton, *Cornwall: A History* (Fowey, 2004), 200.

irreligious, ignoring the Prayer Book rebellion in 1549 and their support of the Anglican church during the Civil Wars. He continues: 'Wesleyanism, which had failed to make any serious impression of the stolid agricultural inhabitants of Devonshire, effected a great work of reformation on the more excitable Cornish, and was one of the chief, possibly it was the main, means of bring the ancient horrors of the Cornish coast to an end.'[48]

The Methodist movement against wrecking began with John Wesley's condemnation of the practice, beginning with his visits to Cornwall in 1743 when he described the Cornish as being 'those who neither feared God nor regarded man', accusing them of murdering shipwreck victims.[49] In 1755, he felt that between the work of Methodists and local clergy, 'in a while, I trust, there will be no more cause on these coasts to accuse *Britannos hospitibus feros*'. He claimed then that the tinners of Mount's Bay had been converted to Methodism, and thus that 'the lions of Breage are now changed into lambs'.[50] However, on a return visit in 1776, Wesley enquired of one of his disciples at Cubert if 'that scandal of Cornwall, the plundering of wrecked vessels, still subsisted'. He received a somewhat ambiguous answer; it still existed '"as much as ever; only the Methodists will have nothing to do with it. But three months since a vessel was wrecked on the south coast, and the tinners presently seized all the goods; and even broke in pieces a new coach which was on board, and carried every scrap away."'[51] Yet, Wesley had supposedly already converted the tinners of Breage, who were accused of the attack. Nevertheless, it is difficult to imagine that the thousands of miners who attended at shipwrecks did not count among their multitudes a large majority of Methodists, as it was with the miners that Methodism had taken root.[52] Indeed, the miners apparently were able to integrate their religious beliefs with wrecking,

[48] Wryde, *British Lighthouses*, 274–275. See also EN/P/463, [Josiah Harris], 'A Voice from the Ocean Grave: An Essay on the deaths of Richard Coombe, John Cockin, Joseph Nettle, and James Hobba, of Holmbush, by Drowning, near Mevagissey, on Sunday, the 11th of September, 1869 ...' (Truro, 1859), 23.

[49] 17 May 1743, diary of John Wesley, quoted in Captain Harry Carter, *The Autobiography of a Cornish Smuggler (Captain Harry Carter of Prussia Cove), 1749–1809*, intro. and notes by John B. Cornish (London, 1900; reprinted Truro, 1971), xix.

[50] Quoted in F.E. Halliday, *A History of Cornwall* (London, 1959), 271

[51] John Pearce, ed. *The Wesleys in Cornwall: Extracts from the Journals of John and Charles Wesley and John Nelson* (Truro, 1964), 158; quoted in Halliday, *A History of Cornwall*, 272. The wreck in question is most likely that of the *Marie Jean*, a French vessel carrying goods of Louis XVI that went aground during a gale at Gunwalloe Cove.

[52] Rule, 'Wrecking and Coastal Plunder', 185; John C.C. Probert, author of *The Sociology of Cornish Methodism* (Truro, 1971), disagrees with this statement and claims that Methodism did not appeal to the miners so much as to the other levels of society, such as rural farmers and urban shopkeepers. He is thus involved in debate with Philip Payton and John Rule. See 'Merritricious?' in the Cornish History Network Newsletter, March 2000.

just as they were able to do with smuggling, another vice Wesley abhorred.[53] In other words, Methodism was syncretised into an existing Cornish culture that included the customs of wrecking and smuggling.[54] Even so, it is not possible to discount the argument that Methodism was an important factor in the decline of wrecking and smuggling. Conversely, however, it also assured the survival of the Cornish reputation for wrecking by promoting the myths through its didactic literature.[55]

Methodism and other dissenting faiths eased the way, claimed Rev. George C. ('Bo'Sun') Smith of Penzance in 1818, to allow him to respond to Methodists Fortescue Hitchins and Samuel Drew's appeal for 'moral and intellectual light' to combat Cornish wrecking. Thus, he was not afraid to travel among the wreckers and smugglers, exhorting them to desist from their unlawful activities.[56] Indeed, a clarion call by the Bishop of St David's in Wales, written in response to depredations on the coast of Cardiganshire and Pembrokeshire, also convinced Smith to go out among his parishioners. The bishop called for the clergy to preach against wrecking and to inform their parishioners of the 'cruel and unchristianlike enormity of plundering wrecks ... and press strongly on their consciences the flagrant criminality of this inhuman practice....'[57] In this he was following statute, which, beginning with 12 Anne in 1714, had mandated that the laws against wrecking be announced in every parish church on the coast four times a year, a requirement that had been neglected by coastal clergy.

Several clergymen in Cornwall took up the bishop's challenge, including Richard Lyne, the rector of Little Petherick. Lyne issued his 'Exhortation against Wrecking', where he claimed that he had heard of wrecked cargo being

---

53 Rule, 'Wrecking and Coastal Plunder', 185; Alan Kent, *The Literature of Cornwall: Continuity, Identity, Difference, 1000–2000* (Bristol, 2000), 91. See also the conversion of one of Cornwall's most famous smugglers in Carter, *The Autobiography of a Cornish Smuggler*.

54 Rule also illustrates how Methodism syncretised with other forms of folk-belief such as magic and superstition. John Rule, 'Methodism, Popular Beliefs and Village Culture, 1800–50' in Robert D. Storch, ed., *Popular Culture and Custom in Nineteenth-Century England* (London, 1982), 64–67.

55 Payton, *Cornwall*, 197. For Methodism's role in assuring the survival of the reputation of the Cornish for wrecking, see Chapter 9. For Methodism's influence on culture, see David Hempton, *Methodism and Politics in British Society, 1750–1850* (London, 1984), Chapter 2 'The Wesleyan Heritage', 20–49; Kayleigh Milden, 'Culture of Conversion: Religion and Politics in the Cornish Mining Communities', *Cornish History Online Journal* (2001); Rule, 'Methodism', 48–70.

56 Fortescue Hitchins and Samuel Drew, *The History of Cornwall: From the Earliest Records and Traditions to the Present Time*, Vol. I (Helston, 1824), 726, quoted by Rev. G.C. Smith, *The Wreckers; or A Tour of Benevolence from St. Michael's Mount to the Lizard Point* (London, 1818), 13. Smith must have read early drafts of the book, since it was not officially published until 1824.

57 Bishop of St David's circular letter, published in *The Times*, 6 January 1817. Six months after the bishop's letter, a wreck bill was placed before the Commons. Failing, it was followed by another bill, with the same results, in 1818. See Chapter 3.

washed ashore in the parish and found by his parishioners. He warned them that:

> I feel it the part of any Office in this Church & Parish to acquaint you, that they who have in any way met with such goods, are required to have them carried & delivered to the Custom house at Padstow or to persons authorized to receive them, for the use and benefit of the unfortunate owners. Which if you who now have such goods in possession, will do, you will thereby do a thing well-pleasing to GOD upon a promise of salvage 'as a reward for your honesty to the poor sufferers' ...[58]

He also cautioned them that the wrecking offence carried the death penalty. Smith did likewise, admonishing his parishioners around Penzance. He outlined his 'Tour of Benevolence' in letters to a 'friend', of which an extract was published in *The Times*. In it he summarised his attempts to preach among the wreckers and to distribute Religious Society tracts along the southern coast from St Michael's Mount to the Lizard, in hopes that he could eliminate 'the natural depravity and the custom of centuries'.

Smith argued that the only effective way to combat wrecking was to 'be the preaching of the gospel, and dissemination of just principles of right and wrong; though some have thought that a well-written tract, something in the form of a dialogue between Wreckers, would be of considerable service'.[59] Although Smith's letters were written in response to the bishop's request, he questioned the bishop's methods for combating wrecking:

> Seldom or ever have I known evil habits and old practices broken by violent threatenings from the pulpit. The understanding is in error, it must be informed; the judgment is wrong, it must be corrected; and the will, if possible, biased by the mild and evangelical persuasions of the gospel. Let this be preached in its purity ... Violent threats against smuggling or wrecking, from the pulpit to the congregation of smugglers and wreckers, would exasperate the people to destroy the preacher; but the fervent and affectionate preaching of Christ crucified would win the heart ... This is my plan and I find it succeed. I speak, therefore, from experience, of preaching among the vilest classes of sinners.[60]

Thus he argued that behavioural change had to be internalised to be effective. Smith claimed that he had proof that his methods of persuasion were far more successful: 'I was happy to receive the concurrent testimony of many persons', he wrote, 'affirming that whatever was obtained by wrecks or smug-

---

[58] P/185/2/3, Richard Lyne, 'Exhortation against Wrecking', 1818.
[59] Smith, *The Wreckers*, 11. Smith was preceded in his idea by the publication in 1768 of the Rev. James Walker's *A Dialogue between a Captain of a Merchant Ship and a Farmer Concerning the Pernicious Practice of Wrecking: as Exemplified in the Unhappy Fate of One William Pearce of St. Gennis, Who Was Executed at Launceston in Cornwall Oct. 12, 1767: Showing Also How the Captain Was Converted to a Life of Much Seriousness and Consideration, etc.* (London, 1768).
[60] Smith, *The Wreckers*, 13.

gling seldom continued long with its possessors; but, in some accountable way, the wrecker was nearly the same at the end of the year as at the beginning, and sometimes much worse.'[61] Smith's work was undoubtedly of some service, since he was well known for his humanitarianism, although it is impossible to know how much effect he truly had on wrecking.[62] Even Hitchins and Drew admitted that by 1818, before Smith and Lyne had begun their work against wrecking, 'this abominable practice [wrecking] is confined to a few western parishes, and that even here no deeds of personal inhumanity towards the unhappy sufferers have been permitted in modern times, even by the plunderers themselves.....'[63] The outlook of Elizabeth Bonham, a Methodist story-teller, is also telling. When describing wrecking on the south coast in the late eighteenth and early nineteenth centuries, she focused on harvest: 'none of the wreckers thought it robbery to seize on anything they might come across, and it was an understood thing that everyone should "catch what they could"'; the plundering of wrecks was not even considered.[64]

It is impossible to measure the effect of clergy such as Rev. Lyne and Rev. Smith on the continued occurrence of wrecking activities, especially since they were imploring against not only the attack of vessels, but against harvest as well. However, the general impression of Hitchins and Drew that wrecking – at least violent plunder – was at an end, is upheld by the other forms of evidence. Indeed, it is illustrative that, as Figure 7 shows, throughout the period the number of shipwrecks actually *increased*, and yet by the time Rev. Lyne and Rev. Smith began their work in 1818, there were few recorded cases of attacks on vessels. Methodism and evangelicalism, then, can be seen as *enhancing* a pre-existing popular morality which operated as a social constraint on plundering, but harvest activities continued to be acceptable behaviour on the part of the coastal populace.[65]

Finally, to complete the consideration of the Cornish wrecker's propensity for plunder, did the existence of large crowds automatically indicate that they were 'prowling round the shore' with 'foul intent the stranded bark explore' as Falconer had alleged? The evidence suggests that to the contrary, the following and attending of shipwrecks cannot be taken as evidence of *intent* to plunder, as some writers maintain. Ships in distress were followed for multiple reasons,

---

[61] Smith, *The Wreckers*, 12.

[62] Smith was a voracious campaigner against what he felt were the ills of society. See *The Extreme Misery of the Off-Islands*, (London, 1818) and *The Scilly Islands and the Famine* (London 1828), among others.

[63] Hitchins and Drew, *History of Cornwall*, Vol. I, 726.

[64] Mrs Elizabeth Bonham, *A Corner of Old Cornwall*, intro. by E.J. Oldmeadow (London, 1896), 169.

[65] For a more general treatment of the role of evangelicalism in moral reform, see M.J.D. Roberts, *Making English Morals: Voluntary Association and Moral Reform in England, 1787–1886* (Cambridge, 2004) and F. David Roberts, *The Social Conscience of the Early Victorians* (Stanford, California, 2002).

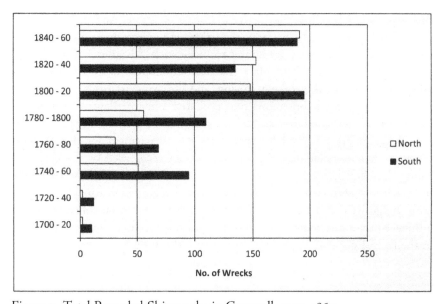

Figure 7. Total Recorded Shipwrecks in Cornwall, 1700–1860.

Source: Compiled from Richard Larn and Bridget Larn, *Shipwreck Index of the British Isles*, Vol. 1 (London, 1995) and additional data from primary research.

including concern for the safety of the crew and passengers, readiness for life-saving and legitimate salvage activity, and for reasons of typical human behaviour: curiosity.[66] Even Customs had to admit that the crowds who assembled on the shore in 1815 when the *Flora* was wrecked on Praa Sands during a gale were beneficial, for 'by the great exertions of the Country People who Assembled on the occasion the Crew were also saved'. Likewise, in 1825, sixteen men making up the French crew of *L'Amietie* 'were saved by the Assistance of the Country People assembled'.[67] Indeed, there are many more accounts of life-saving than of life-taking. It is true that not all individuals were honourable; some did see ships as 'prey'. Behaviour during shipwreck could and did break down. Alcohol was present, as most ships carried large cargoes of wine and spirits. However, it is the extent of such behaviours, and the tarring of all coastal inhabitants with the same brush, that must be doubted.

Wreckers, therefore, were hardly the mass of 'grim hell-hounds prowling round the shore' as popularised into myth by Falconer, or even the evil characters stereotyped in Defoe's descriptive narrative or du Maurier's *Jamaica Inn*. Although to shipwreck victims immersed in such imagery crowds could appear

[66] See *Royal Cornwall Gazette*, 18 November 1819, cited in Larn and Larn, *Shipwreck Index*, Vol. I, n.p.

[67] CUST 68/22, 20 October 1815; CUST 68/29, 20 January 1825.

that way, especially when they arrived *en mass* on shore. And there certainly were some wrecks 'cut to pieces in one tide', as George Borlase alleged, but the charges of inhumanity are harder to make stick.[68] Rather, wreckers came from a rural and coastal populace that had developed its own moral code, and which performed wrecking, salving, and lifesaving activities according to time-honoured social constraints that predated, but were later enhanced, by Methodism. They saved lives and they saved goods, whether those goods were for salvage or appropriated for their own use as payment for their labour. Even so, their popular morality was not always recognised by the elite and ruling classes. The local populace continued to find themselves in a struggle over rights to shipwrecked goods, rights that became increasingly contested with the growth of law enforcement in Cornwall. The social constraints that influenced their behaviour at shipwrecks continued to function, however, even in the face of growing opposition from the authorities.

---

[68] George Borlase to Lt General Richard Onslow, 15 March 1753, in Thomas Cornish, ed., 'The Lanisley Letters: to Lt. General Onslow from George Borlase, his agent at Penzance, 1750–53', *Journal of the Royal Institution of Cornwall*, 6, pt 22 (1880), 379.

# 6

# Wrecking and Enforcement of the Law

*I hope to see y^e wreckers hung in Chains upon the Cliffs*

O N 9 October 1767, the *Sherborne Mercury* reported that 'Last Monday
was executed at St. Stephens, near Launceston in Cornwall, Wm. Pearse
[sic],[1] who was condemned at the last assizes for that county. … He persisted
to the last moment that he was not guilty of the crime he died for.' William
Pearce became the only individual in Cornish history to be executed for
wrecking under the act of 26 Geo. II c. 19, believing to the last that he had
only acted according to custom. He was executed as an example to deter the
rest of the populace from wrecking activities, but Pearce's ritual sacrifice was
a lesson lost: the *Sherborne Mercury* did not even report the crime of which
he was found guilty when it announced his execution. Mention of his crime
was buried in small print in the 31 August issue: at eighty years old, Pearce
had been caught taking an 'inconsiderable quantity of cotton' from a wreck.[2]

William Pearce was unfortunate to be convicted at a time when the ruling
elite wanted to make an example and were not in a mood for lenience. Moreover, they had the act of 26 Geo. II to draw upon. Many legislators argued that
the laws were solid; the problem existed in their enforcement. Local magistrates and lords of the manor were expected to enforce the laws, with the
assistance of Customs, the Preventive Service, the local militia, and soldiers, if
needed. Historians claim that plundering and wrecking continued because of
Cornwall's relative isolation and lack of law enforcement on the coast.[3] They
also argue that even when suspects were caught and indicted, few convictions
followed because of local forms of resistance, such as Cornish particularism;
that even local magistrates and juries closed ranks against outsiders and

---

[1]  Pearce's name is spelled with a 'c' in all other sources, which is the most common form
within Cornwall.
[2]  *Sherborne Mercury*, 31 August 1767.
[3]  John Vivian, *Tales of Cornish Wreckers* (Truro, 1969), 4; Bill Young and Bryan Dudley
Stamp, *Bude's Maritime Heritage: Past and Present* (Bude, 2001), 43.

central government authorities.[4] Indeed, one scholar has gone so far as to say that '[f]or a long time it was generally accepted that no Cornish jury would ever convict a fellow countryman on a wrecking charge', and cites Pearce's case as the lone example.[5] Thus we have the development of a popular belief in which Cornish wreckers were hidden and protected by a community who closed ranks in response to law enforcement measures.

Minimal attention has been given to the role of the law in combating wrecking, however, and there has been no detailed analysis. The forces of governmental control, particularly that of the Coastguard, are often credited with the decline of wrecking, but the process of how this occurred is not ascertained.[6] But what were the relationships of the local elites, the law enforcement officers, and the coastal populace who were involved in wrecking, as it was played out in the arena of the law? By investigating these interactions, the role of mediation and discretion in the quest for justice is revealed, as well as the growing centralisation of State authority – a presence that was increased with the strengthening of the criminal justice system.

At the beginning of the period, law enforcement on the Cornish coast was certainly lacking, making it difficult for local magistrates. At the Launceston Assizes in 1700, it was reported that there were not enough magistrates in Cornwall, and that 'in some Hundreds there are noe Justices at all'. The same session heard about the wreck of an unnamed ship near Padstow, where the goods 'were taken and carried away in a rude and riotous manner … the number of Rioters was so great their threatenings so high and their proceedings so Outrageous that Ordinary Ministers of Justice durst not attempt to suppress them'.[7] Even in 1748, the Customs collector at Penzance complained to London that 'the Civil power can be of no manner of service to us they not daring to appear in our Defence' after the wrecking and plunder of the *Jonge Alcida* in Mount's Bay.[8] John Wesley, too, was particularly critical of both the gentry and the justices, remarking in his diary that 'the gentry of Cornwall may totally prevent it when they please. Let them only see that the laws be strictly executed upon the next plunderers; and after an example is made of ten of these, the next wreck will be unmolested.'[9]

4   John Rule, 'Wrecking and Coastal Plunder', in Douglas Hay, Peter Linebaugh, et. al., *Albion's Fatal Tree: Crime and Society in Eighteenth-Century England* (London, 1975), 181–182.
5   Richard Larn, *Cornish Shipwrecks: The Isles of Scilly* (Newton Abbot, 1971), 20.
6   See Alfonse Esquiros, *Cornwall and its Coasts* (London, 1865), 180; A.K. Hamilton Jenkin, *Cornwall and its People* (Truro, 1932; reprinted Newton Abbot, 1970), 62.
7   PC 1/1/50 Item 4, To Chief Barons all from Cornwall, Launceston Assizes, 18 April 1699/1700.
8   CUST 68/2, 8 December 1748.
9   17 August 1776 in John Pearce, ed. *The Wesleys of Cornwall: Extracts from the Journals of John and Charles Wesley and John Nelson* (Truro, 1964), 158.

The gentry and the magistrates were in a difficult position. Walter Borlase, Chairman of the Quarter Sessions, was frustrated after the wreck of *The Rose in June* near Marazion in 1749. The vessel was plundered

> by the Barbarians of Breage, Germoe &c ... which act of inhumanity and rapine if laid before our superiors in all its flagrant circumstances, will, I fear, produce this natural inquiry. Are there in that County no Justices? Where were they when the Laws were violated in so daring a manner? Or, if they could not prevent such violences what did they do in order to punish them?[10]

Borlase, determined to apprehend the offenders, held meetings with the justices of Penwith and Kerrier, and swore in constables, but to no avail. Despite claims that the identities of the offenders were known, no arrests were forthcoming. Indeed, historian John Rowe asserts that Borlase might have been intimating that the local justices were involved with wrecking themselves.[11] But the situation of the eighteenth-century magistrate was not an easy one. They were not formally trained in the law, they were unpaid, and they had informal judicial practices; it was also difficult to find suitable men to take on the responsibilities.[12] It was no wonder that local authorities had difficulty in the early part of the period.

This is not to say that magistrates were completely ineffective, despite contemporary criticism. Some magistrates were successful in their control of wrecking. Charles Rashleigh MP argued in 1776 that 'the plundering of ships was generally prevented by the assiduity and exertions of the neighbouring gentlemen'.[13] In 1803, the owner of cargo on the wrecked *Rio Novo* packet wrote to Thomas Pascoe JP of his admiration after Pascoe had controlled the plunder of the vessel:

> I am well aware from being myself in the Commission of the Peace for Hampshire & having witnessed in the neighbourhood of my County that in the Isle of Wight Depredations Committed or attempted in all Cases of Wrecks, that their protection must have been greatly assisted by the Activity of a Magistrate, and as I understand you acted alone on that Occasion it is inconceivable with my Ideas of Propriety to remain silent ...[14]

Even Hitchins and Drew, in their county history, credited the work of the 'neighbouring gentlemen' in the fight against plunder in 1824.[15]

---

[10] 8 December 1749, Letter Book of Walter Borlase, quoted in John Rowe, *Cornwall in the Age of the Industrial Revolution* (Liverpool, 1953), 36.

[11] Rowe, *Cornwall in the Age of the Industrial Revolution*, 36.

[12] David Taylor, *Crime, Policing and Punishment in England, 1750–1914* (London, 1998), 107.

[13] 'Debate on Mr. Burke's Bill to Prevent the Plundering of Shipwrecks', 27 March 1776 in *Cobbett's Parliamentary History*, Vol. XVIII (1774–76), 1298.

[14] CRO X/807/39, Pascoe Family Papers. George Ward to Thomas Pascoe, JP, 19 January 1803.

[15] Fortescue Hitchins and Samuel Drew, *The History of Cornwall: From the Earliest Records and Traditions to the Present Time*, Vol. I (Helston, 1824), 726.

## The Use of the Military

Although justices could swear in special constables, as did Walter Borlase in 1750, they frequently resorted to a request for the military when they felt they needed assistance. This was an expedient not taken lightly; magistrates were placed in a position where they had to admit defeat to the Home Secretary and invite in centralised forces.[16] They also invited local opprobrium by bringing in the military. In 1732, Edmund Prideaux, a JP at Padstow, claimed that 'nothing but a good Company of regular troops could have dispersed such a number as were gathered' at a local wreck.[17] The officers of Customs, too, were forced to ask for military assistance during times of what they perceived as extreme need. The Customs officers of Penzance sent numerous requests to London in 1748 and 1749 after the attack on the *Jonge Alcida*.[18] Charles Vyvyan, the Customs collector, claimed that:

> the Insolence of the Smuglers and Wreckers in this neighbourhood is run to such height that tho our Officers have from time to time secured severall Hogsheads it has been by force taken from 'em by numbers of these people assembled together particularly about a Week Since the Officers ... found Two hogsheads of wine part of that Cargoe they were taken from 'em and the Officers forc'd to fly to save their lives ...[19]

His request was in response to the loss of *The Rose in June*, when 'y$^e$ Flax was all destroyed by the Mobb, who came in Such Numb$^r$ as twas impossible to resist without a Millitary force.'[20] By December, Vyvyan once again reiterated his concern when he reported on the attack and burning of the *Squirrel* in Mount's Bay. The last sentence of his report illustrates his frustration: 'we hope y$^r$ Hon$^{rs}$ are by this satisfied there's nothing to be preserved either by Shipwrecks or from smuggling without the assistance of a Millitary force.'[21] Vyvyan finally received a response when troops were sent to Penzance in February 1750. But the situation was not yet solved; the captain informed him that he had no order to assist during shipwrecks. '[A]nd as these things

---

[16] Roy Porter, *English Society in the Eighteenth Century* (London, 1982, 1990), 102.

[17] SP 36/29, f. 91, Edmund Prideaux to Richard Edgcumbe of Mount Edgcumbe, 10 February 1732.

[18] CUST 68/2, Penzance Collector to Board, 2 February 1748/49.

[19] CUST 68/2, 2 February 1748/49. This particular passage is frequently used out of context in popular histories to show the violence of wreckers in plundering vessels, and as such has lent itself to the making of the myth. See Richard Larn and Clive Carter, *Cornish Shipwrecks*, Vol. I: *The South Coast* (Newton Abbot, 1969), 165; Jenkin, *Cornwall and its People*, 52; Vivian, *Tales of Cornish Wreckers*, 7.

[20] CUST 68/2, 21 September 1749.

[21] CUST 68/2, 21 December 1749.

of Late are not to be attempted without all the assistance of a Millitary force', Vyvyan wrote, he needed to apply for an order.[22]

Requests for troops were sent intermittently throughout the eighteenth and early nineteenth centuries, indicating the sporadic need for assistance. All the requests, however, were connected with Customs' battle against smugglers. That the concern was more fervent regarding smuggling makes sense. The defeat of smuggling was 'the "raison d'être" of a large part of the Service'.[23] Wrecking, as a strictly opportunistic event, did not warrant as great a concern. Indeed, throughout the correspondence of the Penzance collectors, wrecking was barely remarked upon in conjunction with the frequent shipwrecks attended by the Customs officers, and after 1768 their requests for military support – made in 1783, 1792, and 1815 – did not even mention wrecking.[24] Indeed, in 1816 the Commissioners of Customs informed Penzance that the Treasury had taken measures to insure that the military would be 'resorted to as extensively as the Service will admit' to combat smuggling.[25] The use of troops against wreckers was thus a result of the smuggling war.

The forces employed against wreckers and smugglers came from several different branches of the military, including the militia, which was reorganised and strengthened in 1757; the Yeomanry, developed in 1794 to protect the coasts from French invasion; the Volunteer Corps, which were also organised in 1794 to serve as part-time auxiliaries for the militia; and the regular army.[26] The army was preferred, as it had professional troops who were thus more disciplined and less inclined to riot.[27] Deployment of soldiers could only be ordered through the Home Secretary, which usually occurred when the Secretary received 'hysterical requests from some provincial magistrates, convinced that revolution was about to break out in their particular parish'.[28] Military detachments were deployed at wrecks at various times throughout the period, though never in large numbers, and often very intermittently. They included the 35th Regiment and the Inniskilling Dragoons.[29] Militia and yeomanry regiments were used during the 1790s after their inception, including the

---

[22]  CUST 68/2, 1 February 1749/50.
[23]  Edward Carson, *The Ancient and Rightful Customs: A History of the English Customs Service* (London, 1972), 12.
[24]  The request made in 1768 only added wrecking as an afterthought. CUST 68/7, 3 November 1768; CUST 68/12, 24 July 1783; CUST 68/16, 12 November 1792; CUST 68/22, 24 January 1815.
[25]  CUST 68/52, Penzance Board to Collector, 28 February 1816.
[26]  David Foster, *The Rural Constabulary Act 1839: National Legislation and Problems of Enforcement* (London, 1982), 4–5; John Brewer, *The Sinews of Power: War, Money and the English State, 1688–1783* (Harvard, Massachusetts, 1990), 32–33.
[27]  John Bohstedt, *Riots and Community Politics in England and Wales, 1790–1810* (Cambridge, Mass. and London, 1983), 49.
[28]  Foster, *The Rural Constabulary Act*, 5.
[29]  CUST 68/1, 20 August 1740.

Penwith Yeomanry Cavalry, the Helston Volunteers, the Mountsbay local militia, the Worcestershire Militia, and the Wiltshire Militia.[30] They were not only used to protect wrecks, but they often performed salvage duties, and thus were often awarded salvage payments.[31] Indeed, the granting of salvage to soldiers was common for most of the period, though occasionally the Customs Commissioners denied them salvage if they were only involved in guarding property rather than physically involved in salvaging. Such was the case with the militia who guarded the *Eudora* near Bude in 1810–11.[32]

The billeting of soldiers was a difficulty. They were viewed by the local populace as a threat, not only because of the lack of quality of the men who made up the force, but also because of what they implied: the control of the Government over local concerns. Here was a 'quasi-alien force, as ready to fight their fellow countrymen as a foreign army'.[33] In no part of the country were soldiers welcomed. To add insult to injury, there were extra costs involved. As George Borlase cautioned Lt General Onslow MP in 1753 regarding the use of troops in Penzance:

> As to the soldiers mencon'd in both yours, unless the rout is as usually subjected to the discretion of the Magistrates and Neighbouring Justices how to dispose of 'em and billett 'em out this Town cannot quarter them. I mentioned them as necessary for the publick and not so much to indulge my own inclinacon because I like 'em. But there is all the reason in the world for part of the detachment to be at Helstone because just on that neighbourhood lye the smugglers and wreckers more than about us, tho there are too many in all parts of this country …

Borlase was adamant that troops were needed regardless of these complications. Ten days later, he again wrote to Onslow, claiming that smuggling and wrecking were on the increase, 'to such a degree as to render them necessary'.[34]

Notwithstanding the difficulties of billeting and the unpopularity of the army, however, troops were often used successfully against wreckers. When the collector at Penzance was questioned as to their efficacy in 1769, he reported that they were necessary support for Customs to perform their duties.[35] Several wrecks were successfully protected by using troops, such as

---

[30] CUST 68/16, 22 March 1794; 14 December 1795; CUST 68/17, 2 January 1797; see CUST 68/24, Petition for salvage charges for the *Victoria*, 8 September 1818.

[31] See CUST 68/39, Petition for salvage, John Millett, Adjutant 2nd, Mount's Bay Volunteer Infantry, to Commissioners of Customs, 16 July 1804.

[32] CUST 69/1, Petition for salvage charges of *Eudora* by T.R. Avery, Boscastle, 2 January 1811.

[33] Ian Gilmour, *Riot, Risings and Revolution: Governance and Violence in Eighteenth-Century England* (London, 1992), 139.

[34] Borlase to Onslow, 5 March 1753 and 15 March, 1753, in Thomas Cornish, ed., 'The Lanisley Letters: to Lt. General Onslow from George Borlase, his agent at Penzance, 1750–53', *Journal of the Royal Institution of Cornwall*, 6, pt 22 (1880), 378.

[35] CUST 68/7, 9 December 1769.

the *Betty* of London in 1741[36] and *Le Dont de Dieu* in 1790, where 'had it not been for the Assistance of the Soldiers we believe that the Vessel never would have been Salved nor but very little of the Cargo, the Country People on this Coast being so very riotous and lawless'.[37] After an initial attack on the brig *John* in 1795 at Poljew Cove, the tinners were put to flight and two were killed.[38] The military proved its effectiveness, for six other ships were reported wrecked or run aground in the following two months; none were reported as being plundered. In 1810, troops were again present during the wreck of the *Eudora* off Bude, the *Mentor* in 1814 in Mount's Bay, and in 1818, they assisted in protecting the *Victoria* and the *Le Eugoine*.[39] Indeed, troops became commonplace at most wrecks from the beginning of the nineteenth century, along with the presence of Customs and Excise officers and the Coastguard. For the most part, however, they were a deterrent rather than an actual fighting force; there were few instances of reported violence. Instead, they were employed in the actual salvage attempts.[40]

The efficiency of the military, however, was also dependent on the mood of the local populace and the timing of the shipwreck event. They were not strong enough when the wreckers were truly bent on plunder, as in the wrecks of the *Vigilantia* and the *Naboths Vinyard* in the winter of 1738/39. Although troops from Helston attended both wrecks, they were too late to prevent plundering.[41] In 1818, although the *Royal Cornwall Gazette* laid great praise on the Penwith Yeomanry Cavalry and Lt G. John, it also reported that some of the cargo 'was plundered by the barbarians in the Neighbourhood'.[42] Even the presence of dragoons could not stop people from harvesting nuts thrown on the beach in December 1819 when the *Montreal* packet wrecked on Loe Bar.[43] The military were a deterrent mainly to stop the more violent forms of wrecking; they were less effective against harvest.

Despite the intermittent requests for military backup, troops were not always needed to combat wrecking. Indeed, in 1785 the collector reported that Customs officers had secured the entire cargo of the brig *Commerce*, which ran aground in Mount's Bay, and that 'it was not plundered or carried away by the Country people'. He emphasised that 'we have no soldiers here ... the Officers were highly necessary to act as Guards independent of their duty

---

[36] CUST 68/1, 28 November 1741.
[37] CUST 68/14, 30 July 1790.
[38] CUST 68/16, 22 November 1795.
[39] CUST 69/1, 31 December 1810; CUST 68/21, 19 March 1814; CUST 68/24, 10 April 1818; CUST 68/25, 28 December 1818.
[40] CUST 68/29, 20 January 1825; CUST 68/30, 8 February 1826.
[41] CUST 68/1, 23 November 1738 and 1 January 1738/39.
[42] Wreck of the *Victoria*, *Royal Cornwall Gazette*, 17 April 1818, quoted in Richard Larn and Bridget Larn, *Shipwreck Index of the British Isles* Vol. I (London, 1995–98), n.p.
[43] CUST 68/26, Account of salvage charges from wreck of the Brig *Montreal Packet*, Tobias Roberts, agent, to Commissioners, 1 January 1820.

as Revenue Officers'.[44] Occasionally it is unclear whether or not troops were in attendance, but the Penzance collector reported in 1798 on two separate occasions that the presence of his officers prevented plunder.[45] Indeed, from that point on, salvage accounts state the role of the attending officers for 'preventing plunderage', for as Collector Ferris remarked,

> had the s[d] Goods not have been secured at the time, they would possibly be endangered by being plundered through the Country People, which is at all times to be dreaded as much as the danger of the Sea. And in every instance of this kind, the Revenue Officers are principally instrumental in counteracting their Designs ...[46]

Officials also reported that they had enough troops at present, or even wished to have them removed. In 1814, the Penzance collector claimed that troops at Truro and Falmouth 'cannot be of any assistance to us'. Two years later, the collector continued to note that the 'distribution of the Military [is] fully sufficient'.[47]

### Preventive Services: The Water Guard and the Coastguard

The use of soldiers to control wrecking and smuggling was soon superseded by other means of governmental law enforcement, particularly with the growth of the Preventive Services. Originally formed in 1698 with the establishment of the Riding Officers, the Preventives were responsible for patrolling the coastal areas for smuggling. In 1809, the Preventive Water Guard was created in response to both the fears of Napoleonic invasion and the problem of smuggling. Officers were drawn from the Royal Navy and were given responsibility for patrolling the coasts; they were also given orders to assist during shipwreck.[48] Additionally, as official orders instructed, the Water Guard was to 'ensure that none of the cargo of the wreck is run or secreted in any manner as to avoid payment thereof'.[49] When the Water Guard was reformed as the Coastguard in 1822, it was given the additional responsibility to act as Receiver of Wreck, taking charge of everything coming ashore.

---

44  CUST 68/12, 13 October 1785; 30 December 1785.
45  CUST 68/17, 15 March 1797; 14 July 1798.
46  See CUST 68/22, wreck of *Delhi*, 23 October 1815; wreck of the *Maria*, 2 December 1815. The role of the officers comes up in salvage reports frequently, as their names are included in receiving salvage for not only salving goods, but for protecting them. However, the commissioners determined that protection could not be included as salvage duties. From that point, the salvage reports emphasise their manual labour in salving, but not in protection. CUST 68/22, 30 March 1816.
47  CUST 68/22, 3 December 1814; 9 May 1816.
48  William Webb, *Coastguard! An Official History of HM Coastguard* (London, 1976), 14.
49  Quoted in Webb, *Coastguard*, 16.

Contemporary evidence indicates that some officers were considered effective. Capt. George Davies RN, the Inspecting Commander of the Coastguard in the Penzance district, received accolades from both the French government and from local shipping agent Richard Pearce. Pearce, as the French Consular Agent, applauded Davis's attendance at the wreck of the *La Meuse*, and his 'determined conduct and example have wrought a remarkable change in the state of affairs in that locality'. However, Pearce also indicated that the presence of the Coastguard in the past had not been as valuable, referring to earlier wrecks of the *Le Landais* (1837) and the *Adele* (1848), in which '[t]he *horrible* scenes of plunder and confusion will not soon fade from memory'. After those particular circumstances, Pearce had been forward in his complaints about the ineffectiveness of the Coastguard in the Penzance district.[50]

Additional evidence for the efficacy, or lack thereof, of the Coastguard is drawn mainly from two different parliamentary select committees, one held in 1839 to inquire into the establishment of a rural constabulary force, and the other held in 1843 to assess the causes of the high numbers of shipwrecks.[51] In both, minor focus was given to the difficulties faced by law enforcement in the struggle against wrecking. The constabulary report, in particular, has been used in wrecking studies without critical analysis;[52] it needs to be used with the utmost caution. Wrecking cases were taken out of context to prove that it was out of control and that a rural constabulary force was needed. The wreck returns from Cornwall, however, can be used conversely to their original intent, to show that the presence of the Coastguard and work of the local magistrates were effective in preventing large-scale cases of plunder. Fowey reported no plundering cases within the previous three years, although in 1830 three foreign vessels were wrecked; they were protected by the Coastguard. In 1834, when a Swedish barque carrying staves was wrecked near Looe, 'no assemblage of persons expressly for plunder' gathered. Falmouth reported no wrecking activity, and Penzance, other than the *Le Landais*, had minimal to no wrecking activity during four different wrecks. Indeed, the *Active* was reported as being protected by the Coastguard cutters. Finally, Padstow reported six wrecks, four in 1834, one in 1836, and one in an unidentified year. Only one, the *Agenard* in 1834 was described as having involved any wrecking (harvesting) activity.[53] (See Appendix 2) The lack of wrecking activity was not only because the cargoes were 'of little value', but because of

50   R. Pearce, French Consular Agent to Captain George Davies, RN, in *Summary of Services in the Royal Navy and Coast Guard; and Services, acting under Civil Power, at Riots, Fires, Wrecks &c. &c. of Capt. George Davies, R.N.; with Documents, Extracts and Testimonials* (Penzance, 1851), 16.
51   PP, *First Report of the Constabulary Force Commissioners* (1839); PP, *First Report from the Select Committee on Shipwrecks; Together with Minutes of Evidence, Appendix, and Index* (1843).
52   Jenkin, *Cornwall and its People*, 60–62; Rule, 'Wrecking and Coastal Plunder'.
53   HO 73/3.

the presence of the Coastguard officers. Thus despite claims to the contrary made by the constabulary report, the Coastguard was showing its effectiveness, at least in Cornwall.[54]

Testimony of Coastguard officers from the 1843 Select Committee on Shipwrecks also indicates that they were for the most part efficacious, except for jurisdictional issues: like Customs, they were only authorised to protect dutiable goods. Indeed, David Williams, Inspecting Commander of the Coastguard at Padstow, was quick to point out that the newspaper report on the plunder of the *Jessie Logan* in 1843 was mistaken, that the Coastguard were not overpowered as had been reported, and that no violence occurred. Although he was protecting his reputation, he also gave credit to the Cornish. He claimed that 'plunder [harvest] always takes place where there is a wreck; when it is scattered along the shore it is impossible for a few men to protect it' but that the only time the local populace would '"steal" property was if it was thrown along the shore'. He added emphatically: 'they were not thieves'.[55] Williams's testimony is indicative of the tone throughout the report. As opposed to the constabulary report, the testimony of those involved with the shipwreck inquiry were more level-headed, giving a picture not that wrecking was out of control, but that the few instances of plundering could be curbed by increasing their jurisdiction over non-dutiable goods and by assuring fair salvage payments.[56] Thus the establishment of the Coastguard, coupled with changes in the popular morality of the coastal populace, had already begun to show itself in the limited cases of violent plunder. Indeed, the efficacy of law enforcement depended on negotiation by both the populace and the law. Otherwise, how could a small group of Customs officers or Coastguard officers hold back, as they described it, 'some thousand Tinners and others attending' for the purpose of plunder? [57]

## Prosecution, Conviction, and Discretionary Justice

Notwithstanding the overall effectiveness of law enforcement, local authorities were not satisfied. They wished to combat all forms of wrecking. Thus they not only requested stronger law enforcement; they occasionally voiced their desire for retributive punishment. Only then could the war on wrecking be won, or so they believed. In 1733, after the wreck of the French ship *Postillion*, local JP Edmund Prideaux stated, 'I have more than once told people in this neigh-

---

[54] *Report of the Constabulary Force Commissioners*, 64.
[55] Testimony of David Williams, *Select Committee on Shipwrecks 1843*, 302.
[56] See testimony of Capt. David Peat, RN; Commander John Wheatley, RN; Inspecting Commander David Williams; Commander James Pulling, RN; Lt John Bulley, RN; and Lt William Viccary, RN, in *Select Committee on Shipwrecks 1843*.
[57] CUST 68/16, 1 December 1794.

bourhood that I hope to see some of y$^e$ wreckers hung in Chains upon the Cliffs, and till some severe examples are made, better is not to be expected.'[58] J.H. Rees, a Welsh magistrate, echoed Prideaux's opinion a hundred years later when he said, 'unless some examples be made of the Major Offenders, these disgraceful scenes will again occur'.[59] The desire for severe punishment was voiced yet again in 1843 by Capt. David Peat RN, despite the fact that the death penalty for wrecking had been repealed only six years previously.[60]

Calls for capital punishment were limited, however. More concern was voiced over the lack of convictions in general. Customs officials charged local juries with particularism at various times when they were frustrated in their attempts to convict known smugglers. Edward Giddy, a magistrate from Tredea near Marazion, was particularly pointed about the problem in his letter to the Customs Board in 1778. After complaining about smuggling, he opined: 'As the Law now Stands, I fear a Criminal Prosecution would be useless at best, for a Reason which shocks one to Mention, that a Cornish Jury would certainly acquit the Smuglers....'[61] Giddy was clearly aggravated by what he saw as an inability to convict smugglers, and feared that the situation would increase their audacity. A similar viewpoint was held by John Julian, the Inspecting Commander for Penzance. He complained to Capt. Bowles RN of the Coastguard in 1824 that although Nicholas Grenfell of St Just had been found guilty of smuggling by the magistrates at Penzance, that 'as its likely that the Grand Jury at the Sessions will be composed principally of Men connected with Smuggling, their [sic] is no doubt they will throw out the Bill'.[62] Julian wanted the accused to be tried at the assizes, so Grenfell could be made an example to the populace. Although neither mentioned wreckers, an analogous situation would most likely apply.

Although there is evidence of particularism by local juries, the reasoning behind the lack of indictments has not been assessed, except for allusions by contemporaries that the juries were themselves involved in smuggling or that people were unwilling to inform against their neighbours.[63] The evidence, however, is more substantial for the existence of complex legal practices that were incorporated into the eighteenth-century justice system throughout England. Recourse to the law and courts was considered to be the last resort, not only by the local authorities, but also by the victims concerned.[64] Indeed,

58  SP 36/29, f. 91, Prideaux to Edgcumbe, February 1732/33.
59  HO 52/23, f. 59, J.H. Rees to Home Office, 26 December 1833.
60  Testimony of David Peat, RN, *Select Committee on Shipwrecks 1843*, 252.
61  CUST 68/42, Edward Giddy JP to Commissioners of Customs, 4 March 1778.
62  CUST 68/29, John Julian to Capt. Bowles, RN, forwarded to the Solicitor of Customs, 9 May 1824.
63  Rule, 'Wrecking and Coastal Plunder', 183.
64  Taylor, *Crime, Policing and Punishment*, 2.

the lack of legal activity may be explained through discretionary processes, that

> although the formal criminal law and legal handbooks sometimes appeared rigid and inflexible, in reality the administration of the eighteenth-century criminal justice system created several interconnected spheres of contested judicial space in each of which deeply discretionary choices were made. Those accused of property offences ... found themselves propelled on an often bewildering journey along a route which can be best compared to a corridor of connected rooms or stage sets. From each room one door led on towards eventual criminalization, conviction, and punishment, but every room also had other exits ...[65]

Indeed, most wreckers encountered rooms with exits. Discretionary justice is thus an important concept involved in the experiences that wreckers had with the law.

### Financial Discretion

Discretion was employed for any number of reasons, but the most common consideration was financial. In the eighteenth century, almost all prosecutions had to be initiated by the victim, at their discretion and at their expense.[66] The sheer cost of apprehending suspects and the ensuing litigation could prove impractical for those who had already suffered loss through shipwreck. Consequently, the victim's first avenue of discretion was to choose whether or not to begin an investigation; it is likely that most did not.[67] Those who decided to institute proceedings had to be ready to incur monetary losses, for complications could increase the costs beyond the value of the goods recovered. Two cases are illustrative of the situation that the victims faced and the costs incurred to bring the plunderers to justice. The first concerns the East India Company, with the loss of *Albemarle* in 1708, and the second involves a smaller conglomerate of French ship and cargo owners, represented by Capt. Jean François Martinot, after the wreck of *La Marianne* in 1763.

After the *Albemarle* went aground on the south Cornish coast near Polperro, the East India Company resolved to punish individuals who plundered its lading, especially 'those of any figure or Substance', and thus they set into motion the required procedures, which illustrate the difficulties of legal recourse.[68] They had to request the Lord Chief Justice's Warrant, which would authorise seizure of any wrecked goods beyond parish and county boundaries;

---

[65] Peter King, *Crime, Justice and Discretion in England, 1740–1820* (Oxford, 2000), 1.
[66] Clive Emsley, *Crime and Society in England, 1750–1900* (London, 1996), 178; J.M. Beattie, *Crime and the Courts in England, 1660–1800* (Oxford, 1986), 36.
[67] See King, *Crime, Justice and Discretion*, 20; Taylor, *Crime, Policing and Punishment*, 109.
[68] East India Company [IOR] E/1/198; James Derriman, 'The Wreck of the *Albemarle*', *Journal of the Royal Institution of Cornwall*, new series II, 1, pt 2 (1992), 128.

apply to the High Court of Admiralty for a commission to search and seize any wrecked goods that had been hidden; and enquire of Customs and Excise regarding duties on the salvaged goods. Delays occurred because of unclear applications and changes in personnel in the Wreck Commission. With each setback, the costs of the enquiry mounted. The managers of the East India Company ordered that the prosecutions should commence against 'the Persons concerned in Plundering the Comp[as] goods in Cornwall against whom there is Sufficient evidence'.[69] Despite their intentions, however, all attempts to prosecute came to nought. Numerous individuals were named and threatened with legal action, and the company managers claimed that 'they would willingly contribute to prevent the like violences in future unhappy occasions', but they 'would not pay too dear for it' in legal costs.[70] And of course, those best able to pay the fines if found guilty, such as Rev. James Cumming, the vicar of Lansallos, hid behind the patronage of Bishop Jonathan Trelawney, brother to the Vice-Admiral.[71] Hence, the East India Company's attempts to capture and punish the plunderers failed and cost the company more than it would have recovered.

The second case involves the wreck of the French vessel *La Marianne*, which ran aground near Perranzabuloe on the north Cornish coast in September 1763. Capt. Martinot sent a petition to the Crown seeking restitution, claiming that he and his crew had been prevented by the local populace from salvaging his cargo as it came ashore, that they had 'hurried the Crew away from the Shore' and then plundered the cargo, including an uninsured chest of 3070 Spanish dollars.[72] He also asserted that he and his crew were stripped of their clothes.[73] The Secretary of State responded that 'should it appear that the poor man was ill-treated, the Solicitor of the Treasury shall prosecute the offenders at His Majesty's expense, not only for satisfaction, but to make such examples of the offenders as shall be adequate to an offence so contrary to justice and humanity'.[74] Unfortunately, for Martinot this did not happen to his satisfaction. He remained in England for the two years of the investigation, during which the king requested the local magistrates to proceed. Goods worth £556 were recovered. The Treasury did not pay for any prosecutions as promised, much less for the salvage expenses; the costs came

---

[69] IOR B/49, Minutes of Court Managers, 2 March 1708/09, 425; Derriman, 'Wreck of the *Albemarle*', 139.

[70] IOR E/1/198, Woolley to Wright, Addis, etc., 30 December 1708, 99–101; Derriman, 'Wreck of the *Albemarle*', 137.

[71] Derriman, 'Wreck of the *Albemarle*', 137.

[72] T 1/450–31, H.S. Conway to the Lord's Commissioners of the Treasury, Enclosure, 15 January 1766.

[73] Petition of John Francis Martinot, PP, *Calendar of Home Office Papers of the Reign of George III, 1760–65* (London, 1878–91), 447.

[74] Earl of Halifax to Lord Edgcumbe, 27 December 1764, No. 1463, in *Calendar of Home Office Papers of the Reign of George III, 1760–65*, 448.

from Martinot's pocket. In the end, he was over £300 in debt. In answer to his complaints of exorbitant salvage charges, the Treasury stated that 'it was true' but since 'the Goods, having been dispersed all over the Country, the collecting and bringing them to a proper place of Sale was necessarily attended with a very great Expence'.[75] Martinot was thus awarded £400 for his pains with the rejoinder that a precedent for indemnification payments should not be set for plundered shipwrecks.[76] Just like the East India Company's experience with the plunderers of the *Albemarle*, the costs incurred outweighed the benefits of investigation and prosecution. If both the East India Company and a merchant backed by the British Government found there was no cost benefit to prosecution, smaller conglomerates of shipping and cargo owners would most likely decide to take their losses. Indeed, the issue of non-prosecution because of cost was a concern in relation to other crimes against property into the beginning of the nineteenth century.[77]

Customs also employed financial discretion in the decision to proceed against smugglers or wreckers indicted as smugglers. Throughout the Penzance Customs records, there are investigations of known smugglers to determine their worth. Often the reports would come back that he was 'not worth anything', or that he 'has no real Estate only what he gets as a fisher man'.[78] However, if the accused was judged to have sufficient means, and was '(to appearance) [in] good Circumstances', then he was deemed suitable for prosecution.[79] Although the records are full of indictments against smugglers, what is lacking is evidence that Customs routinely apprehended wreckers. Officers were occasionally involved in the search for wrecked goods, as in 1763 when Customs obtained a warrant from the Penzance mayor to search the homes of suspects believed to have absconded goods from a wrecked Algerian xebec.[80] But in most cases, wreckers had their goods seized as smuggled contraband, not wreck.[81] The use of discretion, however, not only favoured Customs officers, who received from their seizures more lucrative prize money which was awarded in addition to duty pay, but it inadvertently favoured the offender as well, for smuggling penalties did not include the threat of capital punishment.

---

[75] T 1/450/31–32, H.S. Conway to the Lord's Commissioner of the Treasury, enclosure, 15 January 1766.
[76] Conway to the Lords of the Treasury, 15 January 1766, in *Calendar of Home Office Papers of the Reign of George III, 1766–69*, 5. The Government also paid an indemnity to French merchants after the attack on the *Concord* of Calais, when she ran aground along the Bristol Channel. T 1/469/106–109, Lord Weymouth, re: plunder of French Vessel, 31 October 1769.
[77] Taylor, *Crime, Policing and Punishment*, 14.
[78] CUST 68/4, 13 January 1759.
[79] CUST 68/9, 20 December 1775.
[80] CUST 68/5, 17 January 1763.
[81] See CUST 68/24, 13 April 1818; CUST 68/29, 26 November 1824.

## Discretionary Rewards for Goods and Information

The *Albemarle* and *La Marianne* cases also indicate an additional means in which discretion was exercised. Rather than seeking immediate conviction, victims could choose to offer rewards for the return of the goods. Indeed, this was a common approach.[82] It was also an avenue preferred by local officials so they could enforce the law on a local, less public, basis. By posting notices and offering rewards, officials allowed the populace the opportunity to bring in goods for salvage, rather than become liable for criminal charges. Advertisements were often taken out in local papers, or handbills were attached to prominent locations such as at the Customs House. Christopher Wallis, a Helston attorney, recorded that he had consulted with the local ship's agent regarding the plundered goods of the *Hercules*, in January 1796, as they had been 'greatly dispersed',[83] and accordingly posted handbills offering salvage. This approach must have been effective, for Wallis first used it for the wreck of the *Smyrna* in 1781; he found himself heavily involved in paying out salvage to Helston people for several months afterwards.[84]

Handbills and advertisements were also used to obtain information on offenders and to entice people to inform on those involved in wrecking activities. During the *La Marianne* incident, for instance, it was announced at the Quarter Sessions at Lostwithiel in 1764 that advertisements would be placed in local papers, including the *Sherborne Mercury*, 'that a reward of twenty guineas will be paid' to anyone who would bring information regarding the plunderers, of course providing that there was a conviction.[85] This practice does not appear to be as effective as the salvage notices, although it did lead the authorities to a few suspected wreckers. Wallis employed notices for the wreck of the *John* in 1795, offering a reward for 'all informations suspecting the concealm^t of any part of the cargo'. He must have received some evidence, for he met with the ship's agent and master to advise them about the prosecution of 'several plunderers of the wreck'.[86] In 1812, the Customs collector at Padstow recorded that he had used notices and advertisements to track down those involved in the plunder of the *Magnet* near Newquay. Only two men were apprehended.[87] In 1817, likewise, in response to the harvesting of the *Resolution*, the Customs Commissioners ordered that the Penzance collector initiate an advertisement 'to be published in the Provincial Papers for the Space of a Month if so long a time shall appear necessary offering a reward of £50 for the discovery and apprehension of the Offenders to be paid on convic-

82 Emsley, *Crime and Society*, 182.
83 DJW/1/4, Journal of Christopher Wallis, 3 January 1796.
84 DJW/1/1, Journal of Christopher Wallis, 1 January 1781–12 August 1783.
85 QS/1/2/150, Quarter Sessions, Lostwithiel, 10 January 1764.
86 DJW/1/3, Journal of Christopher Wallis, 1 December 1795; 14, 15 December 1795.
87 CUST 69/1, Padstow Collector to Board, 8 January 1812.

tion'. He was also ordered to post handbills at the Customs House, public throughways, and 'the usual Public Places, and the several toll Gates in your Neighbourhood' as well as in the villages around Mount's Bay.[88] All this effort netted only one possible wrecker; the Customs solicitor had to admit that there was not enough evidence to convict him.[89]

### Prosecutorial Discretion

Magistrates or victims would also frequently determine not to prosecute because of lack of evidence, such as when William Chenhalls was accused by the preventive riding officer at St Just in 1813 of wrecking and smuggling.[90] For not only was the cost of prosecution prohibitive, but evidentiary requirements could also prove problematic. If there was enough evidence for a prosecution, then the next level of discretion would come into play: should the offender be tried? Prosecutorial discretion was enacted during summary court proceedings, usually held in the homes of local magistrates. There, preliminary hearings for felony cases were often heard and the decision made 'whether the accused should be released, dealt with informally, imprisoned for further examination, bailed, or committed to gaol to await jury trial in the major courts'.[91] In 1817, for instance, four fishermen from the parish of Sithney found themselves under summary proceedings from the local JP. They admitted that they had found a box on the beach near Loe Bar and had divided the contents amongst themselves. The JP used discretion to give the men a choice. Rather than face indictment, they swore that they would return the goods to the master of the wrecked vessel, and consequently bypassed more serious allegations.[92]

Constable John Bray of Bude, too, utilised discretion by refusing to testify against a wrecker. He wrote that:

> I would not appear against him to be the causer of hanging a man, not for all the world. If Mr. Dayman [the magistrate] intended any fine for my non-attendance, I must pay it. Then the prisoner was quitted never to do such a bould trick any more. If Hutchings and I had sworn against him he would have been hanged without any benefit of clergy.[93]

88  CUST 68/53, Penzance Board to Collector, 26 June 1817.
89  CUST 68/54, Penzance Board to Collector, 23 September 1817.
90  Emsley, *Crime and Society*, 183; CUST 68/21, J. Richards, Preventive Riding Officer St Just to Commissioners of Customs, 11 August 1813; Customs Commissioners to Penzance Collector, 24 August 1813; Penzance Collector to Board, 8 November 1813.
91  Peter King, 'The Summary Courts and Social Relations in Eighteenth-Century England', *Past and Present*, 183 (2004), 126; Norma Landau, *The Justices of the Peace, 1679–1760* (Berkeley, California, 1984), 6–8, 23–28.
92  RP/244, Case papers: taking of items washed up on Loe Bar from Wrecked Vessel, 1817. This is in keeping with the magistrate's role acting as a mediator to prevent further legal action. See Taylor, *Crime, Policing and Punishment*, 112.
93  John Bray, *An Account of Wrecks, 1759–1830 – On the North Coast of Cornwall*, ed. and transcribed by A.K. Hamilton Jenkin (Truro, 1975), 28.

Discretion also came into play in choosing the form of prosecution. In 1706, Francis Bere and his fellow merchants of Tiverton appointed George Bere of Lanherne to act as prosecutor and attorney to apprehend the plunderers of ninety bags of wool from the *William and Sarah*, which ran aground near Perranzabuloe.[94] By the following year, Bere had instituted proceedings against three men. But rather than take the case to criminal court, Bere instead pressed for penalty of fines. The three men each paid a shilling 'in full satisfaction of all such wooll as … either of them have taken or carried away….' With the payment, Bere acquitted them 'from all manner of trespass and trover for touching or concerning the said wooll'.[95]

Suing for trespass and trover was the most common method of prosecution employed for wrecking offences. In this action, 'trespass' signified that property was appropriated by individuals who had no legal claim to it. 'Trover' was defined by the eighteenth-century jurist Lord Mansfield as a 'remedy to recover the value of personal chattels wrongfully converted by another to his own use'; damages were required rather than a return of the goods.[96] Technically, the law required the offence of wrecking to be tried before judges at the assizes in criminal proceedings, but this was rarely done. Indeed, magistrates, local juries, and merchant-victims did not always agree with statutory law, and thus sought other means of seeking restitution, often using civil proceedings instead.[97] Therefore Symon Tregea, a gentleman from St Agnes, and Ralph Phillips, a yeoman, were sued in an action of trespass and trover at the Exeter Assizes for stealing wool from the *William and Sarah*. The jury assessed the total damages payable by them at £730 40s. However, because the two obviously were not the only guilty parties, and 'divers other persons beside the Defendants … have been discovered, or are verily thought to be guilty', the jury determined that the others should pay a proportionate part of the damages. Tregea and Phillips agreed to apprehend as many others as they could find. As part of their charge, they were to prosecute and collect fines from the other guilty parties, but the sum collected could not exceed £600, leaving the remainder as their share of the fine.[98] Thus the use of discretion came from the merchants and the assize court, who determined that damages

---

94  AR/15/74/1, Appointment of Francis Bere of Tiverton, Merchant to George Bere, to recover wool looted, 18 November 1706.

95  AR/15/74/2, George Bere's acknowledgement of receipt; payment for wool taken from the *William and Sarah*, 25 September 1707.

96  James Oldham, *English Common Law in the Age of Mansfield* (Chapel Hill, North Carolina, 2004), 295–297. The defendant typically entered a plea of 'not guilty', which is the reason for the action. If the verdict is for the plaintiff, usually he is awarded damages which are calculated as the value of the goods with interest, plus the costs of the proceedings. If the award is for the defendant, then he is awarded costs.

97  Emsley, *Crime and Society*, 12; King, *Crime, Justice and Discretion*, 9.

98  AR/15/75, Articles of Agreement concerning wreck at Perranzabuloe, 7 October 1707.

were more likely to be repaid than if the offenders were sentenced under criminal proceedings.

Even during the height of the 'Bloody Code', when wrecking was a capital offence, merchants and magistrates would rather draw up actions of trover against wreckers than force them into criminal court. This is apparent from the journals of Christopher Wallis when he, along with the agent of the wrecked *John*, agreed in 1796 to draw up an action of trover against offenders who had 'plundered', but more likely harvested, goods from the wreck. Indeed, this action occurred after Wallis and the ship's agent had 'consult[ed] on the great plunder made thereon, looking into the wreck acts & Laws, and drawing notice for the plunderers to bring in the goods'.[99] The option of trespass and trover was thus deemed an important alternative to criminal action, which would force the accused into the corridor leading towards capital punishment, an option that few wished to pursue.[100] By taking this route, local magistrates refused to treat wrecking as a capital offence, and illustrated the ways in which 'local decision-makers refused to enforce a ruling that went against their sense of justice, and thus remade the law at a local level'.[101] The Cornish experience is a key example showing the importance of localities in shaping law. It illustrates that law in practice rarely reflected law as written in the statute books. Rather, common law, custom, and local practices served to counteract the much harsher statutory law, and were just as important for the English legal system as anything coming out of Westminster.[102]

## Discretion and the Death Penalty

Finally, the last 'room' and opportunity for discretion came for offenders who had been convicted in criminal court and were awaiting punishment. The option for pardoning the accused lay in the hands of either the assize judge or the monarch by petition through the Secretary of State.[103] Indeed, the government had never proposed that everyone convicted of a capital offence be executed. Rather, situated in the criminal justice system was means that 'not only emphasised the discernment and magnanimity of the ruling elite but also added to the sense of terror as no one could be certain who would be selected to fulfil the sacrificial role'.[104] For those escaping death, their sentence was usually transmuted by pardon to hard labour or transportation, depending on the era in which they were tried.

99  DJW/1/3, Journal of Christopher Wallis, 23 January 1796.
100  Taylor, *Crime, Policing and Punishment*, 111; Beattie, *Crime and the Courts*, Chapter 9.
101  Peter King, *Crime and the Law in England, 1750–1840: Remaking Justice from the Margins* (Cambridge 2006), 7.
102  King, *Crime and the Law*, 8–11, 19, 21–22.
103  King, *Crime, Justice and Discretion*, 297.
104  Taylor, *Crime, Policing and Punishment*, 127.

Thus far, records, although unclear show that only three individuals were executed for wrecking, one in Cornwall (William Pearce in 1767) and two in Wales in 1775 and 1782.[105] Pearce had many local supporters; requests for his pardon were sent to London via Humphrey Morice, the MP for Launceston. Morice wrote that 'the people of this neighbourhood are now more anxious than ever that [Pearce] be saved ... It is very much owing to their having being persuaded that he is not guilty, and that the witnesses on the trial were perjured.' Morice argued that since Pearce was 'above fourscore years, and condemned for stealing rope from the wreck of a ship' he 'should have the same mercy from His Majesty that the other convict has had from the Judge'.[106] While the Under Sheriff of Cornwall on behalf of the 'poor unfortunate old man' sent an additional petition, the king refused to grant mercy.[107] Although pardoning studies have found that age was often a mitigating circumstance and thus a major reason for pardoning, Pearce was not so lucky.[108]

Unfortunately we do not know which ship Pearce was found guilty of plundering, nor do we know much about the crime he committed. If his crime, that he had stolen rope from a wreck, was as asserted, then under the act of 26 Geo. II he would not necessarily have been given the death sentence. That particular punishment was reserved for those who had used violence to attack a ship. But it is apparent that Pearce was not tried for plundering the ship in this manner. Rather the opinion denying his pardon explains further why he was to be executed:

> In some respects the prisoner was not so criminal as others who were not brought to justice ... As there were many common people in court, the Judge took the opportunity of inveighing very warmly against so savage a crime, and of declaring publicly that no importunities whatsoever should induce him to reprieve the criminal ...[109]

Pearce was executed as an example to the rest of the population, rather than for any particular severity of his crime. The only clue we have to the case is

---

[105] John Parry, 'a person of fortune', was executed at Shrewsbury in 1775 for plundering the wreck of the *Charming Jenny* on the coast of Anglesey in 1773. *Gentleman's Magazine*, 45 (1775), 202; *Annual Register* (1774), 148–149, 113–114; (1775), 113–114; Geoffrey Place, 'Wreckers: The Fate of the *Charming Jenny*', *Mariner's Mirror*, 76, no. 2 (1990), 167–168. A farmer 'of some considerable property' near Cardiff, perhaps Parry, was executed at Hereford for plundering a wreck in Glamorganshire in 1775: *Annual Register* (1775), 155; and in 1782, John Webb was executed at Hereford for having plundered a Venetian ship on the Glamorganshire coast: *Annual Register* (1782), 219.

[106] Humphrey Morice to Lord Shelbourne, 4 September 1767, *Calendar of Home Office Papers*, 184. The other convict was condemned for sheep-stealing, but his sentence was transmuted to transportation.

[107] Lord Shelbourne to Humphrey Morice, 30 September 1767, *Calendar of Home Office Papers*, 187–188.

[108] King, *Crime, Justice and Discretion*, 303.

[109] Criminals. Reports, 1767 in *Calendar of Home Office Papers*, 251.

found in a religious tract by Rev. James Walker. Walker suggests that although Pearce was an 'honest farmer', he was executed not for stealing 18 pounds of cotton, but as 'an Accessory in plundering the Ship, whose Cables were cut, and she made a Wreck of as soon as the sailors had left her'.[110]

Despite the severity of the law, there were few convictions for wrecking. Even indictments did not increase until later in the nineteenth century, when the penalty for wrecking was downgraded to transportation, and later, under the Merchant Shipping Act, to fines. Although there were threats, 'the owners of the Ship and Cargo are determined to prosecute the principle offenders, to the utmost Rigour of the law',[111] they were rarely enacted. This is in keeping with the findings of other crime studies, which indicate that escalation of prosecutions began after the reform of criminal law and the professionalisation of trial procedures in the mid-nineteenth century.[112] Indeed, after 1837 mention of individuals and their convictions for plundering appeared with greater frequency in the newspapers.[113] Thomas Ellis senior and his son, or brother – the *West Briton* is not clear – were convicted for stealing staves from the wreck of the French ship *Le Landais*. They came before the Quarter Sessions at Bodmin on 17 October 1837, and although witnesses swore the older man was not guilty of attacking the Lloyd's agent, Richard Pearce of Penzance, the younger Ellis had no such defence. He was sentenced to death, but later received a pardon and was given transportation.[114] *The Times*, on 21 January 1843, reported that nine 'ringleaders' involved in the plunder of the *Jessie Logan* off Boscastle were apprehended. In particular, Hugh Luckey and Robert Chapman were indicted for plundering the ship and stealing cotton. They were found not guilty of the first charge, but found guilty of the second, and thus were sentenced to twelve months' hard labour. Two other men, Joseph Brown and John Boney, were indicted, but found not guilty.[115] Three years later, in 1846, twenty people were committed to Bodmin gaol for the plunder of the *Samaritan*. They were given gaol sentences of between one and four months of hard labour.[116] Twelve years later, Robert Grigg of

---

[110]   Jonas Salvage [Rev. James Walker], *A Dialogue between the Captain of a Merchant Ship and a Farmer Concerning the Pernicious Practice of Wrecking; as Exemplified in the Unhappy Fate of One William Pearce of St. Gennis, Who Was Executed at Launceston in Cornwall, Oct. 12, 1767* (London, Sherborne and Truro, 1768), 4, 17.

[111]   Wreck of the *Endeavour*, reported in the *Western Flying Post*, 19 March 1750.

[112]   Taylor, *Crime, Policing and Punishment*, Chapter 6; Beattie, *Crime and the Courts*, 36.

[113]   Systematic study of the press is needed.

[114]   *West Briton*, 20 October 1837; Clive Carter, *Cornish Shipwrecks, Vol. 2: The North Coast* (Newton Abbot, 1970), 21–22.

[115]   *The Times*, 21 January 1843, 21 March 1843; TNA ASSI 21/60, Bodmin Assizes, Western Circuit, 25 March 1843.

[116]   *The Times*, 23 November 1846; Larn and Larn, *Shipwreck Index*, n.p. Vol. 1 (London, 1995).

Padstow was convicted of stealing cargo from the wreck of the schooner *Flora*. He received just twenty-one days' imprisonment at Bodmin gaol.[117]

Circumstantial evidence drawn from the press thus indicates that the number of reported indictments and convictions increased, almost in direct relation to the lowering of the severity of the penalty and the changes in law which put the onus of prosecution onto the State. But also noticeable within the indictments are the charges. Individuals in the earlier period were brought up on charges of 'plundering' wrecks. Later the language modified to 'stealing', signifying a change in public attitude, although the offences were the same. In reality, they appropriated goods from the wreck, some ostensibly while in the act of lifesaving and salvage, rather than in the physical attack and violent plundering more common in the earlier part of the period. Thus, John Dennis, a farmer from St Gennys on the north coast, was arrested and charged with stealing rope from the wreck of the *Trio* near Crackington Haven in 1859. Although he denied stealing from the wreck while in the act of legitimate salvaging, upon search he was found to have a 34-foot piece of rope coiled around his body under his coat. He was fined double the value of the rope, one shilling, with 9s 9d expenses.[118]

The world of the early eighteenth century, which was characterised by recourse to violence, had changed into the world of Victorian bureaucracy and legal authority, made visible to the wreckers of Cornwall by the increased presence of the Coastguard and of a more stringent, state-controlled criminal justice system. Nevertheless, even earlier, small contingents of law enforcement officers were successful in protecting wrecks from violent attacks. Their very success shows mediation and restraint on the part of those who gathered at the site of shipwreck throughout the eighteenth and nineteenth centuries. Indeed, most shipwrecks were not physically attacked despite fears on the part of those in authority, although they were harvested when goods washed ashore.

Mediation, too, was shown in the legal processes involving wrecking offences, which were typical of the system of discretion also utilised for other crimes in eighteenth- and early nineteenth-century England. What had developed as a popular myth that Cornish communities would close ranks to protect wreckers from the law, and was used as evidence of Cornish particularism, is rather more prosaic. Similar patterns of localism, with centrality of magistrates and their summary courts, were found in areas throughout England, and were an important component in the workings of the criminal justice system.[119] Indeed, summary courts were 'the arena in which the vast majority of the population experienced the law ... these courts would have a much

---

[117]  Larn and Larn, *Shipwreck Index*, n.p.
[118]  Larn and Larn, *Shipwreck Index*, n.p.
[119]  King, *Crime and the Law*.

more formative impact on the everyday lives of the inhabitants and on their attitudes to the law than events that occurred in the assizes town'.[120] Thus despite the punitive punishments required by statutory law and the mandate that they be tried in criminal court for felony, country people rarely had the experience of the law on that level. Rather they were given many options through the mechanism of the discretionary justice system with its attendant lack of prosecutions. Inadvertently, the system allowed them to maintain their belief in their right to harvest because of the contradictory legal discourses about wrecking.

[120] King, 'Summary Courts', 128.

# 7

# Lords of the Manor and their Right of Wreck

*to the use of the Lord of the Franchise*

I<small>N</small> 1835, western Cornwall saw the death of one of the great scions of the local indigenous gentry, Francis Basset of Tehidy, Baron de Dunstanville. Dunstanville's funeral procession took twelve days, travelling from London to Tehidy, and the hearse 'plumed, with pennons bearing the Basset Arms, was drawn by plumed horses carrying velvet cloths'. Behind it were two other mourning coaches, carrying Lady Basset and Sir John St Aubyn of Clowance, the head of another great family. When the procession reached Truro, 800 tenants gathered to follow it into Tehidy. It was probably the largest, most grand funeral ever seen by the local inhabitants. At least 20,000 people were believed to have attended the final interment, and a large monument was erected on top of the highest hill in the area, Carn Brea, in Lord de Dunstanville's memory.[1] St Aubyn followed the Baron de Dunstanville in death four years later, and was himself the subject of a magnificent funeral. Rather than simply being a performance to exemplify the superior authority of the gentry, the funerals also signified something different:

> perhaps in the grandeur of their funeral ceremonies, the mourners sensed they were burying something more than two individuals. They were burying the apogee of a social system. The period of mourning would be a long one, respect for the dead would give illusions of comparable power and influence for decades to come …[2]

The funerals can be seen as a symbolic turning point in Cornish social history; the influence of the Bassets and St Aubyns was waning. Another great Cornish family, the Arundells of Lanherne, had already lost prominence after 1752 when they began to sell off their Cornish estates.

---

[1]  Michael Tangye, *Tehidy and the Bassets: the Rise and Fall of a Great Cornish Family* (Redruth, 1984, 2002), 43–44.
[2]  John G. Rule, 'The Labouring Miner in Cornwall, c. 1740–1870: A Study in Social History' (unpublished Ph.D. thesis, University of Warwick, 1971), 207.

Few studies mention the role of the gentry as lords of the manor with the right of wreck, and of those, most concentrate on the pre-modern period. In more contemporary works, the lord of the manor is little commented upon.[3] One of the few treatments is that of Victorian journalist Cyrus Redding, who included an attack on privilege in his travel and history narrative. Writing in 1842 at the height of the reform movement in wreck law, Redding sought to absolve the guilt of the coastal populace of more violent plundering, just as he wished to explain that they 'were taught by a claim of some lord of the manor in a former time' to plunder vessels or to take any wreck that appeared on the shore. He argued that: 'When an example of this sort of plunder was anciently set by the lord, it was no wonder if the serf availed himself of the same immorality, standing more in need of its produce.'[4] In Redding's mind, the lords were unscrupulous examples, and hence were more accountable for the plundering of wrecks than were the 'country people'. Bert Cowls agreed. After citing a story whereby 'Squire' Penrose and Samuel Coode, lord of the manor at Methleigh, resorted to violence over a wreck at Porthleven in 1743, he censured that 'such behaviour from the squires and magistrates was not calculated to set a good example to the poor miners'.[5] Although the landlords did not occupy a dominant place in the wrecking myths, their representation situates them as being as corrupt as, and perhaps even more dissolute than, the wreckers, since they should have known better. Here we have the development of a myth whereby the commoners are the victims of disingenuous landlords, because they were led astray into the illegal world of wrecking.

These assessments do little to illuminate the relationship manorial lords had with their tenants, or indeed with each other. Nor do they clarify the role and responsibilities manorial lords had in wreck matters in general. The relationships were much more complex; they were accommodating, adversarial, and they were long-standing. They were also based on custom which continued into the beginning of the nineteenth century.

It has been argued that the weak manorial system in Cornwall, as compared to other areas of England, allowed for 'individualistic and independent aspects of Cornish behaviour', which meant that 'differences between social groups were never as clearly marked as elsewhere'.[6] This independence is credited

---

3    See Charles Henderson, *Essays in Cornish History*, ed. by A.L. Rowse and M.I. Henderson (Oxford, 1935; reprinted, Truro, 1963); Clive Carter, *Cornish Shipwrecks*, Vol. 2: *The North Coast* (Newton Abbot, 1970), 57; A.K. Hamilton Jenkin, *Cornwall and its People* (Newton Abbot, 1970), 45–48. Even John Rule leaves out the role of the lord of the manor in 'Wrecking and Coastal Plunder', in Douglas Hay, Peter Linebaugh, et al., *Albion's Fatal Tree: Crime and Society in Eighteenth-Century England* (London, 1975).
4    Cyrus Redding, *An Illustrated Itinerary of the County of Cornwall* (London, 1842), 187–188.
5    Bert Cowls, *'Looking Back to Yesterday': Bygone Days in a Cornish Fishing Village* (Helston, 1982), 48.
6    Arthur C. Todd and Peter Laws, *The Industrial Archaeology of Cornwall* (Newton Abbot, 1972), 214; Edwin Jaggard, *Cornwall Politics in the Age of Reform, 1790–1885* (London, 1999),

as a reason for less deference on the part of the commoners and thus less power and control over commoners on the part of the gentry.[7] And yet, the gentry exerted tremendous influence not only in local proceedings as magistrates, where they employed discretion in wrecking cases, but also in their role as lords of the manor holding rights to wreck. Although not technically 'wreckers' in the contemporary popular sense – gentry were notably absent in the dock at criminal courts – their activities sometimes crossed the border into wrecking. But they also had an important function in legitimate salvage. Thus the lords of the manor inhabited a littoral zone between legal and illegal wrecking; they were also involved in a complex relationship with their tenants, who occupied the same zone.

The Arundells, the Bassets, and the St Aubyns, together with the Duchy of Cornwall and a few other lesser gentry, such as the Penroses, Coodes, Prideaux-Brunes, and Rashleighs, controlled wreck rights along the entire Cornish coast. The Arundells of Lanherne held the great manors including Connerton and the Hundred of Penwith, considered the largest manor in Cornwall from 1086 until the mid-eighteenth century; Lanherne, their Cornish seat; and Carminowe, Winnianton, and Methleigh. These lands, as the Breage vicar Hugh Coulthard lyrically explained, came to the Arundells peacefully: 'the pathway of the Arundells to greatness lay not so much by the way of the tented field as along the flowery paths of successful match-making.'[8] With these acquisitions, the Arundell manorial rights extended around the Cornish coast from St Ives Bay in the north, around Land's End and the Penwith Peninsula, to Mount's Bay and the west coast of the Lizard Peninsula on the English Channel. In geographical terms, then, they claimed rights to wreck along some of the most dangerous and shipwreck-laden areas of Cornwall.

Other parts of the western Cornish coast were held by the Bassets of Tehidy and the St Aubyns of Clowance, though by no means were their holdings as extensive as the Arundells'. The manor of Tehidy on the north coast included rights of wreck between Portreath Island and the Gwithian River (now the Red River), which enters St Ives Bay south of Godrevy. To complicate matters, Tehidy lay within the Penwith Peninsula, the territory of the Arundells; hence there was much conflict between the two over wreck and boundaries.[9] Until the Civil War, the Bassets also held the prominent land- and sea-mark of St Michael's Mount, located in the centre of Mount's Bay on the south coast, but because of their Royalist leanings, they were forced

---

18. Unfortunately most of the work on the manorial system in Cornwall is from the medieval period. More eighteenth- and nineteenth-century studies are needed.

7    Jaggard, *Cornwall Politics*, 12.

8    H.R. Coulthard, *The Story of an Ancient Parish: Breage, with Germoe, With Some Account of its Armigers, Worthies and Unworthies, Smugglers and Wreckers, its Traditions and Superstition* (Camborne, 1913), 116.

9    Tangye, *Tehidy*, 52.

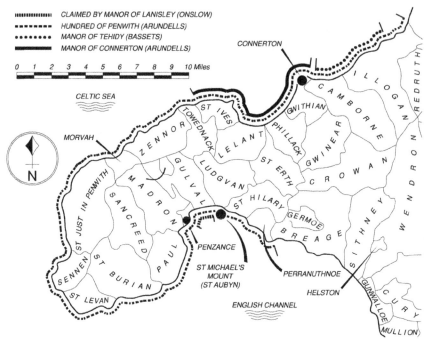

Map 5. Wreck Royalties in Western Cornwall.

to sell it to the Parliamentarian St Aubyn family, who have held it into the twenty-first century.[10] (See Map 5)

The remaining major landowner within Cornwall who held wreck rights was the Duke of Cornwall. The Duchy lands consisted of seventeen demesne manors scattered throughout Cornwall. Also included were several boroughs and towns, including the important towns of Trematon, Saltash, Tintagel, Grampound, Helston, Camelford, Lostwithiel, Launceston, and Liskeard. The Duchy lands encompassed the privileges of 'ancient and new customs' including wrecks, on all parts of the Cornish coast that had not been expressly granted by the Crown.[11]

The issues surrounding the Arundell's right to wreck illustrate some of the more contentious aspects of wrecking history, but they also demonstrate the interrelationships lords of the manor had with the coastal populace. The Arundell claim traced back to the original grant and letters patent for their title to the manor of Connerton and Hundred of Penwith, conferred by

---

[10] Tangye, *Tehidy*, 52; Philip Payton, *Cornwall: A History* (Fowey, 2004), 148; Diana Hartley, *The St Aubyns of Cornwall, 1200–1977* (Chesham, Buckinghamshire, 1977), 11.

[11] John Hatcher, *Rural Economy and Society in the Duchy of Cornwall, 1300–1500* (Cambridge, 1970), 5. Because of the complex history of manorial wreck rights in Cornwall, only a few gentry will be focused upon. They are by no means the only families who maintained wreck rights, though they are the most visible.

Henry II (r. 1154–89). The grant laid out the borders of their territory, which extended 'so far out into the Sea from any part of the Land as a Man may discern a Hamborough Barrell', and bestowed the territory as a liberty – a territorial jurisdiction that gave them legal control rather than the Crown – and granted manorial 'royalties', rights to hunt, shoot, or fish, as well as to profit from resources found within the manors, such as the right of wreck. But those royalties, however, were given in general terms. They were not identified explicitly, which would involve the Arundells in much litigation.[12] Although their patent did not *expressly* state their rights to wreck, legal opinions and court cases from the medieval period to the eighteenth century verified their right by virtue of the legal principle of prescription, which stipulated that rights to wreck had been practised throughout the manor and liberty of Connerton and Penwith continuously from 'time immemorial', that is, from 1189. In keeping with their jurisdiction over the liberty, the Arundells also kept manorial courts, and held pleas in actions of trespass and trover – actions necessary to maintain their claim through prescription.[13] Evidentiary requirements such as affidavits from the oldest manorial tenants and others who brought in shipwrecked goods to the lords of the manor were also considered important in proving the Arundells' right to wreck in the various challenges that they experienced, and thus were crucial as part of the legal proceedings. Indeed, most of the Arundells' manorial records concerning wreck are extant for this very reason.

### Tenant–Landlord Relationships and the Rights of Wreck

The relationship between manorial lords and their tenants regarding rights to wreck was for the most part interdependent and reciprocal. Indeed, the landlords' rights of wreck were in many ways dependent on the tenants' acceptance of their authority.[14] Tenants observed a long-standing practice of conveying wreck to manorial lords in return for a moiety; they were also witnesses whose testimony was critical in verifying their lord's wreck rights in inter-manorial, Admiralty, and Crown conflicts; and they even occasionally found themselves physically at the centre of wreck disputes. The landlord–tenant affiliation was also sporadically adversarial: tenants absconded with wreck for their own use, and were thus in defiance against landlords.

---

[12] CRO X/112/151, Case Papers, rights of wreck, manor of Conarton, [sic] 1753. The Arundell claims for flotsam collected offshore have been used as precedent for wreck law cases in the twenty-first century. Michael Williams, Lecturer of Law, University of Wolverhampton, and legal counsel to the Receiver of Wreck, personal correspondence, May 2005.
[13] CRO X/112/151, Case Papers, right of wreck, manor of Conarton, 1753.
[14] Paul Griffiths, Adam Fox, and Steve Hindle, eds, *The Experience of Authority in Early Modern England* (London and New York, 1996), Introduction, 5.

At the centre of the landlord–tenant relationship was the lord's steward, bailiff, or agent. Men were appointed from diverse localities to act as agents for wreck, which was particularly critical for the widely dispersed mano-rial lands that were characteristic of Cornwall. Indeed, most tenants dealt with the landlord's agents or stewards rather than the landlord himself. In 1714, for instance, John Stevens of St Ives was appointed by the Arundells to take up wreck near St Ives and 'on the Coastes two miles about'.[15] Then, in 1725, John Arundell of Lanherne legally appointed as special agents James Keigwin, Francis Paynter, John Oliver, James Millet of St Just, and Thomas Treluddra of Marazion, along with the continuing appointment of John Stevens of St Ives. In 1729, the Arundells also appointed Edward Penrose of Penrose and Henry Polkinhorne of Helston as agents for the manor of Winnianton,[16] and in 1796 Mr Thomas Arundell of Sithney was appointed for Carminowe and Winnianton.[17] Each of these agents was requested to appoint deputies to assist them, all to cover the territory within the manor of Connerton and Hundred of Penwith. The territory was extensive: it ranged through the parishes of Paul, Madron, St Ives, Towednack, Sennen, Leland, Gwithian, Feock, Perranuthnoe, St Hillary, Ludgvan, St Eval, St Earl, St Just, and Morvah in Penwith. The agents were requested to 'aid each other with full power to each of them severally in the Absence of Each other to do Act and do what Shall be Necessary throughout'. They were also to 'from time to time render their Severall Acco^ts of all Wracks Waifes and Strays … that shall happen and come into their Severall custodys'.[18] The descendants of several of these stewards, including the Paynters and Penroses, eventually became lords of the manor in their own right, by purchasing Arundell lands and by pursuing their own royal grants.

Other landholders also appointed agents to control wreck although their lands were not so extensive. The Rev. Charles Prideaux-Brune, as lord and proprietor of the manor of Padstow, appointed Nicholas Hey, a 'Country Yeoman', as his agent in 1795, stating that Hey was not only to take up wreck but also to use Prideaux-Brune's name 'to ask demand sue for and recover' any wreck which is 'taken up or found at any time or times by any person or persons whomsoever, yielding paying and allowing to the Salvors of such Wreck, such part or parts thereof or such Sum or Sums of Money in lieu thereof as by Law they shall be entitled to have'.[19] Thus the agents had multiple duties: they were to be present at wrecks to handle salvage issues and to protect them from

[15] AR/15/79, Authorisation to take wreck, 19 January 1713/14.
[16] AR/3/307, Appointment of Edward Penrose and Henry Polkinhorne as agents, 1729.
[17] AR/15/193, Appointment of Mr Thomas Arundell to seize wrecks, 1769. It is unclear whether this particular appointment was made official, as the document is a rough draft, and is neither signed, sealed, nor notarised.
[18] AR/13/11, Appointments of agents to take up wreck for Arundells, 1725–26.
[19] PB/5/141, Letter of Attorney to take wrecks, manor of Padstow, 1795.

plunder; claim any wreck that might wash ashore; assign and pay individuals to bury shipwreck victims; and pay out any expenses which might accrue such as 'land-leave' from salvage activities, transportation costs, and 'cellarage' of the salvaged materials.[20] The appointment of agents and their dependability in carrying out their duties was crucial for the optimal working of the land-lord–tenant relationship, as well as for lords of the manors to maintain wreck rights. For in most cases, the agents or stewards were critical to prove 'usage'; this was most vital for the Arundells of Lanherne as we shall see.

The interrelationships of the lord of the manor, the manorial steward, and the local tenants in regards to wreck can be further illuminated by examining manorial court records of the eighteenth century. Of special interest are the court presentments for the Arundells' manor of Connerton, extant from 1704 to 1759.[21] The manorial court was held every October, and all presentments for the preceding year were duly recorded by the steward. Presentments included reports of tenants who had died, or who were fined for such 'misbehaviours' as pulling down hedges, encroaching on one another's lands, sinking a shaft without permission, or not utilising the manorial mill. But most enlightening are the presentments for wrecked items brought in by the tenants. Although the figures are rough – in some years the manorial court may not have been held and the data mostly concerns Penwith – some conclusions can be made. There were a few years where no wreck was presented, yet other years show a large amount of activity, which is in accordance with the overall capricious pattern of shipwreck. Indeed, during the fifty-five-year period analysed, only twenty-five years showed some presentments and thus some income from wreck. There was no wreck presented at all for thirty years, and thus no income. Hence, it illustrates that profit from wreck, whether for the lord of the manor or for those who harvested wreck 'for their own use', was unpredictable because of the vagaries of weather and shipping activity.[22]

By far the most common items presented were hogsheads of wine and brandy, followed by paraphernalia of the ship's structure and fittings – the boats, sails, masts, yards, rigging, pumps, ropes, cables, anchors – and cargoes of butter, iron, and beer. The presentments reveal that tenants were handing over wrecked items to the bailiff in return for a moiety of either the value or

---

[20] Land-leave was a prescribed payment to the lord of the manor whose lands the salvors had to cross in order to access the shipwreck, to take into account any damages to the land or crops that might occur during the salvage operation. It was normally one-fifteenth moiety when figured by owners of the liberty, or a fifth part of what remained after all charges of salvage were paid, when computed according to statute. The holding of the royalty of wreck rights was not necessary to claim land-leave.

[21] See also Appendix 3.

[22] AR/15/68, Copies of Court Presentments, manor of Connerton, 1704–59. Five years had presentments for what appeared to be almost entire shipwrecks – 1708, 1709, 1712, 1726, and 1759.

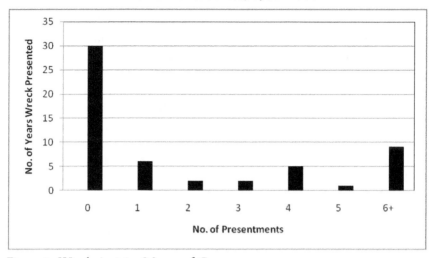

Figure 8. Wreck Activity, Manor of Connerton, 1704–59.

the goods, and that earnings could be substantial when compared to their salary as labourers and fishermen, many of whom earned less than 2s 6d a day.[23] Salvors were paid 3s 4d each for the burial of bodies, including one seaman in 1757, another seaman in 1758, and the bodies of two women and a man in 1759. A piece of mast and a small topyard were divided between Richard Bennets, Isaac Carthew, and a few others, while the other half of the moiety was retained for the lord of the manor in 1721; several casks of brandy salved by Richard Harry and Diggory Hannifer yielded £7 7s in 1756; while a piece of timber found near Sennen was sold for salvor John Jenkins for 7s 6d in 1759.[24] What is clear from the presentments is that salvors often had control of the goods and promptly divided them on the spot, thus bypassing the 'year and a day' legal restriction for defining legal wreck. This activity therefore was multivalent – it was perceived by the owners of the goods as wrecking, but believed by the salvors and the manorial lords as their customary right to salvage.

Records from the medieval and early modern period indicate that the custom of handing over wreck on the Arundell liberty was long-standing. The Penheleg manuscript, compiled when the Arundells were being challenged for their wreck rights by the Tudor state in 1580, describes twenty-nine ships that were recorded as lost on the Cornish coast near Arundell lands; twenty-one were regarded as lawful wrecks, and the cargoes were divided by the bailiff between the 'people of the country' – the finders – and Lord Arundell as 'lord of the Franchise'. Eight shipwrecks had survivors, and thus the cargo was

---

[23] CUST 68/21, Penzance Collector to Board, 5 March 1813.
[24] AR/15/68, Connerton Presentments, 1695–1759.

returned to the proprietary owners, as was required by law.[25] Medieval Duchy of Cornwall records show that this activity extended back beyond the four-teenth century, when goods were divided between the finder and the owner of the wreck rights, 'according to the right and custom of maritime law used in the said county'.[26]

The majority – 75 per cent – of the Connerton presentments show that wreck was handed over to the steward or held by others with cognisance of the steward, 21 per cent of the cases recorded that men appropriated goods 'for their own use', and in 6 per cent of the cases they took items for rival manorial lords. A shipwreck near St Ives in November 1712 illustrates all three outcomes. A part of a mast came ashore near Trenaling Cliffs and was salved by Andrew Stephens for the Arundells, the legal claimant. However, four men, all from the parish of St Ives, 'came to the place where the mast lay & with force & violence cut it up and carried it away'. St Ives fishermen were able to save five puncheons and one hogshead of white wine for Customs, but another hogshead of white wine that came ashore near Lamorna Cove was 'seized and carryed away' by Oliver Hoskyn and other tenants for Sir John St Aubyn, despite Arundell claims to wreck in the cove. A pipe of brandy and a hogshead of wine that came ashore near the St Just cliffs was 'seized' by the Gendalls and William Adams, and 'carryed away & converted for their own use & sold & disposed of a great deal afterwards'. A cask of white wine found washing ashore near St Just was divided into half on site by the salvors, who then proceeded to place the lord's moiety on horseback for delivery to the steward, but five St Just men 'came & took it off the horseback & carryed it away by force'.[27] This instance shows further evidence that wrecking, rather than being condoned by the populace and thus being deemed a social crime, was in fact hotly contested between those who believed in the rights of the lords and those who believed in their personal rights of harvest.

Although the Cornish had a reputation for plundering shipwrecks, and although George Borlase asserted (in his oft-repeated quote) that miners 'cut a large trading vessell to pieces in one tide and cut down everybody that offers to oppose them',[28] there is only one case of outright plunder recorded within the fifty-seven years of Connerton presentments. In 1726, Richard Thomas,

---

[25] P.A.S. Pool, ed., 'The Penheleg Manuscript', *Journal of the Royal Institution of Cornwall*, new series, 3, pt 3 (1959), 163–228.

[26] Duchy of Cornwall Office, 1344/45, in Marianne Kowaleski, *The Havener's Accounts of the Earldom and Duchy of Cornwall, 1287–1356* (Exeter, 2001), 162.

[27] AR/15/68, Connerton Presentments, 1695–1759.

[28] George Borlase, the steward for the manor of Lanisley, was also a shareholder in local mines. He was corresponding with his manorial lord about the passage of new shipwreck legislation. It is often taken out of context to show the wrecking propensities of the Cornish miner, but it is one of the few pieces of evidence illustrating this behaviour. 15 March 1753 in Thomas Cornish, ed., 'The Lanisley Letters: to Lt. General Onslow from George Borlase, his agent at Penzance, 1750–53', *Journal of the Royal Institution of Cornwall*, 6, pt 22 (1880), 379.

George White, and Gregory Stephens cut the cables of a ship stranded between Gwithian and Phillack, and proceeded to plunder her. There is no mention of survivors, but the account gives a substantial list of all the plunderers and approximate amounts and value of the goods carried off. John Harris stole ten shillings worth of butter; Richard Hockin took three barrels of butter and two casks of candles; John Richards and Thomas Reynolds carried off two casks of 'sandy' butter and some candles; John Hockin took 'severall parts of Goods' worth £10, while John and William Cock plundered goods to the value of £40. Richard Bennett took home 'seven or eight hundred weight of beef and butter'. Thomas Carthew also took butter, 'sixty weight' worth. The list is extensive, and for the plunderers it was a windfall, but this kind of occurrence was rare. It is unfortunate that the presentments do not indicate what forms of punishment were in store for those who pushed the boundaries of acceptable behaviour.

Manorial records verify that wreckers, even those who appropriated goods by violence, were not prosecuted by invoking statutory law. Lords of the manor had their own ways of dealing with wreckers, mainly either by fining them in manorial courts, or by suing for trover and trespass. But by the mid-eighteenth century, many manorial lords had lost their right to hold manorial courts, and were thus more dependent upon other courts of justice. Even so, they continued to use discretion as to whether or not they would prosecute a wrecker for 'detaining wreck', for this action was seen as important for maintaining their franchise. In 1813, the dowager Lady Arundell, together with Agnes Wright, sued Samuel Gilbert of Trenance because he had taken eight large barrels of butter from the royalty of Lanherne 'for his own use'.[29] They were unsuccessful. Indeed, although some lords wished to convict wreckers as an example to others to prevent wrecking, they had similar experiences to Lady Arundell. Either the wreckers were too poor to exact damages, or they disposed of the goods before they could be prosecuted.[30] Those who were apprehended and charged with wrecking were dealt with, not by gaol sentences, nor execution, nor transportation as was required by statute, but through the administering of fines and a form of public penance, such as a public apology published in the local newspaper.[31]

Despite the cases of wreck appropriation by the country people, their relationship with their manorial lords could also be advantageous. Lords of the manor and their agents were known to support the coastal populace against claims of Customs, such as in 1755 when the Arundell steward fought for the

[29] CUST 69/1, Agnes Wright, Lanherne, to John Buller, Custom House, London, n.d. February 1813.
[30] AR/15/189/4, Declaration: Basset v. Bryant, Hilary Term, 1728; W/43, H. Willyams to E. Coode, 11 November 1826.
[31] W/43, Willyams to Coode, 26 December 1826.

release of fishermen turned over to the Royal Navy as smugglers by retributive Customs officers, when they had only claimed wreck for Lord Arundell.[32] In 1768 Customs officer Thomas Davies complained that when he and other officers attempted to claim flotsam goods that had washed ashore, they were informed by the local gentleman upon whose royalty the goods were found, as well as by 'the common People', that they had no right to it.[33] And in 1778, Edward Coode also supported his tenants against charges of smuggling by informing the Customs collector that the salvors had not intended to abscond with brandy since they had given 'immediate Notice to his Agent of their having saved the Brandy to his Use'. The collector accepted Coode's statement, as 'he is a gentleman who we are well assured wd not say other then what is strictly true'.[34]

Thus for the tenants, their relationship with their lord of the manor and his steward was based on mutuality. It can be argued that this mutuality was a component of local paternalism, in that the local lords and their agents had a responsibility to look out for their tenants, especially ones who were involved in reciprocity surrounding wreck and salvage. Although some scholars would interpret this responsibility as 'ostentatious paternalism displayed by the indigenous gentry towards their social inferiors [which] enabled them to maintain a stranglehold', the domination/resistance model of social control does not quite fit.[35] Indeed, Cornish manorial tenants were typically more independent than their counterparts in the rest of England because they held more control over their holdings and were thus not as open to landlord coercion or influence. This is not to say that tenants were free from landlord control, however. A few instances of landlord coercion did occur. Sir John St Aubyn sued fisherman for allegedly fishing too close to his royalty as an act of vindictiveness when they voted for the opposing candidate[36] and witnesses were intimidated

---

[32] AR/15/175, The Case of Mr John Harvey master of a Pilchard Sloop called *Mary and Alice* & others who were concerned in saving two casks of brandy near Penzance, 27 December 1755.

[33] CUST 68/6, Thomas Davies to Penzance Collector & Comptroller, 27 April 1768. Interestingly enough, in this case the Commissioners of Customs concurred with the Lord of the Manor. CUST 68/41, Commissioners of Customs to Penzance Collector, 10 May 1768.

[34] CUST 68/11, Penzance Collector to Board, 23 February 1778.

[35] Andy Wood, 'Subordination, Solidarity and the Limits of Popular Agency in a Yorkshire Valley, c. 1596–1615', *Past and Present*, 193 (Nov. 2006), 55. See also James C. Scott, *Domination and the Arts of Resistance: Hidden Transcripts* (New Haven, 1990) and E.P. Thompson, *Customs in Common: Studies in Traditional Popular Culture* (New York, 1993), 36. Thompson would most likely not recognise these actions as paternalism, but rather a 'theatrical style' of 'gestures and postures', a 'dramatic intervention' meant to exact deference on the part of the tenants, that these are not true 'responsibilities' (46). Although his assessment would certainly be true for some cases, it cannot be all inclusive. Thompson's student John Rule acknowledges the important place of paternalism within Cornish society in the eighteenth century in 'The Labouring Miner', 199–201.

[36] Jaggard, *Cornwall Politics*, 11–12, 16.

by the Bassets during a mining claims case in 1793.[37] But these occasions are rare. This lends credence to the suggestion that Cornish tenants were involved in a reciprocal relationship not based solely on the whims of the lord, but which reflected the tenant's sense of agency and individual choice, albeit within the unequal power structure of eighteenth-century society.

### Tenant Testimony and Rivalries between Manorial Lords

Tenants and other commoners were not just involved with reciprocal salvage and wrecking activities. Their testimony, taken as evidence in civil and ecclesiastical disputes, had a crucial function in manorial society. Although their depositions were hardly non-biased accounts, and were 'heavily scripted' and mediated by the court clerks, they further illuminate the tenants' relationship with manorial lords regarding wreck.[38] By invoking collective and personal memory, they clarified manorial boundaries and customary usage, which was especially critical during litigation over wreck rights. The tenants testified that they delivered wreck to the appropriate lord of the manor. For instance, Mathew Jobe of Camborne, a seventy-year-old labourer, testified in 1684 in a case between the Arundells and the Bassets that he found a barrel of butter on the west bank of the Gwithian River. Although he was a tenant on the manor of Tehidy, owned by the Basset family, he handed the butter over to the Arundells' steward, William Willyams. Zennet Wills, another Camborne labourer, testified in the same case that sixty years previously a ship was cast ashore, spewing tallow, butter, and hides along both sides of the Gwithian River. He verified that Willyams and Stephen Pawley, the Arundell bailiff, informed the local people 'not to meddle' with any of the wreck on the east side of the river as it belonged to the manor of Tehidy, and would not be claimed by the Arundells.[39]

John Rowe of Camborne testified in 1676 that he had been involved in the salvage of many wrecks, and had brought the goods to either Sir Francis Basset or his son Sir John. In one instance, he said that he had found some bacon in a cliff near the Gwithian River. He attempted to take it to his mother-in-law for her use, but she insisted that he deliver it to Sir Francis at Tehidy as wreck. This piece of evidence is particularly telling; Rowe claims that she would not even allow him to bring it into her house, and that she 'did severall times tell him that all wrecks between Portreath & Gwythian did belong to

---

[37] A.K. Hamilton Jenkin, *News from Cornwall: With a Memoir of William Jenkin* (London, 1946), 19.
[38] Andy Wood, *The 1549 Rebellions and the Making of Early Modern England* (Cambridge, 2007), 252.
[39] HB/19/60, Basset Papers, Henderson Collection, Vol. 5.

Tehidy Manor'.[40] Thus tenants such as Rowe's mother-in-law held the rights of lords as absolute, and were essential in upholding the manorial custom by insisting that wreck was not always for their own use and a gift of 'providence'.

Although the 'country people' were occasionally accused of embezzling wreck from the lord of the manor, the activities of the stewards of rival manors were seen as more threatening. Indeed, all of the consulted Cornish manorial records and contemporary correspondence covering the right to wreck support this conclusion. Of particular note was a conflict occurring between 1745 and 1768. The Arundells found themselves embroiled in legal disputes with the new lord of the manor at Lanisley, Lt Gen. Richard Onslow, MP for Guildford, who was beginning to assert his claims to wreck through his steward, attorney George Borlase, ironically at the same time he was debating the bill which became 26 Geo. II, making wrecking a capital offence. The testimony of the Arundell tenants was crucial to prove that the Arundells held customary claims to wreck in the area over that of the recent Onslow-Borlase contingent.

The Connerton presentments indicate that in 1757 a piece of timber valued at nineteen shillings was found washed ashore 'on the lands of Dr Borlase', meaning Lanisley, by Charles Lethan and William Jelbert. (Lanisley was owned by Onslow, but as he was an absentee lord, and the Borlases were a well-known indigenous family, the local people described the land as belonging to Borlase.) However, when William Andrews demanded the moiety for Lady Arundell, he claimed that Lethan 'beat and abused him' over it, claiming that it belonged to Borlase. Two years later, a cask of brandy found near Chynadour was 'carried off by Mr Borlase' and a piece of timber salved at Morvah was claimed by Borlase's servant.[41] These actions were regarded as encroachments by the Arundells, who duly sought legal counsel and instituted proceedings against Borlase. Tenant testimony was on their side. Earlier affidavits indicate that the Arundells did, in fact, practise right of wreck at Lanisley prior to 1745. In that year Ralph Corin salved part of a mast, which was duly divided with the Arundell steward. Corin claimed that he had 'never heard of any other claim [except the Arundells'], until lately by Mr Borlase'.[42]

Depositions taken to prove prescriptive rights in 1753 also indicate the Onslow-Borlase claim was recent. Thomas Gamon, eighty-six years old from Long Rock in Mount's Bay, swore that he 'had made it his Business all his Life to follow Wrecks' but 'he had never heard of any Claim by Mr Onslow or any other Except the ffamily [sic] of the Arundells'. The depositions also made it clear that wreck was claimed by the Arundell stewards on other manors located on the coast of the Penwith Peninsula, such as the manors of

---

[40] HB/19/60, Basset Papers, Henderson Collection, Vol. 5.
[41] AR/15/68, Connerton Presentments, 1695–1759.
[42] AR/15/98, Note regarding wreckage and claim by Mr. Borlase, 1745.

Trevedson and Treen, held by Sir Richard Vyvyan; the manor of Lelant; and the manor of the Boscawens, all belonging to important indigenous gentry. As the Arundells' counsel pointed out, 'If the Lords of those Mannors were not Sensible of the Arundells right of Wreck Can it be Imagined these Gent would Suffer them to be Carried off as they were so well able to Control their right if they had any[?]'[43]

Although the Arundell agents admitted that they had not kept up with the Arundell franchise on some manors on the south coast such as St Michael's Mount, and that some wreck had been appropriated by owners of other manors against the Arundell claim, the agents insisted that they had never been lax with the manor of Lanisley. This was borne out by the local testimony. Indeed, the agents made the point that although they had originated in the area, they had never heard of any wreck rights being bestowed on Lanisley, and that:

> it is reasonably concluded that such Wrecks (if any) must have been very inconsiderable in point of value or taken off in a clandestine manner – for had it been carried away publicly as has been always done by the Arundell family when they have taken wrecks – it must have come to the knowledge of some of their agents or friends who then would have had the opportunity of making their Claim. It is therefore presumed no instance of this sort.[44]

If George Borlase took up wreck for the manor of Lanisley, he did not make the claim in the traditional, customary manner. It was also pointed out that the lord of Lanisley had not paid for the burial of shipwreck victims washed ashore on Lanisley, but that Lord Arundell had taken on the responsibility and costs.

The crux of the wreck cases fought by the Arundells in the eighteenth century was, as their steward pointed out, that Arundell rights of wreck traditionally extended beyond the boundaries of their own manors and into the territories of other manors on the Penwith Peninsula, such as Lanisley. This complex geo-political situation was triggered by the Arundells' sale of lands, though not of their wreck rights, after the family married into that of the Arundells of Wardour in Wiltshire. The Arundells had perhaps always been the envy of other local gentry for, as their attorney Charles Bowles explains, they 'must have excited the jealousies in those who under grants and confirmation of them, were considered as dependent Lords on the Lord of the Hundred [the Arundells]'. It must have been particularly galling for them that the 'casual profits from wrecks &c.' went into Arundell pockets. Thus Bowles opined that 'many have been the devices and plans proposed and practised to narrow and circumscribe' the Arundells, especially by 'usurping Lords

---

43  AR/15/147/3/8, Abstract of Mr Paynter, 1753.
44  CRO X/112/151, Case Papers, right of wreck, manor of Conarton, 1753, 7–8.

taking advantage of the supineness of the Lord of the hundred or his agents in watching their rights', and so the rival landlords 'have exercised powers which did not belong to them … the quietly taking possession of part of a wreck on some part of the coast', which 'has emboldened them to deny the legal right of the Lord of the hundred'.[45] Indeed, Lady Arundell was encouraged by numerous legal briefs to bring actions of trespass and trover against anyone who either she or her steward believed was wrongfully claiming wreck.[46]

The conflict between the Arundells and the Onslow-Borlase contingent culminated in 1759 when a vessel was wrecked on the coast near Lanisley, 'without any living Person on Board which was soon Dash'd to pieces'. The masts, ropes, and anchors were salved, valued at approximately £5 9s 6d, but were taken by George Borlase 'the Younger' and at least a dozen Lanisley tenants. The goods were stored in the 'Back Yard' of the elder Mr Borlase, although one of the tenants informed Lady Arundell's agent that he had them in his possession. Lady Arundell's bailiff, John Treluddra, attended the wreck and attempted to claim it, but 'one George Pauley one of the Salvers threatened to knock him down & with a Club struck at him'.[47] Pauley's insolence in attempting to strike Treluddra angered the Arundells' steward, Francis Paynter, but of course worse was the perceived open intransigence of Borlase in claiming wreck for the Onslows. As Paynter remarked to the Arundells' London lawyer in frustration:

> Such a Number of people as the Borlases have always [been] … ready to assist in all these kinds of Enterprizes for they are mostly in that part of the parish M[r] Onslow's Tenants & Borlase is the Steward & commands them, and really I think it's impracticable for either of us to carry off anything without we could Hire a Mob to oppose them, which I presume you wouldn't by any means think an advisable Scheme to be put into practice, for when our Country people are once Set a fighting they are not so easily Stopped in their rage, as you may imagine.[48]

By 1761, the Arundells had had enough, and resorted to the legal system rather than force to stop Borlase's threat. Francis Paynter, as steward, John Treluddra, as bailiff, and Henry Tonkin, Paynter's clerk, filed an action of trover and conversion against George Borlase the Elder and Henry Cowls in the name of Lady Arundell. Witnesses were brought to the Bodmin Assizes from parishes all around the Hundred of Penwith to give evidence. After hearing the witnesses and examining evidence, the court found the defendants,

---

[45] Charles Bowles, *A Short Account of the Hundred of Penwith, in the County of Cornwall compiled from Authentic Documents with an Appendix containing the Original Grants, Confirmations, &c.* (Shaftesbury, 1805), 6–7.
[46] AR/15/146, Opinion of R. Hussey at Temple, 3 November 1760.
[47] AR/15/146, Opinion of R. Hussey at Temple, 3 November 1760.
[48] AR/15/144/2, Francis Paynter to John Purser, Fleet Street London, 1 March 1760.

Borlase and Cowls, guilty and fined them. The cost of the trial, together with all the expenses for the witnesses, including transportation, food and board, and reimbursement for loss of time and salary, amounted to £36 4s 6d.[49]

Of course, the Arundells were not only challenged by the Onslow-Borlase contingent. They had a history of litigation with other gentry such as the St Aubyns, the Duchy of Cornwall, and the Bassets, although not quite so contentious. Around 1753, the St Aubyn lord at St Michael's Mount claimed wreck that his agents salved, and refused to hand it over to Lord Arundell. He claimed that his family had wrecks there 'from time out of mind', and used as evidence the claiming of wreck taken forty years previously. However, as the counsel for the case argued, the St Aubyns 'were mistaken' for the previous instances were shown not to support the St Aubyn claim at all; the wreck had instead been taken up at St Michael's Mount for Sir John Arundell.[50] That was not the first time the St Aubyns had challenged the Arundells. Claims by the St Aubyn family had also occurred even earlier, in 1699. In that year, John St Aubyn wrote a letter to Sir John Arundell complaining about the 'impertincy' of your officer Mr Treledron [Treluddra]', that:

> I think it convenient to acquaint you y$^t$ ab$^t$ 3 or 4 days agoe, there was a 20 Gallon Cask of vinegar thrown in by y$^e$ Sea Just under y$^e$ Mount w$^{ch}$ after my Agent had marked in my name as wreck belonging to y$^e$ Royalty, y$^r$ Officer M$^r$ Treledon made pretentions to it as belonging to you & there [illeg] for y$^e$ future to seize all y$^t$ comes in in y$^r$ name, but supposing y$^t$ his insolency makes him to exceed y$^e$ Commission w$^{ch}$ he pretends to have from you I thought it necessary to acquaint you w$^{th}$ this affair ... there is hardly any thing y$^t$ I would not try y$^e$ continuance of his freindship with unless att y$^e$ Price of a family prerogative or my honour ...[51]

Despite St Aubyn's claims and his concern for family honour, wreck rights near the Mount were legally recognised as belonging to the Arundells, which he was forced to admit. In later years, however, the Arundell interest and claims to the Mount lapsed; the St Aubyns practised wreck rights there with little challenge.

The Arundells also found themselves at odds with the Duchy of Cornwall, though for most of the period the Duchy was relatively quiet when it came to wreck claims. In 1733, a ship laden with empty casks and fish was wrecked in Mount's Bay; the goods were saved by the Arundell agents 'from being Destroy'd by the Country People', and locked in a secure cellar. The

---

[49] AR/17/29/6, Action of Trover by Lady Arundell, 29 October 1761; AR/17/29/10, Papers regarding case of Arundell v. Borlase. This action did not stop Borlase, however, as he began to press claims yet again in 1761 and 1768. Each time, the Arundells were counselled to file trespass and trover charges.
[50] CRO X/112/151, Case papers, right of wreck, manor of Conarton, 1753.
[51] AR/25/122, John St Aubyn of Clowance to Sir John Arundell at Lanherne, 31 March 1698/99.

Customs collector also placed a lock on the cellar, as was normal proceedings. However, soon after, Edward Penrose, acting as an agent for the Duke of Cornwall, claimed the wreck as property of the Duchy. The Arundells applied to the Duchy Board of Council, emphasising that they had 'by Virtue of $y^e$ $s^d$ several Grants, & an <u>uninterrupted</u> Enjoyment' laid claim to the wrecks. The board concurred; they ordered Penrose to remove the Duchy locks from the cellar with the request that the Arundells give security for the value of any claim made by the proprietor or His Royal Highness, a claim that was never pressed forward.[52] Despite this agreement, the Duchy would not be nearly so accepting a hundred years later.

The relationship between lords of the manor over wreck was not always litigious. Indeed, if they could, they preferred to work out the conflicting claims in a more 'gentlemanly fashion'. Lord Falmouth, Lord High Admiral of Cornwall, recognised the Arundell claim when he responded to a letter by Arundell agent John Knill regarding mahogany washed ashore at St Ives in February 1770. Indeed, Falmouth stated that 'Lord Arundell's right is known & has been several times Acknowledged, if the Mahogany is proved to be taken up within his right, which I apprehend is as far as a Barrel can be seen from the Shore, it is incontestable'.[53] This recognition of Arundell's offshore claims by the Admiralty would also eventually be endangered.

Gentlemanly discourse regarding wreck continued into the nineteenth century, when in 1826, Humphrey Willyams of the manor of Carnanton, near Newquay, wrote a deferential note to the Arundells' attorney, Charles Bowles, asking for 'the Favor of $y^r$ Interference in a Case of Right to Wreck'. Willyams was concerned that Lord Arundell's agent, 'young Rawlings has I think improperly interferred', after a piece of wrecked timber washed on shore underneath the cliffs of Trebulzue, Watergate Bay, on the foreshore of Carnanton. Willyams reminded Bowles that wreck had been 'seized by $y^e$ $L^d$ of this Manor as his unquestionable right – I have no Doubt there is some Error in this matter....'[54] Bowles responded in an equally polite manner, claiming that 'Lord Arundell is one of the last Persons in the World to invade the Rights of others, tho' he is desirous of maintaining his own', and asked for time to investigate the extent of the boundaries before giving Rawlings any further directions.[55] Both gentlemen proceeded to research their rights. Willyams admitted that the foreshore had once belonged to the Arundells, but he argued that was no longer the case. To soften his demand, Willyams thanked Bowles and Lord Arundell for asking after his father's health, thus

[52] ML/577, Case Paper re: right to wreck, manor of Conarton and hundred of west Penwith, 1733; AR/15/90, Memorial by Sir John Gifford, 1733; AR/15/91, Order of Duchy Council to Edward Penrose, Receiver General, to remove lock, 26 January 1733.
[53] AR/17/29/2, John Knill to Lord Arundell re: wrecks, 1770.
[54] W/43, Willyams to Bowles, 15 November 1826.
[55] W/43, Bowles to Willyams, 23 November 1826.

maintaining decorum and a sense of civility in the dispute.[56] Bowles must have concurred, for he returned his answer that Willyams had convinced him that his claim to wreck at Trebelzue 'is rock founded, and in consequence I write by this Post to Mr Rawlings to deliver up the Plank to your order, and I am glad you have enabled me to do you Justice'.[57] Thus what could have been a spiteful battle between neighbours over jurisdiction was brought to an end in a peaceful manner, without resort to litigation.[58]

What these cases suggest is that there was a great interest in either maintaining wreck rights or establishing the franchise in eighteenth- and early nineteenth-century Cornwall. However, although wreck could be profitable, especially if a particularly valuable wreck were to come ashore, the chances of this occurring were small in relation to the energy and expense put into litigation, as evidenced by Connerton's presentments. So why did wreck rights generate such activity? For those seeking entry into gentry status, the purchase of manors with their attendant use-rights constituted a move up the social scale, a 'fee for "admission into the charmed circle of English landed society"'.[59] Without land, men could not be considered gentry, no matter their wealth. Cornish society had many opportunities for social mobility; upward movement was 'far from exceptional'.[60] Additionally, there were sound economic reasons for purchasing estates; they were considered secure investments.[61] Wreck rights also afforded the new lords a possible additional income from their lands. Nonetheless, use-rights were sometimes considered 'property' to be sold, but their purchase was not open to anyone. Use-rights had value within the socio-political system as 'a particular structure of political power, influence, interest and dependency'.[62] In other words, wreck rights were not only economic; they were symbolic. They constituted traditional feudal privileges that were not tied to the land, but rather they were a form of cultural capital not necessarily available to everyone seeking entry into gentry status.

[56] W/43, Willyams to Bowles, 23 November 1826.
[57] W/43, Bowles to Willyams, 12 December 1826.
[58] See also EN/1301 for a similar case between Francis Enys of Winnianton and Mr J. Rogers, which was also resolved peacefully.
[59] Quoted in M.J. Daunton, *Progress and Poverty: An Economic and Social History of Britain, 1700–1850* (Oxford, 1995), 77.
[60] Jaggard, *Cornwall Politics*, 19. The openness of movement to landed-elite status within England as a whole has garnered much heated debate, with conclusions diametrically opposed. See H.J. Habakkuk, *Marriage, Debt and the Estates System: English Landownership 1650–1950* (London, 1994); W.H. Rubenstein, *Men of Property: The Very Wealthy since the Industrial Revolution* (London, 1981); Martin J. Weiner, *English Culture and the Decline of the Industrial Spirit, 1850–1980* (Cambridge, 1981); and Lawrence Stone and Jeanne C. Fawtier Stone, *An Open Elite? England, 1540–1880* (Oxford, 1984).
[61] Daunton, *Progress and Poverty*, 16. Peter Earle argues that land was one of the poorest forms of investment, with small returns. See his *The Making of the English Middle Class: Business, Society and Family Life in London, 1660–1730* (Berkeley, California, 1989), 152, 157.
[62] Thompson, *Customs in Common*, 25.

Hence the Arundells' litigation against those whom they found infringing upon their royalties was a necessity for social and economic reasons. But with the waning of Arundell interest in their Cornish lands, increased opportunities for gaining wreck rights on the part of newer lords opened up. The franchise, however, was not always a benefit, for it came with increasing responsibilities.

### Lords of the Manor and Responsibility for Wrecked Goods

Although commentators such as Cyrus Redding argued that the claims of the lord of the manor were based on greed for profit, and that the lord's rights should be extinguished, they overlooked an important function performed by those holding the franchise of wreck. In the eighteenth and early nineteenth centuries, manorial lords had legal responsibilities to put into safekeeping the shipwrecked goods for the requisite year and a day and to be ready to relinquish them if the legal owner appeared with positive proof of ownership. Humphrey Willyams's experiences are a case in point. As Willyams explained to an agent attempting to claim lumber that had washed ashore on the manor of Carnanton:

> With respect to $y^e$ Wreck I think I told you before $y^t$ $y^e$ $L^d$ of a Manor has no Right to give up any wreck unless $y^e$ Property is clearly identified – That not having been done within the Time specified, though the Timber was so peculiarly marked as to be easily proved. I have proceeded as in similar Cases of Wreck to divide it with the Salvors-Men. I in this or in any other instance to give up wreck merely because certain Parties laid Claim to it (& not proved their Property in it) there would always be found Some one to make such Claim & which if allowed would mainly contract $y^e$ manorial privileges and rights.[63]

Willyams had no difficulty handing over wreck if it had been claimed within the requisite 'year and a day', but in this particular case the agent of the *Spring Flower*, which had lost part of her deck load of timber, had waited over a year before contacting him.

If Willyams was pedantic on the time limits, he was even more pedantic in his insistence on positive identification of the property. This was most likely because he had purchased the manor from the Crown only six years previously.[64] Thus, Willyams was asserting his newly acquired wreck rights. His case aptly illustrates the technicalities that could be involved. When the *Kite* was wrecked at Mawgans Porth in 1833, Willyams received notification from the agent that the wreck should be delivered to Rawling's store, where a survey of the goods would be held so they could be auctioned in order to pay

[63] W/43, Willyams to T.R. Avery, 6 December 1826/n.d. January 1827.
[64] W/43, Willyams to Commissioners of Customs, 29 June 1826.

the salvage charges. Willyams was not satisfied when the spars were identified by the agent and the *Kite's* former master in front of his servant; he requested that the property be identified in front of him, or 'to the Satisfaction of any Magistrate'. He would only relinquish them 'on the written authority of the owners, to any person they may please to name'.[65] Willyams's reluctance to deliver the spars could be interpreted in two ways. Either he was hoping that his recalcitrance would ensure that he would be able to maintain possession or, more likely considering the tone of his correspondence, he took his responsibility seriously, if not overly stringently, as a new lord of the manor.

The possession of unclaimed wreck did not always guarantee a profit for the manor; it could even convey monetary loss. Manorial lords were required to pay a moiety for salvage, and progressively more throughout the period, they had to pay duty on an increasing number of goods before they could legally claim them. Indeed, duty was often demanded at the *time* of salvage, even if the wreck clearly was not profitable, much to the chagrin of the lords. This held true on at least three occasions for John Rogers, lord of the manor of Winnianton. In 1813, Customs demanded that he pay duty on three half-full hogsheads of claret that were encrusted with barnacles. Rogers wanted to sell the wine, which was already 'in a perished state', and keep the funds in deposit in the King's Chest at Penzance until the requisite period had lapsed.[66] The Customs Commissioners, however, informed him he had to abide by the act of 52 Geo. III c. 59, which authorised the wine to be kept in his possession, but he had to give security for the payment of the duties.[67] Rogers was not pleased with the order; he had already paid salvors £18, and felt that by the end of the year, the wine would be worthless. He argued that the wine was 'not worth one third of the Duties at present', and requested that it be sold duty free to pay the salvage expenses. In this case, he did not even wish to keep possession of the wine, but instead wanted Customs to remove it from his cellar. He explained, 'I shall be ready to give up my part for nothing. It will be impossible for me to give security for the Payment of the Duties as I should be a very considerable loser instead of a gainer as I ought to be.'[68]

In this case, Rogers found his franchise of wreck to be an inconvenience. He encountered a similar problem in 1816, when thirty-nine casks of red wine, ten boxes of French soap, and one pack of wool was found floating near Gunwalloe, within his liberty. He duly paid salvage immediately, the salvors 'being poor Men with large families'. Upon the expiry of the 'year and a day',

---

[65] W/43, John Tredwen to Humphrey Willyams, with response from Willyams, 30 March 1833; John Tredwen to Humphrey Willyams, with response from Willyams, 23 May 1833.
[66] CUST 68/21, John Rogers of Penrose to Commissioners of Customs, 15 March 1813.
[67] CUST 68/21, Penzance Collector to John Rogers, Penrose, 9 April 1813.
[68] CUST 68/21, J. Rogers, Penrose, to Commissioners of Customs, 26 April 1813.

Rogers applied to Customs to sell the wine duty free to recoup his expenses for salvage, the 'wine being Weak, Sour & of low quality, & as well the Soap in a perishing State'.[69] He included the bill of charges, showing that he had paid thirty-two named individuals, with 'sev$^l$ o$^r$ persons for their labour & assistance with Cart & Horses in bringing the s$^d$ Wine from the Beach and High water mark', for 'Bread Meat & Drink sent to the Salvors during the Nights', as well as salvage charges paid to Customs officers for their assistance and attendance, for a total of £258 2s 6d, quite a substantial sum.[70] He was eventually able to sell some of the goods, but Customs still expected duty on what was not sold, leaving Rogers with a negative total. This would not be the last time, either, and it was by no means an exceptional case.[71] These experiences illustrate the sheer costs involved to the lords of the manor who took their responsibility of wreck and salvage seriously, for they had to be conscientious to their tenant-salvors and to the law. The cases also show that wreck rights were not always profitable, nor was wreck washing ashore on a manor always welcome.

The interrelationships between manorial lords, their agents and tenants were thus complex, based on mutuality as well as antagonism. Salvage customs and wrecking customs were practised side-by-side, occupying that littoral zone between legality and illegality for both lord and tenant alike. Although the lords of the manor occasionally had difficulties with tenants and local peoples in appropriating wreck, and some of the coastal populace refused to recognise the lord's right, they did not always 'loathe each other', as is asserted in popular history.[72] They may have felt that way about Customs officers, a shared foe. Indeed, there is little evidence within the records to suggest the coercive, dominating relationship between lords and commoners such as that suggested by the bi-polar domination/resistance model of E.P. Thompson, James Scott, and Keith Wrightson, at least in regard to wreck and salvage.[73] However, these reciprocal connections underwent modification during the Victorian period, with the tightening of governmental control and bureauc-

[69] CUST 68/23, Petition of John Rogers, Esq, Lord of the Manor & Liberty of Winnianton, to the Commissioners of Customs, 15 February 1817.

[70] CUST 68/23, Charges of Salvage from John Rogers, Esq, forwarded to Commissioners of Customs from the Collector and Comptroller of Customs, Penzance, 18 February 1817.

[71] CUST 68/23, Rogers to Commissioners of Customs, London, 21 April 1817. See also the experience of Edward Coode of Methleigh in 1834: CUST 68/32, 13 February; John Glasson, Agent to the Lord of the Manor of Merthyr [Methleigh], to Commissioners of Customs, 13 February 1834, 20 March 1834.

[72] Bella Bathurst, *The Wreckers: A Story of Killing Seas, False Lights and Plundered Ships* (London, 2005), 232.

[73] Thompson, *Customs in Common*, Chapter 2; Scott, *Domination and the Arts of Resistance*; Keith Wrightson, 'The Politics of the Parish in Early Modern England', in Griffiths et al., eds, *The Experience of Authority*, 10–46.

ratisation. Indeed, in the instance of wreck and salvage, what occurred for lord and commoner alike was the expropriation of customary salvage rights; their mutuality concerning wreck underwent complete transformation. For most, their relationship ceased to exist.

# 8

# Wrecking and Centralised Authority

*the Lord of the Manor and the Salvors were not*
*entitled to any benefit*

ON 27 December 1755, John Harvey, master of the pilchard sloop *Mary and Alice*, along with his crew of eight, put to sea from Penzance pier to cast their nets. Shortly beyond the pier, they spotted two casks of brandy, which they pulled into their boat. All of a sudden, eight Customs officers burst on the scene; they 'bore down upon 'em & order'd them to bring to'. With 'horrid Oaths and Imprecations declar'd they'd fire at 'em, & blow their Brains, and did discharge 2 volleys of Horse Pistols the Wadding of one of which scorch'd John Sampsons Wigg – & Thomas Campion ... was wounded in the left Temple as suppos'd by a Shot from one of the Pistols'. But they were not smugglers. Rather, they were attempting to land the casks 'for the use of Lord Arundell', which would have brought them salvage payment, but they were assaulted before they could do so. The salvors, afraid for their lives, made a dash for the quay, but not before the Customs boat reached Harvey's sloop, and the officers, 'having large Clubbs in their hands, violently assualted [sic] and wounded the Salvors, & threatening to throw them overboard, and, actually would have thrown one over, had not he held by the Shrouds'. The men were saved when Excise Surveyor Young intervened. Young seized the brandy 'for the use of the King', at the same time that Lord Arundell's bailiff, John Treluddra, claimed it as a right of wreck. They agreed that they should secure the brandy until such a time as legal ownership could be ascertained. However, when Young left the scene to speak to the Collector of Customs, 'the Officers most cruelly beat James Lander, So that Blood run out at his Mouth, Nose &c, & almost Killed him & Mr Harvey's Son, and then by Violence took the Brandy away'.[1]

This case contains multiple threads important to wreck history. It illustrates the conflicting legal entitlement between HM Customs, the Admiralty,

---

[1]  AR/15/175, The Case of Mr John Harvey master of a pilchard sloop called *Mary and Alice*, 27 December, 1755.

and the lord of the manor over unclaimed goods. It also demonstrates the ambiguity surrounding the goods: were they smuggled or were they 'wreck', and hence liable to be claimed by the owner of wreck rights? Alternatively, if they were categorised as flotsam, did the goods become the right of the lord, or were they droits – the legal claim – of Admiralty? Finally, the case illustrates, in a very personal way, the centrality of the coastal populace in the conflicts surrounding wreck and wreck rights.

The questions raised by this case were resolved through legal action. Customs and the Admiralty eventually both recognised the claims of the Arundells. Customs admitted that the brandy was not contraband, and the Admiralty conceded that as the casks were found 'as far out to sea as a Hamborough Barrel can be seen on a clear day', as stipulated by the Arundells' royal grant, the goods were found near enough inshore to be considered the right of the lord of the manor. Yet, by the mid-nineteenth century, the very points of evidence upon which this case was won would be negated by the increasing regulatory functions of the State and its attendant bureaucracy. Although wrecking literature and myth focus on the resistance of the common people to governmental encroachment on what they perceived were their customary rights to wreck, the experience of the local lords of the manor in this process has been completely overlooked.[2] By 1854, with the passage of the Merchant Shipping Act, the wreck rights of manorial lords – many of whom were also magistrates – had been severely limited. Four major developments resulting from the centralising of State authority affected their rights: first, the growth of Customs administration; second, the resurgence of Admiralty claims to flotsam; third, the restructuring of the Board of Trade; and fourth, the revival of wreck claims by the Duchy of Cornwall.

### The Ascendancy of Customs

The growing complexity of the Customs administration in the eighteenth century marked the initial curtailing of manorial wreck rights. Customs collected revenue for the State by levying duties on an increasing number of goods, as well as being involved in the battle against smuggling, which grew in relation to the escalating levels of taxation. The charging of Customs duties had gone from a relatively simple system in the 1690s to a system 'so complex that, it was claimed, a lifetime was not sufficient to perfect a knowledge of

---

[2]   Philip Payton, *Cornwall: A History* (Fowey, 2004); John Vivian, *Tales of Cornish Wreckers* (Truro, 1969); John Rule, 'Wrecking and Coastal Plunder', in Douglas Hay, Peter Linebaugh, et al., *Albion's Fatal Tree: Crime and Society in Eighteenth-Century England* (London, 1975), 167–188. Even Roger Prouty, in his *The Transformation of the Board of Trade, 1830–1855: A Study of Administrative Organization in the Heyday of Laissez-Faire* (London, 1957), fails to treat the Board of Trade's role in the regulatory function of wreck rights.

them'.[3] By the 1760s, Parliament had passed some 800 Customs acts; by 1813, it had added another 1300 acts to the total and the methods for figuring duty had become exceedingly complex.[4] The frequent alteration in policies occurred with the exigencies of war and national debt, and with the enacting of trade strategies to protect colonial trade over foreign trade.[5] The status of shipwrecked goods is illustrative of the confusion which this entailed since goods could be defined as legal wreck, smuggled contraband, or flotsam, and even questioned as to whether or not they were liable for duty. Hence, the rapidly changing Customs statutes were not only confusing to the lords; they were unclear to Customs officials, which resulted in an ambiguous and inequitable application of the law.

## Levying of Duties

In the eighteenth century, the Customs' attempts to institute revenue-generating policies and to control dutiable shipwrecked goods provoked reaction on the part of both the lords and commoners throughout the country; neither social group recognised what they perceived as the overreaching of authority.[6] In Cornwall, after several casks of brandy washed ashore in 1763, the lord 'divided part of the Brandy with the Country people and thinks that the King's Officers have nothing to do with it'.[7] Five years later, the coastal populace again rebelled against Customs when salvors from Porthleven broke into a cellar and carried away wine, claiming that since they salved it from a 'dead wreck' Customs had no authority over it. Indeed, jurisdiction and authority were sometimes unclear even to the Customs officers themselves. Thus the collector wrote to London for guidance: 'As accidents of this kind frequently happen ... we pray to be informed whether we are or are not justifiable & whether it is our Duty to Lock up Goods under the above Circumstances or not'.[8] Customs control over wrecked goods was still uncertain in 1778, when a Porthleven smuggler took advantage of the officers' doubt by claiming that the brandy, which the officers had attempted to seize from his house, was

---

[3] Richard Price, *British Society, 1680–1880: Dynamism, Containment and Change* (Cambridge, 1999), 134, 135.

[4] Elizabeth Evelynola Hoon, *The Organization of the English Customs System, 1696–1786* (originally published 1938; Newton Abbot, 1968), 25–33.

[5] John Brewer, *The Sinews of Power: War, Money, and the English State, 1688–1783* (Cambridge, Massachusetts, 1990), Chapter 4; Edward Carson, *The Ancient and Rightful Customs: A History of the English Customs Service* (London, 1972), 92.

[6] William J. Ashworth, *Customs and Excise: Trade Production and Consumption in England, 1640–1845* (Oxford, 2003), 8.

[7] CUST 68/5, Penzance Collector to Board, 29 October 1763. Customs did not name the royalty, but it is suspected that an agent of the Arundells made the claim. Unless otherwise stated, all CUST 68 are from Penzance Collector to Board.

[8] CUST 68/6, 16 January 1768. Unfortunately, the Board's answer is not included within the Board to Collector letterbooks.

'Wreck Goods'. He did not believe that Customs had the power to impose duties on wreck, a belief also held by those holding manorial wreck rights. The officers, too, were hesitant about their authority and were thus anxious that the smuggler's deception of labelling contraband as wreck could be a precedent to other smugglers.[9]

The levying of duties was obviously a major point of contention, and Customs policies were vague, resulting in contradictions in enforcement. In 1798, the Penzance collector reported to London that he imposed duties on 'goods condemned as Droits of Admiralty and also on goods wrecked which become the perquisites of individuals, either as Manorial rights or otherwise unless the duties are remitted by the orders of our Hon[ble] Board to pay Salvage Charges'.[10] However, in 1804, a directive from the Customs Commissioners indicated that lords of the manor were exempt from paying duty on wrecked goods by stating expressly that '... no Duties are due on Wreck[d] Goods which devolve to the Admiralty or Lord of the Manor for want of other legal Claim'.[11] The perplexing issue of whether duties were to be levied on some articles of wreck and flotsam was finally clarified in 1812 by the act of 52 Geo. III c. 159.[12] Its preamble declared that doubts in the status of wreck had allowed tobacco and liquor to be 'sometimes sold and carried into Consumption without any Duties having been paid for ... to the great Loss of His Majesty's Revenue, and Injury of Persons dealing in such Liquors and tobacco....' Consequently, by law, duties were to be charged on wreck and flotsam. Indeed, the act not only obligated the lords to pay duty, but it also required them to place a bond with the Crown for three times the value of the goods if they wished to hold them in their possession for the requisite time. Thus in 1815, a lord of the manor was required to pay duty on two hogsheads of French claret and a pipe of brandy that had washed ashore on his royalty and remained unclaimed, when traditionally the liquor would have been his to claim duty free.[13]

The statute, however, did not clarify the status of all goods. Indeed, duties on timber were unclear, especially since foreign timber from the Baltic was subject to high duties beginning in 1811 while colonial timber incurred preferential lower duties as part of a State policy to limit dependence on supplies

---

9   CUST 68/11, William Hocking and Thomas Davies, Porthleven, to Collector and Comptroller, Penzance, 16 June 1778.
10   CUST 68/17, 24 July 1798.
11   CUST 68/49, Penzance Board to Collector, 10 March 1804.
12   'An Act for charging Foreign Liquors and Tobacco derelict, Jetsam, Flotsam, Lagan or Wreck ... with the Duties payable on Importation of such Liquors and Tobacco'.
13   CUST 28/21, Penzance Collector to J. Rogers, 9 April 1813; CUST 68/22, Penzance Collector to Board, 14 January 1815.

that war could endanger.[14] Evidence from the Penzance Customs records indicates that timber became one of the primary forms of wreck in the nineteenth century, so this issue had major ramifications for manorial lords. In 1833, therefore, Customs allowed Francis Paynter, who had acquired Connerton and its royalty of wreck from the Arundells, to possess wrecked mahogany while they determined whether duties were applicable.[15] Increasingly, though, lords of the manor were charged full duty on all dutiable goods that washed ashore their royalties, including timber. The strengthening of Customs control on the levying of duties thus effectively limited important elements of the manorial lord's right of wreck.

## The Smuggling War

Another key point of contention between Customs and lords of the manor was over the legal status of goods found within the royalties. As smuggling grew endemic from 'free traders' attempting to circumvent the escalating duties, manorial lords found that property they claimed as wreck was being seized by Customs as contraband. The wreck rights of the lords of the manor were thus caught in the middle. From the lords' point of view, this was a vexing encroachment on their rights, for it forced them to establish their claims through legal proceedings in the Court of Exchequer, an action that incurred additional expense.[16] This situation was also exacerbated by the Customs officers' ulterior motive in claiming goods as contraband, for if the goods were prosecuted in the Court of Exchequer, the seizing officer could receive up to one third of the goods or their value.[17] Indeed, Customs officers such as Penzance's Daniel Bamfield were known to make false seizure claims. In 1777, he forced himself into the St Aubyns' cellar and 'placed the King's Mark' upon the casks of gin that had been found flotsam near St Michael's Mount and claimed by Lady St Aubyn's agent. Bamfield then threatened the agent with smuggling charges. Although all the witnesses for Lady St Aubyn, including the Customs officer on the Mount, insisted that there was no evidence on the casks to show they were contraband, the Customs Commissioners opted to believe Bamfield since, they argued, there were no signs of any shipwreck in the vicinity. The commissioners claimed that, 'it is not thereby meant to dispute this Manorial Right in any Just cause', but the St Aubyns lost their claim. In 1787, however,

---

[14] Sarah Palmer, *Politics, Shipping and the Repeal of Navigation Laws* (Manchester, 1990), 57–58.
[15] CUST 68/32, Penzance Collector to Messrs Grylls, Grylls and Hill, 28 March 1833.
[16] CUST 68/10, William Broad, bailiff of the Manor and Liberties of Connerton, to John Scobell, Collector of Customs Penzance, 4 February 1777; CUST 68/42, Penzance Board to Collector, 15 April 1777.
[17] Hoon, *English Customs*, 276.

Bamfield was not so lucky; the Customs Commissioners finally dismissed him for making false seizure claims and for corruption.[18]

The status of goods claimed by manorial lords like the St Aubyns was thus continually questioned by Customs. Indeed, Customs records are full of cases in which officers seized goods from the lords of the manor or their agents, justifying their actions by claiming the goods were contraband.[19] Considering the amount of smuggling on the Cornish coast, and the method of sinking cargoes offshore until they were safe to collect, it is likely that much of the 'wreck' of the eighteenth and early nineteenth centuries was smuggled, but not all.[20] Unfortunately for the lords, however, the onus of proof was on them to produce clear evidence of shipwreck before they could legally claim their rights.

Yet sometimes even verification of shipwreck was not enough for lords to claim their rights to wreck, or if they were allowed to take possession, they were not given the benefit of lower duties for damaged goods. By the early nineteenth century, one manorial lord found that he was denied his right to claim brandy as wreck because it had been shipped in 'a cask which could not legally be imported and consequently could not be admitted to entry for duty'; he was denied his legal and customary right of wreck.[21] Francis Paynter, too, felt deprived of his rights in 1834 after he claimed a quantity of staves from a wreck near St Ives on the manor of Connerton. Customs determined that the staves had come from a cargo that had 'evidently been shipped at a Port in the Baltic, and carried to one of the British Colonies in North America in order that it might be imported into Great Britain at low duties'. Because of 'this mode of evading duties', Customs concluded that the lord of the manor and the salvors were 'not entitled to any benefit'! Thus Paynter and his tenants were penalised and charged the 'highest rates on the Goods in possession', although they were not the ones who had attempted to evade the duties. To add insult to injury for Paynter, the shipping of Baltic timber through the colonies was not made illegal until the following year.[22] The threat to the manorial right of wreck by Customs' battle against smuggling and the system of revenue generation through duties was not alleviated until after 1842. In that year, Sir Robert Peel removed duties on over 600 items and lowered

---

[18] CUST 68/11, Declaration of Witnesses, 30 March 1779; CUST 68/43, Penzance Board to Collector, 20 April 1779; CUST 68/45, Penzance Board to Collector, 19 July 1787; CUST 68/43, Edward Coode to Commissioners, 4 February 1778.

[19] CUST 68/1, 6 November 1740; CUST 68/10, 27 February 1777, 27 March 1777; CUST 68/43, Penzance Board to Collector, 7 March 1778.

[20] See Mary Waugh, *Smuggling in Devon and Cornwall, 1700–1850* (Newbury, Berkshire, 2003), 33, for methods used by smugglers to deceive Customs and Preventive officers.

[21] CUST 68/31, 24 November 1828.

[22] CUST 68/32, 28 February 1834; Palmer, *Navigation Laws*, 58.

duties on many more, eliminating many of the incentives for smuggling.[23] However, by that time, manorial rights to wreck had already been extensively curtailed.

## Loss of First Possession of Shipwrecked Goods

The first possession of shipwrecked goods held during the requisite 'year and a day' became another point of controversy between lords of the manor and Customs, which again resulted in the abatement of manorial rights. Similar to the confusion over the levying of duties, the policies of possession were unclear. In 1801, Humphrey Bridgeman took possession of tobacco and allspice that had been found at sea within the limits of his lord's royalty, and proceeded to 'claim and Secure the Goods for & in his [the lord's ] behalf' when they were landed at Land's End. He brought the goods to his home, not realising that, according to Customs, 'it was subject to Forfeiture upon removing'. Under this pretence, the goods were seized.[24] Even so, other Customs officials were not necessarily clear about who should have first possession. Ten years later, the collector from Padstow was informed by the commissioners that legally 'whether the Lord of the Manor or the Officers of the Revenue get first possession of Stranded goods neither of them can until a year and a day has elapsed take them out of the other's possession'.[25]

By the early nineteenth century, manorial first possession of wreck was becoming increasingly bypassed and even totally ignored by Customs. When 100 gallons of brandy washed on the beach between Penzance and Marazion in 1803 both Customs and Excise determined that it was wreck, and not smuggled. Nevertheless, neither agency contacted the Arundells, who had legal claim. Rather, they were more concerned about competing with each other over rights to secure it, and thus reap the rewards.[26] Indeed, the claim of the Arundells was not put forth until a year later, when no proprietary owner appeared and the brandy was legally defined as wreck. Unfortunately it is not recorded if Lord Arundell ever received what he claimed as 'his Perquisite and right'.[27]

By 1824, lords of the manor were still attempting to hold possession and deny the levying of duties. Humphrey Willyams, a lord of the manor as well as local magistrate and deputy lord lieutenant of Cornwall, had altercations with Customs which show the misunderstandings the lords had over the

---

[23] Geoffrey Morley, *The Smuggling War: The Government's Fight against Smuggling in the 18th and 19th Centuries* (Stroud, Gloucestershire, 1994), 157.

[24] CUST 68/18, William Richards and John Julyan to Collector and Comptroller, Penzance, 25 May 1801; Penzance Collector to Board, 28 May 1801.

[25] CUST 69/1, Padstow Collector to Board, 20 August 1811. The Board referred to the Statute of Westminster, which defined wreck and gave the prerequisite 'year and a day' time limitation.

[26] CUST 68/18, 29 January 1803.

[27] CUST 68/18, 25 January 1804.

changing Customs policies, and the power plays that resulted. When a piece of timber washed ashore Willyams's royalty of Carnanton, he duly reported it to Customs, but he was determined to maintain possession of it until he could claim it by law. However, he received a notice from the Chief Officer of the Coastguard at Newquay, Nicholas Marshall, informing him that the timber belonged to a vessel driven into Padstow, and that the import duties had not been paid. Marshall's letter was extremely accusatory, stating that:

> You must be aware, Sir, that all Foreign Timber or Goods is liable to pay a Duty ... in case of Receiving Information where any Uncustomed Goods may be secreted to evade payment of Duties, We are directed to make Search with writ of Assistance from the Court of Exchequer ... and to make Seizure of the Same ... but I am sorry to perceive you think my Conduct <u>unjustifiable</u> and <u>unlawful</u> ...[28]

Willyams responded that he retained the timber as a right of the lord of the manor, and since no claim had yet been put forward, 'no one but myself has a right to interfere with it'. He was adamant, and exclaimed that 'on these Grounds I consider your Conduct "unjustifiable & unlawful"' and that:

> So far also from my having secreted the Timber, you will be pleased to understand that ever since it came into my Possession it has been lying uncovered & exposed by the side of a much-frequented Highway – & so far from wishing to act clandestinely I shall be ready to shew other Pieces of Timber which I have on the Premises to any one who wishes to prove their Property in them – indeed you must be well aware that I am the last Person to interfere with the Proceedings of any Authorities when conducted legally and correctly.[29]

At this point, both combatants determined to send their missives to the Commissioners of Customs in London.[30] Willyams forwarded his own letter to the commissioners, much more deferential in tone, asking them to take into account his objections. He protested the duty on the timber, which he claimed 'is so novel' that 'I cannot suppose it was intended that the rights of Lords of Manors & particularly of royal Manors (that of Carnanton was purchased of y^e Crown only about 5 or 6 years since) are to be annihilated by a lately worded clause in an act relative to Customs'.[31] Willyams argued that the clause of 6 Geo. IV c. 107 cited by Customs did not specify duties on timber, but that it only applied to 'liquors and tobacco', and most importantly, even if it did apply, the timber had washed on shore and come into his possession before the act came into force, that is, before 5 January 1826. He closed with a promise to pay the duties if the Customs solicitor disagreed

---

[28]  W/43, Marshall to Willyams, 5 June 1826.
[29]  W/43, Willyams to Marshall, 8 June 1826.
[30]  W/43, Marshall to Willyams, 10 June 1826.
[31]  Willyams was referring to 6 Geo. IV c. 107.

with him. Nevertheless he explained that 'in resisting the Claim, I am sure the hon^ble y^e Comm^rs will see that I have only used my efforts to maintain the Rights and Privileges which have been just granted me by the Crown – a large portion of which I shall be deprived of if they are to be subject to the above Clause'.[32] Unfortunately for Willyams, the commissioners determined that the act applied to the timber.[33] Willyams paid the duty and sent an apology to the commissioners, pleading 'the novelty of the case'. In so doing, however, he also signified his displeasure by stating that he would 'resist the Illegal Conduct of any Officer (as in the present Instance) who may proceed to a Sale' before the lord of the manor could claim the goods, 'which the Act requires'.[34] Thus with the changes in statutes applying to Customs duties, the lords of the manor saw their rights 'annihilated' as Willyams predicted.

By the end of the 1850s, lords of the manor had become accustomed to paying duties on the wide range of imported goods as required by law, despite the fact that they were lawful wreck. Indeed, in 1854, Rev. John Rogers of Penrose found himself paying duty at the British colonial rate for mast, a spar, and eight deals that had washed ashore his manor.[35] Thus the lords of the manor, who once controlled the wreck that washed ashore on their lands, and who were able to claim the goods duty-free as part of their franchise, were at the end of the period liable to pay duty on pieces of a wrecked ship itself.

### The Admiralty and the Manorial Rights to Flotsam

Claims to flotsam, jetsam, and lagan had been legally defined whereby articles found at sea were considered 'droits of Admiralty', and articles found near the shore were considered the right of the lords of the manor.[36] Manorial lords had traditionally claimed goods that were found floating offshore of their royalty, 'as far out to sea as a Hamborough barrel can be seen on a clear day', according to the Arundells' charter. Indeed, even in 1770 Lord Falmouth as Lord High Admiral recognised the Arundell claim to flotsam off Connerton and the Hundred of Penwith.[37] However, by 1836, flotsam was considered solely the legal possession of the Admiralty. The new classification, which denied possession of inshore flotsam to the manorial lords, resulted from the consolidation of the Customs acts, and from three landmark court cases.

---

[32] W/43, Willyams to Commissioners of Customs, 29 June 1826.

[33] W/43, Commissioners of Customs to Collector and Comptroller, Padstow, 13 July 1826.

[34] W/43, Willyams to Commissioners of Customs, 26 July 1826.

[35] CUST 68/35, Rogers to Commissioners of Customs, 8 February 1854.

[36] Sir Henry Constable's case (1601), in James C. Hannen and W. Tarn Pritchard, *Pritchard's Digest of Admiralty and Maritime Law*, Vol. II (London, 1887), 2317.

[37] AR/17/29/2, John Knill to Lord Arundell re: wrecks, 1770.

From the start, the 1836 Customs Act was confusing to both Customs officers and lords of the manor, despite its intention to clarify the tangle of former legislation. Of special concern was the status of flotsam. The Penzance collector requested clarification from the Receiver General of Droits of Admiralty, informing the receiver that jetsam, flotsam, and lagan found on the shore, or 'within the flow of the sea', had traditionally been claimed by the lords of the respective royalties. 'Thus I presume', he wrote, 'the clause in question does not interfere with their rights, but I should be obliged by your informing me how I should proceed when such claims are urged in the future.' The receiver informed him that the goods thus found *were* droits of the Admiralty; lords of the manor had no claim. The Penzance collector recognised that this pronouncement would cause confusion. He informed the receiver that 'there is no doubt that the respective Lords of the Manor will still retain possession of all Goods taken up near their Manors, their notion on the Subject being that they are entitled to all Goods as far out at Sea as a Hambro' Cask can be seen floating'. [38] He was correct; there was much misunderstanding.

Rev. Charles Prideaux-Brune, lord of the manor of Padstow, found himself constrained by the new legislation the following year. In question was a quantity of timber salved within his royalty, and seized by the local Customs collector. Although Prideaux-Brune had applied to Customs for the timber, they denied him possession under the 1836 act. In the ensuing case paper, Sir William Follett remarked that he did not think that the act applied to the lord of the manor if the goods were thrown upon the shore beyond the reach of the sea. Rather it would apply to articles found in the sea, or on the shore within reach of the sea.[39] Thus, the act and its judicial interpretation expressly denied lords of the manor that which their royal grants had conferred, and which both the Admiralty and Customs had recognised in the eighteenth century.

### The Rights to Flotsam in Common Law

The loss of offshore wreck rights, and in some cases foreshore wreck rights, was heralded by three landmark court cases: the King *v.* 49 Casks of Brandy in 1836; the King *v.* Two Casks of Tallow in 1837; and the *Pauline* in 1845. Although none of the cases involved Cornwall per se, the decisions directly affected manorial rights throughout the country. In '49 Casks', the lord of the manor at Corfe Castle in Dorset claimed brandy salvaged within 3 miles of his manor. Although he showed that the Crown formerly accepted the liberty, and even upheld it on a *quo warranto* in 1664, Victorian judges chose to interpret the law differently. In particular, Sir John Nichols denied that manorial

[38] CUST 58/33, Penzance Collector to Receiver General, Droits of Admiralty, 7 December 1836.
[39] PB/6/769, Case paper, right of wreck, manor of Padstow, 1837.

boundaries extended into the sea; rather they extended to the foreshore only. Therefore, any goods found in the sea belonged rightfully to the Admiralty as droits.[40] Indeed, with this case, wreck rights became highly complicated: if the goods were found above high water mark, and thus aground, they would belong to the manorial lord as *wreccum maris*. If the goods were found below low water mark, and floating, they would become droits of Admiralty. However,

> ... those which were afloat between high and low-water marks, but being afloat never having even touched the ground, had not become wreck of the sea, and those which had been found on the ground, the tide being out, were wreck of the sea; that those which were found on the ground, though still moved by the waves, the sea at one time surrounding them and at another leaving them dry, were doubtful, but ought to be considered wreck of the sea, because they had struck ground.[41]

This case had severe ramifications, for the next year the lords of the manors of Caistor Pastons and Caistor Bardolfs in Norfolk claimed rights to two casks of tallow salved and taken to Customs at Great Yarmouth. Although they claimed the casks by prescription, the Admiralty denied their rights, instead arguing that the salvors had claimed the casks before they had grounded on the beach. The lords maintained that the casks had been grounded; it was only with the reversal of the tide that they were floating. Sir John Nichols made the determination that since the casks were floating, they were no longer considered wreck of the sea. He stated, 'I cannot agree to the proposition that things having once touched the ground, thereby necessarily become the property of the lord of the manor.' He forewarned that 'What might be the law in the case of things having become fixed on the shore, and afterwards the sea leaving them, may be a question hereafter....'[42]

The 'question hereafter' arose with the case of the *Pauline*, which occurred in 1845 when the ship wrecked at the mouth of the River Exe. Both the Admiralty and the earl of Devon as lord of the manor of Kenton claimed her, literally at the same time. Men from both camps boarded the ship to salvage her; it was admitted by all that she was within the low-water mark and within the

---

[40] Nichols based his decision on a possible 'legal fiction', that the office of Lord High Admiral existed from 'time immemorial' – before 1189 – and thus predated any manorial claims to flotsam. All manorial claims through prescription or express grant after 1189 were declared void. However, Michael Williams has uncovered evidence that express grants may have existed prior to 1189, predating any claim of the Lord High Admiral. In addition, Williams points out that Professor Marsden has argued that there is no evidence for the office of Lord High Admiral prior to 1360. This argument has opened the way for manorial court cases being contested at the time of writing. Michael Williams, 'Manorial Rights of Wreck', unpublished paper presented at the Nautical Archaeology Society Conference, University of Plymouth, March 1995. Special thanks to Mr Williams for sharing his paper with me.

[41] Stuart A. Moore, *A History of the Foreshore*, 3rd edition (London, 1888), 468.

[42] Quoted in Moore, *Foreshore*, 469.

manor for most of the time. However, Dr Stephen Lushington of the High Court of Admiralty determined the case against the lord of the manor by arguing that the ship was within Admiralty jurisdiction, that she was 'lying on land covered with water'. He found for the manorial lord only in respect to a few casks that had come ashore, quoting the case of 'Two Casks of Tallow'.[43]

It is evident that lords of the manor attempted to fight the new legislation, and feared the restriction of their rights. In Cornwall, the Penzance Customs collector, appointed as the local agent to the Receiver General of Droits, complained to the receiver in 1837 that he was having difficulty with the local lords. He had stated in 1836 that the manorial lords were insisting on maintaining possession of wrecked goods, and were adamant that they were entitled to goods taken at sea; the situation had not changed. Indeed, the collector did not seem to be convinced of the change in the law either:

> ... the Lord of the Manor (who states he has a Royal Grant) persists in claiming derelict Goods as formerly and has given me notice that he shall proceed against me in the Event of my detaining any such Goods which he calls his rights –; I believe the claim has been allowed here from time immemorial, and since my residence at this port as Collector of Customs embracing a period of 40 years, the Lord of the Manor has always taken possession of Goods if within 3 miles of the Shore ...[44]

Thus, not only were commoners attempting to maintain their customs and rights in the face of governmental intervention and changing policy, so too were the gentry.

## Ascendancy of the Board of Trade

With the enactment of the Merchant Shipping Act of 1854, administration of wreck rights transferred to the newly reconfigured Board of Trade. One of its mandates was to examine manorial rights of wreck. This would allow receivers to identify and contact legal claimants, ostensibly so they could receive payment for wreck that had washed ashore on their royalties. In 1855, the Board of Trade assigned the investigation to James O'Dowd, a Customs solicitor, who was to travel to the coastal areas of the United Kingdom to examine existing wreck claims. Prior to his visit, the Board of Trade requested that receivers of wreck at the various Customs ports send

---

43  Moore, *Foreshore*, 469. Dr Lushington is credited with largely shaping salvage law from 1838 to 1867. See S.M. Waddams, *Law, Politics and the Church of England: The Career of Stephen Lushington, 1782–1873* (Cambridge, 1992), 195–6.

44  CUST 68/33, Penzance Collector to Alexander Callandar, Receiver General of Droits of Admiralty, 7 December 1836; Collector Ferris to Charles Jones, Solicitor of the Admiralty, 4 November 1837.

in names and addresses of landed proprietors whom they believed to have wreck rights. Many of these receivers also conveyed letters to the lords asking them to send information regarding their claims, the date and nature of their grant, along with the geographical extent of their franchise. J.D. Bryant, the receiver at Padstow, admitted to Humphrey Willyams that he was aware that Willyams's claim had been upheld against the Crown, but counselled him that the evidence would be 'requisitioned' by the Board of Trade. Willyams was forewarned that 'you are no doubt aware that the Duchy of Cornwall claim the wreck on <u>all the Coasts of the County</u> and that such claim is conflicting with yours among many others'.[45] Bryant thus alluded to the third and fourth developments that resulted in the curtailing of manorial rights of wreck: the centralising policies of the Board of Trade and the re-emergence of the Duchy of Cornwall's claims to wreck.

With three court decisions fresh on the books that legally denied manorial lords their traditional (and originally legal) right to flotsam, and the resurgent claims of the Duchy, Cornish lords of the manor were apprehensive about the plans of the Board of Trade. The Board must have been aware of these concerns, for in its circular sent out to the lords, Secretary Thomas Henry Farrer sought to assure them:

> To remove the erroneous impression that the inquiry may subject Lords of the Manor to expense and inconvenience, I beg to observe, that a rigid and formal investigation of Title is not intended; but such an inquiry, as may lead to a safe & reasonable conclusion as to the rights of several claimants, with a view of enabling the Board of Trade to give receivers of Wreck the necessary instructions, as to parties entitled to receive unclaimed Wreck, or the proceeds thereof ... This being the sole object of the inquiry ...[46]

O'Dowd's task was not an easy one, as the wreck rights for Cornwall had severe entanglements, as we have seen. He was aware of the conflicting rights, and while he had no legal authority to determine whose rights were to be upheld, he wished to recognise those appearing to be sound. In particular, O'Dowd realised that he would need to acknowledge the claims of the Duchy of Cornwall. He felt he had a duty to require evidence for claims that were alleged to be 'antecedent to the creation of the Duchy of Cornwall and in any cases in which I admitted the validity of a title by prescription'. He emphasised that he 'did so upon such ancient and uninterrupted evidence of the

---

[45] W/43, J.D. Bryant, Receiver of Droits of Admiralty, Padstow, to Humphrey Willyams, manor of Carnanton, 7 July 1855.
[46] BT 212/1, Board of Trade Warning Letter on O'Dowd's impending visit regarding wreck rights, n.d.

user as led to the presumption of a grant from the Crown previous to such creation.'[47]

In June 1857, O'Dowd reported that he had completed his investigation into manorial wreck rights for whole of England, after a period of only eighteen months. His first reports, sent to the Board of Trade, claimed that the investigation had ended favourably.[48] However, the undercurrent of dissatisfaction in Cornwall belied his remarks. Ironically, Farrer, as 'the architect of the nineteenth-century Board of Trade', believed that the state's duty was to protect 'as much individual freedom as is consistent with the welfare of an organised society'.[49] Yet, the Cornish lords would have disagreed that Farrer was carrying out that philosophy. Instead, their experiences were the reverse. The investigation underscored their continuing loss of individual wreck rights.

O'Dowd's survey, which included additional investigations completed intermittently between 1867 and 1869, recognised several manors as having rights to unclaimed wreck. Manors such as those of John Rogers, Edward Coode, and Humphrey Willyams were accepted.[50] But O'Dowd also reported on other manors that he felt lacked evidence, and thus they were denied recognition by the Board despite Farrer's claim that 'a rigid and formal investigation of Title is not intended'.[51] On the denial list was the application of the Rt Hon. John Francis, Lord Arundell of Wardour, who claimed for the remaining few smaller Cornish manors still left in his holdings. For each of the claims, O'Dowd remarked that there was no evidence of title, and that the Arundell solicitor had failed to show any evidence of rights through prescription. However, O'Dowd did allow the manor of Lanherne to retain its manorial rights to wreck, proven through prescription.[52]

An even more controversial decision on the part of O'Dowd concerned the remaining parcels of the manor of Connerton and Hundred of Penwith. By 1840, the manor and hundred had been sold to the Paynter family, descendants of the Arundell chief stewards. Catherine Augusta Paynter claimed title

---

[47] BT 243/262, Duchy of Cornwall: legislation of right of wreck, 1856–1952, Case for opinion of the Law Officers of the Crown, n.d. 1861.
[48] BT 243/262, Duchy of Cornwall: legislation of right of wreck, 1856–1952, O'Dowd, Custom House Sligo to Board of Trade, 8 June 1857.
[49] T.H. Farrer, *The State and its Relation to Trade* (1883), 178, quoted in John Davis, 'Thomas Henry Farrer,' *Oxford Dictionary of National Biography* (Oxford, 2004; online edition May 2009), accessed 9 August 2009.
[50] The original report has not been found, and no other work has been discovered other than the amendments to the original lists. BT 212, Series Details. The enormous job this entailed, and the costly loss of this information, is indicated by the fact that some 691 claims were enumerated; 635 of these were exclusive of the Duchy.
[51] BT 212/1, Board of Trade Warning Letter on O'Dowd's impending visit regarding wreck rights, n.d.
[52] Lord Arundell's title was eventually accepted in 1869. See MT 9/5982, Duchy of Cornwall and parts of Devon, Manorial Rights, Boundary Claimants to Manors.

for unclaimed wreck, but was initially denied. O'Dowd remarked that there was some support for her claim, but he maintained that 'no mention of Wreck is made in any of these Grants'. He recognised that there was evidence that the Arundells had practised right of wreck through prescription, which he would have considered sufficient, except that there was also evidence the earls and dukes of Cornwall claimed wreck within the Hundred, 'both anterior and subsequent to the creation of the Duchy'. Therefore, 'the <u>prima</u> <u>facie</u> case of the Claimants in support of the title by prescription failed, both as to the manor and the Hundred'.[53] This opinion was unforeseen, considering the plethora of evidence that the Arundells had practised rights of wreck through prescription, and that the rights had been upheld in legal decisions throughout the eighteenth century, using the same evidence. Indeed, even the High Admiral had recognised Arundell claims. Nevertheless, O'Dowd denied recognition to what were once one of the largest, most visible manors in western Cornwall. But rather than completely denying the claims, and, 'to prevent possible future litigation', Mrs Paynter's solicitors offered an ultimatum to the Duchy. They would agree to withdraw their claims for the Hundred of Penwith if the Duchy gave up the claim for Connerton. An agreement was thus drawn up.[54]

O'Dowd also denied the claim of William Rashleigh for the manors of Tywardraeth, Trenant, and Polruan. Although Rashleigh's solicitor brought evidence that the right of wreck had been practised, O'Dowd remarked that 'this was not satisfactory to us'. He requested further court rolls and documentation, but Rashleigh appeared to be tired of the whole proceeding. Indeed, O'Dowd observed that Rashleigh 'was not disposed to enter further into the matter', and thus he denied claim to the manors.[55] O'Dowd's list is quite revealing, for it shows that by the mid-nineteenth century, the great gentry families of eighteenth-century Cornwall had lost not only their claims to wreck found offshore their manors, but also their claims to the right of wreck within the manors themselves.

## Claims of the Duchy of Cornwall

Not only were some of the gentry frustrated with the Board's inquiry, so too was the Duchy of Cornwall. The Duchy was particularly disgruntled, and put forth strong assertions that led to a stalling of the proceedings. The resurgence of the Duchy's claims to wreck was a result of reorganisation that

53 MT 9/5981, 'Schedule B: A Return of Parties in the County of Cornwall whose titles to receive unclaimed wreck are adversely reported upon'.
54 MT 9/5981, 'Schedule B: A Return of Parties in the County of Cornwall whose titles to receive unclaimed wreck are adversely reported upon'.
55 MT 9/5981, 'Schedule B: A Return of Parties in the County of Cornwall whose titles to receive unclaimed wreck are adversely reported upon'.

occurred in 1842 when the Crown appointed Prince Albert as Lord Warden of the Stannaries. He reformed the Duchy from its medieval guise, in which its revenue production had stagnated, into a stronger economic enterprise.[56] The issue of manorial title was a particularly important one for the Duchy. As Secretary James Gardiner of the Duchy declared: 'the prerogative right of the Crown to wreck of the Sea was so far as regards the entire County of Cornwall <u>inalienably</u> settled by the Legislature in the reign of Edward the 3rd upon the Heir Apparent of the Crown'. Therefore, he argued, the Merchant Shipping Act did not apply to Cornwall, and neither did the jurisdiction of the new Board of Trade.[57] In other words, the Duchy claimed that the Board of Trade's investigation into wreck rights was illegal, and that all other manorial claims in Cornwall were invalid except for those conferred by the Crown and Duchy. This had strong implications for the rights of all other manorial lords holding the royalty of wreck.

The Duchy specifically wanted information on all of the lords of the manor whose claims O'Dowd had determined should be admitted: the names, the nature of the titles, the dates of the grants from the Crown, and the length of time in which prescription was practised. Farrer refused to hand over all this data because O'Dowd had assured the lords' confidentiality. Moreover, Farrer argued that the Duchy had 'no right to see the Titles – we had no power to compel their production – but they were produced for our own satisfaction and security – and the condition that they should be divulged was under the circumstances a perfectly fair one.'[58] Gardiner was incensed not only at the Board's refusal to share information, but that 'they seem to have assumed that there is no distinction between the County of Cornwall and other parts of the Kingdom and have dealt or propose to deal with the subject as if no distinction existed.'[59]

This most contentious and far-reaching issue, whether Cornwall was part of England and thus included within the Merchant Shipping Act or a separate entity strictly under Duchy jurisdiction, was to be determined by an inquiry to the Law Officers of the Crown. For the lords of the manors, the decision would have severe ramifications on their rights of wreck. Farrer, too, was concerned that if the Law Officers found for the Duchy, the act would need to be amended to extend to Cornwall, or 'otherwise there will be no jurisdiction for the protecting of wrecks in that part of the country which

---

[56] Graham Haslam, 'Modernisation', in Crispin Gill, ed., *The Duchy of Cornwall* (Newton Abbot, 1987), 48–49; Payton, *Cornwall*, 209–210.

[57] BT 243/262, J. Gardiner, Duchy of Cornwall to Mr Booth, President, Board of Trade, 7 December 1860.

[58] BT 243/262, Farrer, BT, to Gardiner, Duchy of Cornwall, 5 October 1860; BT 243/262, Minute Paper No. 2434, 21 February 1861.

[59] BT 243/262, Gardiner, Duchy of Cornwall, to Booth, President, BT, 7 December 1860.

most require it.'[60] Farrer was thus concerned that if the Duchy had its way, it would open up the possibility of increased wrecking activity.

While the issue was being referred to the Law Officers, claims for wreck were put into abeyance, and the manorial lords were advised of the Duchy claims. O'Dowd was not pleased. He told Farrer about a Chancery Court proceedings whereby the lord of the manor of Killinack was legally granted wreck rights because 'the Council of the Duchy have never interfered'. O'Dowd explained that the Duchy's 'zeal on this point has not been heard of until lately indeed so little so, that I firmly believe they cannot establish a single instance of their having enforced the chartered right to Wreck which they now appear anxious to establish against proprietors some of whose titles run back to the days of the first Bishops of Cornwall'.[61]

The proprietors were not enthralled with the proceedings, either, especially since the investigation dragged on, and no one saw any payment for the wreck for which they felt entitled. In 1862, James Delmar, the solicitor for Lord John Thynne and John Hockin, informed the Board of his clients' situation, that Lord Thynne's title 'has nothing to do with the Duchy of Cornwall ... his Lordship resting his claim on an antecedent title to that of the Prince of Wales'. Hockin's claim, Delmar argued, 'has been twice submitted to Duchy Officers and it would appear a great hardship that he should be at the Cost of defending rights – bona fide paid for – '.[62] Although Farrer tried to assure Delmar that his client's rights, and wreck profits, would be taken into account, 'my Lords still think it desirable to postpone any further inquiry until the issue of the pending negotiations is known.'[63]

Delmar was not the only attorney frustrated by the lapse in proceedings. George Allens of St Columb, representative for Humphrey Willyams, also voiced his displeasure. He reiterated that Willyams's claims had been 'established ... I believe to M[r] O'Dowd's perfect satisfaction, to all Wreck found within the manor of Carnanton, formerly a Crown manor'. But tersely, he added, 'Since that time twenty wrecks have been handed over to the Receiver of Droits & now M[r] Willyams has respectively applied to him for an account of the Sales, but has hitherto failed in receiving any.'[64] Allens received the same answer as the other solicitors: negotiations were still pending.

John J. Rogers, lord of the manor of Penrose and county magistrate, also had issues with the Board over the abeyance of wreck rights. In particular,

---

[60] BT 243/262, Minute Paper No. 2434, 21 February 1861.
[61] BT 243/262, O'Dowd to Farrer, 17 April 1861.
[62] BT 243/262, James Delmar, Stratton, Cornwall to T.H. Farrer, Secretary, BT, 28 January 1862.
[63] BT 243/262, Farrer to Delmar, 3 February 1862.
[64] BT 243/262, George B. Allens, Esq, St Columb, attorney to Humphrey Willyams, to T.H. Farrer, BT, 10 September 1862. Rather than implying that there were twenty shipwrecks, Allens was saying that twenty pieces of wreck had been turned over to the receiver.

he was concerned that the lords had received no notice from the receivers of any wreck found:

> I feel strongly that if our rights are still to be held in abeyance (as they have now been most unjustly & injuriously for three years past) ... & the proceeds unaccounted for, we should at least receive from the Receiver a form notice of each [illeg] of Lord's wreck by him stating date & value, or proceeds if sold, in order that the Lord may have some knowledge of the way in which the account is kept on their behalf by the Board of Trade.[65]

Rogers' complaint stemmed from a policy set forth by the Board of Trade in 1856, in which receivers would eventually be forwarded admitted claims. But, 'in the meantime Receivers are not in any way to admit *any* such claim or title to unclaimed wreck, and are to be careful not to report wreck to Lords of Manors without the express sanction of the Board of Trade.'[66] The Board, working with Customs, had, despite Farrer's protestations to the contrary, explicit control over manorial wreck, not only in determining which claims would be admitted, but also in possessing the wreck itself and in suppressing information of its existence. Not only was Rogers contemptuous of the way the Board was handing his affairs, he issued a warning that the 'present state of interregnum is not only injurious in many ways to the Lords of wreck rights, but that it is not beneficial to the shipowners, whose interests the Board should protect, because that state operates as an inducement to poor men along shore to commit plunder of wreck'.[67] Accordingly, Rogers employed the threat of plundering, for despite its cessation as a major Cornish concern, the spectre still haunted popular consciousness.

Some proprietors determined to take the issue into their own hands. Rather than fight Duchy claims, Sir Samuel Spry purchased the wreck rights of his manor directly from the Duchy.[68] Other proprietors took a more challenging position. Receiver J.D. Bryant informed the Board in September 1862 that William Drewe, lord of Carnewas, a claimant accepted by the O'Dowd inquiry, had 'picked up a piece of fir Timber and declined either to report it or deliver it to me – although requested to do so – assigning as a reason that the Timber is his private property and that no one has the right to interfere with it'. Bryant felt that the incident could prove fatal: 'if unchecked, will prove subversive to all order in the District ... shall I have him summoned

---

[65] BT 243/262, John Rogers of Penrose to BT, 2 April 1862.
[66] CUST 33/38, Receivers of Wreck: Instructions for Customs Staff, *Supplemental Instructions in Respect to Wreck & Casualties Issued by the Board of Trade under the Merchant Shipping Act 1854* (London, 1856), sec. 112, 13.
[67] BT 243/262, Rogers to BT, 2 April 1862.
[68] BT 243/262, Secretary of the Duchy of Cornwall to T.H. Farrer, 4 December 1862.

before the Justices for not reporting and delivering as directed by the Act? It is a very clear case, I think.'[69] Thus in language reminiscent of the apprehensions of eighteenth-century Customs officers against wreckers and smugglers, a lord of the manor was threatened with legal action for claiming what he believed was his customary and lawful right. The major difference was, of course, that the rights of the lords of the manor *had* been legally recognised in the past. Bryant thought it was a 'clear case', but the Customs solicitor was more cautious. Although the Board's president requested that he send Drewe a warning of the penalties to be incurred for failing to report and deliver wreck to the receiver as required in section 450 of the Merchant Shipping Act, the solicitor was unsure whether the clause applied to legal owners of wreck rights. Farrer, however, pointed out that Drewe had been informed of the Duchy negotiations; his wreck claims were still in abeyance.[70] Thus by the mid-nineteenth century, the definitions of criminality relating to wreck had been extended to lords of the manors themselves through bureaucratic sleight of hand.

Wreck claims of lords of the manor continued in abeyance even though the Law Officers informed the Board of Trade in March 1862 that the Merchant Shipping Act did, in fact, apply to Cornwall. Although the news was relayed to the manorial lords at that time, they would not see any profit from their rights until six years later. Indeed, after the legal decision a new committee, formed through the cooperation of the Board of Trade and the Duchy of Cornwall, instituted a new inquiry into the claims of wreck rights in Cornwall. At its conclusion in 1868, Farrer wrote: 'This is I hope the end of a very long and troublesome business. The Duchy were at first very wrong in [illeg] us to use our Statutory powers to help them against the Landowners – And then M^r O'Dowd's inquiries were endless – Now the Duchy are reasonable and the Landowners I hope satisfied.'[71]

Why was there so much concern over wreck rights? Occasionally, as has been seen, wreck rights could be profitable, though only in windfall situations. By the mid-nineteenth century, however, profitability had decreased. For example, the Board of Trade reported the following profit from wreck:

[69] BT 243/262, J.D. Bryant, Receiver of Wreck, Padstow, to T.H. Farrer, 2 September 1862.
[70] BT 243/262, Minute Paper No. 9758, Farrer note to Customs Solicitor, 2 October 1862.
[71] MT 9/5982, Minute Paper, 9 March 1868.

Table 7. Profits from Wreck in Cornwall, 1862–64

| Receivers Districts/ Customs Ports | Amount received 1862 £ s d | Amount received 1863 £ s d | Amount received quarter ending March 1864 £ s d |
|---|---|---|---|
| Falmouth | –– | 28.5.8 | 3.19.2 |
| Padstow | 25.16.9 | 2.10.9 | 9.17 |
| Penzance | 91.5.1 | 21.7.8 | –– |
| Scilly | 107.10.11 | 31.10.7 | –– |
| Plymouth | 12.1.7 | 3.9.1 | 39.10.5 |
| Bideford | 22.2.2 | –– | 3.4.7 |
| Total | 262.5.1 | 134.13.4 | 95.10.7 |
| Deduct Expenditure in Excess of Income | | | |
| Falmouth | 10.1.7 | –– | –– |
| Bideford | –– | 19.7 | –– |
| Padstow | –– | –– | 2.11.11 |
| Scilly | –– | –– | 3.5.8 |
| Total | 252.3.6 | 133.13.9 | 89.13.0 |

Source: TNA MT 9/22. Draft Returns of all sums of money received by the Board of Trade or by their Receivers in the County of Cornwall, in Continuation of Parliamentary Paper No. 456 of Session 1862, 1864. Totals as given in the original table.

In analysing the above figures, it is clear that the profit from wreck, once expenses and salvage payments were taken into account, amounted to little for each owner. Farrer recognised the low profitability when he discussed the proceeds of wreck in 1858. As he argued, 'not only is the whole sum already observed very trifling but the amount rising from wreck found afloat is very small indeed as compared with wreck found ashore'; neither amounted to a large profit.[72] Indeed, even Charles Gore, Secretary of the Office of Woods, remarked to the Treasury that 'the value of Wreck as a matter of Revenue is very small, and is likely to diminish with an improved administration.'[73]

Rather than reflecting concern about profitability, the correspondence of the Board of Trade indicates that by the mid-nineteenth century, the right of wreck was constituent with wider concerns, especially that of the foreshore. As a memorandum from the Board of Trade put forth in 1858, the right of wreck 'is looked upon by the Courts of law as one of the strongest proofs of a right to the shore itself'. It quoted a court case at Brighton whereby a member of the jury asked the judge if 'the Lord is entitled to Wreck should

---

[72] MT 9/6, Right of Crown to Wreck, Titles Admitted by Crown, Minute Paper, 17 August 1858.

[73] MT 9/6, Charles Gore, Office of Woods to Treasury, cc'd to Board of Trade, 29 May 1858.

your Lordship think he would be entitled to the Soil?' The judge's answer was affirmative.[74]

In spite of possible foreshore claims, and because of governmental and Duchy pressures, many lords of the manor lost interest. The lack of profitability from wreck made fighting for their rights a losing proposition. Either they did not put forth the effort and expense to prove their rights or they began to sell them off. Even the claims of the Arundells, held since the twelfth century, were eventually sold to the Duchy for a mere £7 10s in 1964. As the Ministry of Transport solicitors admitted: 'Valuable wreck which is cast ashore is usually claimed by the owners and a perusal of the records of the past ten years shows that no monies deriving from the acquisition of unclaimed wreck have been paid to the manor of Lanherne.'[75] They could have probably added that little profit was made in the past hundred years, either.

The increasing state domination not only slowly curtailed local control of the lords of the manor; it also directly affected the customary rights of the local populace. Gone was the custom of receiving a moiety of either the goods or their value for salvage, paid almost immediately by the agents or bailiffs upon receipt of the goods. In its place were bureaucracy and red tape, and endless delays of waiting for compensation. It is no wonder that many continued to act in the way that they always had, to 'harvest' the beaches 'for their own use'. It is also no wonder that many of the lords of the manor opted to sell their wreck rights to the Board of Trade or to the Duchy and disown the entire business.

The actual custom of wrecking, therefore, whether practised by the coastal populace as 'providence' or 'moral entitlement', or by the lords of the manor as their right of wreck, experienced shifting definitions of criminality through the course of the eighteenth and early nineteenth centuries, and was subject to increasing governmental control. Consequently, after the eighteenth century, when customary rights ranging from common-land use to perquisites had been lost, and such previously legitimate activities had been criminalised, the loss of legitimate wreck rights in the nineteenth century became another example of 'the disruption of custom, the triumph of law'.[76] The gentry have been excluded from this model, and from the narratives and myths of popular culture that emphasised wrecker resistance, but their experiences show that they, too, suffered loss of power at the hands of government.

If lords of the manor rarely profited from their wreck rights because so little wreck came ashore, the same could be said for the common people. The

---

[74] MT 9/6, Right of Crown to Wreck, Titles admitted by Crown, 1858, Memorandum on Letter from the Board of Trade respecting Wreck of the Sea, 19 June 1858.

[75] BT 243/131, Messrs Eland Hore Patersons, Solicitors for the Ministry of Transport regarding Lanherne Manor, 17 November 1964.

[76] Douglas Hay and Nicholas Rogers, *Eighteenth-century English Society: Shuttles and Swords* (Oxford, 1997), 97–113.

chances of profit through all forms of wrecking were limited, especially as the nineteenth century progressed and technology advances changed ship design from sail to steam and from wood to iron. Indeed, the very lack of profitability is another indicator that wrecking was not as widespread and invidious as popular belief allows. But if it was not, how did it become part of the popular imagination, and more importantly, how did it become almost completely tied to Cornwall, when wrecking was practised in all coastal areas of the British Isles? To answer these questions, it is important to go beyond the actualities of wrecking and to enter into an examination of wrecking discourse, in essence to perform the 'unravelling of myths and reflections on the making of "common knowledge".[77]

---

[77] Miri Rubin, 'What is Cultural History Now?', in David Cannadine, ed. *What is History Now?* (London, 2002), 83.

# 9

# The Wrecker, the Press, and the Pulpit

*those greedy Cormorants waiting for their Prey*

IN 1751, the *Sherborne Mercury*, one of the first regional papers in the West Country, reported the loss of a vessel near Porthleven on 18 March:

> the cliffs, as usual, were covered with hundreds of those greedy Cormorants, waiting for their Prey, which no sooner came within their Reach but was Swallowed up by them, more barbarous in their Nature than Cannibals ... Amongst these greedy Wolves there were many of their Kind that made so free with the Spirit, and were so exasperated with each other, that they stripped even to their Buff and fought like Devils.

Thus begins one news account of a wrecking event, illustrating an evolving representation of the wrecker as someone who was less than human – a 'folk devil'.[1] To appreciate the development of the wrecking myth and its solidification into popular consciousness, we need to consider the role of the press, the public pronouncements of the clergy, and the didactic function of the novel. Not only were these practices important to spread information and news, they also had an impact in influencing societal mores and shaping identity. Although the language of the *Sherborne Mercury* article was particularly hostile, its author applied metaphors and reporting conventions commonly employed to describe wrecking events in many parts of the country, not just in Cornwall. Therefore, sensationalist reporting by the media, as also the tone of comments by the clergy, was a factor in mythologising the wrecker as a 'folk devil' and a source of 'moral panic'. Although the myth of the Cornish wrecker was in existence before the advent of the eighteenth century, it is in the eighteenth and nineteenth centuries that popularisation of the motif gained momentum. The modern uses of such sources, without taking into account their historicity and bias, solidified the myth in shipwreck accounts of the twentieth century.

---

[1] Stanley Cohen, *Folk Devils and Moral Panics: The Creation of the Mods and Rockers*, 3rd edition (originally published London 1972; London, 2002).

The press's influence in popularising the rapacious wrecker image began in the early eighteenth century after regional printers gained freedom to establish provincial newspapers. Of importance to the West Country, and especially to Cornwall, was the *Sherborne Mercury*, which began printing in 1737.[2] It was not rivalled for Cornish news coverage until the establishment of the *Royal Cornwall Gazette* in 1803 and the *West Briton* in 1810.[3] With the boom in provincial newspapers, literacy levels also increased. Whatever the precise level of literacy, it is clear that more of the populace had access to newspapers, whether as readers or as listeners, which increased the numbers encountering viewpoints of the press.[4]

Since trade and shipping were vital for the national economy, newspapers featured special sections dedicated to shipping movements and shipwreck reports. Indeed, the topic of shipwreck permeated British culture in the eighteenth and early nineteenth centuries, whether as reality or metaphor, and the public had a voracious appetite for shipwreck narratives that were also published in pamphlet form.[5] But because of the pervasiveness of shipwreck reporting, whether by local, regional, or national newspapers, or by magazines, the reports of shipwrecks are almost impossible to quantify, making a full statistical examination of media accounts of shipwrecks difficult. Nevertheless, examples given are representative of the tone and convention of the contemporary press.

Wrecking reports in the media during the eighteenth and nineteenth centuries ranged from hostile to neutral to total disregard, a spectrum that needs to be acknowledged to understand the proportionality, and hence the persuasiveness, of the sporadic hostile accounts. Not all column space on shipwrecks was devoted to the vilification of the country people's activities during the shipwreck event. Indeed, more often than not reports of shipwrecks do not

[2] The *Sherborne Mercury* later merged with other West Country-based papers, such as the *Western Flying Post* in the 1750s.

[3] R.M. Barton, ed., *Life in Cornwall in the Early Nineteenth Century, Being Extracts from the West Briton Newspaper in the Quarter Century from 1810 to 1835* (Truro, 1970), preface. The *West Briton* eventually outsold its rival, with twice the circulation of the *Royal Cornwall Gazette* by 1835. The two papers were eventually merged in 1951 to become the *West Briton and Royal Cornwall Gazette*. The *West Briton* is still in print, though it is a district paper rather than county-wide. See also Brian Elvins, 'Cornwall's Newspaper War: The Political Rivalry Between the *Royal Cornwall Gazette* and the *West Briton*, Part One, 1810–1831', in Philip Payton, ed., *Cornish Studies* 9, second series (Exeter, 2001), 145–172, and 'Part Two, 1832–1855' in Philip Payton, ed., *Cornish Studies* 11, second series (Exeter, 2003), 57–84.

[4] Jonathan Barry, 'Literacy and Literature in Popular Culture: Reading and Writing in Historical Perspective', in Tim Harris, ed., *Popular Culture in England, c. 1500–1850* (London, 1995), 69–94. See also Hannah Barker, *Newspapers, Politics, and Public Opinion in Late Eighteenth-Century England* (Oxford, 1998).

[5] See George P. Landow, *Images of Crisis: Literary Iconology, 1750 to the Present* (London and Boston, 1982) for a discussion of the cultural importance of both religious and secular iconology of shipwreck. See also Keith Huntress, ed., *Narratives of Shipwrecks and Disasters, 1586–1860* (Ames, Iowa, 1974).

contain any reference at all to wrecking activity. Rather the reports are basic, simply listing the name of the vessel, master, destination, place of wreck, and cargo, if known. Occasionally wrecking activity was remarked upon, but with a neutral tone. *Gentleman's Magazine* tended to describe the plundering of wrecks in dispassionate, though still slightly condemnatory, terms. In January 1751, just a month before the emotive report by the *Sherborne Mercury* that opened this chapter, a small brig wrecked near Looe, with all hands lost. *Gentleman's Magazine* recounted that Customs officers attempted to save the valuable cargo and materials, 'but the townsmen whom they would have appointed as a guard, pillaged for themselves, and the whole country poured in, as well reputable farmers and tradesmen as the poor, and in defiance of the officers, loaded horses and even carts with their plunder'.[6] Thus, although full-scale plundering was reported, extreme language is absent. Even in the coverage of the *Charming Jenny* wrecked off the Welsh coast in 1773, in which the corpse of the captain's wife was reported to have been robbed, *Gentleman's* used neutral reporting techniques.[7] Indeed, the magazine rarely described any wrecking events with emotion, and only once in the survey of the period 1751 to 1783 did they accuse a population of inhumanity – and that was aimed at the Portuguese when an English shipwreck was plundered near Oporto.[8]

The *West Briton*, too, sometimes left out reference to wrecking in its shipwreck accounts. It described the great gale of 1829 in which twenty-five vessels were either wrecked or damaged near Padstow. Five vessels ran aground and one was lost with all hands, but the article did not mention a single instance of wrecking, although beach harvest must assuredly have occurred. Rather, the account claimed that several of the vessels were 'saved', through local assistance.[9] Even the *West Briton's* announcement of the total loss of the Danish brig *Ospra* on the Lizard, with a cargo of sugar and coffee worth £10,000, did not merit the mention of a single case of wrecking.[10] Similarly, entries in *The Times* and the *Annual Register* simply cite the loss of a vessel, giving no details or else commending country people for their lifesaving and salvage efforts.[11] The *West Briton* also praised the local populace. It reported that two poor fishermen of Mevagissey were rewarded by the Russian government for saving the crew of the Russian brig *St Nicholas* in December 1831, and the men of Looe were acclaimed in 1838 for saving the crew of the London brig *Bellis-*

6   *Gentleman's Magazine*, 21 (1751), 41.
7   *Gentleman's Magazine*, 43 (1773), 89.
8   *Gentleman's Magazine*, 36 (1766), 340.
9   *West Briton*, 18 September 1829.
10  *West Briton*, 11 May 1832.
11  See *The Times*, loss of the *Friendship*, where the 'honesty and activity of the country people in general' around Dunbar 'merit particular commendation', 14 January 1786. See also *Gentleman's Magazine*, 40 (1770), 187, and 42 (1772), 597.

*sima* – they 'carried a boat on their shoulders a distance of two miles before she could be launched, owing to a boisterous sea'.[12]

The relative absence of hostile language could be indicative of isolated instances of wrecking on the British coast, or it could be that wrecking, as with other customary activities, was pervasive enough not to warrant comment and was thus underreported.[13] Indeed, the underreporting of harvest activities fits this assertion, evidenced by social acceptance of the coastal populace and the occasional turning of a blind-eye by officers of the Customs Service. It is doubtful, however, that the violent plundering of shipwrecks would warrant the public's disregard. As E.P. Thompson suggests regarding journalistic silence, customary practice was 'not considered worthy of report, unless some additional circumstance (humorous, dramatic, tragic, scandalous) gave it interest'. And wrecking, just like wife sales, 'became newsworthy contemporaneously with the evangelical revival ... [and] redefined a matter of popular "ignorance" into one of public scandal'.[14] In other words, the media reported on violent wrecking events because they were uncommon and attention-grabbing. Benign wrecking activities were 'scandalous' and thus had the attention of evangelicals. However, the majority of press reports did not indicate any wrecking activity, although from the mid-eighteenth to the mid-nineteenth century intermittent hostile reports of wrecking appeared as a form of moral commentary, which created an entrenched cultural construct of the wrecker as a 'folk devil' and solidified the myth. It is the use of such rhetoric as a form of symbolic violence against the coastal populace and its implied cultural meaning that is the focus of this chapter.

The reputation of the Cornish and the ubiquity of the myth would have us believe that an overwhelming number of wrecking reports, with or without pejorative comment, would be limited to Cornwall. This is not the case. Indeed, *Palmer's Full Text Online* of *The Times* articles from 1802 to 1867 identifies forty-six reports of wrecking in sixty-five years; only five short articles deal with Cornwall. One of the articles reported the plundering of *Resolution* in 1817; two recounted the plunder of *Jessie Logan* and subsequent indictment of Luckey and Chapman in 1843; one commented on the attack of *Samaritan* in 1846; and the final article involving Cornwall was a reprint of a letter by a Penzance clergyman in response to an account of wrecking in Wales. The balance of *The Times* articles covers wrecking all over the British Isles, but mainly in Scotland, Wales, Essex, Dorset, and Kent. In fact, most column space was given in 1866 to wrecking events on the Kent coast near Deal,

[12] *West Briton*, 5 August 1831; 30 November 1838.
[13] Robert Bushaway, *By Rite: Custom, Ceremony and Community in England 1700–1880* (London, 1982), 21.
[14] E.P. Thompson, *Customs in Common: Studies in Traditional Popular Culture* (New York, 1993), 410.

implicating the Deal boatmen.[15] By examining the cases of hostile rhetoric, we can also see that Cornwall was not singled out. Wreckers from other regions received the same treatment as the Cornish. The inhabitants of Whitstable 'live by the plundering of wrecks and smuggling'; they were 'lawless people'.[16] Wreckers were described as 'infest[ing] the Kentish coast',[17] and, although wreckers in Cornwall were given the epithet 'ruffians',[18] the people of Carlisle were 'heartless scoundrels' who were involved in 'unfeeling work'.[19] For the London press these sporadic cases of wrecking, wherever they occurred, were used to raise issues about the immorality of the coastal poor.

### The Rhetoric of Wrecking

Hostile press coverage and clerical writings of wrecking events, no matter whether they happened in Cornwall or other areas of the British Isles, was characterised by all or some of these most salient features: exaggerated images of mob action; formulaic descriptions of wreckers; caricatures of drunkenness; emotional portrayals of women and children; and perceived threats to cherished values and national reputation. By the beginning of the nineteenth century, the 'lament' also becomes evident. These stereotype-producing rhetorical devices had a significant role in shaping the cultural representation of the wrecker.

Descriptions of wrecking events commonly involved some form of mob action. The *Western Flying Post* on 19 March 1750 reported that the Customs officers and gentlemen of the district of Looe were successful in saving a wreck

> against a mob of obstinate and lawless villains, who came down upon them
> in great Fury, and would doubtless have plundered and destroyed all … These
> worthless Wretches were arm'd with rugged sort Bludgeons, and had distin-
> guished themselves by a Private Mark, that they might not destroy one another
> in this wicked Enterprise …

'Swarms of plunderers' were feared to carry away ships' cargoes 'piecemeal'.[20] The *West Briton* in 1815 focused on the 'barbarians of Breage and Germoe', who 'came down in such numbers, that before assistance could proceed … had nearly torn the vessel to pieces'. When the militia arrived, they 'could scarcely restrain the wretches from completing the work they had so actively begun'.[21]

---

15 See a long series of correspondence published in *The Times* beginning 19 October 1866.
16 *The Times*, 30 December 1802.
17 *The Times*, 7 April 1843.
18 *The Times*, 15 January 1817.
19 *The Times*, 19 December 1821.
20 *West Briton*, 21 April 1815, quoted in Barton, *Life in Cornwall*, 58.
21 *West Briton*, 27 October 1815, quoted in Barton, *Life in Cornwall*, 61.

In January 1817, the *West Briton* again reported on the activities of the Breage and Germoe wreckers: 'The shore was covered by hundreds of barbarians.'[22] When this wreck, identified as the *Resolution*, was reported in *The Times*, the account said that the vessel was entered by 'thousands of ruffians', and that the dragoons from Helston 'were wholly unable to restrain the ferocious multitude that crushed in on all sides.'[23]

We can see in such reports a linkage with societal fears of the mob and rioting which have been identified by historians as a feature of eighteenth- and early nineteenth-century British history. Although the real threat from wreckers was minimal, for many it was just one more example of the lower orders endangering societal values by threatening the forces of law and authority. This fear of the poor was exacerbated by the Gordon Riots in 1780 and continued through demobilisation from the French Revolutionary and Napoleonic Wars to the 1840s, and on occasions of economic depression. By the mid-eighteenth century the law increasingly defined property as sacred; in Lockean terms 'government has no other end but the preservation of property'.[24] Thus elite belief about the depravity of wrecking was fashioned from anxiety about the masses and apprehensions about threats to property. The prevailing discourse served to create the perfect platform for the mythogenesis of the wrecker.

In line with the view of the collective mob as more organism than human, the press characterised the wreckers as 'fierce', 'ravenous', 'barbarous', 'cruel', 'inhuman', and 'savage devourers'. Or, as in the above descriptions of mob actions, wreckers were conceptualised as 'obstinate and lawless villains', 'worthless Wretches', 'greedy Wolves', 'Cannibals', and 'Devils'. Religious tracts of the period used similar descriptors. In *The Wreckers, or a View of What Sometimes Passes on our Sea Coast*, written by an anonymous clergyman who was a former lieutenant in the Royal Navy and who had been shipwrecked, wreckers were described as 'hard-hearted' and 'wretches'. He set his sermon to verse, stating that it was not an exaggeration, but a true representation, instituting the validity principle on what was actually hyperbole. As the ship finds itself in distress, the 'wreckers, as cruel [as wolves and tigers] do savagely prowl; Round the shores of the dark troubled main ...

> These sights, so afflicting, to *wreckers* were dear,
>    Who live by fell rapine and crime;
> Whose eyes never shed soft compassion's sweet tear,
> Whose hearts never learnt e'en their Maker to fear,
>    Or to reflect on the end of their time.

[22] *West Briton*, 31 January 1817, quoted in Barton, *Life in Cornwall*, 74.
[23] *The Times*, 15 January 1817.
[24] John Locke, *Two Treatises of Government*, ed. Peter Laslett (Cambridge, 1963), 347.

Now shoreward the masts, and their tackling swing round,
   And the *wreckers* begin their glad toil;
They curse and blaspheme, while they cover the ground
With spars, and with sails, and whatever is found;
   For each seizes his share of the spoil. ...

The news of the wreck it soon spread along shore,
   And women and men ran for gain;
Thus numbers they harden each other the more,
Till mercy and justice their hearts close the door,
   That love of curst money may reign.[25]

The terminology used to describe the wreckers serves to separate the 'rabble', or the 'mob', from the ruling elite. Indeed, it is indicative of the process of dehumanisation by using symbolic violence. If we analyse the lines from one of the most vituperative reports, which opened this chapter, we can fully envisage the dehumanisation process and the creation of 'folk devils'. Although the author of the *Sherborne Mercury* was caustic in his description, his text utilises commonly understood symbolism, a cultural code of 'representative images that conveyed something of importance'.[26] Cormorants in Renaissance figurative language were insatiably greedy, with a voracious appetite. This image is followed by the statement that when the 'prey' reached them, it 'was Swallowed up by them'. Readers well versed in literary symbolism would also recognise the undertones of evil; after all, in Milton's *Paradise Lost*, the cormorant signified Satan. The use of the term 'cormorant' for the Cornish had a long history, invoked by Parliamentarian pamphleteers during the Civil Wars as a pejorative against the mainly Royalist Cornish.[27] The phrase 'more barbarous than Cannibals', as well, held certain well-understood connotations. The word 'barbarian' had been borrowed from the Greeks, especially the works of Aristotle, to denote the 'prototype of the wild man ... savages represent[ing] man in his degenerate rather than his primitive form'.[28] If this degeneracy were not enough, the report emphasised that the wreckers were even worse than 'Cannibals', referring to the strongest taboo in Judeo-Christian religion, and thus the most potent image of savagery.[29] Like the methods of labelling non-Western cultures as the Other – as cannibals and barbarians – to justify the colonising process, the same mechanisms were applied to wreckers.

[25] Anon, *The Wreckers, or a View of What Sometimes Passes on Our Sea Coast: Written By a Clergyman of the Church of England, etc.* (London, 1820?), 1–8. The tract was published several times without publication dates.
[26] Landow, *Images of Crisis*, 17.
[27] Mark Stoyle, *West Britons: Cornish Identities and the Early Modern British State* (Exeter, 2002), 79.
[28] Quoted in J.H. Elliott, *The Old World and the New, 1492–1650* (Cambridge, 1970), 42.
[29] Gustav Jahoda, *Images of Savages: Ancient Roots of Modern Prejudice in Western Culture* (New York, 1999), 97; see also Frank Lestringant, *Cannibals: The Discovery and Representation of the Cannibal from Columbus to Jules Verne* (Berkeley, 1997).

But rather than justifying conquest, the labelling served to focus attention on groups perceived to be involved in degenerate activities. Thus the meanings of representation utilised by the authors were dialogic, in that they drew on powerful pre-existing cultural ideas which served to solidify the images into popular consciousness and to differentiate the wreckers from the 'better sorts' of society, thereby emphasising social distance.

Another important theme that runs through the hostile press coverage and sermons concerns drunkenness during wrecking events. Granted, alcohol was one of the universal cargoes; most ships carried some form of alcohol or spirits, a major source of government income through import duties. Thus alcohol was a seemingly ubiquitous commodity that washed ashore. However, it is impossible to know the true extent of drunkenness during the wrecking event. Just like the gin craze, the magnitude of public concern over drunkenness bore little relation to the actual level of occurrence.[30] At the root of anxiety about drunkenness were fears that excessive alcohol would lead to sin and degeneracy, fears that found voice in sixteenth-century sermons and pamphlets, and which were conveyed into the nineteenth century.[31] It is telling that news reports and sermons used wrecking as a form of moral commentary to dramatise the depravity of drunkenness on the part of the lower orders. Class fears were readily apparent, for drunken behaviour on the part of the gentry and upper classes was ignored. Indeed, James Silk Buckingham, a well-known proponent of the temperance movement originally from Falmouth, maintained society believed that 'intoxication' was the 'mark of a gentleman, as indicative of high breeding', and that 'the higher classes, clergy as well as laity, seemed more frequently inebriated than the lower'.[32] Thus, any movement on the part of the lower classes to partake in higher quality spirits such as those available through shipwreck and smuggling, rather than local rough beer, was seen as an affront, a threat to the social fabric, and evidence that the poor were living 'above their station'.[33] In other words, spirits were a form of cultural capital not to be in the possession of the coastal poor.

It is therefore significant that in many wrecking accounts drunkenness, resulting in either the moral or physical danger – even death – of the wrecker is featured. For example, the *London Journal* reported in November 1720 that when a Dutch ship laden with brandy and saffron ran aground near Falmouth, 'some of those plunderers having drunk so much brandy, and being

30  Jessica Warner, *Craze: Gin and Debauchery in an Age of Reason* (New York, 2002), 4; Jonathan White, 'The "Slow but Sure Poyson": The Representation of Gin and its Drinkers, 1736–1751', *Journal of British Studies*, 42 (January 2003), 38.
31  Dana Rabin, 'Drunkenness and Responsibility for Crime in the Eighteenth Century', *Journal of British Studies*, 44, no. 3 (July 2005), 459, 465.
32  James Silk Buckingham, *Autobiography of James Silk Buckingham: Including his Voyages, Travels, Adventures, Speculations, Successes and Failures ...* Vol. I (London, 1855), 33–34.
33  Warner, *Craze*, 37.

busy in the hole [hold] with a candle, they set fire to the brandy by which means the ship and cargo were destroyed and two of the ruffians perished in the flames'.[34] *The Times*, reporting on the wreck of the *Resolution* in 1817 in Mount's Bay, also stressed that the wrecking was dangerous. One man from Wendron was drowned while attempting to save some of the cargo, but more especially, 'two other persons got so much intoxicated with wine, that they were unable to reach home, and were next day found dead by the roadside, having perished through the inclemency of the weather'.[35]

If the newspapers did not report on physical danger and death that awaited the wrecker, they underscored the negative behaviour that could result. The *West Briton* described drunkenness at the wreck of the *Ocean* in 1826, when, it claimed, some of the male plunderers 'knocked in the heads of three or four casks of wine, into which they dipped their hats and drank what they took up in them. As the day advanced, the plunderers, male and female, became intoxicated, and a variety of contests, some of them of the most ludicrous description, took place'.[36] Of more concern, however, than 'ludicrous' behaviour was the fear that alcohol would inflame violence. Thus the *General Evening Post* reported in 1751 that the people of Looe were 'so used to night work, so Habituated to Defiance of any Authority and Contempt of Laws, and generally more or less so inflamed with Spirituous Liquors that they are ever ready to perpetuate any Villainy that their Violent Temper and Love of Lucre shall prompt them to'.[37]

These reports of drunkenness were not limited to Cornwall. The country people of Wales, when plundering a Bristol merchant ship in 1758, 'broached the wine and spirits, got immediately drunk, and committed the most violent outrages'.[38] They were again reported to have imbibed too much alcohol during a wreck in 1817, when 'hundreds of men and women were reduced to nearly a state of insensibility through intoxication'.[39] *The Times* reported on mass drunkenness after a shipwreck near Kirk Maughold in Scotland, when a large hogshead was discovered by locals, who proceeded to 'tap the admiral'. Thus some individuals were 'carried home on men's backs, others on horseback, some in carts, others remained on the field of battle till next morning, so completely in that state familiarly but significantly known as "dead drunk," that their very mouths had to be opened with spoons, knives, &c., in order to

34 *London Journal*, 18 November 1720, quoted in John Vivian, *Tales of Cornish Wreckers* (Truro, 1969), 5–6.
35 *The Times*, 15 January 1817.
36 *West Briton*, 14 April 1826.
37 *General Evening Post* (London), January 1751, quoted in Vivian, *Tales of Cornish Wreckers*, 8–9.
38 *Annual Register*, November 1758, 113.
39 *Annual Register*, September 1817, 90.

prevent even more serious consequences'.[40] One of the most sensationalistic passages describing alcohol comes from the *Limerick Chronicle*, reprinted by the *Annual Register*. The wreckers were 'already excited by the taste of ardent spirits', when one of their number was shot by a coastguard. The wreckers then 'commence[d] a scene of indiscriminate wreck and plunder ... Many of these inhuman wretches were seen stretched upon the beach like pigs, in a beastly state of stupefaction from the liberal draughts of whiskey they had imbibed; and several died from too frequently indulging in this poisonous liquid!'[41]

The clergy exploited similar rhetoric regarding the dangers of alcohol. In an extract of a letter written by 'a Clergyman of Penzance', actually Rev. George C. Smith, the hazard of alcohol at wrecks is illustrated: 'Should a vessel be laden with wine or spirits, she brings them certain death: the rage and fighting to stave in the casks and bear away the spoil in kettles, and all kinds of vessels, is brutal and shocking; to drunkenness and fighting succeed fatigue, cold, wet, suffocation, and death!'[42] If alcohol did not exacerbate wrecking behaviours during the event, then it was blamed for causing people to be involved in wrecking in the first place. Rev. Eden pleaded with his congregation that they should not have spent their earnings in the alehouse or beer-shop during the summer; drinking was the cause of their misfortune during the winter, and hence the source of their temptation to go wrecking.[43]

The newspaper and clerical accounts warning of the perils of wrecking also emphasised the potential danger to women and children; the presence of women and children at wrecks was not unusual, as we have seen. Nevertheless, the noting of their attendance was not intended to comment on the everyday activities of the country people, but rather to underscore the depravity of an activity that would use women and children. Some accounts find humour in the women's activity, while others are scandalised. The *West Briton* delighted in a report of competition between 'ball maidens' (female mine workers) and 'a party of damsels who were on the lookout for secreted plunder'. The struggle over the goods – a hidden box of figs – 'lasted for two hours, in the course of which some of the combatants were reduced to a state approaching nudity. In the end the ball maidens were victorious, and carried off the prize.'[44] After the wreck of the *Ocean* in 1826, the same paper also targeted women: 'a greater part of the miscreants were women, who carried off whatever they could lay their hands on, and were very dexterous in concealing bottles of wine and

---

40  *Mona's Herald*, reprinted in *The Times*, 22 December 1842.
41  *Limerick Chronicle*, reprinted in the *Annual Register*, December 1833, 172–173.
42  *The Times*, 22 September 1818.
43  Rev. Robert Eden, *An Address* [on Ephes. IV.28] *to Depredators and Wreckers on the Sea Coast* (London, 1840), 19.
44  *West Briton*, 5 February 1819.

other things, so as to elude the search'.[45] The presence of children, too, was employed by the press to epitomise the degeneracy of wreckers. The *General Evening Post* of London reported in January 1751 that at the wreck of a brigantine near Looe, 'even the children were proud to stagger under the Burden of a painted board'.[46] Women and children outside of Cornwall were also shown as involved in the business. When the smack *Grampus* wrecked near Carlisle in 1821, *The Times* noted that 'even women assisted in the unfeeling work'.[47]

A more sympathetic view of women and children was provided by Rev. George C. Smith. He describes Predannack, near Mullion, as an area 'sadly infested with wreckers'. He continues: 'The moment the vessel touches the shore she is considered fair plunder, and men, women, and children are working on her to break her up, night and day', adding that 'the precipices they descend, the rocks they climb, and the billows they buffet, to seize the floating fragments are the most frightful and alarming I ever beheld'. Smith was not condoning wrecking, however. Indeed, he underscored his concern about his wrecker parishioners: 'Imagine to yourself 500 little children in a parish, brought up every winter this way, and encouraged, both by precept and example, to pursue this horrid system.'[48] Smith was most certainly exaggerating the numbers of children involved in wrecking, especially since he was declaring his success in turning his parishioners away from the activity. But for Smith, the presence of children sent out a message: wrecking was self-perpetuating because young children were inducted into it at an early age. This was a moral outrage that had to be prevented through religious education.

The perceived threats offered by unruly mobs of drunken wreckers, coupled with the deleterious effects on the family and social order through the involvement of women and children, served to support yet another elite apprehension. Wreckers were threatening cherished values and national reputation, hence many of the epithets used against them. Of particular salience is the use of the binary opposition of barbarity versus civility. The *Western Flying Post* expressed this in a report from 1768: 'Notwithstanding immediate assistance was sent from this town [Plymouth] to ships lately wrecked on our coasts, such was the inhumanity of the Country People, that they stole the greatest part of their cargoes – What vile behaviour. Is this a civilised country?!'[49] Fifty-three years later, *The Times* opined that the behaviour of the country people 'was most disgraceful to a civilized country', when they

---

45  *West Briton*, 14 April 1826.
46  *General Evening Post* (London), January 1751, quoted in Vivian, *Tales of Cornish Wreckers*, 9.
47  *The Times*, 19 December 1821.
48  Rev. G.C. Smith, *The Wreckers; or a Tour of Benevolence from St Michael's Mount to the Lizard Point* (London, 1818), 8–9. He also published an extract of the letter in *The Times*, 22 September 1818.
49  *Western Flying Post*, 29 February 1768.

plundered the *Mercury* wrecked at Duddon.[50] The identification of wreckers with 'barbarous' natives of North America is explicitly drawn by Rev. Thomas Francklyn of Dorset in a 1761 sermon. In fact, in his mind the wreckers were even more barbarous, for even 'the very native <u>Indians</u> of <u>Virginia</u> use all possible Hospitality and Civility to Persons in Distress.'[51] He was echoing the juxtaposition of barbarity and civility that was being levelled by contemporary philosophers and writers such as Montaigne, Swift, and Voltaire against those Europeans who were deemed to be perpetuating cruelty among their own people, or against those who were societal outcasts.[52]

The use of such rhetoric to emphasise the danger wrecking posed to the established order and to national reputation was common currency. As we have seen in Chapter 3, politicians used the same language in debates over wreck bills, and it also appears in sermons of the period. Francklyn exhorted his flock to desist from wrecking, not only because of the 'Terrors of an Act of Parliament, threatening Pains, and Penalties, and Death', but because he wished the local gentry to distribute his sermon 'among their Neighbours and Tenants on the Sea-Coast, to try what may be done towards stopping the Progress of an Evil generally complained of, and justly styled in the Act itself, "An Enormity that is a Scandal to the Nation".'[53]

Clergy also stressed the theme of national reputation to shame their parish-ioners into desisting from wrecking. In 1840, Rev. Eden of Leigh, in Essex, exhorted his parishioners to turn in wrecked goods they had secreted by refer-ring to the reputation of wreckers of the past, whose 'fiendish habit was to rejoice in every wreck which occurred, to gloat with savage pleasure over the groans and agonies of the perishing sufferers … a plunder which was often stained with blood …', but, he added to shame them, 'And well I remember thinking that it could not be possible, that *Englishmen* could so act.'[54] His own parishioners, it seems, were beginning to follow the sins of the wreckers of old. To combat this slide into depravity, Eden had his sermon published, 'hoping that it may be of service in other parishes on the sea-coast.'[55]

Occasionally, commentators drew on experiences from other countries to suggest ways to counter wrecking. In 1843 one New Romney inhabitant wrote in to *The Times* recommending that the French example be followed: the French had recently arrested, tried, and condemned to prison plunderers

---

[50] *The Times*, 19 December 1821.
[51] Thomas Francklyn, *Serious Advice and Fair Warning to All that Live Upon the Seacoast* (London, 1761), 43.
[52] See Lestringant, *Cannibals* and Claude Rawson, *God, Gulliver and Genocide: Barbarism and the European Imagination, 1492–1945* (Oxford, 2002).
[53] Francklyn, *Serious Advice*, 10. This sermon was in response to the passage of 26 Geo. II c. 19.
[54] Eden, *An Address to Depredators and Wreckers*, 12.
[55] Eden, *An Address to Depredators and Wreckers*, 1.

of the wrecks of the British ships *Reliance* and *Conqueror*. He maintained that, 'It would most signally be aiding the cause of humanity if the authorities on Romney Marshes would follow the example set them by their neighbours; for such wholesale plunder as has taken place here lately I never would have believed had it not come under my observation.'[56] His opinion was seconded by the members of the parliamentary Select Committee on Shipwrecks who had come to the same conclusion.[57] Thus even England's mortal enemy, France, was able to control wrecking, which highlighted England's failure. Others did not offer specific suggestions, but instead issued calls for reform to save the national reputation. After reporting on the deaths of wreckers by intoxication after the *Resolution* wreck in 1817, the Plymouth paper opined, 'Surely some step ought to be taken to prevent the reoccurrence of scenes which, by the eyes of strangers, stamp such disgrace on the country at large.'[58]

The rhetoric applied to wrecking discourse contained the same elements as other forms of public dialogue in the eighteenth and nineteenth centuries. It emphasised elite apprehensions of the physical threat to trade, combined with 'self-deprecation, even self-flagellation', characteristics which 'featured ... in contemporary discourse, especially when Protestant doctrine, accentuated by successive waves of evangelical fervour, took command'.[59] The presence of wrecking, therefore, was a national embarrassment. This was intensified by the ruling elite's perceptions that wrecking was effectively managed not only by France, but by countries of the Mediterranean, a situation untenable to those who believed in Britain's place as an exceptional example to the world. John Henniker, an MP for New Romney who had suffered through two shipwrecks, summed it up during the debate over Burke's wreck bill in 1776. In northern England, 'the gentlemen in the neighbourhood gave every assistance in their power, but with very little purpose', while in the Mediterranean, 'he had everything returned that was saved; and when he offered gratuity for the trouble, the answer received was "No, you have already enough in the loss of our ship, we will take nothing."'[60] William Falconer, too, commented on the lack of wrecking activity in the Mediterranean as opposed to England's 'bloodhound train, by rapine's lust impell'd', consequently engaging in the

56 *The Times*, 28 February 1843.
57 See PP, *First Report from the Select Committee on Shipwrecks*, 10 August 1843.
58 *The Times*, 15 January 1817.
59 Paul Langford, *The Short Oxford History of the British Isles: The Eighteenth Century, 1688–1815* (Oxford, 2002), 12. See also Peter Mandler, *The English National Character: The History of an Idea from Edmund Burke to Tony Blair* (New Haven, 2006).
60 'Debate on Mr. Burke's Bill to prevent the Plundering of Shipwrecks', 27 March, 30 April, 1776, in *Cobbett's Parliamentary History*, Vol. XVIII (1774–76), 1298–1302.

self-flagellating national rhetoric.[61] Thus wrecking was a threat to the values central to English identity – patriotism and commercial prowess.[62]

Eighteenth-century rhetoric incorporated the barbarity and civility dichotomy as a means of categorising commoners within society, but this language could also be utilised in another way. Rhetoric and symbolism were used by the press as a form of social control to persuade locals to behave, in other words, to eschew superstitious beliefs and to act with civility.[63] Reports of wrecking, like reports of superstitious beliefs, were often prefaced by comments in the form of 'laments'; this is especially evident by the nineteenth century. A good example comes from the *West Briton*: 'it is scarcely credible, though unfortunately too true, that some of the ruffians ... actually robbed the Captain of his watch and plundered all the unfortunate seamen of the clothes they endeavoured to save' and

> we are sorry to state, that on the first intimation of the disaster, a number of persons ... crowded down with the view of plundering the stores. We state these facts with shame and sorrow, but truth requires that they should be stated in order that effective measures may be taken to prevent a repetition of scenes so disgraceful, on the occurrence of any future disaster of a like melancholy description.[64]

By reporting such incidences, and sensationalising the activities, local communities could be 'shamed' into proper, civilised behaviour.[65] Incidentally, after the *West Briton* reported the attack on the French ship *Ocean* on 14 April 1826, prefaced by a 'lament', it published a recantation a week later: 'False report in previous issue: conduct good'.

Whether commentators' concern was for the safety of property, or national reputation, or for moralistic reasons, they wished to see the end of the practice of wrecking. They used the newspapers as a vehicle to sway public opinion: 'depredators ... should be sought after, and made an example, to deter others from following up a system of plunder so infamously brutal, and endeavour

---

[61] William Falconer, *A Critical Edition of the Poetical Works of William Falconer*, ed. by William R. Jones (Lewiston, Queenstown, Lampeter, 2003).

[62] See Linda Colley, *Britons: Forging the Nation, 1707–1837* (New Haven and London, 1992), where she discusses the rise and role of patriotic rhetoric in the development of 'Britishness'.

[63] Although there is much debate encircling the concept of 'social control', I will use the meaning not of an achieved state, but of the action of the dominant classes in seeking to 'modify the behaviour of another in its own interests'. Morag Shiach, 'Popular Culture and the Periodic Press 1830–1855', in *Discourse on Popular Culture: Class, Gender and History in Cultural Analysis, 1730 to the Present* (Oxford, 1989), 71–100. See also Herman Roadenberg and Pieter Spierenburg, eds, *Social Control in Europe*, Vol. 1: *1500–1800* (Ohio, 2004), introduction.

[64] *West Briton*, 21 April 1815; 14 April 1826.

[65] Owen Davies, 'Newspapers and the Popular Belief in Witchcraft and Magic in the Modern Period', *Journal of British Studies*, 37 (April 1998), 147–149. For a discussion of the press's educational mandate, see Mark Hampton, *Visions of the Press in Britain, 1850–1950* (Chicago, 2004).

to bring some of the principal ruffians to justice'.[66] The press also reported on the indictment of wreckers, holding up their fate as an example. In 1820, after Thomas Moore of Moreton, in Chester, was convicted of stealing rope from a wreck and given the death sentence, *The Times* opined, 'It is to be hoped, that all persons who have hitherto looked upon wrecking as a lawful trade, will learn from his sentence, that by the law of the land, as well as the laws of humanity, it is considered a most atrocious crime'.[67] At least one Cornish clergyman, however, saw moral transformation rather than the law as the solution: 'nothing short of moral and intellectual light in universal diffusion can accomplish its entire suppression' – thereby acknowledging the deep hold wrecking had on his parishioners.[68]

## Wrecking as Moral Panic

The prevalence and tone of such wrecking rhetoric found in newspapers and sermons, as also in public political discussion, suggests that wrecking was the subject of sporadic 'moral panics'. The concept was first coined in the 1960s, but has proven to be a useful paradigm to explain outbursts of concern about a group of people or their activities which are perceived to threaten the fabric of society.[69] Moral panics follow typical patterns.[70] First, they can erupt in reaction to the public's concern over transgressive behaviours that are perceived as dangerous. Second, moral panics usually pinpoint a suitable enemy who is believed to be the cause of the threat, usually an outcast group which has little power and which can easily be publically condemned and made a scapegoat. The target is 'preferably without even access to the battle-field of cultural politics'.[71] The wreckers were especially ideal: the descriptions emphasised a population who were poor, without easy recourse to law. None of the accounts identifies wreckers from other societal levels with the same language. Mention of the involvement of gentry, local merchants, and businessmen, or other 'gentlemen', is notably absent. An important component of

[66] *The Times*, 15 January 1817.
[67] *The Times*, 8 May 1822. Moore ultimately escaped this final penalty.
[68] 'The Wreckers' extract of a letter written by a Clergyman of Penzance, *The Times*, 22 September 1818.
[69] For historical studies utilising the moral panic model, see Peter King 'Moral Panics and Violent Street Crime 1750–2000: A Comparative Perspective', in Barry S. Godfrey, Clive Emsley, and Graeme Dunstall, eds, *Comparative Histories of Crime* (London, 2003), 53–71 and Jennifer Davis, 'The London Garotting Panic of 1862: A Moral Panic and the Creation of a Criminal Class in mid-Victorian England', in V.A.C. Gatrell, Bruce Lenman and Geoffrey Parker, *Crime and the Law: The Social History of Crime in Western Europe since 1500* (London, 1980).
[70] Erich Goode and Nachman Ben-Yehuda, *Moral Panics: The Social Construction of Deviance* (Oxford, 1994), 33–41.
[71] Cohen, *Folk Devils and Moral Panics*, xi.

the scapegoat criterion is that moral panics need a suitable 'victim' with whom to identify and to feel moral outrage for.[72] In this case, the injured parties were either the shipwreck victims themselves, if the call was for humanity, or the merchants and insurers of Britain, if the concern was for the trade and commerce of the nation.[73] Third, there needs to be a consensus that the group or activity is a threat to society, and that the threat is not an isolated incident; it could become pervasive. Wreckers were not only plundering vessels along the entire coast of Britain, but if left unchecked, their activities could jeopardise the nation's commerce, and thus endanger the economic underpinnings of society. Commentators also argued that national reputation was at stake. It was in consensus-building that the moral entrepreneurs had the most vital role. A flurry of letters debating the guilt of the Deal boatmen of wrecking, published in *The Times*, illustrates this function: the press are the 'archetypal carriers', of moral panics and sensationalised reporting.[74] Fourth, moral panics are typically initiated by an extreme or dramatic case, rather than a volume of cases, but their reporting is disproportionate.[75] The introduction of the first wreck bill of the eighteenth century came with agitation from the East India Company after it lost the *Albemarle* in 1708; John Knill's wreck bill, promoted by the Cornish elite, came after the wreck and plunder of the *Brielle* in 1792; the Bishop of St David's clarion call came after several wrecks on the Cardiganshire and Pembrokeshire coast in 1816; and Rev. Eden's sermon was published after the wreck of the brig *Ewen* on the Essex coast in 1840.[76] Several news reports published in *The Times* in 1843 regarding the plundering of the *Jessie Logan* were used as examples by William Palmer to provide recommendations in his *The Law of Wreck, Considered with a View to its Amendment*.[77] These cases were reported as if they were indicative of mass wrecking activity, but as we have seen, they were actually isolated events.

The press not only sensationalised wrecking events; it was involved in outright misrepresentation which resulted in symbolic violence against the coastal populace, and thus created mythologised 'folk devils'. These cases of misrepresentation also illustrate the reflective and performative aspects of the myths. For example, in a 1774 Welsh wrecking case the local newspaper reporters falsified details, claiming that the wreckers had employed false lights to lure ashore the *Charming Jenny*; the captain's testimony did not corroborate

---

[72] Cohen, *Folk Devils and Moral Panics*, xi.

[73] *The Times*, 18 May 1810.

[74] Cohen, *Folk Devils and Moral Panics*, xiii, xxiii.

[75] Cohen, *Folk Devils and Moral Panics*, xii, xxii.

[76] CA/B/46/99, Knill's Wreck Bill, 1792; Circular Letter of the Bishop of St David's, *The Times*, 6 January 1817; Eden, *An Address to Depredators and Wreckers*, 1.

[77] *The Times*, 21 January 1843, 28 March 1843; William Palmer, *The Law of Wreck, Considered with a View to its Amendment* (London, 1843).

their report.[78] In 1792, Joseph Banfield professed that the local press's claims that the coastal people had 'plunder[ed] the people of their cloaths as they came ashore' after the wreck of the *Brielle* was 'totally destitute of the truth.'[79] Likewise, Coastguard Inspecting Commander David Williams of Padstow asserted that the events surrounding the wreck of the *Jessie Logan* in 1843 were misrepresented by the press.[80]

Another important Cornish case which was falsified and used as evidence of wrecker depravity, and which was thus mythologised, includes events surrounding the 1817 wreck of the *Resolution* in Mount's Bay. The veracity of the reports on the wreck has heretofore not been scrutinised. Rather, the events have been described in popular history as a 'full-scale orgy', that even the Inniskilling Dragoons could not hold the wreckers back. The wreckers 'drove the soldiers from the beach and continued drinking well into the next day'.[81] The source of the story, although not identified, is an article quoted in *The Times* on 15 January 1817 from the *Plymouth Gazette*. The report claimed that after the *Resolution* had come ashore,

> the vessel was entered by thousands of ruffians, who proceeded to plunder. As the private property of the Captain and crew was carried off; the heads of the pipes and hogsheads were staved in, and kegs, &c. filled with liquor; [Of] the whole of the cargo of 375 pipes and 25 hogsheads of wine, only between 50 and 60 pipes were saved by agents. Several contests took place between the plunderers, each being anxious to secure the greatest booty. About 14 dismounted dragoons from Helston came to the spot, but they were wholly unable to restrain the ferocious multitude that crushed in on all sides ... Almost the whole of the cargo might have been saved, had it not been for the infamous conduct above described.

The Customs account initially reporting the wreck did not mention that any plundering had occurred.[82] So what did happen? Further investigation shows us that a conflict between the Customs officers and a self-appointed agent for the *Resolution*, Francis Symons of Falmouth, is at the centre of the matter. Symons vindictively accused the Customs officers and the official agent of the *Resolution* of neglect of duty when he failed to receive salvage payment for work he claimed to have done. Indeed, he alleged that *he* was the official

---

[78] Geoffrey Place, 'Wreckers: The Fate of the *Charming Jenny*', *Mariner's Mirror*, 76, no. 2 (1990), 167–168.

[79] HO 43/4, Joseph Banfield to Mr Knill, 28 February 1792, Falmouth. Extract of letter also given in John G. Rule, 'Wrecking and Coastal Plunder', in Douglas Hay, Peter Linebaugh, et al., *Albion's Fatal Tree: Crime and Society in Eighteenth-Century England* (London, 1975), appendix, 187.

[80] Testimony of David Williams, PP, *First Report from the Select Committee on Shipwrecks*, 10 August 1843, 302.

[81] Bella Bathurst, *The Wreckers: A Story of Killing Seas, False Lights and Plundered Ships* (London, 2005), 241.

[82] CUST 68/23, Penzance Collector to Board, 13 January 1817.

agent. Testimony, including that by the salvors, indicated that he had not even been in attendance at the wreck. It was almost assuredly Symons who instigated the claims that Customs had been negligent and had allowed the ship to be plundered, charges which were eventually picked up and sensationalised by the press.[83] The Customs collector admitted to the Customs Board that some 'plundering' had occurred, that 'the Country People who assembled in large Numbers ... certainly manifested a disposition to plunder, and actually carried off in Milk Pails, Pitchers, small Casks, and in many Instances in their Hatts & even Shoes, small quantities of the Wine'. But, he stressed, the officers and dragoons recovered a large quantity of the wine. In answer to the charge that he had failed to control the 'ferocious multitude', that he had lost the majority of the cargo and failed to find the perpetrators, he declared that 'it did not appear necessary to us, to adopt legal Measures for securing or prosecuting the Persons in question, nor do we understand that any such Measures were thought necessary by the Agents or other Persons concerned in salving the Cargo –'.[84]

Although the collector described widespread wrecking – actually harvesting – he was not unduly concerned about it. He explained that the attention of the Customs officers was on salving the cargo itself, 'a Measure, in our judgement, more beneficial to the Revenue & the Parties interested than the pursuit & attempt to apprehend the petty Depredators'. He was emphatic that there 'was no report ... of any extensive or aggravated Instances of Plunder'.[85] In other words, the accounts from Symons and the press were without merit. The board must have concurred, as the collector was allowed to resume his duties. Thus there is little evidence to corroborate the more sensationalistic assertions of *The Times* article.

The portrayal of the wreck of the *Resolution* may have been used as means of spicing up the reports to sell more papers. This objective has been noted as a factor behind the increased reporting of crime in general, as the *Chelmsford Chronicle* admitted in 1786: 'it has long been a general complaint that our public papers during the recesses of parliament, especially since the return

[83] See CUST 68/52, Penzance Board to Collector, 14 May 1817, where the Customs Board reported to Penzance that detailed complaints had been filed 'at the request of an agent of that place [Falmouth]'. See also CUST 68/22, F.S. Symons, Falmouth, to Penzance Collector, 17 January 1817; Penzance Collector to Board, 18 January 1817; Symons to Falmouth Collector, 8 January 1817; Penzance Collector to Symons, 20 January 1817, 10 February 1817; Petition of Frances Stansfield Symons to Commissioners of Customs, 12 March 1817; Richard Pearce to Commissioners of Customs, 15 March 1817; Penzance Collector to John Borlase, esq, Solicitor, Helston, 24 March 1817; Penzance Collector to Board, 9 April 1817, 5 May 1817; CUST 68/52, Board to Penzance Collector, 14 May 1817; CUST 68/23, Penzance Collector to Board, 20 May 1817; CUST 68/53, Board to Penzance Collector, 30 May 1817, 26 June 1817; CUST 68/24, 8 October 1817.
[84] CUST 68/73, Penzance Collector to Board, 20 May 1817.
[85] CUST 68/23, Penzance Collector to Board, 20 May 1817.

of peace ... have become exceedingly dull and unentertaining'.[86] And there was nothing like lurid stories of crime to attract readership. Additionally, the account of the *Resolution*, in leaving out the personal vendetta which gave genesis to the negative reporting, shows not only the reflective properties of the myth in shaping perceptions of the press – the country people must have been guilty because they are wreckers – but also how the press reinforced the use of symbolic violence against the Cornish coastal populace. The article consequently became a vehicle for the transmission of the myth into popular consciousness. Therefore, in moral panics, the 'untypical is made typical ... the insulting labels are applied to all'.[87] The language of the reports did not differentiate between harvest activity and violent plunder, and a misleading impression is given of the nature and extent of violent plundering. Finally, moral panics involved the repetition of metaphors and themes, such as those discussed above. As Erich Goode and Nachman Ben-Yehuda point out, 'one indication that a moral panic is taking place is the stereotypical fashion with which the subject is treated in the press'.[88]

If we can see that wrecking is a subject of moral panic, what underpinned this reaction? Why were the elite, as represented by the press and clergy, so interested in popularising the wrecking problem by using such emotive and dramatic rhetoric? On the surface, the rhetoric against wrecking was a control and power issue: a revenue issue precisely. Why worry about oranges that are in a 'perishing state', or destroy damaged tobacco rather than let it fall into the hands of the populace? But even more crucially, why describe these people as 'barbarians' and 'plunderers' when for the most part they were only involved in the harvesting of wrecked cargo, mostly damaged, from the beach? Clearly, for the eighteenth century, the issues of cultural and economic capital came into play, as well as the elite's view of the proper ordering of society and fears of popular uprising. By the advent of the nineteenth century, the 'moral revolution' and the rise of the 'culture of sensibility' had an effect on the wrecker stereotype. British culture underwent a change in national character which was the result of the combined movements in morality by religious evangelicals, dissenters, and secular moral entrepreneurs. How these movements altered and affected the attitudes of the lower classes and what their role was in the 'civilising process' need further study.[89] A secondary result of this movement was less toleration of violence in society, which made it appear that there was

[86] Quoted in Peter King, *Crime, Justice and Discretion in England, 1740–1820* (Oxford, 2000), 165.
[87] Cohen, *Folk Devils and Moral Panics*, xix.
[88] Cohen, *Folk Devils and Moral Panics*, xxvii–xxx; Goode and Ben-Yehuda, *Moral Panics*, 26.
[89] Robert Shoemaker, *The London Mob: Violence and Disorder in Eighteenth-Century England* (London, 2004), 290. See also Norbert Elias, *The Civilizing Process: The History of Manners and State Formation and Civilization*, trans. by E. Jephcott (Oxford, 1994).

increasing crime.[90] The elite conceptualised their views of crime, including wrecking, as consisting only of certain groups. The 'degenerates' emerge as a clearly defined 'problem' for which 'solutions' can be recommended. By stereotyping images of crime, and creating a simplified view, the elite had the 'luxury of reacting to crime with a stock response rather than thinking too deeply about the issues involved',[91] a process that is clearly evident in the reporting of wrecking. Consequently, the wreckers themselves were collectively demonised within press accounts, which resulted in increasing visibility of the subjectified wrecker image.[92] In addition to its conceptualisation as a crime, the 'moral' aspect of the moral panic is the central to the survival of wrecking as a popular myth. It also shows us why wrecking became most identified with Cornwall.

## Methodism and Wrecking as Popular Myth

The continued popularising of the wrecker motif gained further momentum by its use not only by the press and clergy, but also by Methodist writers who adopted identical rhetoric and hyperbole for didactic purposes. Indeed, it is not an exaggeration to claim, as does Simon Trezise, that 'the primary written source for the villainous wrecker is the literature of Methodism'.[93] The stereotype of the wrecker, and hence the wrecking motif, was exploited by Methodist writers for their morality tales, with the majority of novels being produced after the 1840s. The writers not only adopted the reporting conventions already established, but they also imposed the additional trope of deliberate wrecking by false lights, making wreckers even more heinous, and thus a more flagrant example of immorality. In this, the Methodists employed a metaphor which was similar to that already recognised as a 'cultural code', the shipwreck. Shipwreck metaphors had been used to denote 'punishment, test, or trial, or as a means of spiritual education' for centuries.[94] The most influential of the nineteenth-century narratives used Cornwall as their backdrop – writers perceived it as a marginalised locale because of distance, geography,

---

90  Clive Emsley, *Hard Men: The English and Violence since 1750* (London, 2005).

91  J.A. Sharpe, *Crime in Early Modern England, 1550–1750* (London, 1984, 1992), 165–166.

92  See also Geoffrey Quilley, 'The Imagery of Travel in British Painting: With Particular Reference to Nautical and Maritime Imagery, circa 1740–1800' (unpublished Ph.D. thesis, University of Warwick, 1998), Chapter 7, 'The Negative Face of the Sea: Smuggling and Wrecking', 237–259, for a useful discussion of the wrecker in art.

93  Simon Trezise, 'The Sea-Dog, the Smuggler and the Wrecker: Literary Representations of Maritime Life in the West Country' (conference paper, University of Exeter, 20 October 2001), 26.

94  Landow, *Images of Crisis*, 17.

and Celticity.[95] These tales include James Sheridan Knowles's 'The Wreckers: A Cornish Tale' (1844); Rosa Kettle's *The Wreckers* (1857); and Malcolm Errym's *Sea Drift; or the Wreckers of the Channel: A Tale Ashore and Afloat* (1860). One of the most intriguing novels, in that it lent a window to other aspects of folk culture within Cornwall, was William B. Forfar's *The Wizard of Penwith*, printed in 1871. But it was the publication five years later in 1876 of James F. Cobb's Methodist morality tale, *The Watchers of the Longships*, which instigated further developments of the myth. Republished at least thirty-five times, most recently in 2005, it became a major if erroneous source for histories such as Hardy's *Lighthouses: Their History and Romance*, which in turn was used by Michael Oppenheim in his error-laden maritime history chapter in *Victoria County History of Cornwall* (1906), itself a major basis for Cornish shipwreck histories.[96] Cobb's book describes the wrecker:

> to the lazy and evil-disposed, who live from hand to mouth, and whose real trade was smuggling and wrecking, it [the clear weather] was by no means so welcome. The storms indeed which had heralded the approach of winter ... had brought the Sennen wreckers a rich harvest; but all these ill-gotten gains had long since been spent on drink; women and children were famishing; men, gaunt and morose, hung around the alehouse, or lounged on the beach, uttering curses upon the weather, the lighthouse, or the parson, whichever at the moment seemed to them the cause of their present poverty and misery – never once reflecting that their own evil and idle conduct was alone to blame for this.[97]

Thus Cobb's wrecker has multiple characteristics that were employed as examples of degeneracy: he transgresses societal rules by deliberately causing shipwrecks and preying on the misfortunes of the innocent; and he epitomises the evils of sloth and drink, a major theme of evangelicalism and moral reform. He also violates the work ethic through the sin of laziness, another sign of degeneracy.[98] The wreckers in Cobb's novel inhabit the Sennen district near Land's End; they are tinners, the group who bore the brunt of the sinful wrecker reputation. As vividly described by Andy Wood, miners and other industrial workers were viewed by the elite as 'lewd in their manners, profligate in their spending and irreligious in their habits ... a culturally degenerate and socially subversive isolated mass, cut off from normal society: the arche-

---

[95] See Simon Trezise, *The West Country as a Literary Invention: Putting Fiction in its Place* (Exeter, 2000) and Ella Westland, ed., *Cornwall: The Cultural Construction of Place* (Penzance, 1997).

[96] Michael Oppenheim, 'Maritime History', in *Victoria County History of Cornwall*, Vol. I (London, 1906), 475–511.

[97] James F. Cobb, *The Watchers of the Longships: A Tale of Cornwall in the Last Century* (London, 1877), 190.

[98] Michel Foucault, *Madness and Civilization: A History of Insanity in the Age of Reason*, trans. by Richard Howard (New York, 1965), 55–56.

typal "many-headed monster", inhabiting the "dark corners of the land".[99] And that description was not even taking into consideration the miner's known proclivities for wrecking! Even as far back as 1753, George Borlase accused tinners of laziness when they were wrecking rather than working.[100] By the mid-Victorian era, poverty was interpreted as a failure of character, and evidence of profligacy, idleness, and sin.[101] Therefore, the poor miner was the epitome of a lost soul who needed didactic material that would show him the error of his ways, and give him a datum point from which to measure his moral evolution.

Although popular Cornish belief holds that the stereotype of the wrecker was placed upon the county by non-Cornish authors, the stereotype was most likely both adopted and indigenous.[102] It was promoted by Cornish authors themselves, many of whom were Methodist. This is a point made by W.H. Hudson in 1908 when he claimed facetiously that 'the books containing these veracious statements, so flattering to the Cornish, are exceedingly popular for keeping these fables alive'.[103] Indeed, wrecking and smuggling were two Cornish themes that novelists found useful as literary devices since they were social problems that needed commentary and reform. Thus the stories were 'given a narrative "make-over" in order to make them acceptable, entertaining, and sometimes morally correct for the age's readership; a reader that was present both inside and outside Cornwall'.[104]

Ultimately, the press, clergy, and Methodist writers transformed wreckers from actual individuals into a mythic stereotype through the vehicles of the press, sermons, and novels. Antiquarian writers and folklore collectors such as Rev. Robert Hawker, Rev. Sabine Baring-Gould, Robert Hunt, and William Bottrell also had an important role in shaping the myth, but they were most likely influenced by the dominant discourse. As a result, the reality of inter-mittent wrecking reports was overshadowed by the use of moralising dialogue and by the telescoping of events characteristic of moral panics, making it appear that wreckers were out of control and a threat to society. The stereo-

---

99   Andy Wood, 'Custom, Identity and Resistance: English Free Miners and Their Law, c.1550–1800', in Paul Griffiths, Adam Fox, and Steve Hindle, eds, *The Experience of Authority in Early Modern England* (London and New York, 1996), 254.

100   Borlase to Onslow, 1 February 1753; 5 March 1753, in Thomas Cornish, ed., 'The Lanisley Letters: to Lt. General Onslow from George Borlase, his Agent at Penzance, 1750–53', *Journal of the Royal Institution of Cornwall*, 6, pt 22 (1880), 374, 377.

101   F. David Roberts, *The Social Conscience of the Early Victorians* (Stanford, California, 2002), 140–141, 144.

102   Peter Pern, ed., *Cornish Notes and Queries: Reprinted from the* Cornish Telegraph (London and Penzance, 1906), 292–297 and *Mariner's Mirror*, 70 (1984), 44, 388.

103   W.H. Hudson, *The Land's End: A Naturalist's Impressions in West Cornwall* (originally published London, 1908; reprinted London, 1980), 136.

104   Alan M. Kent, *The Literature of Cornwall: Continuity, Identity, Difference, 1000–2000* (Bristol, 2000), 130.

type became reflexive, in that popular writers told and retold the myths as fact. Indeed, as Goode and Ben-Yehuda explain, 'because the tale confirmed a certain public image of the events and who perpetrated them, it was repeated and believed as true', with little regard for what actually occurred.[105] The stories thus doubled back on the wrecker so that even his reality was interpreted without recognition of the shroud of mythical layers, or of the power of elite perception in shaping the dominant narratives. Thus the wrecker was altered from someone who practised varying forms of wrecking and who came from a population which had developed its own popular morality regarding its legitimacy to an objectified symbol of evilness, a 'folk devil' who became part of popular consciousness.

[105]  Goode and Ben-Yehuda, *Moral Panics*, 25.

# Conclusion
## Myths and Reputations Reconsidered

With the typecasting of the Cornish as wreckers in popular consciousness, their actions in relation to shipwrecks have been interpreted in terms of that identity, no matter their record of lifesaving. Indeed, the stereotype has been magnified in the popular press even in the early twenty-first century: witness the BBC headlines that opened this book – 'Timber galore for Cornish wreckers' after the 2002 wreck of the *Kodima*. The Cornish are conflicted about their wrecking past, and have contradictory reactions regarding their labelling as wreckers. As other marginalised groups have done, they have attempted to 'own' the myths through a retelling of the stories in their own way, whether in the yarns told to willing listeners, or through more permanent means of literature, theatre, and film.[1] And yet defensiveness is also apparent, played out in local denial whenever the topic of wrecking is introduced. Indeed wrecking is a sensitive subject. At the root of Cornish defensiveness is the accusation that they lured ships ashore using false lights, not that they were involved in the plunder of shipwrecks. A germane example illustrating their concerns comes from one recent popular history, where it is facetiously claimed:

> ... despite all this evidence – the victims, the lords, the shipowners, the sea-captains, the vicars, the officials – the locals remain adamant that there is no such thing as a real Cornish wrecker. In the bookshops and libraries, in museums and harbours, in bars, shops, hotels and tourist traps, the answer is always the same: the Cornish never deliberately wrecked ships and they never used false lights.[2]

It is true that the Cornish deny that they deliberately wrecked ships with false lights – there is no evidence for it, despite the above assertion – but they do not deny that they were wreckers. Thus, it is the conflation of the myth with reality that is at the heart of Cornish concerns, a conflation that does not take into account the sheer complexity of wrecking activities, the ubiquity of the

---

[1] See 'Wreckers', a musical written by Cornish teacher Timothy Tuck and performed by Maitland Area School in 1998, and 'The Wrecking Season', a film by Nick and Jane Darke (2005), which seeks to explain and extend the wrecker motif to emphasise the importance of wrecking-as-beachcombing. Cornwall has also adopted Daphne du Maurier, who transmitted the image of the mythic wrecker more than any other novelist in the twentieth century with her *Jamaica Inn* (1936).
[2] Bella Bathurst, *The Wreckers: A Story of Killing Seas, False Lights, and Plundered Ships* (London, 2005), 242.

practice in other coastal regions, or the historicity of the custom. Wrecking was not unique to Cornwall.

While the myth and the actuality of wrecking are intertwined, it has been possible to examine some of the strands separately; it has been equally important to recognise how those strands have influenced each other, and how they relate to wider culture – the reflective and performative aspects of myth-making – which sustained the image in popular consciousness. The myths of wrecking reflect societal concerns and the interests of their audiences; they are also performative in that they shaped those cultural views, as the Cornish can attest. Thus, the mythic stereotype became reified – touted as an accurate description of real wreckers – while the realities of wrecking were buried under accretions of moral, media, and entertainment discourses. It is perhaps telling that not only are contemporary accounts of explicit, conclusive cases of violent plundering limited, so too are independent versions of the wrecking myth. Indeed, the process of what Raphael Samuel describes as 'displacements, omissions, and reinterpretations through which myths in personal and collective memory take shape' is readily apparent, and the lineage of the many renditions of the wrecking myths can be traced from the few extant sources.[3] In other words, 'dynamics of corruption' have resulted in errors and biases that have crept in through the retellings to create substantially different fictional narratives that have become more a part of popular consciousness than are the actualities of wrecking.

But whether those wrecking narratives are told through Methodist novels, through dramatic films, or backdrops or plots for contemporary television programming, the actualities are just as intriguing. We can get beyond the popular and reductionist mythic view of wrecking, and can begin to understand with more sophistication the world of the coastal populace and their relationship to shipwrecks. E.P. Thompson's quest to 'rescue' the poor 'from the enormous condescension of posterity' has inspired many researchers to study the marginalised populations of history.[4] Wreckers can be included in the rescue. Although few would argue that wreckers per se have been lost to posterity, their reality has been clearly subsumed by the myth and was in desperate need of salvage.

The act of historical 'beach-combing', then, has revealed wrecking as a multifaceted, sophisticated cultural practice and cultural construct, made up of a complexity of attitudes and multiple points-of-view. It can no longer be understood as a straightforward example of an eighteenth-century elite

---

3  Raphael Samuel and Paul Thompson, *The Myths We Live By* (London and New York, 1990), 5. See for example Cathryn J. Pearce, '"Neglectful or Worse": A Lurid Tale of a Lighthouse Keeper and Wrecking in the Isles of Scilly', *Troze, the Online Journal of the National Maritime Museum Cornwall*, 1, no. 1 (September 2008).

4  E.P. Thompson, *The Making of the English Working Class* (London, 1963, 1980), 12.

assault on customary rights, nor can it be seen as a custom that was wholly practised and accepted by the coastal poor of Cornwall. The coastal populace, which included the poor and gentry alike, had their own popular morality, including the use of mediation and constraint, which allowed them to practise wrecking, salvage, and lifesaving simultaneously. And they had their own understanding of the law, a law that was murky and ill-understood by even the most educated elite.

Violent wrecking, although not as widespread and invidious as popular histories allow, has become part of the past. However, the popular conviction that individuals have the right to whatever they find washing ashore – harvesting, now called 'beach-combing' – remains strong into the twenty-first century despite its historic legal prohibition. The practice of wrecking-as-harvest shows continuity of both belief and practice throughout the British Isles and beyond. Wrecking is therefore much more nuanced than its survival in popular culture has indicated. Despite wrecking's historical complexity and its ability to offer an intriguing window on past practices, however, the vision of the more simplistic mythic wrecker will keep on grabbing the popular imagination because it continues to speak to the imagination. As Virginia Woolf so aptly phrased it, 'It is far harder to kill a phantom than a reality.' But behind the phantom the historical wrecker now lurks, a multi-dimensional figure who, for the most part, represents normal individuals who chanced upon 'gifts of the sea'.

# Appendix 1

## *Wreck Bills and Statutes, 1700–1854*

| Year | Title | Results | Statute Name |
|------|-------|---------|--------------|
| 1708 | To prevent Embezzlement of Goods and Merchandizes cast away upon, or near, the Coast of Great Britain … | Dropped by HC | |
| 1714 | For the preserving of all such Ships and Goods thereof which shall happen to be forced on Shore, or Stranded upon the coasts … | Passed | 12 Anne st. 2 c. 18 |
| 1718 | For enforcing and making perpetual an Act of the Twelfth Year of her late Majesty … | Passed | 4 Geo. I c. 12 |
| 1724 | To continue several acts therein … for preventing frauds … | Passed | 11 Geo. I c. 29 |
| 1736 | To render the Laws, now in being more effectual for saving and recovering Ships and Goods wrecked, or driven on the Shore … | Dropped by HC | |
| 1737 | For the better preserving of all such Ships, and Goods thereof, which shall happen to be stranded upon the Coasts … | Dropped by HL | |
| 1753 | For enforcing the Laws against Persons who shall steal or detain ship-wrecked Goods; and for the Relief of Persons suffering Losses thereby … | Passed | 26 Geo. II c. 19 |
| 1776 | For Preventing the inhuman practice of Plundering Ships that are shipwrecked on the Coasts of Great Britain … | Failed in HC | |
| 1792 | Knill's 'for more effectually preventing the plundering of wrecks' | To Home Office, but not to HC | |
| 1803 | For making effectual Provision for the Punishment of Offences in wilfully casting away, burning, or destroying ships or vessels … | Passed | 43 Geo. III c. 113 |
| 1808 | For preventing frauds and depredations on merchants, shipowners, and underwriters, within the jurisdiction of the Cinque Ports, and for remedying defects in the adjustment of salvage under the Statute of Anne … | Passed: Temporary Act | 48 Geo. III c. 130 |

| 1809 | For preventing frauds and depredations ... | Passed: Temporary Act | 49 Geo. III c. 122 |
|------|------|------|------|
| 1812 | For charging foreign liquors and tobacco derelict, Jetsam, Flotsam, Lagan or Wreck | Passed | 52 Geo. III c. 159 |
| 1813 | For preventing frauds ... to continue and amend 48 & 49 Geo. III | Passed | 53 Geo. III c. 87 |
| 1818 | For the more effectual Preservation of Property, in cases of Wreck, in England and Ireland ... | Dropped by HC | |
| 1821 | To continue and amend certain acts for preventing frauds ... and also for remedying certain defects relative to the adjustment of Salvage in England under an Act made in the twelfth year of Queen Anne | Passed | 1 & 2 Geo. IV c. 75 |
| 1827 | For consolidating and amending the Laws in England relative to malicious injuries to property | Passed | 7 & 8 Geo. IV c. 30, s. 9–11 |
| 1836 | Customs Act | Passed | 6 & 7 Will. IV c. 60 |
| 1837 | To amend the Laws relating to Burning or Destroying Buildings and Ships | Passed | 1 Vic c. 89, s. 4–7 |
| 1840 | To improve the Practice and Extend the Jurisdiction of the High Court of Admiralty | Passed | 3 & 4 Vic. c. 65, s.5 |
| 1845 | For the general regulation of Customs; as relates to Persons being in possession of Goods derelict Jetsam, Flotsam, or Wreck, and the disposal of such Goods | Passed | 8 & 9 Vic. c. 86 |
| 1846 | For Consolidating and Amending the Laws Relating to Wreck and Salvage | Passed | 9 & 10 Vic. c. 99 |
| 1850 | Mercantile Marine Act of 1850 | Passed | 13 & 14 Vic. c. 93 |
| 1854 | Merchant Shipping Act | Passed | 17 & 18 Vic. c. 104 |
| 1854 | Merchant Shipping Acts Repeal | Passed | 17 & 18 Vic. c. 120 |
| 1854 | Amendment of law relating to Wreck and Salvage | Dropped HC | |

## Cornish Wreck Returns, Constabulary Report 1837[1]

| District | Ships Plundered?[2] | Wrecks?[3] | Property Depredation?[4] |
|---|---|---|---|
| Fowey | None within past three years: 'but in December 1830 three Foreign Vessels (Viz.) a Russian Brig – a French schooner and a Dutch Galliot were wrecked at Port Holland (lives saved) 4 miles East of Nare Head when a great Body of people assembled for the purpose of plunder – but were in a great measure prevented from doing so by the Coast Guards – in January 1834 a Swedish Barque was wrecked near Looe laden with Staves – no assemblage of persons expressly for plunder.' | None | Nil |
| Falmouth | 'Only two Wrecks, small Coasting Vessels … This was in the River Helford, where it was not probable there would be any Assemblage for the purpose of Plunder, and to the W$^d$ of the Lizard.' | Two | None |
| Penzance | 'The Lower Classes of inhabitants more particularly, assemble for the purposes of plunder, very few act as Salvors. On the 1st October last, the French brig Le Landais was wrecked near St Just, three or four thousand persons assembled, the greater part continued during 36 hours to plunder as much as they could or whenever they could.' | Zephyr (1834)<br><br>Active (1834) | Not any – went to pieces a long way out.<br><br>Case of champagne, value £1400. Protected by Coast Guard Boats. |

[1] Compiled from HO 73/3, Questionnaires returned by coastguard stations around the British coast surveying wrecking activities for the Royal Commission on a Rural Constabulary, 1836–37.

[2] The question reads in full: '2. On the occurrence of Wrecks, have there been any and what extent of assemblages for the purposes of plunder? – Will you state instances?'

[3] 'What wrecks have occurred on the station within your command during the last three years?'

[4] The final category was enumerated on the back page of the questionnaire: 'Description and Value of Property, if any, supposed to be lost through Depredation.'

| | | | |
|---|---|---|---|
| | | *Le Reaux* (1834) | Not of any consequence. Driven on shore and dismasted. |
| | | *Le Landais* (1837) | 'About one fourth plundered & carried away, also the sails, Rigging &c by Men with hatchets and Knives one fourth destroyed to prevent loss of life and a general fight.' |
| Padstow | 'When a wreck takes place on this Coast the Assemblage is generally very Great. On the instance of the within mentioned wrecks I have known from two or three Thousands, many out of Curiosity, and many for the purpose of Plunder and committing depredations.' | *Prosperous* (1834) | 'All the Wrecks that have Occurred on this Coast for the last three years have been <u>coasting vessels</u> with cargo of little value.' |
| | | *Union* (1834) | |
| | | *Brothers* (1834) | |
| | | *Agenard* (1834) | 'More than half the cargo [butter and oats] value not known.' |
| | | *Ocean* (1836) | [left blank] |
| | | *Britannia* (1837) | 'Not worth picking up.' [apples] |

The *First Report of the Constabulary Force Commissioner*'s wrecking focus lay with the experiences with wreckers on the Cheshire coast, which, unlike Cornwall, lacked the presence of the Coastguard. The testimony, as well, is clearly based on hearsay and contains obvious class-based rhetoric. By taking wrecking cases out of context, the report attempted to prove that wrecking was out of control and that a rural constabulary force was needed. The Cornwall returns, as shown above, had only one major reported case of plunder, that of the *Le Landais* in 1837 at Sennen. All other districts of Cornwall which were surveyed reported either no or minimal wrecking activity. Indeed, the constabulary report manipulated the Cornish evidence through its frequently quoted assertion that '[w]hilst on other parts of the English coast the persons assemble by hundreds for plunder on the occurrence of a wreck, on the Cornish coast they assemble on such occasions in thousands.'[5] The Padstow

5   PP, *First Report of the Constabulary Force Commissioners*, 64; Michael Oppenheim, 'Maritime History', in *Victoria County History of Cornwall*, Vol. I. (London: 1906), 508; A.K. Hamilton

return, from which the impression originated, contained the key phrase, that when the crowds of 'two or three Thousands' gathered, the crowds included 'many out of Curiosity'. Indeed, as can be seen above, even the original questions were leading. Despite these issues, the *Report* can be used with caution.

Jenkin, *Cornwall and its People* (originally published Truro 1932; reprinted Newton Abbot, 1970), 62; John G. Rule, 'Wrecking and Coastal Plunder', in Douglas Hay, Peter Linebaugh, et al., *Albion's Fatal Tree: Crime and Society in Eighteenth-Century England* (London, 1975, 1988), 185.

# Appendix 3

## Presentments, Manor of Connerton, 1704–59

Sources: CRO AR/15/68 and [AR/149]

| Year | Wreck presented |
|------|-----------------|
| 1704 | 2 small boats |
| 1705 | |
| 1706 | |
| 1707 | |
| 1708 | 8 barrels of butter turned in by various tenants; one boat; a shattered plank; timber |
| 1709 | Oak beam; 15 gallons white wine; unspecified amount of wine; piece of mast, yard; 3 hogsheads of wine; sail, ropes and rigging; mast; 20 gallons rum; piece of a sail and a piece of a yard; piece of a tree; 4 casks; unidentified goods; yard; rigging |
| 1710 | |
| 1711 | Pieces of timber |
| 1712 | 2 pieces of topmast; part of a mast; 5 puncheons 1 hhd of brandy; 15½ hogsheads of white wine; 4 casks wine; mast and yard; 1 pipe brandy; 2 hhd brandy; cask of brandy; 1 cask (48 gallons) red wine; mast; small piece of timber<br>[cask of wine at Newlyn] |
| 1713 | |
| 1714 | |
| 1715 | |
| 1716 | |
| 1717 | |
| 1718 | |
| 1719 | |
| 1720 | |
| 1721 | 80 gallons of oil; one piece of mast and one small top yard; one water cask; two pieces of timber |
| 1722 | 1 barrel cast iron; other iron collected by six other men and not presented; poles (iron?) |
| 1723 | Timber pump |
| 1724 | 1 piece timber, 6–7 foot |
| 1725 | 8 deal boards; piece of timber; 2 boats |
| 1726 | Plundered shipwreck: butter, candles, anker of wine, two casks sandy butter, timber, 'goods', beef (amounts not given) |
| 1727 | Hull of a ship |
| 1728 | 1 cannon |
| 1729 | |
| 1730 | |

1731
1732
1733    Mast of a ship; piece of timber; part of a fish
1734
1735    Topmast
        *[piece of a mast at Chyandour; piece of Pervian]*
1736
1737    *[boat at Mousehole]*
1738    *[ropes &c. at Gulval –]*
1739    *[piece of timber at Marazion sands –]*
1740
1741
1742
1743
1744
1745    *[Ralph Corin carried away a piece of timber at Chyandour –]*
1746
1747
1748
1749    2 pieces of mast, some cordage; 'pinns of iron'; 2 brass shraves; large topmast
        *[2 pieces cordage at Paul parish –]*
1750
1751    3 pieces of small timber; boat
        *[boat between Long Rock and Chyandour –]*
1752    12 hoops; 3 casks of beer; piece of timber
1753    Cable, mast, small ropes and timber; small stream cable; old iron, 'olde nails' and a block; iron chains; part of a ship's anchor; piece of a mast; yard; large cable
        *[bag of cotton at Long Rock; bag of cotton at Gulval Church Town; 2 broken anchors, E. Cudden Pt –]*
1754    2 pieces of timber; boat, 'canoe'; pump
        *[boat at Favell's Cove; Canoe between Long Rock and Chyandour; piece of timber, Cliff Fields, Marazion. –]*
1755    7 hogsheads of unspecified wine; 3 hhd of claret wine; small cask of white wine
1756    Piece of a mast; yard, 6 'pieces of fforeign brandy'; plank of oak; an 'Ore'; piece of mast
1757    Piece of a yard, and other small pieces of timber and bolts; piece of a yard; small pieces of plank; piece of rope; piece of a pump; small pieces of timber; cask of wine; body of a dead seaman; piece of oak; unspecified pieces of timber picked up by various people
1758    'broken Body'; small boat; piece of timber; ship's pump
1759    Piece of timber; 2 pumps; piece of a pump; 18 gallons brandy; 12 gallons 'Rhenish wine'; yard; cask of brandy; 'image part of a wrecked ship'; 2 dead women; 1 dead man; 40 gallons unspecified wine; 4 hhds red wine; topmast; bowsprit

# *Bibliography*

## Primary Sources

### Manuscript Sources

### British Library

*Additional Manuscripts*

| | |
|---|---|
| Add.37825 | Hedgeland, Philip, vicar of Penzance, Papers, 1876 |
| Add.38270 | Liverpool Papers |

*East India Company Collection*

| | |
|---|---|
| B/35–37, 49 | Minutes of the Court of Directors, 1678–84 |
| D/91 | Memoranda of the EIC Committee of Correspondence, 1700–10 |
| E/1/198–199 | Secretary's Out-letters. |
| E/3/90 | Letter Books |
| L/Mar. | Maritime Section |

### Cornwall Record Office

| | |
|---|---|
| AD/392/29 | Bill for further relief of owners and masters of ships, 1798 |
| AD/448/35 | Extracts from original documents re: to wrecking, 18th century |
| AD/514/27, 29 | Diaries, incl. references to shipwrecks, 1823–62 |
| AD/604, AD/1041 | Bodmin Quarter Sessions, 1786–1812 |
| AD/1426/2 | George John, attorney & mayor, Penzance, Journal, 1793–1834 |
| AR/1, 3, 8, 13, 15, 17, 25 | Arundell Papers, 17th, 18th, and 19th centuries |
| BL/1 | Bolitho Papers, wreck of the *Mentor*, 1814 |
| CA/B/42, 46 | Croft Andrew Papers, anti-wrecking bills |
| EN | Enys Papers, shipwrecks |
| G/1723 | Gregor Family of Trewarthenick Papers, salvage account, 1737 |
| J/1881, 2104 | Hawkins and Johnstone Papers, case papers – wreck, 1751–54, 1824 |
| ME/1552, 2840–1 | Mount Edgcumbe Papers, right of wreck, 1690–18th century |
| ML/577, 653 | Millaton Papers, right of wreck, 1733; anti-wrecking bill, 1818 |
| P/185 | Little Petherick Ecclesiastical Papers. Sermon: 'Exhorta- |

|  | tion against wrecking after the sermon in Little Petherick Church', 1818 |
| PB/1, 5–6 | Prideaux-Brune Papers, right of wreck Padstow, 18th–19th centuries |
| QS/1/2/150 | Quarter Sessions, Lostwithiel 1764 |
| R/3901 | Case paper, right of wreck, manors of Lantyan and Thretheake, 1745 |
| R/4517 | Accounts and estimate for wrecks, and a bill for burial of a body, 1775–1801 |
| R/5085 | Papers re: salvage and wreck, 1774–1800 |
| R/5584 | Report of the Association for the Preservation of Life and Property from Shipwreck, Padstow Harbour, 1838 |
| RH/352 | Quitclaim, right to wreck, St Michael's Mount, 1838 |
| RP/2, 17, 237 | Rogers of Penrose Papers, salvage accounts |
| RS/1/1068–1077 | Rashleigh of Menabilly Papers, shipwreck records, 18th century |
| T/1369, 1894–95 | Tremayne Papers, wrecking, 1743, 1790s; re: anti-wrecking bill, 1792 |
| W/43 | Willyams Papers, papers relating to wrecks, 1822–55 |

*Miscellaneous Papers*

| X/106/26–35 | Broadsheets, various wrecks, 1822–59 |
| X/112/151 | Case papers, right of wreck, manor of Conarton, 1753 |
| X/117/44 | Affidavits of masters of ships wrecked or stranded off Bude, 1850–55 |
| X/155/371 | Mayor's Account, six shipwrecked Dutchmen, 1700–01 |
| X/309/1 | Pamphlet, vessels wrecked and stranded near Padstow harbour, 1800–26 |
| X/498/58 | Henry Trengrouse Papers |
| X/807/39 | Pascoe Family Papers |

**Guildhall**

*Corporation of Trinity House*

| MS 30004 | Court Minutes, 1676–1879 |
| MS 30008 | Court Summons Books, Vol. 2: 1838–1913 |
| MS 30010 | Minutes, 1646–1875 |
| MS 30048 | Correspondence: Letter Books, Vol. 1: 1685–89 |
| MS 30051 | Correspondence: Select Entries, 1670–85 |
| MS 30052 | Correspondence: Select Papers and Reports, 1872–76 |
| MS 30072 | Copy Letters Patent, Vol. 1: Lizard, Scilly, 1665–87 |

Lloyds Marine Collection. Cornish Wrecks 1800–37, Research Box 3. File #3.

## National Maritime Museum, Greenwich

Marine Department, Wreck Registers, 1855–98

## The National Archives of the UK (formerly Public Record Office)

| | |
|---|---|
| ASSI 21/60 | Bodmin Assizes, Western Circuit |
| BT 212, 243, 297 | Board of Trade Records, Right of Wreck |
| CUST 33/38 | HM Customs: Board of Customs: Receivers of Wreck: Instructions for Customs Staff |
| CUST 67–69 | HM Customs Outport Records |
| HO 43–44, 52, 73 | Home Office Papers, wreck and plunder cases and correspondence |
| MT 9 | Ministry of Transport Records, Right of Wreck |
| PC 1/1/50 | Privy Council records, pillage of wreck, 1700 |
| SP 36 | State Papers Domestic, plundering of wrecks, 1732–45 |
| T 1/436, 450, 469 | HM Treasury Papers, plundering of wrecks, 1760s |

## Royal Institution of Cornwall, Truro

| | |
|---|---|
| DJW/1/1–11 | Journal of Christopher Wallis |
| HB/19/60 | Henderson Collection, Basset Papers |

Gary Hick's Maritime Shipwrecks Database, 18–20th centuries

## Contemporary Newspapers and Magazines

*Annual Register*
*Cornish Telegraph*
*Gentleman's Magazine*
*New York Times*
*Notes and Queries*
*Royal Cornwall Gazette*
*Sherborne Mercury*
*The Times*: Palmer's full text online, 1790–1905
*West Briton*
*West Briton and Cornwall Advertiser*
*Western Morning News and Mercury*

## Government Reports

*Calendar of Charter Rolls*, Vol. I: *Henry III AD 1226–1257.*
*Calendar of Home Office Papers of the Reign of George III*, 1760–65; 1766–69; 1773–75; 1776–79.
*Calendar of State Papers Domestic*, 1553–58.
*Cobbett's Parliamentary History*, Vols X (1737–39); XVIII (1774–76).
England, Departments of State and Official Bodies, Board of Trade. 'Instructions to Receivers of Wreck and Droits of Admiralty, and to Officers of the Customs and Coast Guard, concerning their duties in respect of wrecks, casu-

alties and salvage, under the "Merchant Shipping Act, 1854," "The Merchant Shipping Repeal Act, 1854," and "The Merchant Shipping Act Amendment Act, 1855". London, 1859.

——. 'Instructions to Receivers of Wreck and Droits of Admiralty, and to Officers of the Customs and the Coast Guard, etc. [with supplemental instructions]'. London, 1865.

*Hansard's Parliamentary Debates.* Vols XIV (1747–53); XV (1753–65); XXXVIII (1818). 3rd series.

*Journal of the House of Commons.* Vols XVI–CIX (1708–1859).

*Journal of the House of Lords.* Vol. XXVII (1753–56).

Parliamentary Papers. *First Report of the Constabulary Force Commissioners*, 1839, Vol. XIX.

——. *First Report from the Select Committee on Shipwrecks; Together with Minutes of Evidence, Appendix, and Index*, 1843, Vol. IX.

——. *Report from the Select Committee Appointed to Inquire into the Causes of Shipwrecks, With the Minutes of Evidence, Appendix and Index*, 1836, Vol. XVII.

——. *Report from the Select Committee on Shipwrecks of Timber Ships; with Minutes of Evidence*, 1839, Vol. XVII.

*The Statutes at Large, from Magna Charta to … 1761*, ed. D. Pickering. 24 vols. Cambridge: J. Bentham, 1762–69.

Statutes. Act of Parliament. 3 Edw. I c. 4; 27 Edw. III c. 13; 8 Eliz. c. 13; 12 Anne st. 2 c. 18; 4 Geo. I c. 12; 11 Geo. I c. 29; 26 Geo. II c. 19; 26 Geo. III c. 101; 28 Geo. III c. 25; 43 Geo. III c. 113; 48 Geo. III c. 75; 48 Geo. III c. 130; 49 Geo. III c. 122; 52 Geo. III c. 159; 53 Geo. III c. 87; 1 & 2 Geo. IV c. 75; 7 & 8 Geo. IV c. 30; 6 & 7 Will. IV c. 60; 1 Vic. c. 89; 3 & 4 Vic. c. 65; 8 & 9 Vic. c. 86; 9 & 10 Vic. c. 99; 13 & 14 Vic. c. 93; 17 & 18 Vic. c. 104 (Merchant Shipping Act of 1854); 17 & 18 Vic. c. 120; 25 & 26 Vic. c. 63 s. 53.

**Published Primary and Contemporary Sources: Books and Articles**

Anon. *Chronicles of the Sea: or Faithful Narratives of Shipwrecks, Fires, Famines, and Disasters Incidental to a Life of Maritime Enterprise …*, Vol. I. London: William Mark Clark, 1838.

Anon. *Summary of Services in the Royal Navy, and Coast Guard; and Services, acting under Civil Power, at Riots, Fires, Wrecks, &c. &c. of Capt. George Davies, R.N.; with Documents, Extracts and Testimonials.* 31 January 1851. Penzance: printed by T. Beare, Bookseller, Market Place, 1851.

Anon. *The Shipwreck.* London: The Religious Tract Society, 1830.

Anon. [Defoe, Daniel?] *The Storm: or, a collection of the most remarkable casualties and disasters which happened in the late dreadful tempest, both by sea and land.* London: G. Sawbridge, 1704.

Anon. *The Wreckers, or a View of What Sometimes Passes on Our Sea Coast: Written By a Clergyman of the Church of England, etc.* London: F. Collins, J. Nisbet, c. 1820.

Archibald, John Frederick. *The Justice of the Peace, and Parish Officer.* 3 vols. Vol. 2. London: Shaw and Sons, 1840.

Arnold, Morris S. ed. *Select Cases of Trespass from the King's Courts, 1307–1399*, Vol. 1. London: Selden Society, 1985.

Association for the Protection of Commercial Interests as respects Wrecked and Damaged Property. *Report on the Subject of Wreck and Salvage on the Coast of Kent*. London: Lloyd's Salvage Association, 1867.

——. *Report on Wrecking in the Bahamas*. London: Lloyd's, Salvage Association, 1868.

Barton, R.M. *Life in Cornwall in the Early Nineteenth Century, Being Extracts from the West Briton Newspaper in the Quarter Century from 1810 to 1835*. Truro: D. Bradford Barton, 1970.

——. *Life in Cornwall in the Early Nineteenth Century, Being Extracts from the West Briton Newspaper in the Two Decades from 1835–1854*. Truro: D. Bradford Barton, 1971.

——. *Life in Cornwall in the Early Nineteenth Century, Being Extracts from the West Briton Newspaper in the Two Decades from 1855–1875*. Truro: D. Bradford Barton, 1972.

Blackstone, Sir William. *Commentaries on the Laws of England*, 9th edition, ed. R. Burn. 4 vols. London: 1783.

Blight, J.T. *A Week at Land's End, and A Week at the Lizard*. Truro: Lake & Lake, 1893.

Borlase, William. *Antiquities, Historical and Monumental, of the County of Cornwall*. London: W. Bowyer and J. Nichols, 1769.

——. *Observations on the Antiquity of Cornwall*. Oxford: W. Jackson, 1756.

Bottrell, William. *Traditions and Hearthside Stories of West Cornwall*, with Illustrations by Mr Joseph Blight. 2 vols. Penzance: printed for the author by Beare and Son, 1870, 1873.

Bowles, Charles. *A Short Account of the Hundred of Penwith, in the County of Cornwall compiled from Authentic Documents with an Appendix containing the Original Grants, Confirmations, &c.* Shaftesbury: R. Hurd, 1805.

Bray, John. *An Account of Wrecks, 1759–1830 – On the North Coast of Cornwall*. Edited and transcribed by A.K. Hamilton Jenkin. Truro: Trevithick Society and the Institute of Cornish Studies, 1975.

Browne, Austin L. *Corporation Chronicles: Being Some Account of the Ancient Corporations of East Looe and of West Looe in the County of Cornwall*. Plymouth: John Smith, 1904.

Buckingham, James Silk. *Autobiography of James Silk Buckingham: Including his Voyages, Travels, Adventures, Speculations, Successes and Failures ...* 2 vols. London: Longman & Co., 1855.

Burke, John. *A Genealogical and Heraldic History of the Commoners of Great Britain and Ireland*. 4 vols. London: Henry Colburn, 1838.

Carew, Richard of Antony. *The Survey of Cornwall*. Ed. F.E. Halliday. Originally published London, 1602; London: Andrew Melrose, 1953, 1969.

Carter, Captain Harry. *The Autobiography of a Cornish Smuggler (Captain Harry Carter of Prussia Cove), 1749–1809*. Introduction and notes by John B. Cornish. London: Gibbings & Co, Ltd., 1900. Reprinted Truto: D. Bradford Barton, 1971.

Clifton, C.F.C. *Bude Haven: Bencoolen to Capricorno, a Record of Wrecks at Bude, 1862 to 1900*. Manchester: J.E. Cornish, 1902.

Cooke, James Herbert, FSA. *The Shipwreck of Sir Cloudesley Shovell on the Scilly Islands, in 1707 from the Original and Contemporary Documents Hitherto Unpublished*. Gloucester: John Bellows, 1889. (Read at a Meeting of the Society of Antiquities, London, 1 February 1883; reprinted by Isles of Scilly Museum, No. 6, n.d.)

Cornish, Thomas, ed. 'The Lanisley Letters: to Lt. General Onslow from George Borlase, his agent at Penzance, 1750–53'. *Journal of the Royal Institution of Cornwall*, 6, pt 22, 1880, 374–379.

Coulthard, Hugh Robert. *The Story of an Ancient Parish: Breage, with Germoe, With Some Account of its Armigers, Worthies and Unworthies, Smugglers, and Wreckers, its Traditions and Superstitions*. Camborne: Camborne Printing & Stationery Co., 1913.

Courtney, Leonard. Baron Courtney of Penwith. *A Week in the Isles of Scilly*. Truro: Lake & Lake, 1883.

Cummings, Rev. Alfred Hayman. *The Churches and Antiquities of Cury and Gunwalloe in the Lizard District including Local Traditions*. Truro: W. Lake; London. E. Marlborough and Co., 1875.

Dalrymple, Sir David, 3rd Bart, Lord Hailes, and John Sinclair, Archdeacon of Middlesex. *Wrecking; or the Duty of Christians to Shipwrecked Sailors. A Sermon which Might Have Been Preached in East Lothian, on the 25th October 1761*. London: n.p., 1860.

Davies, Capt. George C. *Summary of Services in the Royal Navy and Coast Guard; and Services, under Civil Power, at Riots, Fires, Wrecks &c. &c. of Capt. George C. Davies, RN with Documents, Extracts and Testimonials*. London: n.p., 1851.

Defoe, Daniel. *An Historical Narrative of the Great and Tremendous Storm Which Happened on Nov. 26$^{th}$, 1703*. London: printed for W. Nicholl, in St Paul's Church-yard, 1769.

——. *A Tour through the Whole Island of Great Britain*. Originally published 1724. Introduction by G.D.H. Cole and D.C. Browning. London: J.M. Dent & Sons, Ltd, 1962, 1974.

Dowdeswell, George Morley. *Merchant Shipping Acts, 1854 & 1855, with a Readable Abridgement of the Former Act, and an Explanation of the Law Relating to It*. London: V. & R. Stevens & G. S. Norton, 1856.

Eden, Rev. Robert. Canon of Norwich. *An Address [on Ephes.iv.28] to Depredators and Wreckers on the Sea Coast*, London: n.p., 1840.

Eden, Sir William. *Principles of Penal Law*. London: B.White and T. Cadell, 1771.

Esquiros, Alfonse. *Cornwall and its Coasts*. London: Chapman and Hall, 1865.

Falconer, William. *A Universal Dictionary of the Marine*. London: n.p., 1769.

Fiennes, Celia. *The Journeys of Celia Fiennes*. Edited by Christopher Morris. London: The Cresset Press, 1947.

Francklyn, Thomas, Rector of Langton-Herring and Vicar of Fleet, Dorset. *Serious Advice and Fair Warning to All that Live Upon the Sea-Coast*. London: n.p., 1761.

Gairdner, James, ed. *The Paston Letters, 1422–1509 AD*. Edinburgh: John Grant, 1910.

Glover, Fred. R.A. *Harbours of Refuge, Not Dangerous Decoys, Ship Traps, Nor Wrecking Pools*. London: E. Stanford, 1859.

Halliwell, J.O. *Rambles in Western Cornwall by the Footsteps of the Giants; with Notes on the Celtic Remains of the Land's End District and the Islands of Scilly*. London: John Russell Smith, 1861.

Harper, John A.W. *Report on the Subject of Wreck and Salvage on the Coast of Kent*. London: Lloyd's Salvage Association, 1867.

Harris, G.G., ed. *Trinity House of Deptford Transactions, 1609–35*. London: London Record Society, 1983.

Harvey, Rev. Edmund G. *Mullyon: Its History, Scenery and Antiquities, etc*. Truro and London: n.p., 1875.

Hawker, Rev. Robert S. *Footprints of Former Men in Far Cornwall*. London: John Russell Smith, 1870, 1903.

Hawker, Rev. Robert S., and C.E. Byles. *The Life and Letters of R.S. Hawker (Sometime Vicar of Morwenstow) by his Son-in-Law C.E. Byles*. London: John Lane, The Bodley Head, 1906.

Heath, Robert. *The Isles of Scilly: the First Book on the Isles of Scilly*. Originally published London: R. Manby and H.S. Cox on Ludgate Hill, 1750; reprinted Newcastle-upon-Tyne: Frank Graham, 1967.

Hitchins, Fortescue, and Samuel Drew. *The History of Cornwall: From the Earliest Records and Traditions, to the Present Time*. 2 vols. Helston: W. Penaluma, 1824.

Holdsworth, Sir William. *A History of English Law*, 17 vols. London: Methuen & Co., 1903–1972.

Hunt, Robert. *Popular Romances of the West of England: or the Drolls, Traditions and Superstitions of Old Cornwall*. London: John Camden Hotten, Piccadilly, 1865.

Jagoe, John. *The Wreck and Salvage Act, 9 & 10 Vict. c. 99 with Copious Notes, Analysis Proceedings and Forms …* London: n.p., 1846.

James, E. Boucher. *Letters Archaeological and Historical Relating to the Isle of Wight*, Vol. I. n.p. Henry Frowde, 1896.

Kowaleski, Maryanne, ed. *The Havener's Accounts of the Earldom and Duchy of Cornwall, 1287–1356*. Vol. 44. Exeter: Devon and Cornwall Record Society, 2001.

Laing, Joseph. *Observations on the … Grievances Inflicted upon Merchant Seamen, by the Maritime Laws and Customs of England, in Cases of … Shipwreck, with Suggestions for their Redress*. London and Tynemouth: Hamilton, Adams, & Co., 1841.

Lambert, Sheila, ed. *House of Commons Sessional Papers of the Eighteenth Century*. Vol. 27, *George III Bills, 1774–75 and 1775–76*. Delaware: 1975.

Law, Palmer. *The Cornish Shipwreck*. London: Elliot Stock, c. 1865.

Lloyds Salvage Association. 'Translation of a report entitled "Wreckers on the English coast," issued by the Societé centrale de Sauvetage des Naufragés'. Paris: Municipal and other Institutions, Societies, etc., Société Centrale de Sauvetage des Naufragés; reprinted London: A. Williams, 1867.

Locke, John. *Two Treatises of Government*. Edited by Peter Laslett. Cambridge: Cambridge University Press, 1963.

Mallison, William Henry. *Plan of an Institution for Rendering Assistance to Shipwrecked Mariners, Preserving their Lives, and the Property of Our Merchants, When Wreck Occurs*. London: n.p., 1810.

Marsden, Reginald G. ed. *Select Pleas in the Court of Admiralty*. 2 vols. London: Bernard Quaritch for the Selden Society, 1892–97.

Maskell, William. *Bude Haven: A Pen-and-Ink Sketch, with Portraits of the Principal Inhabitants*. London: n.p., 1863.

Murton, Sir Walter. *Wreck Inquiries: The Law and Practice Relating to Formal Investigations into Shipping Casualties, etc.* London: Stevens & Sons, 1884.

Palmer, William, MA. *The Law of Wreck, Considered with a View to its Amendment*. London: n.p., 1843.

Pearce, John, ed. *The Wesleys in Cornwall: Extracts from the Journals of John and Charles Wesley and John Nelson*. Truro: D. Bradford Barton, 1964.

Penaluna, William. *The Circle, or Historical Survey of Sixty Parishes and Towns in Cornwall*. Helston: printed and published by William Penaluna, 1819.

Pern, Peter, ed., *Cornish Notes and Queries: Reprinted from the* Cornish Telegraph. London: Elliot Stock; Penzance: The Cornish Telegraph Office, 1906.

Polsue, Joseph. *Lake's Parochial History of the County of Cornwall*. 4 vols. Reprinted Wakefield: EP Publishing for Cornwall County Library, 1974.

Polwhele, Richard. *The History of Cornwall, 1760–1838*. Reprint of 1803–08 and 1816 edition, Dorking: Kohler and Coombes, 1978.

——. *Traditions and Recollections: Domestic, Clerical and Literary*. 2 vols. London: John Nichols and Son, 1826.

Pool, P.A.S., ed. 'The Penheleg Manuscript', *Journal of the Royal Institution of Cornwall*, new series, 3, pt 3, 1959, 163–228.

Redding, Cyrus. *An Illustrated Itinerary of the County of Cornwall*. London: How and Parsons, 1842.

Shearme, Rev. John. *Lively Recollections*. London: John Lane, 1917.

Smith, Rev. G.C. *The Extreme Misery of the Off-Islands*. London: n.p. 1818.

——. *The Scilly Islands and the Famine*. London: W.K. Wakefield, 1828.

——. *The Wreckers; or a Tour of Benevolence from St Michael's Mount to the Lizard Point*. London: W. Whittemore, 1818.

Smith, William. *A full account of the late ship-wreck of the ship called the President, which was cast away in Montz-bay in Cornwal on the 4th of February last, as it was deliver'd to his Majesty (both in writing and discourse) by William Smith and John Harshfield, the only persons that escaped in the said wreck. Together with all the remarkable adventures in the said voyage from their sailing out of the Sound at Plimouth on May-Day 1682, particularly their engagement with six pirate-ships at once on the coast of Malabar. The whole relation being taken in private conference with the said William Smith*. London: printed for Randal Taylor near Stationers' Hall, 1684.

Stenton, Doris Mary, ed. *Pleas Before the King or His Justices, 1198–1202*. Vol. II: *Rolls or Fragments of Rolls from the Years 1198, 1201 and 1202*. London: Selden Society, 1952.

——. *Rolls of the Justices in Eyre, being the Rolls of Pleas and Assizes for Yorkshire in 3 Henry III (1218–19)*. London: Bernard Quaritich for the Selden Society, 1937.

Studer, Paul. *Oak Book of Southampton*. 2 vols. Southampton: Southampton Record Society, 1910–11.

Tait, Thomas R. *Early History of Lighthouses, with a Short Account of Lighthouse Legislation in the United Kingdom; and Excerpts from Existing Acts Affecting the Commissioners of Northern Lighthouses*. Glasgow: James Hedderwick & Sons, 1902.

Thomas, Charles, ed. *Three Early Accounts of the Isles of Scilly: James Beeverell, 1707, Graeme Spence, 1792, Henry Spry, 1800*. Redruth, Cornwall: Penwith Books, 1979.

Thomas, Henry Grills. *A Cornish Shopkeeper's Diary, 1843: The Diary of Henry Grills Thomas, Draper and Grocer of St Just-in-Penwith, Cornwall, and Thirteen Letters Written to his Wife Between 1846 and 1854*. Transcribed and annotated by Richard G. Grills. Truro: Dyllansow Truran, 1997.

Thompson, William Harding. *Cornwall: A Survey of its Coast, Moors, and Valleys, with Suggestions for the Preservation of Amenities*. Member of the Town Planning Institute, for the Cornwall Branch of the Council for the Preservation of Rural England. With notes on the Antiquities of Cornwall by Charles Henderson, MA, Fellow of Corpus Christi College, Oxford, and a Preface by Sir Arthur Quiller-Couch, D. Litt, FRSL. London: University of London Press, 1930.

Tregellas, Walter H. *Cornish Worthies*, Vols I and II. London: Elliot Stock, 1884.

Trengrouse, Henry. *Shipwreck Investigated, for the Cause of the Great Loss of Lives with which it is Frequently Attended; and a Remedy Provided in a Portable, Practicable Life Preserving Apparatus; Which is Calculated For, and Is Necessary to Become, a Part of Every Ships Equipment*. Falmouth: James Trathan, 1817. Troutbeck, John. *A Survey of the Ancient and Present State of the Scilly Islands, etc.* Sherborne: Goadby and Lerpiniere, 1796.

Twiss, Travers, ed. and trans. *The Black Book of the Admiralty*. 4 vols. Rolls Series 55. London: n.p., 1871–76.

van Caenegem, R.C., ed. *English Lawsuits from William I to Stephen (Nos 1–345)*, London: Selden Society, 1990.

——. *Royal Writs in England from the Conquest to Glanvill: Studies in the Early History of the Common Law*. Selden Society 77. London: Bernard Quaritch, 1959.

Walker, Commodore George. *The Voyages and Cruises of Commodore Walker*. Edited and notes by H.S. Vaughan. Originally published London: A Millar, 1760; reprinted London: Cassell, 1928.

Walker, Rev. James [used pseudonym 'Jonas Salvage']. *A Dialogue between the Captain of a Merchant Ship and a Farmer Concerning the Pernicious Practice of Wrecking; as Exemplified in the Unhappy Fate of One William Pearce of St. Gennis, Who Was Executed at Launceston in Cornwall Oct. 12, 1767. Showing Also How the Captain Was Converted to a Life of Much Seriousness and Consideration, etc.* London, Sherborne and Truro: n.p. 1768.

Whitaker, Rev. John. *The Ancient Cathedrals of Cornwall Historically Surveyed.* 2 vols. London: Stockdale, 1804.

White, Walter. *A Londoner's Walk to the Land's End, and a Trip to the Scillies,* London: Chapman and Hall, 1855 .

Whitfield, Rev. H.J. *Scilly and its Legends.* Originally published Penzance: 1852; facsimile reprint Felinfach: Llanerch Publishers, 1992.

Williams, T. *Everyman His Own Lawyer,* 2nd edition. London: n.p., 1818.

Woodley, Rev. George. *A View of the Present State of the Scilly Islands: Exhibiting their Vast Importance to the British Empire; the Improvements of Which they are Susceptible; and a Particular Account of the Means Lately Adopted for the Amelioration of the Conditions of the Inhabitants, By the Establishment of their Fisheries.* London: printed by J. Carthew, County Library, Truro, 1822.

## Secondary Sources

### Unpublished Secondary Sources: Conference Papers

Davey, Francis. 'Cornish Medieval Piracy'. Paper read at the First Cornish Maritime History Conference, National Maritime Museum Cornwall, 25 September 2004.

Doe, Helen. 'Cornish Ships and Shipbuilding in the Nineteenth Century'. Paper read at the First Cornish Maritime History Conference, National Maritime Museum Cornwall, 25 September 2004.

Pawlyn, Tony. 'Fishermen Smugglers'. Paper read at the First Cornish Maritime History Conference, National Maritime Museum Cornwall, 25 September 2004.

——. 'Some Notes and Observations on Cornish Wreckers: Or – Wreck Recycling'. Unpublished manuscript, April 2003.

Pearce, Cathryn. 'Lured by False Lights: Cornish Wrecking and Victorian Myth'. Paper read at the 5th International Congress of Maritime History, University of Greenwich, 23–27 June 2008.

Trezise, Simon. 'The Sea-Dog, the Smuggler and the Wrecker: Literary Representations of Maritime Life in the West Country'. Conference paper, University of Exeter, 20 October 2001.

Williams, Michael. 'Manorial Rights of Wreck'. Unpublished paper read at the Nautical Archaeology Society, University of Plymouth, March 1995.

### Unpublished Secondary Sources: Theses and Dissertations

Doe, Helen. 'Small Shipbuilding Businesses during the Napoleonic Wars: James Dunn of Mevagissey, 1799 to 1816'. M.A. dissertation, University of Exeter, 2003.

Muskett, Paul. 'English Smuggling in the Eighteenth Century'. Ph.D. thesis, Open University UK, 1996.

Probert, William Bernard. 'The Humanitarian, Technical and Political Response to Shipwreck in the First Half of the Nineteenth Century. The 1836 Inquiry and its Aftermath'. Ph.D dissertation, University of Southampton, 1999.

Quilley, Geoffrey. 'The Imagery of Travel in British Painting: With Particular Reference to Nautical and Maritime Imagery, circa 1740–1800'. Ph.D. thesis, University of Warwick, 1998.

Rule, John G. 'The Labouring Miner in Cornwall c. 1740–1870: A Study in Social History', Ph.D. thesis, University of Warwick, 1971.


## Published Secondary Sources: Books

n.a. *Shipwrecks around the Isles of Scilly*. St Ives, Cornwall: Beric Tempest & Co., Ltd., n.d.

Anderson, Benedict. *Imagined Communities: Reflections on the Origin and Spread of Nationalism*. London and New York: Verso, 1983, 2000.

Ashworth, William J. *Customs and Excise: Trade, Production, and Consumption in England, 1640–1845*. Oxford: Oxford University Press, 2003.

Baehre, Rainer, ed. *Outrageous Seas: Shipwreck and Survival in the Waters off Newfoundland, 1583–1893*. Montreal: Carleton University Press, 1999.

Balchin, W.G.V. *Cornwall: An Illustrated Essay on the History of the Landscape*. London: Hodder and Stoughton, 1954.

Baring-Gould, Sabine. *The Book of West Cornwall*. First published London: Methuen, 1899; reprinted London: Wildwood House, 1981.

——. *The Vicar of Morwenstow: Being the Life of Robert Stephen Hawker, M.A.* London: Methuen & Co., 1899.

Barker, Hannah. *Newspapers, Politics, and Public Opinion in Late Eighteenth-Century England*. Oxford: Clarendon Press, 1998.

Barthes, Roland. *Mythologies*. Translated by Annette Lavers. New York: Hill and Wang, 1972.

Barton, Denys Bradford. *Essays in Cornish Mining History*. Truro: D. Bradford Barton, 1968.

——. *A History of Copper Mining in Cornwall and Devon*. Truro: D. Bradford Barton, 1961.

——. *A History of Tin Mining and Smelting in Cornwall*. Truro: D. Bradford Barton, 1965.

Bathurst, Bella. *The Wreckers: A Story of Killing Seas, False Lights and Plundered Ships*. London: Harper Collins, 2005.

Beattie, J.M., *Crime and the Courts in England, 1660–1800*. Oxford: Oxford University Press, 1986.

Berg, Maxine. *Luxury and Pleasure in Eighteenth-Century Britain*. Oxford: Oxford University Press, 2005.

Berg, Maxine and Elizabeth Eger, eds. *Luxury in the Eighteenth Century: Debates, Desires and Delectable Goods*. Basingstoke: Palgrave Macmillan, 2003.

Berger, Stefan, Heiko Feldner and Kevin Passmore, eds. *Writing History: Theory and Practice*. London: Hodder Arnold, 2003.

Berry, Claude. *Cornwall*. London: Robert Hale, 1949.

Blackmore, Josiah. *Manifest Perdition: Shipwreck Narrative and the Disruption of Empire*. Minneapolis: University of Minnesota Press, 2002.

Blumenberg, Hans. *Shipwreck with Spectator: Paradigm of a Metaphor For Existence*. Translated by Steven Rendall. London and Cambridge, Massachusetts: MIT Press, 1997.

Boak, A.E.R., ed. *University of Michigan Historical Essays*. Ann Arbor: University of Michigan Press, 1937.

Boase, George Clement, and William Prideaux Courtney. *Bibliotheca Cornubiensis: A Catalogue of the Writings, both Manuscript and Printed, of Cornishmen, and of Works relating to the County of Cornwall with Biographical Memoranda and Copious Literary References*. 3 vols. London: Longmans, Green Reader, and Dyer, 1878.

Bohstedt, John. *Riots and Community Politics in England and Wales, 1790–1810*. Cambridge, Mass. and London: Harvard University Press, 1983.

Bonham, Mrs Elizabeth. *A Corner of Old Cornwall*. Introduced by E.J. Oldmeadow. London: The Unicorn Press, 1896.

Bourdieu, Pierre. *Outline of a Theory of Practice*. Cambridge: Cambridge University Press, 1977.

——. *Practical Reason: On the Theory of Action*. Stanford, California: Stanford University Press, 1998.

Bowley, E.L. *The Fortunate Islands: The Story of the Isles of Scilly*. St Mary's, Isles of Scilly: W.P. Kennedy, 1945.

Brandon, David. *Stand and Deliver! A History of Highway Robbery*. Stroud, Gloucestershire: Sutton Publishing, 2001.

Brendon, Piers, *Hawker of Morwenstow: Portrait of a Victorian Eccentric*. London: Pimlico, 1975, 2000.

Brewer, John. *The Sinews of Power: War, Money and the English State, 1688–1783*. Cambridge, Massachusetts: Harvard University Press, 1990.

Brewer, John, and J. Styles. *An Ungovernable People? The English and their Law in the Seventeenth and Eighteenth Centuries*. London: Hutchinson, 1980.

Briggs, John, Christopher Harrison, et. al. *Crime and Punishment in England: An Introductory History*. London: UCL Press, 1996, 1998.

Broeze, Frank, ed. *Maritime History at the Crossroads: A Critical Review of Recent Historiography*. Research in Maritime History 9. St John's Newfoundland: International Maritime Economic History Association, 1995.

Brown, Lucy. *The Board of Trade and the Free-Trade Movement, 1830–1842*. Oxford: Clarendon Press, 1958.

Burke, Peter. *Popular Culture in Early Modern Europe*. New York: Harper & Row, 1978.

——. *Varieties of Cultural History*. Cambridge: Polity Press, 1997.

Bushaway, Robert. *By Rite: Custom, Ceremony and Community in England, 1700–1880*. London: Junction Books, 1982.

Brice, Geoffrey. *Maritime Law of Salvage*. 3rd edition. London: Sweet and Maxwell, 1999.

Cabantous, Alain. *Les côtes barbares: Pilleurs d'épaves et sociétés littorales en France, 1680–1830*. Paris: Fayard, 1993.

Cannadine, David, ed. *What is History Now?* London: Palgrave Macmillan, 2002.

Carson, Edward. *The Ancient and Rightful Customs: A History of the English Customs Service.* London: Faber & Faber, 1972.

Carter, Clive. *Cornish Shipwrecks, Vol. 2: The North Coast.* Newton Abbott: David & Charles, 1970.

Clark, Peter, ed. *The Cambridge Urban History of Britain, Vol. II: 1540–1840.* Cambridge: Cambridge University Press, 2000.

Clifton, C.F.C. *Bude Haven: Bencoolen to Capricorno: A Record of Wrecks at Bude, 1862 to 1900.* Manchester: J.E. Cornish, 1902.

Coate, Mary. *Cornwall in the Great Civil War and Interregnum, 1642–1660: A Social and Political Study.* Oxford and New York: Clarendon Press, 1933.

Cohen, Stanley. *Folk Devils & Moral Panics: The Creation of the Mods and Rockers.* 3rd edition. Originally published: London: MacGibbon and Kee, 1972; London: Routledge, 2002.

Colley, Linda. *Britons: Forging the Nation, 1707–1837.* New Haven and London: Yale University Press, 1992.

Cornwall County and Diocesan Record Office. *Handlist of Maritime Sources at the Cornwall Record Office.* Truro: Cornwall County Council, 1998.

Cotton, Sir E., and Sir C. Fawcett. *East Indiamen.* London: Butterworths, 1949.

Couch, Jonathan. *The History of Polperro: a Fishing Town on the South-Coast of Cornwall.* First published 1871; Newcastle upon Tyne: Frank Graham, 1965, abridged.

Cowls, Bert. *'Looking Back to Yesterday': Bygone days in a Cornish Fishing Village.* Helston: B. Cowls, 1982.

Crispin, Gill. *The Duchy of Cornwall.* Newton Abbot: David & Charles, 1987.

Cubitt, Geoffrey, ed. *Imagining Nations.* York Studies in Cultural History. Manchester: Manchester University Press, 1998.

Cunliffe, Barry. *Facing the Ocean: The Atlantic and its Peoples, 8000BC–AD1500.* Oxford: Oxford University Press, 2001.

Daunton, M.J., ed. *The Cambridge Urban History of Britain, Vol. III: 1840–1950.* Cambridge: Cambridge University Press, 2000.

——. *Progress and Poverty: An Economic and Society History of Britain, 1700–1850.* Oxford: Oxford University Press, 1995.

Davis, Ralph. *The Rise of the English Shipping Industry in the 17th and 18th Centuries.* London: Macmillan for the National Maritime Museum, 1962; reprinted Newton Abbot: David & Charles, 1972.

Dell, Simon. *Policing the Peninsula (1850–2000): A Photographic Celebration of Westcountry Policing over the Last 150 Years.* Devon and Cornwall Constabulary, 2000.

Doe, Helen. *Enterprising Women and Shipping in the Nineteenth Century.* Woodbridge, Boydell Press 2009.

Doty, William C. *Mythography: The Study of Myths and Rituals.* 2nd edition. Tuscaloosa: The University of Alabama Press, 2000.

Duffin, Patricia Anne. *The Political Allegiance of the Cornish Gentry, c. 1600–c.1642.* Exeter: University of Exeter, 1989.

Earle, Peter. *Sailors: English Merchant Seamen, 1650–1775.* London: Methuen, 1998.

——. *The Making of the English Middle Class: Business, Society and Family Life in London, 1660–1730*. Berkeley: University of California Press, 1989.

Elias, Norbert. *The Civilizing Process: The History of Manners and State Formation and Civilization*. Translated by E. Jephcott. Oxford: Oxford University Press, 1994.

Elliott, J.H. *The Old World and the New, 1492–1650*. Cambridge: Cambridge University Press, 1970.

Emsley, Clive. *Crime and Society in England, 1750–1900*. London: Longman, 1996.

——. *Hard Men: The English and Violence since 1750*. London: Hambledon Continuum, 2005.

Fidler, Kathleen, and Ian Morrison. *Wrecks, Wreckers, and Rescuers*. London: Lutterworth Press, 1977.

Fisher, Stephen, ed. *Ports and Shipping in the South-West: Papers presented at two seminars on the maritime history of the South-West of England, held at Dartington Hall, 19–20 October 1968 and 18–19 October 1969*. Exeter: University of Exeter, 1971.

——. *Studies in British Privateering, Trading Enterprise and Seamen's Welfare, 1775–1900*. Exeter: University of Exeter Press, 1987.

——. *West Country Maritime and Social History: Some Essays*. Exeter: University of Exeter, 1980.

Foster, D. *The Rural Constabulary Act 1839: National Legislation and Problems of Enforcement*. London: Bedford Square Press, 1982.

Foucault, Michel. *Discipline and Punish: The Birth of the Prison*. London: Penguin 1977.

——. *Madness and Civilization: A History of Insanity in the Age of Reason*. Translated by Richard Howard. New York: Random House, 1965, 1988.

Fowles, John. *Shipwreck: Photography by the Gibsons of Scilly*. London: Jonathan Cape, 1974.

Gater, Dilys. *Historic Shipwrecks of Wales*. Llanrwst, Gwynedd: Gwasog Carreg Gwalch, 1992.

Gatrell, V.A.C. *The Hanging Tree: Execution and the English People, 1770–1868*. Oxford: Oxford University Press, 1994.

Gatrell, V.A.C., Bruce Lenman, and Geoffrey Parker, eds. *Crime and the Law: The Social History of Crime in Western Europe since 1500*. London: Europa, 1980.

Gibson, Jeremy, and Colin Rogers. *Coroners' Records in England and Wales*. 3rd edition. Bury, Lancashire: The Family History Partnership, 2009.

Gill, Crispin, ed. *The Duchy of Cornwall*. Newton Abbot: David & Charles, 1987.

Gilmour, Ian. *Riot, Risings and Revolution: Governance and Violence in Eighteenth-Century England*. London: Pimlico, 1992.

Godfrey, Barry S., Clive Emsley, and Graeme Dunstall, eds. *Comparative Histories of Crime*. London: Willan Publishing, 2003.

Goode, Erich, and Nachmann Ben-Yehuda. *Moral Panics: The Social Construction of Deviance*. Oxford: Blackwell, 1994.

Griffiths, Paul, Adam Fox, and Steve Hindle, eds. *The Experience of Authority in Early Modern England*. London and New York: Macmillan Press, 1996.

Habakkuk, H.J. *Marriage, Debt and the Estates System: English Landownership 1650–1950.* London: Clarendon Press, 1994.

Halliday, F.E. *A History of Cornwall.* London: Duckworth, 1959.

Hampton, Mark. *Visions of the Press in Britain, 1850–1950.* Chicago: University of Illinois Press, 2004.

Hannen, James C., and W. Tarn Pritchard. *Pritchard's Digest of Admiralty and Maritime Law.* 3rd edition, Vol. II. London: Butterworths, 1887.

Hardy, William. *Lighthouses: Their History and Romance.* London: Religious Tract Society, 1895.

Harris, Tim, ed. *Popular Culture in England, c. 1500–1850.* London: Macmillan Press, 1995.

Hartley, Diana. *The St Aubyns of Cornwall, 1200–1977.* Chesham, Buckinghamshire: Barracuda Books, 1977.

Hatcher, John. *Rural Economy and Society in the Duchy of Cornwall, 1300–1500.* Cambridge: Cambridge University Press, 1970.

Hathaway, Eileen. *Smuggler: John Rattenbury and his Adventures in Devon, Dorset, and Cornwall, 1778–1844 (Including Memoirs of a Smuggler, 1837).* Swanage: Shinglepicker, 1994.

Hattendorf, John B. *Maritime History,* Vol. 2: *The Eighteenth Century and the Classic Age of Sail.* Malabar, Florida: Krieger Publishing, 1997.

Hay, Douglas, Peter Linebaugh, et al. *Albion's Fatal Tree: Crime and Society in Eighteenth-Century England.* London: Allen Lane, 1975; reprinted London: Penguin, 1988.

Hay, Douglas, and Nicholas Rogers. *Eighteenth-Century English Society: Shuttles and Swords.* Oxford: Oxford University Press, 1997.

Hempton, David. *Methodism and Politics in British Society, 1750–1850.* London: Hutchinson, 1984.

Henderson, Charles G. *Essays in Cornish History.* Edited by A.L. Rowse and M.I. Henderson. Foreword by Sir Arthur Quiller-Couch. First published Oxford University Press, 1935; reprinted Truro: D. Bradford Barton, 1963.

Hill, Sir George. *Treasure Trove in Law and Practice: From the Earliest Time to the Present Day.* Oxford: Clarendon Press, 1936.

Hilton, Boyd. *A Mad, Bad and Dangerous People? England, 1783–1846.* Oxford: Clarendon Press, 2006.

Hobsbawm, Eric, and Terence Ranger, eds. *The Invention of Tradition.* Cambridge: Cambridge University Press, 1983.

Holdsworth, Sir William. *A History of English Law.* Vols I–II. London: Methuen, 1938.

Hoon, Elizabeth Evelynola. *The Organization of the English Customs System, 1696–1786.* Originally published 1938; Newton Abbot: David & Charles, 1968.

Hoppit, Julian, ed. *Failed Legislation, 1660–1800: Extracted from the Commons and Lords Journals.* London: Hambledon Press, 1997.

Hudson, W.H., *The Land's End: A Naturalist's Impressions in West Cornwall.* Originally published London: Hutchinson & Co., 1908; reprinted London: Wildwood House, 1980.

Hunt, Alan. *Governance of the Consuming Passions: A History of Sumptuary* Law. New York: St Martin's Press, 1996.

Huntress, Keith, ed. *Narratives of Shipwrecks and Disasters, 1586–1860.* Ames: Iowa State University Press, 1974.

Jaggard, Edwin. *Cornwall Politics in the Age of Reform, 1790–1885.* Royal Historical Society, Studies in History. London: Boydell Press and the Royal Historical Society, 1999.

Jahoda, Gustav. *Images of Savages: Ancient Roots of Modern Prejudice in Western Culture.* New York: Routledge, 1999.

Jenkin, A.K. Hamilton. *Cornish Seafarers: The Smuggling, Wrecking & Fishing Life of Cornwall.* London: J.M. Dent, 1932.

——. *Cornwall and its People.* Truro, 1932; reprinted Newton Abbot: David & Charles, 1970

——. *News from Cornwall: With a Memoir of William Jenkin.* London: Westaway Books, 1946.

Johns, Jeremy Rowett. *The Smugglers' Banker: The Story of Zephaniah Job of Polperro.* Polperro: Polperro Heritage Press, 1997.

Jones, D.J.V. *Crime, Protest, Community, and Police in Nineteenth-Century Britain.* London: Routledge & Kegan Paul, 1982.

Jones, Dwyryd W. *War and Economy in the Age of William III and Marlborough.* Oxford: Basil Blackwell, 1988.

Jupp, Peter. *The Governing of Britain, 1688–1848: The Executive, Parliament and the People.* London: Routledge, 2006.

Kent, Alan M. *The Literature of Cornwall: Continuity, Identity, Difference, 1000–2000.* Bristol: Redcliffe Press, 2000.

King, Peter. *Crime, Justice and Discretion in England, 1740–1820.* Oxford: Oxford University Press, 2000.

——. *Crime and the Law in England, 1750–1840: Remaking Justice from the Margins.* Cambridge: Cambridge University Press, 2006.

Landau, Norma. *The Justices of the Peace, 1679–1760.* Berkeley: University of California Press, 1984.

Landow, George P. *Images of Crisis: Literary Iconology, 1750 to the Present.* London and Boston: Routledge & Kegan Paul, 1982.

Langford, Paul. *A Polite and Commercial People: England, 1727–1783.* New York: Oxford University Press, 1992.

——. *The Short Oxford History of the British Isles: The Eighteenth Century, 1688–1815.* Oxford: Oxford University Press, 2002.

Larn, Richard. *Cornish Shipwrecks: The Isles of Scilly.* Vol. 3. Newton Abbot: David & Charles, 1971.

——. *Shipwrecks of Great Britain and Ireland.* Newton Abbot: David & Charles, 1981.

Larn, Richard, and Clive Carter. *Cornish Shipwrecks, Vol. I: The South Coast.* Newton Abbot: David & Charles, 1969.

Larn, Richard, and Bridget Larn. *Shipwreck Index of the British Isles.* 5 vols. London: Lloyd's Register of Shipping, 1995–98.

Lecky, William E.H. *History of England in the Eighteenth Century*, Vol. II. London: Longmans, Green and Co., 1892.

Lestringant, Frank. *Cannibals: The Discovery and Representation of the Cannibal from Columbus to Jules Verne*. Berkeley: University of California Press, 1997.

Linebaugh, Peter. *The London Hanged: Crime and Civil Society in the Eighteenth Century*. Cambridge: Cambridge University Press, 1992.

Lowry, Henry Dawson. *Wreckers and Methodists, and other Stories*. London: W. Heinemann, 1893.

Lüdtke, Alf. *The History of Everyday Life: Reconstructing Historical Experiences and Ways of Life*. Translated by William Templer. Princeton: Princeton University Press, 1995.

McKendrick, Neil, John Brewer and J.H. Plumb. *The Birth of Consumer Society: The Commercialization of Eighteenth-Century England*. London: Europa, 1982.

McLynn, Frank. *Crime and Punishment in Eighteenth-Century England*. London: Routledge, 1989.

Macpherson, David. *Annals of Commerce: Manufactures, Fisheries and Navigation, with Brief Notes*. 4 vols. London: Nichols and Son, 1805.

Mandler, Peter. *The English National Character: The History of an Idea from Edmund Burke to Tony Blair*. New Haven: Yale University Press, 2006.

Matthews, John H. *History of the Parishes of St Ives, Lelant, Towednack and Zennor in the County of Cornwall*. London: Elliot Stock, 1892.

Minchinton, Walter, ed. *Reactions to Social and Economic Change, 1750–1939*. Exeter: University of Exeter Press, 1979.

Moore, Stuart A. *A History of the Foreshore*. 3rd edition. London: Stevens and Haynes, 1888.

Morley, Geoffrey. *The Smuggling War: The Government's Fight against Smuggling in the 18th and 19th Centuries*. Stroud, Gloucestershire: Alan Sutton Publishing, 1994.

Nance, R. Morton. *A Glossary of Cornish Sea-Words*. Edited by P.A.S. Pool, M.A. Truro: The Federation of Old Cornwall Societies, 1963.

Noall, Cyril. *Cornish Lights and Ship-Wrecks, including the Isles of Scilly*. Truro: D. Bradford Barton, 1968.

——. *The Story of Cornwall's Ports and Harbours*. Truro: Tor Mark Press, 1970.

Noall, Cyril, and Grahame Farr. *Cornish Shipwrecks*. Truro: Tor Mark Press, n.d.

Oldham, James. *English Common Law in the Age of Mansfield*. Chapel Hill, North Carolina: University of North Carolina Press, 2004.

Palmer, Sarah. *Politics, Shipping and the Repeal of the Navigation Laws*. Manchester: Manchester University Press, 1990.

Parnall, Roger. *Wreckers and Wrestlers: A History of St Genny's Parish*. St Austell: n.p., 1973.

Pawlyn, Tony. *The Falmouth Packets, 1689–1851*. Truro: Dyllansow Truran, 2003.

Payton, Philip. *Cornwall: A History*. Fowey: Cornwall Editions, 2004.

——. *The Making of Modern Cornwall: Historical Experience and the Persistence of 'Difference'*. Redruth, Cornwall: Dyllansow Truran, 1992.

Perkin, Harold. *The Origins of Modern British Society, 1780–1880*. London: Routledge & Kegan Paul, 1969.

Peter, Thurstan C. *A Compendium of the History and Geography of Cornwall, by the Reverend J.J. Daniel.* 4th edition by Thursten C. Peter. Truro: Netherton and Worth; London: Houlston & Sons, 1906.

Popplewell, Lawrence. *Coastguard and Preventive upon the Shipwreck Coast.* Southbourne: Melledgen, 1990.

Porter, Roy. *English Society in the Eighteenth Century.* London: Penguin, 1982, 1990.

Price, Richard. *British Society, 1680–1880: Dynamism, Containment and Change.* Cambridge: Cambridge University Press, 1999.

Probert, John C.C. *The Sociology of Cornish Methodism.* Truro: Cornish Methodist Historical Association, 1971.

Prouty, Roger. *The Transformation of the Board of Trade, 1830–1855: A Study of Administrative Organization in the Heyday of Laissez-Faire.* London: William Heinemann, 1957.

Radzinowicz, Leon. *A History of English Criminal Law and its Administration from 1750.* 4 vols. London: Stevens & Sons, 1948.

Randall, Adrian. *Riotous Assemblies: Popular Protest in Hanoverian England.* Oxford: Oxford University Press, 2006.

Rawson, Claude. *God, Gulliver and Genocide: Barbarism and the European Imagination, 1492–1945.* Oxford: Oxford University Press, 2002.

Reay, Barry, ed. *Popular Cultures in England, 1550–1750.* London and New York: Longman, 1998.

Roadenberg, Herman, and Pieter Spierenburg, eds. *Social Control in Europe,* Vol. 1: *1500–1800.* Ohio: Ohio State University Press, 2004.

Roberts, F. David. *The Social Conscience of the Early Victorians.* Stanford, California: Stanford University Press, 2002.

Roberts, M.J.D. *Making English Morals: Voluntary Association and Moral Reform in England, 1787–1886.* Cambridge: Cambridge University Press, 2004.

Roddis, Roland J. *Penryn: The History of an Ancient Cornish Borough.* Truro: D. Bradford Barton, 1964.

Rogers, J.J. *John Knill, 1733–1811.* Helston: R. Cunnack, Market-place, c. 1871.

Rowbotham, Judith, and Kim Stevenson, eds. *Behaving Badly: Social Panic and Moral Outrage – Victorian and Modern Parallels.* Aldershot, Hampshire: Ashgate, 2003.

Rowe, John. *Cornwall in the Age of the Industrial Revolution.* Introduction by A.L. Rowse. Liverpool: Liverpool University Press, 1953.

Rowles, Jean C., and Ian Maxted, eds. *Cornwall: Bibliography of British Newspapers.* London: British Library, 1991.

Rowse, A.L. *Tudor Cornwall: Portrait of a Society.* London: Jonathan Cape, 1941.

Rubenstein, W.D. *Men of Property: The Very Wealthy since the Industrial Revolution.* London: Croom Helm, 1981.

Rudé, George. *The Crowd in History: A Study of Popular Disturbances in France and England, 1730–1848.* London: Lawrence and Wishart, 1964, 1981.

Rule, John G. *Cornish Cases: Essays in Eighteenth and Nineteenth Century Social History.* Southampton: Clio Publishing, 2006.

———. *The Labouring Classes in Early Industrial England, 1750–1850.* London: Longman, 1986.

Rule, John G., and Roger Wells. *Crime, Protest and Popular Politics in Southern England, 1740–1850*. London: Hambledon Press, 1997.

Salmon, Arthur P. *The Cornwall Coast*. London: T. Fisher Unwin, 1910.

Samuel, Raphael. *Theatres of Memory*, Vol. I: *Past and Present in Contemporary Culture*. London: Verso, 1994.

Samuel, Raphael, and Paul Thomas. *The Myths We Live By*. London and New York: Routledge, 1990.

Scholl, Lars U., ed. *Merchants and Mariners: Selected Writings of David M. Williams*. Research in Maritime History 18. St John's, Newfoundland: International Maritime Economic History Association, 2000.

Scott, James C. *Domination and the Arts of Resistance: Hidden Transcripts*. New Haven: Yale University Press, 1990.

Seal, Jeremy. *Treachery at Sharpnose Point: Unraveling the Mystery of the* Caledonia's *Final Voyage*. New York: Harcourt, 2001.

Sharpe, J.A. *Crime in Early Modern England, 1550–1750*. London: Longman, 1984, 1992.

Shiach, Morag. *Discourse on Popular Culture: Class, Gender and History in Cultural Analysis, 1730 to the Present*. Oxford: Basil Blackwell, 1989.

Shoemaker, Robert. *The London Mob: Violence and Disorder in Eighteenth-Century England*. London: Hambledon Continuum, 2004, 2007.

Shore, Commander H., RN. *Old Foye Days: An Authentic Account of the Exploits of Smugglers in and Around the Port of Fowey*. London: n.p., 1907.

Smyth, Admiral W.H. *The Sailor's Word Book, an Alphabetical Digest of Nautical Terms*. London: Blackie & Son, 1867.

Spraggs, Gillian. *Outlaws & Highwaymen: The Cult of the Robber in England from the Middle Ages to the Nineteenth Century*. London: Pimlico, 2001.

Starkey, David J. *British Privateering Enterprise in the Eighteenth Century*. Exeter: University of Exeter Press, 1990.

——. *Devon's Coastline and Coastal Waters: Aspects of Man's Relationship with the Sea*. Exeter: University of Exeter Press, 1988.

Starkey, David J., and Alan G. Jamieson, eds. *Exploiting the Sea: Aspects of Britain's Maritime Economy since 1870*. Exeter: University of Exeter Press, 1998.

Stevenson, John. *Popular Disturbances in England, 1700–1870*. London and New York: Longman, 1979.

Stone, Lawrence, and Jeanne C. Fawtier Stone. *An Open Elite? England, 1540–1880*. Oxford: Oxford University Press, 1984.

Storch, Robert, ed. *Popular Culture and Custom in Nineteenth-Century England*. London: Croom Helm, 1982.

Stoyle, Mark. *West Britons: Cornish Identities and the Early Modern British State*. Exeter: University of Exeter Press, 2002.

Tangye, Michael. *Portreath: Some Chapters in its History*. Redruth, Cornwall: Dyllansow Truran, 1968.

——. *Tehidy and the Bassets: The Rise and Fall of a Great Cornish Family*. Redruth, Cornwall: Dyllansow Truran, 1984, revised 2002.

Tangye, Nigel. *Cornwall Newspapers, 18th & 19th century: Gazetteer and Finding List*. Redruth, Cornwall: n.p., 1980.

Taylor, David. *Crime, Policing and Punishment in England, 1750–1914*. Social History in
Perspective Series. London: Macmillan Press, 1998.

Thomas, Charles. *Methodism and Self-Improvement in Nineteenth Century Cornwall*. Redruth: Cornish Methodist Historical Association Occasional Publication, 1965.

Thompson, E.P. *Customs in Common: Studies in Traditional Popular Culture*. New York: The New Press, 1993.

——. *The Making of the English Working Class*. London: Penguin, 1963, 1968, 1980.

——. *Whigs and Hunters: The Origin of the Black Act*. London and New York: Penguin, 1975, 1990.

Thompson, Hilary. *A History of the Parish of Gerrans, 1800–1914*. 2 vols. Porthscatho: H. Thompson, 1995.

Todd, Arthur C. *The Cornish Miner in America*. Truro: D. Bradford Barton, 1967; reprinted Spokane, Washington: Arthur H. Clarke Co., 1995.

Todd, Arthur C. and Peter Laws, *The Industrial Archaeology of Cornwall*. Newton Abbot: David and Charles, 1972

Todd, Malcolm. *The South West to AD 1000*. London and New York: Longman, 1987.

Todorov, Tzvetan. *Mikhail Bakhtin: The Dialogical Principal*. Translated by Wlad Godzich. Minneapolis: University of Minnesota Press, 1984.

Trubshaw, Bob. *Explore Mythology*. Loughborough: Heart of Albion Press, 2003.

Turner, Victor. *The Anthropology of Performance*. Preface by Richard Schechner. New York: PAJ Publications, 1987.

Trezise, Simon. *The West Country as Literary Invention: Putting Fiction in its Place*. Exeter: University of Exeter Press, 2000.

Uren, J. G. *Scilly and the Scillonians*. Plymouth: Western Morning News, 1907.

Vivian, John. *Tales of Cornish Wreckers*. Truro: Tor Mark Press, 1969.

Vyvyan, C.C. *The Scilly Isles*. London: Robert Hale, 1953, 1954.

Waddams, S.M. *Law, Politics and the Church of England: The Career of Stephen Lushington, 1782–1873*. Cambridge: Cambridge University Press, 1992.

Walsham, Alexandra. *Providence in Early Modern England*. Oxford: Oxford University Press, 1999, 2003.

Warner, Jessica. *Craze: Gin and Debauchery in the Age of Reason*. New York: Random House, 2002.

Waugh, Mary. *Smuggling in Devon and Cornwall, 1700–1850*. Newbury, Berkshire: Countryside Books, 1991, 2003.

Webb, William. *Coastguard! An Official History of HM Coastguard*. London: HMSO, 1976.

Weiner, Martin J. *English Culture and the Decline of the Industrial Spirit, 1850–1980*. Cambridge: Cambridge University Press, 1981.

Westland, Ella, ed. *Cornwall: The Cultural Construction of Place*. Penzance: The Institute of Cornish Studies, University of Exeter, 1997.

Whetter, James. *Cornwall in the 13th Century: A Study in Social and Economic History*. Gorran, Cornwall: Lyfrow Trelyspen, The Roseland Institute, 1998.

——. *Cornwall in the 17th Century: An Economic History of Kernow.* Padstow: Lodenek Press, 1974, 2002.

——. *The History of Falmouth.* Redruth: Dyllansow Truran, 1981.

Wood, Andy. *The 1549 Rebellions and the Making of Early Modern England.* Cambridge: Cambridge University Press, 2007.

Wryde, J. Saxby. *British Lighthouses: Their History and Romance.* London: T. Fisher Unwin, 1913.

Young, Bill, and Bryan Dudley Stamp. *Bude's Maritime Heritage: Past and Present.* Bude, Cornwall: Bill Young, 2001.


**Published Secondary Sources: Articles**

Barry, Jonathan. 'Literacy and Literature in Popular Culture: Reading and Writing in Historical Perspective', in Tim Harris, ed., *Popular Culture in England, c. 1500–1850.* London: Macmillan Press, 1995.

Beik, William. 'The Violence of the French Crowd from Charivari to Revolution', *Past and Present*, 197 (November 2007), 75–110.

Berg, Maxine and Elizabeth Eger, eds. 'The Rise and Fall of the Luxury Debates', in *Luxury in the Eighteenth Century: Debates, Desires and Delectable Goods.* Basingstoke: Palgrave Macmillan, 2003.

Burt, Roger, and Michael Atkinson. 'Mining', in Crispin Gill, ed., *The Duchy of Cornwall.* Newton Abbot: David & Charles, 1987.

Bushaway, Robert W. 'Ceremony, Custom and Ritual: Some Observations on Social Conflict in the Rural Community, 1750–1850', in Walter Minchinton, ed., *Reactions to Social and Economic Change, 1750–1939.* Exeter: University of Exeter Press, 1979.

Campbell, S.M. 'The Haveners of the Medieval Dukes of Cornwall and the Organisation of the Duchy Ports', *Journal of the Royal Institution of Cornwall*, new series, 4 pt. 2 (1962), 113–144.

Childs, Wendy. 'The Commercial Shipping of Southwestern England in the Later Fifteenth Century'. *Mariner's Mirror* 83, 2 (1997), 272–292.

Chynoweth, John. 'The Wreck of the *St. Anthony*', *Journal of the Royal Institution of Cornwall*, new series, 5 pt. 4 (1968), 385–406.

Davies, Owen, 'Newspapers and Popular Belief in Witchcraft and Magic in the Modern Period', *Journal of British Studies*, 37 (April 1998), 139–165.

Davis, H.W.C. 'The Chronicle of Battle Abbey', *English Historical Review*, 29 (July 1914), 426–434.

Davis, Jennifer. 'The London Garotting Panic of 1862: A Moral Panic and the Creation of a Criminal Class in mid-Victorian England', in V.A.C. Gatrell, Bruce Lenman, and Geoffrey Parker, eds., *Crime and the Law: The Social History of Crime in Western Europe since 1500.* London: Europa, 1980.

Derriman, James. 'The Wreck of the *Albemarle*', *Journal of the Royal Institution of Cornwall.* New series II, 1, pt 2 (1992), 128–148.

Doe, Helen. 'Politics, Property and Family Resources: The Business Strategies Adopted by Small Shipbuilders in Fowey and Polruan, Cornwall, in the 19th Century', *Family and Community History*, 4, no. 1 (2001), 59–72.

——. 'Waiting for Her Ship to Come In? The Female Investor in Nineteenth

Century Sailing Vessels', *Economic History Review*, 63, no. 1 (February 2010), 85–106.

Elvins, Brian. 'Cornwall's Newspaper War: The Political Rivalry between the *Royal Cornwall Gazette* and the *West Briton*, 1810–1831, Part One', in Philip Payton, ed. *Cornish Studies* 9 (second series), Exeter: University of Exeter Press, 2001.

———. 'Cornwall's Newspaper War. The Political Rivalry between the *Royal Cornwall Gazette* and the *West Briton*—Part Two 1832–1855', in Philip Payton, ed. *Cornish Studies* 11 (second series), Exeter: University of Exeter Press, 2003.

Fernández-Arnesto, Felipe. 'Epilogue: What is History Now?', in David Cannadine, ed., *What is History Now?* London: Palgrave Macmillan, 2002.

Fox, Howard, 'The Lizard Lighthouse', *Journal of the Royal Institution of Cornwall*, 6, pt 14 (1879), 319–336.

Gatrell, V.A.C. 'The Decline of Theft and Violence in Victorian and Edwardian England', in V.A.C. Gatrell, Bruce Lenman and Geoffrey Parker, eds, *Crime and the Law: The Social History of Crime in Western Europe since 1500*. London: Europa, 1980.

Gray, Todd. 'Turks, Moors and the Cornish Fishermen: Piracy in the Early Seventeenth Century', *Journal of the Royal Institution of Cornwall*, new series II, 10 (1990), 457–478.

Hamil, Frederick C. 'Wreck of the Sea in Medieval England', in A.E.R Boak, ed., *University of Michigan Historical Essays*. Ann Arbor: University of Michigan Press, 1937.

Haslam, Graham. 'Evolution', in Crispin Gill, ed., *The Duchy of Cornwall*. Newton Abbot: David & Charles, 1987.

———. 'Modernisation', in Crispin Gill, ed., *The Duchy of Cornwall*. Newton Abbot: David & Charles, 1987.

Hatcher, John. 'Non-manorialism in Medieval Cornwall', *Agricultural History Review*, 18 (1970), 1–16.

Hay, Douglas. 'Property, Authority and the Criminal Law', in Douglas Hay, Peter Linebaugh, et al., *Albion's Fatal Tree: Crime and Society in Eighteenth-Century England*. London: Allen Lane, 1975; reprinted. London: Penguin, 1988.

Henderson, Charles. 'Cornish Wrecks and Wreckers: Plundered Ships and Sailors', *Western Morning News and Mercury*, Monday 21 January 1929.

Hudson, Pat. 'Economic History', in Stefan Berger, Heiko Feldner, and Kevin Passmore, eds, *Writing History: Theory and Practice*. London: Hodder Arnold, 2003.

Hughes, Helen. '"A Silent and Desolate Country": Images of Cornwall in Daphne du Maurier's *Jamaica Inn*', in Ella Westland, ed., *Cornwall: The Cultural Construction of Place*. Penzance: Institute of Cornish Studies, University of Exeter, 1997.

Innes, Joanna. 'Governing Diverse Societies', in Paul Langford, ed., *The Short Oxford History of the British Isles: The Eighteenth Century, 1688–1815*. Oxford: Oxford University Press, 1995.

Innes, Joanna, and John Styles, 'The Crime Wave: Recent Writing on Crime and Criminal Justice in Eighteenth-century England', in Adrian Wilson, ed., *Rethinking Social History: English Society 1570–1920 and its Interpretation*. Manchester and New York: Manchester University Press, 1993.

Jackson, Gordon. 'Ports 1700–1840', in Peter Clark, ed., *The Cambridge Urban History of Britain*, Vol. II: *1540–1840*. Cambridge: Cambridge University Press, 2000.

——. 'Seatrade', in John Langton and R.J. Morris, eds., *Atlas of Industrializing Britain, 1780–1914*. London: Methuen, 1986.

Jenkin, A.K. Hamilton. 'Smuggling, Wrecking and Fishing in Cornwall', *The Listener*, 26 September 1934.

Kennett, David H. 'The *Magic*: A West Country Schooner in the Mediterranean, 1833–9', in Stephen Fisher, ed., *West Country Maritime and Social History: Some Essays*. Exeter: University of Exeter, 1980.

King, Peter. 'Decision Makers and Decision-Making in the English Criminal Law, 1750–1800', *Historical Journal*, 27 (1984), 25–58.

——. 'Moral Panics and Violent Street Crime 1750–2000', in Barry S. Godfrey, Clive Emsley, and Graeme Dunstall, eds, *Comparative Histories of Crime*. London: Willan Publishing, 2003.

——. 'The Summary Courts and Social Relations in Eighteenth-Century England', *Past and Present*, 183 (2004), 125–172.

Langbein, John. 'Albion's Fatal Flaws', *Past and Present*, 98 (1983), 96–120.

Lawrence, Jon. 'Political History', in Stefan Berger, Heiko Feldner, and Kevin Passmore, eds, *Writing History: Theory and Practice*. London: Hodder Arnold, 2003.

Lemire, Beverly. 'The Theft of Clothes and Popular Consumerism in Early Modern England', *Journal of Social History*, 24, no. 2 (1990), 255–276.

Lincoln, Margarette. 'Shipwreck Narratives of the Eighteenth and Early Nineteenth Century. Indicators of Culture and Identity', *British Journal for Eighteenth-Century Studies*, 20, no. 2 (1997), 155–172.

Maza, Sarah. 'Stories in History: Cultural Narratives in Recent Works in European History', *American Historical Review*, 101, no. 5 (December 1996), 1493–1515.

Melikan, Rose. 'Shippers, Salvors, and Sovereigns: Competing Interests in the Medieval Law of Shipwreck', *Journal of Legal History*, 11 (1990), 153–182.

Middlebrook, Louis F. 'The Laws of Oléron', *Marine Historical Association*, 1, no. 10 (22 April 1935), 171–183.

Milden, Kayleigh, 'Culture of Conversion: Religion and Politics in the Cornish Mining Communities'. *Cornish History Online Journal* 2001.

Monad, Paul. 'Dangerous Merchandise: Smuggling, Jacobitism and Commercial Culture in Southeast England 1690–1760', *Journal of British Studies*, 30, 2 (1991), 150–182.

Mooers, Stephanie L. 'A Reevaluation of Royal Justice under Henry I of England', *American Historical Review*, 93, no. 2 (April 1988), 340–358.

North, Christine. 'The Arundell Archive', *Journal of the Royal Institution of Cornwall*, new series II, 1, pt 1 (1991), 47–57.

Oppenheim, Michael. 'Maritime History', in *Victoria County History of Cornwall*, Vol. I. London: 1906.

Palmer, Sarah. 'Ports 1840–1950', in Martin J. Daunton, ed., *The Cambridge Urban History of Britain*, Vol. III: *1840–1950*. Cambridge: Cambridge University Press, 2000.

——. 'Seeing the Sea: The Maritime Dimension in History', *Inaugural Lecture Series*, University of Greenwich, 11 May 2000.

Passmore, Kevin. 'Poststructuralism and History', in Stefan Berger, Heiko Feldner, and Kevin Passmore, eds, *Writing History: Theory and Practice*. London: Hodder Arnold, 2003.

Payton, Philip. 'Cornwall in Context: The New Cornish Historiography', *Cornish Studies*, second series, 5 (1997), 9–20.

Pearce, Cathryn J. '"Neglectful or Worse:" A Lurid Tale of a Lighthouse Keeper and Wrecking in the Isles of Scilly', *Troze: The Online Journal of the National Maritime Museum Cornwall*, 1, no. 1 (September 2008).

——. 'Review of Bella Bathurst's *The Wreckers: A Story of Killing Seas, False Lights and Plundered Ships*', *International Journal of Maritime History*, 17, no. 2 (December 2005), 411–412.

Place, Geoffrey, 'Wreckers: The Fate of the *Charming Jenny*', *Mariner's Mirror*, 76, no. 2 (1990), 167–168.

Pounds, Norman J.C., 'The Population of Cornwall Before the First Census', in E. Minchinton, ed., *Population and Marketing*, Exeter Papers on Economic History 11. Exeter: University of Exeter Press, 1976.

Price, Jacob M. 'Competition between Ports in British Long Distance Trade, c. 1660–1800', *Puertos y Sistemas Portuarios (Siglos XVI–XX): A Clas del Coloquio Internacional*, El Sistema Portuario Español, Madrid, 19–21 October 1995, 19–36.

Probert, John C.C. 'Meritricious?' Cornwall History Network Newsletter, March 2000.

Rabin, Dana. 'Drunkenness and Responsibility for Crime in the Eighteenth Century', *Journal of British Studies*, 44, no. 3 (July 2005), 457–477.

Rodger, N.A.M. '"A little navy of your own making," Admiral Boscawen and the Cornish Connection in the Royal Navy', in Michael Duffy, ed., *Parameters of British Naval Power, 1650–1850*. Exeter: University of Exeter Press, 1992.

Rubin, Miri. 'What is Cultural History Now?', in David Cannadine, ed., *What is History Now?* London: Palgrave Macmillan, 2002.

Rule, John. G. 'Explaining Revivalism: the Case of Cornish Methodism', *Southern History*, 20–21 (1998–99), 168–188.

——. 'Methodism, Popular Beliefs and Village Culture in Cornwall, 1800–50', in Robert Storch, ed., *Popular Culture and Custom in Nineteenth-Century England*. London: Croom Helm, 1982.

——. 'Social Crime in the Rural South in the Eighteenth and Early Nineteenth Centuries', *Southern History*, 1 (1979), 135–153.

——. 'Some Social Aspects of the Cornish Industrial Revolution', *Exeter Papers in Economic History*, 2 (1970), 71–106.

——. 'Wrecking and Coastal Plunder', in Douglas Hay, Peter Linebaugh, et al., *Albion's Fatal Tree: Crime and Society in Eighteenth-Century England*. London: Allen Lane, 1975.

Runyan, Timothy, 'The Rolls of Oléron and the Admiralty Court in Fourteenth Century England', *American Journal of Legal History*, 19 (1975), 95–111.

Schofield, Bertram. 'Wreck Rolls of Leiston Abbey', in *Studies Presented to Sir Hilary Jenkinson*, ed. J. Conway Davies. Oxford: Oxford University Press, 1957.

Southward, Alan, Gerald Boalch, and Linda Maddock, eds. 'Climatic Change and the Herring and Pilchard Fisheries of Devon and Cornwall', in David J. Starkey, ed., *Devon's Coastline and Coastal Waters: Aspects of Man's Relationship with the Sea*. Exeter: University of Exeter Press, 1988.

Starkey, David J. 'British Privateering against the Dutch in the American Revolutionary War, 1780–1783', in Stephen Fisher, ed., *Studies in British Privateering: Trading Enterprise and Seamen's Welfare, 1775–1900*. Exeter: University of Exeter Press, 1987.

——. 'Growth and Transition in Britain's Maritime Economy, 1870–1914: The Case of South-West England', in David J. Starkey and Alan G. Jamieson, eds, *Exploiting the Sea. Aspects of Britain's Maritime Economy since 1870*. Exeter: University of Exeter Press, 1998.

Stoyle, Mark J. '"The Dissidence of Despair:" Rebellion and Identity in Early Modern Cornwall', *Journal of British Studies*, 38 (1999), 423–444.

——. 'English "Nationalism", Celtic Particularism and the English Civil War', *Historical Journal*, 43, no. 4 (December 2000), 1113–1128.

——. '"Pagans or Paragons?" Images of the Cornish during the English Civil War', *English Historical Review*, 111 (1996), 299–323.

Thomas, Paul. 'The Population of Cornwall in the Eighteenth Century', *Journal of the Royal Institution of Cornwall*, new series, 10, pt 4 (1990), 416–456.

Trezise, Simon. 'The Celt, the Saxon and the Cornishman: Stereotypes and Counter-Stereotypes of the Victorian Period', in Philip Payton, ed., *Cornish Studies 8* (2000), 54–68.

Vernon, James. 'Border Crossings. Cornwall and the English Imagination', in Geoffrey Cubitt, *Imagining Nations*. Manchester: Manchester University Press, 1998.

Welskopp, Thomas. 'Social History', in Stefan Berger, Heiko Feldner, and Kevin Passmore, eds, *Writing History: Theory and Practice*. London: Hodder Arnold, 2003.

Wheeler, Sara. 'Whose Loot is it Anyway? A review of Bella Bathurst's *The Wreckers*', *The New York Times*, 17 July 2005.

Whetter, James C.A. 'The Rise of the Port of Falmouth, 1600–1800', in Stephen Fisher, ed., *Ports and Shipping in the South-west: Papers presented at two seminars on the maritime history of the South-West of England, held at Dartington Hall, 19–20 October 1968 and 18–19 October 1969*. Exeter. University of Exeter, 1971.

White, Jonathan. 'The "Slow but Sure Poyson": The Representation of Gin and its Drinkers, 1736–1751', *Journal of British Studies*, 42 (January 2003), 35–64.

Whitley, H. Michelle. 'The Treasure Ship of Gunwallo', *Journal of the Royal Institution of Cornwall*, 10, pt 1 (1890), 106–108.

Williams, David. 'James Silk Buckingham: Sailor, Explorer, and Maritime Reformer', in Stephen Fisher, ed., *Studies in British Privateering, Trading Enterprise and Seamen's Welfare, 1775–1900*. Exeter: University of Exeter, 1987.

Williams, Michael, 'A Legal History of Shipwreck in England', subsequently published in *Annuaire de Droit Maritime et Océanique* (Tomexu: Centre de Droit Maritime et Océanique Faculte de Droit et des Sciences Politique, Université de Nantes, 1997), 71–92.

Winslow, Cal. 'Sussex Smugglers', in Douglas Hay, Peter Linebaugh, et al., *Albion's Fatal Tree: Crime and Society in Eighteenth-Century England*. London: Allen Lane, 1975.

Wood, Andy. 'Custom, Identity and Resistance: English Free Miners and their Law, c.1550–1800', in Paul Griffiths, Adam Fox, and Steve Hindle, eds, *The Experience of Authority in Early Modern England*. London and New York: Macmillan Press, 1996.

——. 'Subordination, Solidarity and the Limits of Popular Agency in a Yorkshire Valley, c. 1596–1615', *Past and Present*, 193 (November 2006), 41–72.

Wright, R.F. 'The High Seas and the Church in the Middle Ages, Part II', *Mariner's Mirror*, 53, no. 1 (February 1967), 115–135.

Wrightson, Keith. 'The Politics of the Parish in Early Modern England', in Paul Griffiths, Adam Fox, and Steve Hindle, eds, *The Experience of Authority in Early Modern England*. London and New York: Macmillan Press, 1996.

Wynter, Andrew. 'Wrecks and Wreckers on the English Coast', *Peeps into the Human Hive*, Vol. 2. London: n.p., 1874.

## Literary and Dramatic Sources

Baring-Gould, Sabine. *In the Roar of the Sea: A Tale of the Cornish Coast*. Originally published Methuen & Co., 1892; London: Corgi Books, 1977.

Cobb, James F. *The Watchers of the Longships: A Tale of Cornwall in the Last Century*. Originally published 1877; 8th edition, New York: Thomas Y. Crowell & Co., 1882.

Darke, Nick and Jane. 'The Wrecking Season'. 59 minutes. 2005.

du Maurier, Daphne. *Jamaica Inn*. First published London: Victor Gollancz, 1936; reprinted London: Pan Books, 1976.

Errym, Malcolm J. [James Malcolm Rymer]. *Sea Drift; or, the Wreckers of the Channel: A Tale Ashore and Afloat*. New York: Frederic A. Brady, c. 1860.

Falconer, William. *A Critical Edition of the Poetical Works of William Falconer*. Edited by William R. Jones. Studies in British Literature 71. Lewiston, Queenstown, Lampeter: The Edwin Mellen Press, 2003.

Forfar, William Bentinck. *The Wizard of West Penwith: a Tale of Land's End*. Penzance: n.p., 1871.

Hawker, R.S. *Ecclesia, a volume of poems*. Oxford: Rivington, 1840.

——. *Cornish Ballads and Other Poems*. Ed. with an intro by C.E. Byles. London: John Lane, 1904.

Hyland, William. [A Farmer in Sussex]. *The Shipwreck: A Dramatick Piece in Prose*. London: n.p., 1746.

Kettle, Mary Rosa Stuart. *The Wreckers*. n.p. 1857.

Knowles, James Sheridan. 'The Wreckers. A Cornish Tale'. *Tegg's Magazine of Knowledge*. London: Thomas Tegg, 1844.

## Internet Sources

BBC. 'Floods continue amid heavy rain', 4 February 2002. news.bbc.co.uk/l/hi/uk/1799659.stm

——. 'Timber galore for Cornish wreckers', 4 February 2002. news.bbc.co.uk/hi/english/uk/england/newsid_1801000/1801109.stm

Magnusson , Sigurdur Glylfi. 'Social History-Cultural History-Alltagsgeschichte-Microhistory: In-Between Methodologies and Conceptual Frameworks', *Journal of Microhistory* (2006). Accessed 2 January 2009 at www.microhistory.org

Sandford, Mark. 'The Sinking of the Barque "John". A collection of news stories from the *Plymouth and Stonehouse Journal*, 1855. Accessed 9 April 2010 at www.rsandthefaces.pwp.blueyonder.co.uk/fh/john/index.html

'Treasure Island – Related Topics. Wrecks and Wreckers.' Accessed 6 December 2001 at www.stockportmbc.gov.uk/treasure_island/wrecks.htm

# Index